Praise for *Openings*

Larry Peacock is a friend and a gifted brother on the spiritual journey who has poured his spiritual insight into the pages of this wise book. I am convinced that as we discover the depths of prayer, we will, as Teilhard de Chardin suggested, "discover fire for the second time."

—MARTIN SHEEN

Like a fresh spring, *Openings* invites those thirsty for God to "come to the waters" (Isa. 55:1). Larry Peacock's simple yet wonderfully wise ponderings and prayer practices refresh the spiritual traveler and help to uncover the source of blessing hidden in each day.

—WENDY M. WRIGHT, Ph.D.
Professor of Theology
John C. Kenefick Chair in the Humanities
Creighton University

Using a wide variety of resources—lives of saints from every age, psalms, personal guides for reflection, and suggestions for practice—Larry Peacock has written a wonderfully helpful, wise book for anyone hungry for a richer prayer life. No matter where you may be in your exploration of prayer and meditation, Peacock is an excellent guide to a deeper, more sustaining experience of authentic spirituality.

—REV. DR. TED LODER
Author of *Guerrillas of Grace*

Adhering faithfully to daily prayer requires an approach that provides the ease of a familiar practice as well as stimulating variety. Meeting this need, Larry Peacock has written a creative and rich resource for prayer that nicely blends scripture, reflection on saintly lives, and helpful suggestions for new ways of praying. Sensibly down-to-earth, he offers a guidebook that will appeal to Christians of all denominations who want to stay alive to the Spirit one day at a time.

—WILKIE AU, Ph.D.
Associate Professor
Department of Theological Studies
Loyola Marymount University

Karl + Brenda
For all the days
of your journey!
Larry J. Peacock

OPENINGS

A DAYBOOK OF SAINTS, PSALMS, AND PRAYER

LARRY JAMES PEACOCK

UPPER ROOM BOOKS®
NASHVILLE

OPENINGS: A Daybook of Saints, Psalms, and Prayer
Copyright © 2003 by Larry James Peacock
All rights reserved.

The Upper Room® Web site: www.upperroom.org

Unless otherwise indicated, scripture quotations are from the New Revised Standard Version Bible, copyright © 1989, Division of Christian Education of the National Council of the Churches of Christ in the United States of America. Used by permission. All rights reserved.

Scriptures marked KJV are from the King James Version. Additional scripture notices are on page 435.

At the time of publication all Web sites referenced in this book were valid. However, due to the fluid nature of the Internet, some addresses may have changed or the content may no longer be relevant.

An extension of the copyright page is on page 435.

Cover design: Christa Schoenbrodt/Studiohaus
Cover photo: Father Vince Hovley
Interior design and implementation: Nancy Cole-Hatcher
First printing: 2003

Library of Congress Cataloging-in-Publication Data

Peacock, Larry James, 1949–
Openings : a daybook of saints, Psalms, and prayer / Larry James Peacock.
    p. cm.
ISBN 0-8358-9850-4
1. Devotional calendars. 2. Bible. O.T. Psalm—Meditations. 3. Christian saints—Prayer-books and devotions—English. I. Title.
BV4811.P327 2003
242'.2—dc21   2003004631

Printed in the United States of America

To my family
Anne Broyles
Trinity and Justus Peacock-Broyles
for loving support and encouragement

To the Upper Room Academy for Spiritual Formation
one of the finest programs in spiritual formation
and a community and team that affirmed
my call and gifts in this area

To the people of Malibu United Methodist Church
who have tried most everything in this book
and loved me along the journey

To family and friends
who provided hospitality to write
and encouragement to share
what I have been living and praying

Contents

Acknowledgments

I want to express my gratitude to the following:

* the Upper Room Academy 15 leadership team at Mercy Center, San Francisco, for letting me be the focus of a Clearness Committee and for helping me discern the call to write this book.

* Father Luke, Sister Teresa, and the monks of Saint Andrews, Valyermo, California, for their hospitality as I began writing this book. The snow and the power failure made writing an interesting challenge.

* Bill Broyles and Joan Scott, my brother- and sister-in-law, for the use of their guesthouse for many weeks of writing in the solitude and warmth of the Arizonan desert.

* my Academy leadership team for continually calling forth my gifts in the area of spiritual formation and writing. I have been blessed with five wonderful friends and colleagues: Suzanne, Odis, Elise, Kathy, and Dick.

* my wonderful spiritual directors and teachers from traditions outside my own. I have been blessed to have spiritual guides from the Quaker, Episcopal, and Roman Catholic traditions.

* all the persons who have encouraged my writing, especially those who have used *Water Words,* the prayers and liturgies I have published for ten years.

* my family and the people of Malibu United Methodist Church for gracing me with time away from normal activities of home and church. Thanks to all those who picked up extra tasks to free me to write.

* JoAnn Miller of Upper Room Books, who shepherded this book and encouraged my writing; and Anne Trudel, Sarah Schaller-Linn, and Denise Duke, who guided me through the details, permissions, and edits. Such gracious support!

An Invitation

Our hearts are restless till they find rest in Thee.

—Augustine

*T*he words of Saint Augustine shape the invitation of this book. I invite you to come close to God through remembering the saints, reading the Psalms, and practicing prayer.

We are restless until we connect with our Creator. From our central relationship with God and from our awareness of this centrality, we discover our true identity and enter into healthy relationships with others and with all of creation. From living in the presence of the sacred, we discover our vocation of service to others. As we deepen our relationship, we raise our voices in praise to God. "It was you who formed my inward parts; you knit me together in my mother's womb. I praise you, for I am fearfully and wonderfully made" (Ps. 139:13-14). From a living and breathing connection to God, praise and joy erupt.

Yet today, life's pressures and distractions often keep us from knowing God. Busyness invades our life so that we do not have or take the time to deepen our connection with the Source of life. Full calendars, packed days, endless demands occupy the present and threaten the future. Work, school, or family—sometimes all of them—compete for our minutes and our focus.

One writer says he tries to do some serious reading every day but laments that distractions threaten to prevail. It is hard to sit and do one task without our mind, phone, or pager calling us to something else. We have so many options for how to spend our time; the choices can overwhelm us. Distractions and busyness keep us from noticing the movements of the Spirit, from hearing the whispers of God, from walking with Jesus.

Deep in our hearts we feel restless. Deep in our souls we want to be more aware of and attuned to the Ruler of the universe, the Giver of life. Yet often we do not act on this hunger of the heart. Why don't we do what our heart yearns to do? Paul wrestled with this question as he acknowledged how he usually ended up doing what he didn't want to do and ignoring what he wanted to do (Rom. 7:15).

I pray that this book helps move your restless heart into the presence of God, providing you with examples of faithful living, challenging thoughts, prayer practices, and daily scripture reading. I hope it becomes a simple and trusted companion as you create a space to commune with God and develop a prayer practice to combat the distractions in your life.

In this book each daily meditation features a saint or event to remember and receive as comfort or challenge. Next I invite you to read from the Psalms and other selected scripture passages. By the end of the year, you will have read all 150 psalms and prayed the prayer book of the Hebrew people. A time of pondering, an invitation to reflect on the psalm and sometimes on the saint, follows the reading. Finally each day I suggest a method or pattern of prayer and invite you to practice this pattern in the hopes of guiding you closer to the God who created you and desires your prayer and witness.

SAINTS AND EVENTS

We humans seem to have short memories. We try to live independently, to pull ourselves up by our own bootstraps. In so doing we miss the encouragement and wisdom from the past. In the church we talk about the communion of the saints, the cloud of witnesses who have gone before us and who carry us in their prayers. Yet most Protestant churches give attention to saints only one day a year, All Saints' Day (Nov. 1). Some churches do not even celebrate this day, since it does not always fall on a Sunday.

Thank God for that one day at least, but we need to hear and know the stories of people who can teach us something about faith, goodness, sacrifice, and compassion. The "saints" mentioned in these pages come from the margins and mainstreams of life. Some have been formally canonized by the Roman Catholic Church, but many have not. Some you will have heard of, while others will be new to you. Some still live, but most belong to the great cloud of witnesses who have died. They are not perfect people to be put on a pedestal and either adored or ignored. Rather, they exemplify faith and creative responses to the needs of their particular time, and they challenge us to be equally faithful, creative, and even courageous in our witness and service.

I have chosen a few "saints" who are not part of the Judeo–Christian heritage. I believe God's love crosses boundaries and appears in women and men of faith in many religious traditions. I receive encouragement to be a better Christian from the social compassion of a Gandhi or the spiritual poetry of a Rumi. God's blessings come from many, often surprising, sources.

Robert Ellsberg says, "We are formed by what we admire."[1] In this book's daily meditations, I lift up people other than the sports and movie stars receiving so much media attention today. We need to cultivate a deeper look at history that moves beyond the popular or successful to recognize people who are faithful, noble, and good. Our young people need models of commitment and service. We all need witnesses who, in their humanity and ordinariness, remind us of a life centered on God and lived out in love, sacrifice, and generosity. As Ellsberg says so simply, "To call someone a saint means that his or her life should be taken with the utmost seriousness. It is a proof that the gospel can be lived."[2]

Psalms

The Psalms comprise the prayer book of the Hebrews and the early Christian church, and for good reason. In this collection of 150 prayers, you find every emotion and the varieties of human experience transformed into the ingredients of private and public prayer. The Psalms gave voice to the writers' anger and hatred, frustration and despair, sorrow and pain, hope and joy. The psalmists directed prayer to God, the One who hears and responds, weeps and rejoices, receives and acts.

Praying the Psalms connects us to a community. We are not the first to pray these psalms; rather, we join our hearts with ancient and contemporary people in using these words to take us into the heart of God. We join our voices with the Hebrews in exile; with Teresa of Avila in reforming religious communities; with Dietrich Bonhoeffer in prison in Nazi Germany; with Thomas Merton in the monastery near Louisville, Kentucky; with the small church in our town; and with the lonely one who prays in the middle of the night.

The Psalms provide us with a language of intimacy and feeling. These writings let us know that we can approach God with any emotion—joy or sorrow, depression or oppression. The Psalms can enable us to turn our strongest feelings and our most amazing or puzzling life experiences into prayer.

Over this year, I invite you to read all 150 psalms and to let their incredible richness deepen your practice of prayer. The psalms themselves suggest various ways of prayer, from praise to lament, from thanksgiving to tears. Above all, I hope that the Psalms will lead you into the presence of God, giving you a language to speak to God and a way to listen to God.

PRAYER AND PRACTICE

To have a life of prayer, one must pray. *Openings* provides thoughts, reflections, and practices to help you pray. The practice of prayer undergirds the heart of any faith. You can pray in the comfort of a chair in front of a fire or in the company of a choir singing Handel's *Messiah.* Your prayer practice may involve you in serving the poor at a soup kitchen or in praying with a small group for healing of the sick. Individuals and groups can practice hundreds of ways of prayer. The abundance of varieties can overwhelm one and inhibit the spiritual journey. However, you must begin somewhere and sometime. Now is a good time, and this book can serve as your companion and guide for the journey.

Initially, the prayer practices may seem like just another obligation to add to an already full schedule. But my intent is for the prayer practices to shape your life every moment of the day so that you may indeed "pray always" and "without ceasing" (Luke 18:1 and 1 Thess. 5:17). I invite you to move from *saying* prayers to *living* a life of prayer, a life constantly aware of the presence of God. Such communication and communion with God can happen in the ordinary activities of life.

Setting aside time for prayer practice (and to read this book) remains important. The discipline of scheduling time for prayer practice, for "saying prayers," teaches us to be more prayerful. Our intentional time of prayer rehearses the way we want to live and act. Our time of focused prayer lets us express our gratefulness and our connectedness.

HOW TO CREATE A DAILY PRAYER PRACTICE

Creating a daily prayer practice takes discipline. The goal is not to be rigid but faithful. Here are some hints to guide you:

- *Find a time that works for you.* Spend from fifteen minutes to an hour in a focused time of reading and praying. Many people find mornings best, before activities impact the day.

- *Find a space that works for you.* Choose a quiet, uninterrupted place, a warm and inviting space. Find a comfortable chair or pillow. Light a candle, open a Bible, and consider creating an altar or table with objects that evoke quiet or prayer. Some like to sit near a window that looks out on nature.

- *Find a balance of sound and silence that works for you.* Allow for solitude. Not only do you want to talk with God but also to listen. Minimize distractions and interruptions.

- *Consider using music as an aid to prayer and as a way to move from the noise of the day into a time of prayer.* Music can help you connect with your emotions, taking you into sadness or dancing.

- *Keep a Bible, a journal for writing reflections, and this book with you as your prayer companions.* You may also think of other spiritual books or tapes that you want to have accessible.

- *Consider copying the prayers that begin each month* and posting them so that you can pray them each day of the current month.

Words of Encouragement

Don't wait for all the perfect conditions or the perfect setting. *Begin where you are, as you are.* Notice God's presence.

You will not connect with all the practices. Try them all; see which ones bring you to a deeper awareness of God and which ones increase your capacity to love. Some practices will stretch you, yet I encourage you to try them. God desires your growth.

Stay flexible; treat yourself gently. If you miss a day or change your rhythm to meet a situation, don't be too hard on yourself. God forgives.

Look for companions, but don't make comparisons. Other people can hold us accountable to our promises, but each person's spiritual journey is unique and follows its own time line.

As the poet Rumi said so beautifully:

Work. Keep digging your well.
Don't think about getting off from work.
Water is there somewhere.

Submit to a daily practice.
Your loyalty to that
is a ring on the door.

Keep knocking, and the joy inside
will eventually open a window
and look out to see who's there.[3]

My prayers are with you as you open your heart and the windows of your soul to discover the amazing presence of God.

January

Loving God, journey with me this year
so that I may feel your presence,
abide in your forgiveness, grow in your strength,
and dwell in your love.
Give me an open heart,
an open mind,
and open eyes
so that I may sing your praise
and follow your path always and everywhere. Amen.

January 1

REMEMBER

Mary of Nazareth (first century), a woman of exceptional faith, responded to God's invitation to bear God's son by saying, "I am the Lord's servant! Let it happen as you have said" (Luke 1:38, CEV).

READ

Psalm 1

PONDER

Both Mary and the psalmist express openness to God. Mary trusts in God and yields to the incredible promise that she will bear God's child. The openness and surrender evident in her prayer soon give way to a song of praise called the Magnificat. "My soul magnifies the Lord, and my spirit rejoices in God my Savior" (Luke 1:47). Like Mary, the psalmist knows the delight in opening to the presence of God, meditating on God's truths, and drinking from the depths of God's wisdom. Rooted like a tree planted near water, the psalmist feels fruitful and alive, nourished and productive in the Creator's blessings. Praise bubbles forth and joy flows freely: "Happy are those . . . (whose) delight is in the law of the LORD" (Ps. 1:1-2).

PRAYER/PRACTICE

This year, make some promises to yourself about your spiritual growth.

- What books do you wish to read?

- In what ways do you want to dwell with scripture?

- What relationships do you want to deepen and grow?

- What witness to justice do you want to make?

- How might God be calling you to deepen your faith, to walk more closely with the One who created you?

Write down your promises. Pray for openness to God's leading and for courage to keep your promises in this new year. Thank God for a whole year to practice prayer and to live gratefully and lovingly.

January 2

REMEMBER

Saint Basil and Saint Gregory (fourth century), monks, friends, and defenders of the faith, supported the growth of monasticism and encouraged individual monks (hermits) to meet together in community.

READ

Psalm 2

PONDER

A brand new day and year unfold. New possibilities, new challenges, and new beginnings await. How do we begin? "Worship God in adoring embrace, Celebrate in trembling awe" (Ps. 2:11, THE MESSAGE).

Whereas the first psalm spoke to individuals, this psalm expands the horizons to include nations and rulers. "O kings, be wise; be warned, O rulers of the earth" (v. 10). Leaders and all people are instructed to serve God, to be wise and sensible. The psalmist invites us to order our lives according to God's guidance and commands and thus to live in joy, awe, and reverence before God.

PRAYER/PRACTICE

Esther de Waal says, "Now I know that there is no necessary connection between physical discomfort and holy thoughts. So sit, or kneel, or lie, or use a prayer stool."[1] As you begin this new year of prayer, I invite you to remain open to trying new ways and patterns of prayer. Choose any posture that allows you to feel comfortable and alert—sitting in a comfortable chair, lying on the bed, or sitting on the floor. Each day open yourself to the God who loves you and wants you to live with abundant joy and compassionate care. Choose a posture that allows you to remain open to the whispers of God. Ask God for the courage to serve this year with joy, reverence, and awe.

January 3

REMEMBER

Lucretia Mott (1793–1880), a Quaker traveling minister born this day, lived out her faith as a pacifist and women's rights pioneer. Active in the struggle to abolish slavery and to gain the right for women to vote, Mott helped organize the first women's rights convention in 1848 in Seneca Falls, New York. She adhered to the Quaker belief that God dwells in each person, even those denied rights by society.

READ

Psalm 3

PONDER

The Hebrew word *ruach* translates as wind, breath, or spirit. Our breathing connects us to the Spirit. We live by breathing; we live by Spirit. Our actions flow from the liberating and compassionate Spirit of God. God sustains us in our waking and sleeping (v. 5). Awareness of our breathing focuses and deepens our prayer and meditation. Through focusing on our breathing, we can release worries and concerns and connect with the divine breath.

PRAYER/PRACTICE

Every breath can serve as a prayer. Pay attention to your breathing right now. Is it shallow, mostly in the chest, or does it reach down to your belly (diaphragm)? Is the rhythm of your breathing regular, or does it come in fits and starts? Take a big breath and exhale slowly. Notice how your stomach expands and relaxes. Does your breath feel like a sigh of relief? Can you feel your body come to a deeper rest?

Several times today focus on your breathing. Take a deep breath and let it out slowly. The air you breathe is the wind of the Spirit. Relax and breathe deeply of God.

January 4

REMEMBER

Elizabeth Ann Seton (1774–1821) opened the first American Catholic parochial school, established the first American Catholic orphanage, and founded the American Sisters of Charity. She was the first U.S. native to be declared a saint by the Roman Catholic Church.

READ

Psalm 4

PONDER

Psalm 4 occupies a traditional place in the service of evening prayer. If you visit a monastery and stay for the night service, you will probably pray this psalm. The psalmist cries for help in the midst of trouble, evidencing deep trust that God hears hurt and pain. One paraphrase ends the psalm with these words: "In peace will I spend my days and sleep at night; For You alone, my Beloved, take away my fears" (Ps. 4:8, PFP). With glowing confidence in God, the psalmist, monastic communities, and many others have found comfort in praying this psalm before going to sleep.

PRAYER/PRACTICE

When you take fast, shallow breaths, your body responds with increased heart rate and blood pressure. When you take slow, deep breaths, your body responds with rest and peace.

Focus again today on your breathing. Take a deep breath (what some call a letting-go breath or a big sigh breath) and then shift to belly breathing, watching your diaphragm expand and relax. After another deep sigh breath, spend a minute or two practicing slow belly breathing.

Practice deep breathing several times today. Center your mind on God breathing in and through you.

January 5

REMEMBER

Joseph Jean Lanza del Vasto (1901–1981), called the Servant of Peace by his teacher Gandhi, founded the Community of the Ark in France. This community based itself on common work, religious life, and nonviolence. Del Vasto sought to bring Gandhi's principles to the West and actively campaigned against injustice and violence.

READ

Psalm 5

PONDER

Many people find morning to be the best time for prayer. The psalmist says, "In the morning you hear my voice; in the morning I plead my case to you, and watch" (v. 3).

Some fitness trainers say that people who exercise in the morning will more likely remain faithful to this discipline. It's a good practice to exercise or pray before the tasks and busyness of the day clamor for attention and tempt one to skip morning rituals. The mind and body can be tempted to think, *I'll exercise (or pray) later.* Usually "later" turns into "I did not pray (or exercise) today. I'll try again tomorrow." Certainly one can pray anytime of the day, but the psalmist speaks words of wisdom from the past. Begin the day with some morning time for God.

PRAYER/PRACTICE

A meditation class I took suggested counting breaths in order to focus the mind on one's breathing. This day, after a deep sigh breath, on your next inhalation, mentally focus on the number 4. Lightly blow out all the air as you keep your mind focused on the number 4. On the next inhalation and exhalation, focus on 3, then 2 and 1 on successive breaths. Repeat the counting of breaths for about five minutes. Remember to use your belly (diaphragm) breathing. If thoughts come to your mind, notice them and return your focus to the number. Repeat this exercise two or three times during the day.

January 6

REMEMBER

The Magi from the east followed the star to the Christ child and presented gifts to the child. Warned in a dream not to return to Jerusalem, they went home a different way, disobeying King Herod's command.

READ

Matthew 2:1-12

PONDER

Epiphany, the celebration of the visit of the Magi, marks the end of the Christmas season. Eastern Orthodox communities claim this as the most important celebration, for Epiphany symbolizes that Jesus came for the stranger and the foreigner. The shepherds' visit to the manger symbolizes that Jesus came for the poor. The birth of Jesus affects the whole world, rich and poor, stranger and friend.

The Sundays following Epiphany tell the stories of the wedding feast at Cana, the baptism of Jesus, and the beginning of Jesus' ministry of calling, teaching, and healing. These Epiphany days give a glimpse into the wonder of Jesus, who draws us and the stargazing Magi into his presence.

PRAYER/PRACTICE

One of our family traditions involves keeping on the dining room table a symbol of whatever church season we are celebrating. During Epiphany, we bring out three kings (minus any other nativity scene figures) and place them on the table. We also hang stars over the table and in doorways.

Consider ways you might decorate your home this Epiphany season. Go outside and look at the stars. Let go of worry and fear, and trust that God will place a star on your horizon to guide you. Inside the house, light a candle to symbolize God's light in the darkest time of the year.

Remember also to practice your breathing today.

January 7

REMEMBER

Zora Neale Hurston (1903–1960), an author, anthropologist, and African American folklorist born this day, revealed insights into the black heritage in both fictional and factual accounts.

READ

Psalm 6

PONDER

The Psalms touch the deepest emotions with unflinching honesty. These writings bring all of life—the hidden dungeons and the surprising ecstasies—to God. In this penitential psalm, one of seven so designated, we find a question frequently on our lips as we confront illness or injustice: "How long, O God, how long?" The psalmist implores God to respond and even gives God reasons to act: "Save me, if you love me; for in death there is no remembrance of you; who can sing your praises in Sheol?" (vv. 4-5, JB).

The strong language of lament usually ends in a word of trust or praise. "For Yahweh has heard the sound of my weeping; Yahweh has heard my petition, Yahweh will accept my prayer" (vv. 8-9, JB). The lament psalm moves from hopeless despair to confident assurance. Thanks be to God!

PRAYER/PRACTICE

Focusing on our breathing helps us begin to befriend silence, one of the simplest and best gifts to deepen prayer. In prayer we both talk to and listen to God. For most people today, listening is harder. Words and images bombard us all day long, and if we stop to be silent, our minds still whirl with the events of the day and undone tasks. We need to befriend silence so we can listen to the whispers of God.

Today, after a big sigh breath, instead of counting, try saying two words from Psalm 46 as you breathe in and out, using belly breathing: "Be still." As you inhale, say "Be"; as you exhale, say "still." Try this breath prayer for five minutes several times today.

January 8

REMEMBER

A. J. Muste (1885–1967), a Christian pacifist, lived a long life of integrity and witness to nonviolence, speaking out against the Cold War, the Vietnam War, and the insanity of nuclear weapons.

READ

Psalm 7:1-11

PONDER

"There is no way to peace, peace itself being the way."[2] These words of A. J. Muste remind us of the interconnection of ends and means. We cannot create a peaceful community if we harbor resentments, anger, and hatred. Our frantic worry, obsessive zeal, and lack of peace often taint our good intentions and well-meaning actions.

Likewise, the writer of 1 John says, "Those who say, 'I love God,' and hate their brothers or sisters, are liars, for those who do not love a brother or sister whom they have seen, cannot love God whom they have not seen" (1 John 4:20). Love must become a part of our actions, our prayers, and our whole way of being.

PRAYER/PRACTICE

In *The Hunger of the Heart*,[3] Ron DelBene suggests the breath prayer as a way to enter God's presence. The breath prayer consists of a short sentence or phrase of adoration and petition repeated over and over while inhaling and exhaling. The Jesus Prayer ("Lord Jesus Christ, have mercy on me") is a well-known breath prayer.

Develop your own breath prayer. In a time of silence, ask yourself these questions: What image or title for God do I use in prayer? If God or Jesus asked me, "What do you want or need the most?" how would I respond? Your breath prayer will arise from your deepest needs. (Example: "Holy God, help me know your love.")

Keep on working with the words until you have a prayer of six to eight syllables. Say part of the prayer as you inhale and the rest as you exhale. Repeat your breath prayer several times today as you practice deep breathing.

January 9

REMEMBER

Galileo Galilei (1564–1642), an Italian astronomer, believed that the earth revolved around the sun. This radical idea challenged the accepted and rigid views of society and the church. Even under the threat of torture by the religious hierarchy, Galileo remained a person of deep faith.

READ

Psalm 7:12-17

PONDER

Trees that bend with the wind stand a better chance of not breaking. Though deeply rooted, they can remain supple and flexible. The psalmist chooses this image as a model for institutions and people. We need to establish our roots in God but not become so brittle and rigid that we have trouble moving to the fresh wind of God, which often comes from unlikely sources.

Many years passed before the church could repent of what it did to Galileo. The church hierarchy finally realized the truth of the psalm. They had dug a pit of faulty perceptions and had fallen into their own narrow view (v. 15). The psalmist said, "Their mischief returns upon their own heads" (v. 16).

PRAYER/PRACTICE

Some people take awhile to find their breath prayer. If you think of several ideas or have trouble discovering your breath prayer, try answering this question: How would it feel if what you want comes true? Or you might ask: What do I want that would make me feel most whole? The answer to either of these questions forms the petition part of your prayer. Write down your thoughts and eliminate or combine some to come up with a six- to eight-syllable prayer that fits one inhalation and exhalation. Some prayers place the name for God at the beginning; others work best with it at the end. What rhythm works for you?

The purpose of a breath prayer is to bring you into God's presence and to help you pray unceasingly. Practice your breath prayer fifteen to twenty times during the day.

January 10

REMEMBER

Evagrius Ponticus (345–399), a desert hermit, became one of the earliest persons to speak of the value of contemplative prayer. He wrote about the spiritual life of monks and described stages of spiritual growth.

READ

Psalm 8

PONDER

Perhaps the psalmist composed this psalm at night while looking at the moon and stars or perhaps while looking at a baby. However the psalm came to be written, it testifies to the sense of awe and wonder humans experience when they consider the works of the Creator. The words of this psalm echo in countless hymns and songs. We often begin prayers of praise and express our gratitude to the Creator by saying, "How majestic is your name in all the earth!" (v. 1).

In the stage version of Jane Wagner's book, *The Search for Signs of Intelligent Life in the Universe*, Lily Tomlin plays a bag lady named Trudy. Delightfully quirky and uncommonly wise, Trudy suggests that all people should do "awe-robics" every day.[4] Praying Psalm 8 is a good way to begin. Use Psalm 8 as your prayer of awe and wonder. Stand outside or in the presence of a baby and express your awe and thanksgiving to the Creator.

PRAYER/PRACTICE

Any good spiritual discipline grows and deepens with practice. I invite you to try out and practice a number of spiritual disciplines over the course of this year.

Your breath prayer, a wonderful gift to use in your time of prayer, can focus the mind and calm the body, preparing you to listen to the still small voice of God.

Today, pray your breath prayer several times. You may wish to write your breath prayer on cards and put them around the house, office, or wherever you spend most of your time. Every time you see a card, say your breath prayer. Try to say it twenty times today.

January 11

REMEMBER

Someone who helped you learn how to pray. It may be a family member, someone at church, or even an author or teacher.

READ

Psalm 9:1-10

PONDER

The psalmist gives thanks for God's deeds and for being "a stronghold in times of trouble" (v. 9). Thanksgiving weaves its way through many of the Psalms and models for us the practice of gratitude. "I will give thanks to the LORD with my whole heart" (v. 1). The simple words *thank you* mean so much to people around us. I heard someone remark, "Saying thank you moves beyond good manners to honoring God and deepening our spirituality." The Psalms teach us and give us a vocabulary of praise and thanksgiving that goes beyond good manners.

PRAYER/PRACTICE

Today consider writing or calling someone who has assisted you on your spiritual journey to express your thanks. Who taught you to pray? Who has listened to your questions and your struggles? Who remembers you in prayer? If your teachers or guides are no longer living, offer a special prayer of thanks for their gifts to you.

Today practice saying thank you. Remain aware of big and little occasions to say thanks. You might also wish to consciously say grace before all your meals.

Continue to practice your breath prayer. Be aware that your name or title for God constitutes a way of adoration, and your request forms a prayer of petition. You may also count your breaths as a way to meditate.

January 12

REMEMBER

Evelyn Underhill (1875–1941), a British mystic and writer, emphasized the importance of worship, pacifism, and spiritual direction. Her book *Mysticism* remains a classic on the subject.

READ

Psalm 9:11-20

PONDER

"For the needy shall not always be forgotten, nor the hope of the poor perish forever" (v. 18). Though a gifted writer on mysticism, the spiritual life, and worship, and though a sought-after spiritual retreat leader, Evelyn Underhill knew she needed to balance her prayer life and spiritual work with active service to the needy. Her spiritual director, Baron von Hügel, occasionally advised her to go serve the poor, for he thought that her blood lodged too much in the brain and not enough in the hands and feet. Underhill's life became a testimony of service to the poor and offered leadership for the church. Thank God for the Psalms and for friends who remind us to care for the poor and needy.

PRAYER/PRACTICE

You can use your breath prayer throughout the day. Whenever you find yourself waiting at a traffic light, standing in line, or waiting in a doctor's office, say your breath prayer. Any time you spend waiting becomes an opportunity to pray.

You may also find support for developing your prayer life by sharing your breath prayer with others. When they remember you, they will know the deepest prayer of your heart. You may also share your breath prayer with a small group (and invite other group members to share their breath prayers) and thus pray for one another.

Share your breath prayer with at least one person, and ask him or her to remember you in prayer sometime during the day.

Keep practicing breathing and praying.

January 13

REMEMBER

George Fox (1624–1691), founder of the Society of Friends (Quakers), believed that the "seed of God" was present in everyone, enabling them to live righteous and holy lives. He paid no attention to social hierarchy, and he opposed war and violence. The Society of Friends still witnesses to peace, friendship, and the importance of silence and remaining attentive to the inner life.

READ

Psalm 10:1-13

PONDER

In a time when crime seems to pay, the greedy get more, and no one pays attention to the justice of God, read today's psalm again and again. The psalmist begs for God to arise, for justice to be done, for the wicked to see that they cannot get away with oppressing and cheating. "Rise up, O LORD; O God, lift up your hand; do not forget the oppressed" (v. 12).

The Quakers model persistence in doing good. Their witness for peace, attempts at living simply, and efforts for reconciliation remain constant. Give thanks for their founder, George Fox. Give thanks for their faithfulness to living out the gospel in a peaceful and simple way.

PRAYER/PRACTICE

Another way of using the breath in prayer involves focusing the mind on a single word while breathing slowly. Many call this centering prayer, a prayer practice based on a fourteenth-century book titled *The Cloud of Unknowing* and popularly taught by Thomas Keating. (See Appendix A.)

In centering prayer, you select a single word that connects you to God, for example, *holy, Lord,* or *peace.* As you breathe, silently say this word and focus on it with each breath. The prayer word may fall away and enable you to sit silently in the presence of God. If your mind wanders, return to using your prayer word. Try this way of praying today.

January 14

REMEMBER

Martin Niemöller (1892–1984), a Lutheran pastor, founded the Confessing Church in Germany to resist Nazism. Imprisoned for his opposition to Hitler, he became a spokesperson for disarmament after the war.

READ

Psalm 10:14-18

PONDER

These verses of Psalm 10 affirm that God sees and responds to the needs of people, especially the poor and orphans. Contrast God's attention and compassion with our own reluctance to care, as Martin Niemöller expressed in his writing about World War II:

> First they came for the socialists, and I did not speak out—
>   because I was not a socialist.
> Then they came for the trade unionists, and I did not speak out—
>   because I was not a trade unionist.
> Then they came for the Jews, and I did not speak out—
>   because I was not a Jew.
> Then they came for me—and there was no one left to speak
>   for me.[5]

PRAYER/PRACTICE

Choose any method you have been practicing for stilling your mind and body and opening your heart to the God of peace. Take a deep sigh breath and choose from these practices:

- counting your breaths

- repeating a mantra phrase like "Be still"

- saying your breath prayer

- centering prayer, using your prayer word

Spend at least five minutes twice today in your chosen way of prayer.

January 15

REMEMBER

Martin Luther King Jr. (1929–1968), a Baptist pastor, assumed leadership of the civil rights movement with the Montgomery, Alabama, bus boycott. He articulated a dream for all of God's children and backed up that dream with nonviolent marches, sit-ins, and stirring sermons and speeches. The witness of Gandhi and the radical love of Jesus shaped King's philosophy and practice. He won the Nobel Peace Prize in 1964.

READ

Psalm 11

PONDER

"When the world crumbles, what can the good hope to do?" (v. 3, AP). The psalmist's anguishing question leads to the words and witness of Martin Luther King Jr. In the segregated world of the 1960s, many must have felt there was no hope. But not Dr. King.

> Truth crushed to earth will rise again. How long? Not long! Because no lie can live forever. How long? Not long! . . . Because the arc of the moral universe is long but it bends toward justice.[6]

> When our days become dreary with low-hovering clouds and our nights become darker than a thousand midnights, let us remember that there is a great benign Power in the universe whose name is God, and [God] is able to make a way out of no way, and transform dark yesterdays into bright tomorrows. This is our hope for becoming better men [and women]. This is our mandate for seeking to make a better world.[7]

PRAYER/PRACTICE

Martin Luther King Jr. challenged people to live out of a new dream of justice and peace where all of God's children would be free to enjoy equal opportunity and access to God's blessings.

Think of deeds of kindness and acts of justice you can do. Choose one simple deed to do today. In your prayer time, reflect on ways you help build the new community of justice and peace.

January 16

REMEMBER

Frank Laubach (1884–1970), a modern mystic and missionary to the Philippines, India, and other countries, created a literacy program using symbols and pictures that proved effective in underdeveloped countries. Many know this literacy program as "Each One Teach One."

READ

Psalm 12

PONDER

The psalmist anguishes and despairs over the disappearance of the faithful (v. 1) and being surrounded by flagrant lies (v. 2) and double hearts (v. 2). In anger, the psalmist prays that God will "cut off all flattering lips and every boastful tongue" (v. 3, NIV).

Frank Laubach worked with words so that they did not cover up evil but communicated the gospel in foreign lands. His teaching methods allowed people to read, to become literate, and even to teach others. His compassion for others carried out God's promise of care for the poor and needy (v. 6).

PRAYER/PRACTICE

A strong intention, a deep desire, and a ready will are gifts that deepen one's prayer life. Ask God for a fervent desire to remain faithful to your spiritual journey and for help in practicing daily awareness of the divine presence.

Continue to use your breath prayer for a focused time (five to ten minutes) and during periods of waiting you encounter during the day.

January 17

REMEMBER

Saint Anthony of Egypt (c. 251–356) left a prosperous life in Egypt, sold all his possessions, and went to live in the desert with God. His wisdom from wrestling with inner demons, which he described as wild beasts, and his radiance in following Christ attracted disciples. Anthony organized his followers into a community bound by a rule of life, and he became abbot of this early monastic community.

READ

Psalm 13

PONDER

The Psalms provide us with a structure for lamenting. Many happenings in our lives and in the world cause us pain and discouragement. The Psalms invite us to take our anguish to God in prayer.

Usually the lament psalms begin by calling God's name, making the complaint or concern known in strong language, and asking for God's help. Sometimes they give reasons for God to act and even suggest what God should do in the situation. After all these words, one can almost sense a deep sigh; then the lament ends with gratitude that God hears and responds. Often a doxology, a short verse of praise, concludes the psalm. Notice the lament structure of this brief, poignant psalm.

PRAYER/PRACTICE

A good prayer practice often begins with writing your own prayers. When you start to write, you will find words buried in your heart, longing to be expressed.

Today try writing a lament. What events or circumstances in your life or in the world disturb you so much that you wish God would intervene? You might begin by evaluating whether you have some lingering grief, wound, or hurt. Use that memory as a beginning for your lament. Use the pattern suggested above to write your own lament.

January 18

REMEMBER

Priscilla (first century) and her husband, Aquila, important members of the early Christian community, opened their home as the base for Paul's ministry in Corinth and surrounding areas.

READ

Psalm 14

PONDER

There is a difference between a "fool for Christ" and a fool. "Fools for Christ" willingly step out of line, away from the ordinary, to follow Christ. They are not embarrassed or ashamed of their love for Christ even if others make fun of them. They may fall, but they get up.

Fools, on the other hand, say there is no God, and their behavior and deeds are corrupt (v. 1). That is no laughing matter, says the psalmist. "Don't they know anything, all these imposters? Don't they know they can't get away with this?" (v. 4, THE MESSAGE).

PRAYER/PRACTICE

Continue to practice your breath prayer or centering prayer. As you breathe, remain mindful that God dwells all around and within you. God, the Creator, made you. God dwells as close as your breath.

Take a deep sigh breath and let go of anxiety and worry about the day. Rest in God's presence, knowing that God wants to grant you the desire of your breath prayer. Sit confidently and quietly in that awareness of God. Breathe in the presence of the Spirit.

January 19

REMEMBER

In Celtic tradition, a spiritual companion or soul friend is called an *anmchara*. Saint Brigit of Ireland is believed to have said, "Anyone without a soul-friend is a body without a head."[8] Remember one of your spiritual companions.

READ

Psalm 15

PONDER

The term *soul friend* reminds us of the long tradition of spiritual guidance. We all need companions on the spiritual journey. Sometimes we feel the need for one person to notice and give special attention to the movement of the Spirit in our lives. We look for someone wise enough to know how to listen with care and respond without judgment. We long for someone attentive to his or her own spiritual journey so that he or she can notice pitfalls or sunsets on our path. We long for those persons who "walk blamelessly, and do what is right, and speak the truth from their heart" (v. 2).

PRAYER/PRACTICE

If you do not already have a spiritual director, this year you may wish to find and experience the blessings of a soul friend. Look at nearby retreat centers or check with a pastor, priest, rabbi, or spiritual friend. Spiritual Directors International publishes a directory of spiritual directors by regions of the world. (See Appendix A. We will explore more about spiritual direction in June.)

Lines or images from psalms provide a good beginning for prayer, whether written or silent. Psalm 15 lists attributes of people who live on God's holy hill. Begin your prayer like this: "I want to be among those who _____." Fill the blank with attributes that can take you to the holy hill of God.

January 20

REMEMBER

Madame Jeanne Guyon (1648–1717) left French aristocratic society to write about prayer and the devotional life, especially about abandoning oneself to God's will. She remained faithful to God even though arrested several times for her beliefs.

READ

Psalm 16:1-6

PONDER

"You, LORD, are all I have, and you give me all I need; my future is in your hands. How wonderful are your gifts to me; how good they are!" (vv. 5-6, GNT). Resounding with confidence and assurance, this psalm represents the other side of lament. One senses the psalmist looking back over life, rejoicing to have turned from the errors of the past and looking forward to a future God prepares. The future may not be well-defined, but the shape and boundaries rest in God's hands. The future God prepares looks bright and beckoning. Do you have that same trust and confidence about your future?

PRAYER/PRACTICE

Some persons like to use a line from scripture or from a hymn or song for their breath prayer or mantra. Associating words with a melody can make it easier to remember and pray those words as a breath prayer. Music can also evoke a sense of peace or joy.

What scripture verses or songs help you feel the confidence and trust expressed in Psalm 16? Consider these hymn possibilities:
"Blessed Assurance"
"Amazing Grace"
"Jesus, Remember Me" (Taizé tune)

January 21

REMEMBER

Saint Agnes (d. 304?) refused to give in to a patriarchal culture that said she must be married. Because of her martyrdom at age twelve or thirteen, she became known as the patron saint of chastity.

READ

Psalm 16:7-11

PONDER

God desires that we walk the good path; as we do so in God's presence, we experience fullness of joy (v. 11).

A traveler, hopelessly lost in Ireland, stopped the car and asked directions of an old country gentleman walking alongside the road. "Do you know the way to Kildare?" The old man bent down, looked in the window at the traveler, and in a thick Irish accent said, "Do you have the time to go the beauty way?" Ah yes, do you have the time to dwell in beauty, to notice the flowers, to see the smile of a impish three-year-old, to look up at the sky?

PRAYER/PRACTICE

The Psalms, laden with many wonderful images, not only inspire our written prayers of thanksgiving or lament, but they can also inspire our artistic side. You might try drawing or painting your road or path of life. Or you might try drawing a wagon wheel with your life as the hub and each spoke a joy or pleasure you celebrate as a gift from God.

Notice your breathing throughout the day. If it is fast and shallow, take time to do a deep sigh breath and then some belly breathing with one of your prayer words. Today pay attention to the beauty and joy all around you. Look for the "beauty way."

January 22

REMEMBER

Bartimaeus (first century), a blind beggar, called out to Jesus and then got up, cast off his begging robe, and went to Jesus when the crowds said, "Take heart; get up, he is calling you" (Mark 10:49).

READ

Psalm 17:1-7

PONDER

Both Bartimaeus and the psalmist testify to the importance of stating our needs, of crying out to God for help. Bartimaeus cried out, "Jesus, Son of David, have mercy on me!" (Mark 10:47). The psalmist said, "Hear a just cause, O LORD; attend to my cry" (v. 1).

A baby cries for what it needs. As we get older, though, we often stifle our requests. We fear disappointment, rejection, disregard. We fear we won't like the answer, so we don't even ask. Yet God desires our prayers, our petitions, our cries, and our shouts.

PRAYER/PRACTICE

As we continue to explore ways to pray the Psalms, let Psalm 17 invite you to make your deepest desires known to God. You might use this verse as the beginning of your prayer: "Listen to my heart, O Love Divine; hear the cry within me!" (v. 1, PFP).

Write your prayer in your journal or speak it aloud in some private place. Be as honest and real as you can. Your writing can be for your eyes only.

January 23

REMEMBER
A grandparent who lived a life of faith and showed special care and love.

READ
Psalm 17:8-15

PONDER
You are special to God, the apple of God's eye, one of God's beloved hidden under God's protective wings. We sometimes forget the words of affirmation woven through scripture.

Perhaps we need human faces to let us know and experience God's love. When I was young, my family went several times a year to visit my grandparents, who lived on a farm. My grandmother, though slowed by multiple sclerosis, could still sit in the kitchen and cook. Fresh home-baked bread awaited us when we city folk arrived at the farm. I always felt special as the smell of fresh bread greeted me and my grandmother welcomed me to the farm. Even today the smell of fresh bread evokes memories of my grandmother's special love.

PRAYER/PRACTICE
Henri Nouwen, a Catholic priest and prolific writer, collected a number of "beloved" verses from scripture in his book *Life of the Beloved.* Meditate on these verses today, letting their truth wash over you and flow within you.

> I have called you by name, from the very beginning. You are mine
>   and I am yours. You are my Beloved, on you my favor rests.
> I have molded you in the depths of the earth and knitted you
>   together in your mother's womb.
> I have carved you in the palms of my hands and hidden you in the
>   shadow of my embrace . . .
> I will not hide my face from you.[9]

Don't forget that you are the apple of God's eye (v. 8).

January 24

REMEMBER

Saint Francis de Sales (1567–1622), a bishop and spiritual director, wrote *An Introduction to the Devout Life.* The simply written yet wise book continues to guide people to a more holy and spiritual life.

READ

Psalm 18:1-6

PONDER

Rock-solid. Rock-hard. We know the meaning of these words. The psalmist uses rocks as one of many strong images for God. God is a fortress, a rock of refuge, a shield, a stronghold (v. 2). Whatever trials or battles the psalmist and we might face, we can depend on God, the rock of ages, a mighty fortress, and a strong deliverer. Those powerful images emerge in many hymns and songs. Look in a hymnal for the words to "A Mighty Fortress Is Our God," "Rock of Ages," "How Firm a Foundation," or "Source and Sovereign, Rock and Cloud." Sing about the strength of God.

PRAYER/PRACTICE

The first two verses of this psalm overflow with images for God. Indeed, scripture abounds with words, titles, and images for God. Why, then, do many Christians think Father is the only title we can use for God? For some persons, the image of father evokes painful and hurtful memories of abusive or absent fathers. Addressing God as Father in these instances hinders rather than aids prayer.

Today's psalm gives us other choices. Try using an image from this psalm to begin your prayer. Or try a new image that grows out of your own experience.

January 25

REMEMBER

The story of Paul's conversion, recorded in Acts 9, reveals an incredible transformation.

READ

Psalm 18:7-15

PONDER

Sometimes dramatic, almost cataclysmic, changes occur in our lives or in our world. Paul experienced a life-changing moment on the road to Damascus. Likewise, the psalmist must have experienced a great storm or tremendous victory that gave rise to these verses in Psalm 18. Sometimes it seems that a big or dramatic event must happen to get our attention. We plow through life with heads down and hearts weary, failing to notice that God still acts in the world, bringing hope in the midst of despair, bringing light in the midst of darkness, and sometimes even knocking us off our mount in order to set us on a new path.

PRAYER/PRACTICE

Pray your breath prayer today to keep you aware of God's presence in all the events of the day. Consciously say your breath prayer as you take a drink of water or as you sit down to eat. Say it before you make a phone call or respond to an e-mail. Pray your breath prayer to give thanks for God's presence each time you meet another person or engage in conversation. Take time to notice the sky; keep your breath prayer on your lips and remain aware of God's grandeur.

January 26

REMEMBER

Timothy and Titus (first century), companions of Paul, became early bishops of the church.

READ

Psalm 18:16-24

PONDER

I remember driving late one evening down a major highway in Michigan and seeing a church with a big neon sign that said, "Jesus Saves." Here, in the middle of the eighteenth psalm, flashes a big neon sign: "God saves." God reaches down and delivers David from his enemies. God saves.

In her wonderful paraphrase of the Psalms, Nan Merrill says the enemies are often within us. "You delivered me from the fears that bound me, and from ignorance that blinded me; for they threatened to overcome me, to separate me from You. . . . yet You, O Merciful One, were ever present. You brought me forth into the Light; You released my fears, You delighted in me" (vv. 17, 19, PFP).

PRAYER/PRACTICE

As you reflect on the theme of this psalm, let arise in you a prayer of thanksgiving for all the times and ways you have experienced God's amazing grace, God's amazing love and forgiveness. Borrow some of these thoughts to start your prayer.

> Merciful One, how many times have you rescued me, but I did not say thank you? How many times have I thought there was no way out, but there you were? How many times have you exchanged my fear for trust and I thought it was my own doing? Merciful One, give me a grateful heart this day and always. Amen.

January 27

REMEMBER

John Bunyan (1628–1688), a pastor and author, wrote *The Pilgrim's Progress,* a popular allegory of a Christian's pilgrimage in trusting God's grace from birth until death.

READ

Psalm 18:25-30

PONDER

David, named as the author of this psalm, pushes the limits of exaggeration and stretches the metaphors for God's actions in his battles. "With your help I can advance against a troop; with my God I can scale a wall" (v. 29, NIV). David talks not about a hedge, but a fortress-big, castle-tall wall. This psalm lays the foundation for understandings and powerful images in the New Testament. "I have the strength to face all conditions by the power that Christ gives me" (Phil. 4:13, GNT). With such faith, obstacles in our lives do not frighten us; rather they become opportunities for us to trust in the help and guidance of God, who helps us leap over walls of problems.

PRAYER/PRACTICE

Today's psalm may inspire a new prayer as you continue to practice your breathing. As you breathe in, pray "With God"; as you exhale, say "all is possible." If you feel joyful and playful, pray "Mighty God" on the inhalation and "watch me leap (or soar)" on the exhalation.

When I need energy and strength, such as when I prepare to speak before a group or lead a retreat, I use a similar breath prayer. I trust in God to fill me so that I may leap and soar for God. What bold breath prayer can you carry with you?

January 28

REMEMBER

Saint Thomas Aquinas (1225–1274) is regarded as the most outstanding and influential theologian of the Middle Ages. Despite opposition from his family, he became a Dominican friar and spent most of his life in Paris as a teacher and writer.

READ

Psalm 18:31-42

PONDER

The strong words in this passage assault our sensibilities, our desire for peace, our commitment for working things out. "I struck them down, so that they were not able to rise; . . . those who hated me I destroyed"(vv. 38, 40). Who or what are our enemies today? Fear? anger? racism? hatred? prejudice related to class, gender, or sexual orientation? greed? Would we not want to use strong words, send in our skillful warriors, and draft our best battle plans to strike these from our world, from our communities?

PRAYER/PRACTICE

What weapons do you need to fight injustice? What plans would you develop for subduing hatred, containing anger, overcoming prejudice? Such decisions and strategies need to be bathed and formed in prayer. And prayer becomes one of the garments we put on when we go to face hatred and prejudice.

Today make a list of what you need to face your fears. Make another list of what you need to face the injustices of the world. Pray for God's strength, guidance, and love.

January 29

REMEMBER

Saint Andrei Rublëv (c. 1360–c. 1430), a Russian Orthodox monk and influential artist, painted icons and murals. His most famous icon, *Old Testament Trinity,* uses a biblical subject and striking colors to represent harmony and sacrifice in the life of Christ.

READ

Psalm 18:43-50

PONDER

The artist helps us see. In the Eastern Orthodox Church, the painting of icons—highly spiritualized depictions of Christ, Mary, and the saints—developed as a window for glimpsing the divine. By prayerfully gazing at these icons, one could gradually see beyond the art to view the spiritual reality it represented. The making of icons was itself a spiritual work, usually undertaken after prayer and fasting.

The Psalms also help us see. At the end of the eighteenth psalm, the poet views God's work as deliverance and our work as praise. "Blessed be my rock, and exalted be the God of my salvation"(v. 46).

PRAYER/PRACTICE

The Psalms are prayers, and they also initiate and form our life of prayer. Today you may wish to write a psalm of praise or thanksgiving. Look back over your life and offer God your song of praise. Use bold language and several different titles for God.

Or, today you may wish to begin exploring the use of icons in your meditation. Several books describe the use of icons, and you can purchase icons in some religious bookstores. (See Appendix A.)

January 30

REMEMBER

Mohandas Gandhi (1869–1948) witnessed to the power of love and nonviolence to change individuals and nations as he helped lead India to freedom from rule by Great Britain. Though a devoted Hindu, Gandhi believed in the teachings of Jesus, even if he considered Christians less than exemplary in living up to the loving ways of Jesus.

READ

Psalm 19:1-6

PONDER

While the psalmist saw the grandeur of the heavens, Gandhi saw the power of the ordinary. Gandhi encouraged simple acts of resistance that caused the whole nation of India and indeed the whole world to see injustice. Whether Gandhi fasted, walked, or sat at a spinning wheel, the world paid attention. In his life and witness he embodied the teachings of Christ in the Sermon on the Mount (Matt. 5). Though he remained a committed Hindu, Gandhi helped people realize the power of simple acts of nonviolence and the power of love.

PRAYER/PRACTICE

I invite you to try writing a hymn to creation. Stand outside, if it is not too cold, and gaze at the world in front of you. What prayer wells up inside you? If you lack an opening line, you might begin with Psalm 19:1, "The heavens are telling the glory of God . . ."

Today would also be a good day to watch the movie *Gandhi* or to read a book about him. He influenced many Christians, including Martin Luther King Jr., and helped many realize the strength and nonviolence of Jesus' teachings about love and forgiveness.

January 31

REMEMBER

Any saint from this month.

READ

Psalm 19:7-14

PONDER

The psalmist shifts from poetry about the glories of the heavens to verses expounding the virtues of God's law. Carroll Stuhlmueller writes, "The Law enables us to walk through life *with enough restraint* that we do not hurt or destroy what is fragile or delicate, *with enough direction* that we can move easily and even spontaneously without stopping every minute for new decisions, *with enough harmony* that we enjoy the peace of family and neighborhood." [10]

The two distinct parts of Psalm 19 are linked together by God, who works through the majesty and beauty of creation (vv. 1-6) and the wisdom and guidance of the law.

PRAYER/PRACTICE

Many religious communities recite a psalm prayer after reading a psalm. This short prayer consists of three to five sentences that repeat the themes or images of the psalm and lift them in prayer. Psalm prayers became a shorthand way to remember the psalm, especially long ones.

Try writing a psalm prayer for this psalm, weaving together a word about creation and about law. You may wish to end with the wonderful benediction, "Let the words of my mouth and the meditation of my heart be acceptable to you, O LORD, my rock and my redeemer" (v. 14).

February

God of the winter sky, fill the night with stars,
for I need to lift my eyes and raise my weary soul
from shadows and short days,
from dreary tasks and unending lists.
Shine bright lights into the darkness
and remind me that new life and dormant seeds
gather strength in the depths of the earth.
Open me to the newness inside me
waiting to be born. Amen.

February 1

REMEMBER

February is Black History Month in the United States. Langston Hughes (1902–1967), an African American writer, emerged as a major figure in the Harlem Renaissance, a flowering of music and literature in the 1920s as blacks moved from the South to the North.

READ

Psalm 20

PONDER

"Some may boast of wealth and personal power . . . But our pride is in the name of the Lord our God" (v. 7, PFP). Nations boast of armies and weapons, but if no one worships God, all this armament amounts to nothing. They boast of gross national product and exports, but if no one shows compassion for the poor or honors God, all this wealth is empty. Nations boast of nuclear capabilities and a nuclear shield, but if no one senses that God loves the world and no one negotiates skillfully, all this weaponry amounts to death and destruction. "O Beloved, You who have created us, hear our call, make your home in our hearts!" (v. 9, PFP).

PRAYER/PRACTICE

For most people in the Northern Hemisphere, February continues the darkness and cold of winter. The days after Epiphany, often called Ordinary Time on the church liturgical calendar, continue until the season of Lent. Even in the cold and ordinary days, I invite you to remember God's warmth and love. God knows you and calls you beloved.

Claim these words from the writings of Henri Nouwen to focus your prayer and warm your heart:

> [God says] "I look at you with infinite tenderness and care for you with a care more intimate than that of a mother for her child. I have counted every hair on your head and guided you at every step. Wherever you go, I go with you, and wherever you rest, I keep watch. . . . You know me as your own as I know you as my own. You belong to me."[1]

February 2

REMEMBER

Today we honor the presentation of Jesus, when Mary and Joseph took the infant Jesus to the Temple to offer a prayer and offering for their child in order to fulfill requirements of the law of Moses.

READ

Luke 2:22-40

PONDER

Forty days ago we celebrated the birth of Jesus. The law of Moses excluded a woman from public life for forty days after childbirth. On the fortieth day, the mother was required to go to the Temple to make an offering for purification. Usually the offering consisted of a young lamb and a pigeon or dove. If the family was poor, an offering of two doves or pigeons was acceptable.

Mary and Joseph brought the offering of the poor, yet they received rich blessings (and most likely a little worry) from the words of Simeon and Anna. The son of Mary and Joseph would bring light, glory, and salvation to all the world.

PRAYER/PRACTICE

Simeon's words—"Now let your servant depart in peace, for my eyes have seen your salvation" (vv. 29-30, AP)—almost shape themselves into a song. Indeed, song texts abound for the Canticle of Simeon. In monastic traditions this canticle usually is sung during the last service of the day. The assurance of trust, confidence in God, and willingness to place oneself into God's hands for whatever happens form a comforting blessing before bedtime.

Find a text or musical version of the canticle and commit it to memory. (See Appendix A for sources.) Pray it throughout this week as a bedtime prayer.

February 3

REMEMBER

Brother Lawrence (1611–1691), a member of the Carmelite Order in Paris, dispensed wisdom as well as food during thirty years as a cook at his monastery. His simple and wise counsel was published in a now-classic book, *The Practice of the Presence of God.*

READ

Psalm 21:1-7

PONDER

Brother Lawrence believed that God looks more at the love with which an action is performed than at the greatness or bigness of the work. God's love shone through Brother Lawrence's humble work and his simple wisdom of living mindfully in the presence of God. He revealed his consciousness of God's abiding presence in a famous statement: "The time of business is no different from the time of prayer. I possess God as tranquilly in the noise and clatter of my kitchen, where sometimes several people ask me different things at the same time, as if I were on my knees before the Blessed Sacrament."[2] Indeed, every time and place can offer an opportunity to lift one's heart to God, who is always near and ready to hear.

PRAYER/PRACTICE

Today I invite you to begin exploration of practicing the presence of God. How can you recognize God's presence in the ordinary experiences of your day?

In some countries, particularly in Latin America, small wooden crosses stand alongside the roads. They usually mark where someone died, and they can serve as a call to prayer and to caution.

Think about a typical day in your life and the places you go. Establish some markers that call you to awareness of God and to prayer. The tree you pass can call you to give thanks for the seasons. The stream or river you cross can call you to remember your baptism. The school you drive by can call you to pray for children. Name some markers that will nudge your prayer and awareness of God.

February 4

REMEMBER

Rosa Parks (b. 1913) prompted the Montgomery, Alabama, bus boycott by refusing to give up her seat to a white person and move to the back of the bus. Her courage and the subsequent leadership of Martin Luther King Jr. during the boycott awakened the United States to the civil rights movement.

READ

Psalm 21:8-13

PONDER

It would be a long time before African Americans could sing the last lines from this psalm: "We praise you, LORD, for your great strength! We will sing and praise your power" (v. 13, GNT). When Rosa Parks remained seated in the bus, she started a movement of active resistance to segregation and racism. For much of the 1960s, Rosa Parks, Martin Luther King Jr., and many others led a struggle against the evil policies and practices that had kept African Americans separate and unequal. Songs and prayers focused the civil rights movement on God's yearning for justice for all. We find the basis of this hunger for justice in the Psalms and in the strong words of the prophets in the Hebrew Scriptures.

PRAYER/PRACTICE

Yesterday you set up markers on your travel through a day. Today think of people you meet, work with, or study with each day. As you visualize these people, think of them as being Christ to you or as opportunities for you to be Christ to them. Imagine the light of Christ surrounding each person, loving each individual you meet. Invite Christ's presence into each of your encounters throughout the day. Know that Christ goes before you into each meeting.

Now you have places and people that call you to prayer and awareness as you practice the presence of God in the ordinary experiences of life.

February 5

REMEMBER

Brother Roger Schutz (b. 1915) founded the ecumenical religious community in France called Taizé, which is known for its music, ministry with youth, and work for reconciliation and justice around the world.

READ

Psalm 22:1-5

PONDER

Jesus quoted part of this psalm from the cross: "My God, my God, why have you forsaken me?" (v. 1). The verse gave vent to his feelings of abandonment. Yet the psalm also lifts up the memory of a people who trusted in God and whom God did not disappoint. "In you our ancestors trusted; they trusted, and you delivered them" (v. 4). Even in his agony, Jesus probably remembered the rest of this psalm. What sounds like hopelessness and anguish to us, on a deeper reading, becomes a prayer of hope addressed to the One who hears and responds. "To you they cried, and were saved" (v. 5).

PRAYER/PRACTICE

"Prayer around the Cross," a popular meditative prayer service from Taizé, usually happens at night in a darkened sanctuary lit by candles. Taizé music is sung and chanted by a choir, soloists, and the congregation, and times of silence and scripture reading intersperse with the singing. Toward the end of the service, a large cross is placed on the floor, and people come forward to kneel and pray around the cross. Sometimes each person who comes to pray lights a candle. Music continues, quietly sung by the congregation, as people come to pray.

I invite you to find and attend a Taizé service near you. You may also wish this evening to light a candle, play some quiet music (especially music from the Taizé Community), and kneel for a time of prayer.

February 6

REMEMBER

Saint Paul Miki and Companions (d. 1597) were the first Christian martyrs of Japan in Nagasaki, the center of Christianity in Japan.

READ

Psalm 22:6-11

PONDER

"Do not be far from me, for trouble is near and there is no one to help" (v. 11). Such would have been a prayer of sixteenth-century Japanese Christians. Christianity arrived in Japan in 1549, quickly establishing itself with many converts. But by the turn of the century, repression and persecutions had begun, and from the middle of the seventeenth century until the 1860s, Christianity essentially disappeared from Japan. Despite no clergy and no leadership for two hundred years, a small remnant managed to keep the faith alive and pass it on in hopes of attaining freedom to practice Christianity openly. Nagasaki became a main center of Christianity with a large cathedral, which, sadly and ironically, served as a target for the dropping of the atomic bomb.

PRAYER/PRACTICE

As you continue to practice awareness of God's presence today, notice objects around you that might serve as a call to prayer. Do you have any religious art at home or at work upon which you can intentionally gaze? Some people set up a small altar in their home with special objects to help them focus in prayer. Do you have any religious symbols sacred to you? A cross? A chalice? A bowl and towel? A baptism candle or membership certificate? Imagine two hundred years without church. What symbols and objects would help you keep the faith? Name some objects that will call you to prayer.

February 7

REMEMBER

Dom Helder Camara (1909–1999), a prophetic Roman Catholic bishop in Brazil, encouraged the church to make an "option for the poor." Though small in physical stature, he unsettled big government by his persistent and passionate calls for social justice.

READ

Psalm 22:12-21

PONDER

Either personal tragedy or societal injustice could give rise to the sentiment of this psalm. "O my help, come quickly to my aid!" (v. 19). Archbishop Camara habitually arose at 2 A.M. for prayer to center his work for the poor in the compassion of God. Trusting in God's aid, he spoke out about human rights abuses and encouraged the poor to become agents for social transformation. He chose to wear a wooden cross instead of the customary gold or silver, moved out of the archbishop's mansion, and lived in a humble house. In his lifestyle and in his words, Dom Camara trusted God and lived faithfully, courageously demonstrating the compassion of Christ.

PRAYER/PRACTICE

Two o'clock in the morning may not be your best time to pray, but naming certain times of the day as special times for prayer remains important. The most common times of the day for prayer are morning, evening, and at meals. If you do not have a pattern of prayer at these times, consider choosing one of them as a call to prayer. You might practice your breath prayer during a morning time of sitting for five minutes. You might choose to use the Canticle of Simeon (see Feb. 2) in the evening. Or perhaps you can pray while at the gym, as you drink a morning cup of coffee or an afternoon cup of tea, as you shower, while you walk, or before you go to sleep. Write down your schedule and choose some times to serve as your calls to prayer.

February 8

REMEMBER

Martin Buber (1878–1965), a Jewish theologian interested in interfaith dialogue, influenced Christianity with his book *I and Thou.*

READ

Psalm 22:22-31

PONDER

The twenty-second psalm does not end in anguish and complaint but resounds with gratefulness and praise. "'[God] does not neglect the poor or ignore their suffering; . . . does not turn away from them, but answers when they call for help.' In the full assembly I will praise you for what you have done" (vv. 24-25, GNT). God hears our laments, our anger, and our fear and still works for good even in the midst of our pain. God never looks away even when we wander from the path, give in to greed, or lose our patience. God looks at us with love and forgiveness. Such good news, such love, and such compassion prompt a chorus of praise, an anthem of thanksgiving.

PRAYER/PRACTICE

Places, people, objects, and times of the day all can serve as calls to prayer. Review your thoughts over the last week. How many markers did you set up as calls to prayer?

Do not try to create so many markers that praying feels like a burden—one more task to do in an already too busy day. Be gentle with yourself, yet seek to increase your awareness of God's presence by marking some places, people, objects, and times in your daily rhythm as conscious calls to prayer. These elements constitute the core of practicing the presence of God.

Give thanks for your growing awareness, and ask God to keep you mindful of blessings throughout the day.

February 9

REMEMBER

Alice Walker (b. 1944), an African American novelist, wrote *The Color Purple*, which opened people's eyes to the experience of faith among black people. Read some of her work during Black History Month.

READ

Psalm 23

PONDER

One of the best known and most beloved texts in the entire Bible, the Twenty-third Psalm speaks of a deep confidence in the presence of God, who renews and refreshes us in the splendor of creation; who guides us through dark valleys, shadows, and death; who leads us to our home at the table in the house of the Lord. The psalm does not cover up death, evil, enemies, or weariness; yet through all these situations remains the shepherd with sure and gentle strength, leading us on our path in life. A quiet, strong assurance abides in the words of this psalm. The psalm creates an inner space where we can go often and find rest for our souls and strength for our journeys.

PRAYER/PRACTICE

Henri Nouwen once wrote an article titled "What Do You Know by Heart?" I don't remember much of the content, only that Nouwen said we should know some things by heart. Words of poems, songs, and prayers lodged in the memory and heart can sustain us in all times and seasons. Psalm 23 certainly merits your committing to heart.

Another way to discover the power of assurance in this psalm is to write its opposite. Write about the difficulties, disappointments, and disasters in your life. You might begin with, "The Lord is not my shepherd; I am abandoned, worn out, confused. . . ." After writing your complaints in the most picturesque language possible, take a deep breath and pray the wonderful assurance of Psalm 23. Let its truths sink into your consciousness and refresh you. The Shepherd abides with you; guides you in all times; and lifts you from the difficulties, disappointments, and disasters of life.

February 10

REMEMBER

Saint Scholastica (c. 480–c. 543), twin sister of Saint Benedict, served as abbess of a convent near her brother.

READ

Psalm 23:1-3

PONDER

As a child, I loved to lie on the lawn, feel the grass against my bare feet, and simply enjoy the wonder of sky, grass, and summer. Nowadays I and so many others seem to have fewer hours to rest. When we want to experience nature, we load up tents, recreation vehicles, binoculars, cameras, all-terrain vehicles, or bikes and go off to have an experience we can capture on digital film, DVD, or video.

The simplicity of the first verses of Psalm 23 calls us to slow down, lie down, and sit down in the meadow, by the stream, or near the lake. God beckons us to breathe deeply and let our souls be restored, our lives be without want, and our spirits be at rest.

PRAYER/PRACTICE

The psalm invites us to experience God in nature. If possible today, spend some time outside. Take a walk, go to a park, or gaze at the sky. Visit a lake, walk by a stream, sit under a tree. If indoors, look at a flower, water a plant, gaze at the landscape. Visit an arboretum, a nursery, or a greenhouse.

Remember times when you felt the presence of God in nature. Plan to regularly restore your soul by spending time beside green meadows, gentle waters, well-worn paths.

Thank God for trees that stretch our eyes to the heavens, for streams of water that echo God's constant flow of grace, and for stars that carry us into awe. Consider writing your own prayer of thanks to the Creator.

February 11

REMEMBER

Saint Aelred of Rievaulx (1110–1167), a Cistercian monk, wrote about the friendship of God and led his monastery as a "school of love."

READ

Psalm 23:4-6

PONDER

"Even though I walk through the darkest valley, I fear no evil; for you are with me" (v. 4). This verse has sustained many persons during times of grief. I still remember this passage from the King James Version: "Yea, though I walk through the valley of the shadow of death, I will fear no evil: for thou art with me." Death indeed feels like an emotional jumble of valleys and shadows. Yet the psalmist speaks of hope, implying that we walk *through* the valley rather than staying in the valley. And we do not walk alone. Jesus likewise instructed us to have the courage to mourn, for if we walk through the valley of shadows and death, we shall be comforted (Matt. 5:4).

The psalm concludes with another word of promise that offers hope to the grieving, that we "shall dwell in the house of the Lord forever" (v. 6, AP). The psalm offers us comfort on the journey through the valley of grieving and also lifts up the promise of Christ and the hope of eternal life. Hear the echoes of Jesus' words in John 14, where he says he goes to prepare a room for us. Jesus has gone before us, and so have our loved ones who have died.

PRAYER/PRACTICE

I invite you to draw or visualize a table of any size or shape and see your loved ones, family members, and friends who have died seated at the table. Whom do you see at the table? What does the table look like? What food or drink is on the table? Do you see or sense the presence of Christ? Can you hear any music? Can you feel the prayers of the persons seated at the table? What words of encouragement or support do they have for you? Offer a prayer of thanks for this community of saints that remembers you and has inspired and guided you.

February 12

REMEMBER

Abraham Lincoln (1809–1865), as American president, fought to keep the Union together and to free the slaves. Also remember the founding of the National Association for the Advancement of Colored People (NAACP) in 1909.

READ

Psalm 24:1-6

PONDER

"Who is suited to climb God's mountain and to stand in God's holy place? Whoever has integrity—those who do not chase shadows or live lies. God will bless them and bring them justice" (vv. 3-5, AP). The psalmist cares less about physical strength needed to climb mountains than about inner integrity, personal honesty, and appropriate reverence. Though the dates between them span one hundred years, Abraham Lincoln and the NAACP share the virtue of integrity and the willingness to struggle for justice for minorities and the less fortunate.

PRAYER/PRACTICE

Practicing the presence of God, one of our prayer themes for February, includes living each day in greater awareness of God. I suggested setting up markers in your days—places, people, times, and objects that call you to prayer. Recall the markers you set.

Practicing the presence of God happens in the ordinary experiences of the day. As you get ready for the day, you can do the common tasks of cleansing and dressing in awareness of God. The water used in bathing can remind you of being cleansed for a new day, of your baptism, of God's forgiveness. As you put on your clothes, each garment can signal God's love and blessing. Or you can recall Paul's encouragement to put on the armor of God, the belt of truth, the breastplate of righteousness (Eph. 6:10-17). Create your own images for the items you put on—for example, the dress of beauty, the shirt of kindness, the socks of humility. How can your time of getting ready in the morning serve as an adornment of prayer?

February 13

REMEMBER

Georges Rouault (1871–1958), a French artist, chose bold colors to depict the pathos of the human situation and used bold strokes for his engravings on the passion and death of Christ.

READ

Psalm 24:7-10

PONDER

"Open the doors and gates for the one who is coming"(v. 7, AP). The sentiment of this psalm is appropriate for the seasons of Advent and Lent as Christians prepare to receive either the baby born in a manger or the humble king riding on a donkey into Jerusalem. The psalmist invites us as individuals and as a community to prepare to receive the strong and mighty one, the King of glory. Yet we know this king was born in a stable and crucified on a cross. The Resurrection overturns all preconceptions of the strong and mighty and makes it possible for us to open ourselves to greet the King who acts like no worldly king but still claims our worship and praise.

PRAYER/PRACTICE

Teacher and author Flora Wuellner suggests several ways to remain aware of God's presence as you face your day:

> Early in the day, or on the way to work, reflect on the tasks and the varied experiences ahead. Claim Jesus' promise that he will go ahead of you, preparing the way for you. Picture the Healer already at your place of work (or wherever you go) filling it with light, so that when you get there you will feel welcomed and strengthened.[3]

Try visualizing Christ going before you into this day. See in your mind's eye all the places you will go and people you will meet; see Christ already present.

February 14

REMEMBER

Saint Valentine (d. 269), a priest in Rome, helped Christians persecuted by Emperor Claudius II. Eventually arrested, imprisoned, and martyred because he refused to renounce his faith, Valentine is remembered for his kindness.

READ

1 Corinthians 13

PONDER

I heard a story, which may be true, about a young boy with learning disabilities who decided to make a valentine for every child in his class. Despite misgivings, the boy's mother helped her son painstakingly make and address a valentine for each classmate. She worried that the children would not appreciate the work involved and, even worse, that her son would not receive many, or perhaps no, valentines. When he arrived home after the big day in school, his mother noticed his thin valentines sack, and her heart sank. But the boy smiled and she heard him say, "I didn't forget anyone."

Kindness counts: to classmates, to children, to spouses and partners, to friends and colleagues, to those in prison.

PRAYER/PRACTICE

This is a good day to practice kindness, especially toward persons who may not receive many expressions of kindness. Prisoners and prison employees are often forgotten, shunted off to some isolated place; a card or a letter of encouragement could mean a lot to them. Regularly writing to an inmate may extend Valentine's Day into a ministry of compassion. Church communities can offer support in the process of rehabilitation.

This is also a good day to make your own valentine cards or a gift. What words or images would really express your care and thanks? Look within yourself and less at the advertising around you. Have fun. Be creative and share your cards with others.

February 15

REMEMBER

C. F. Andrews (1871–1940), an English missionary to India, befriended the poor and became a close friend of Gandhi.

READ

Psalm 25:1-5

PONDER

The psalmist voices our desire to know and do what God wants. Of all the great teachers in the world, God, the supreme one, shows us the right paths and how to live. We can trust God to guide us in the ways of truth, to lead us through valleys and shadows, to bring us hope and salvation. Through reading the Bible and developing a life of prayer and other spiritual disciplines, we cultivate a spirit of openness to God's leading; we become attentive students of the wisest teacher.

PRAYER/PRACTICE

Throughout your day, intentionally stop and let the miracles of God's creation remind you of the Creator. Touch or hold an apple or a seashell and marvel at its color, design, shape. Stop to smell a rose or listen to the sound of a bird or a loud clap of thunder. Gaze at a sunset, a cloud formation, snow-covered trees, or a rainbow. Such moments of contemplation sensitize us to the beauty the Creator has placed around us. Today practice thankful awareness by pausing from your normal busyness to look at, smell, touch, listen, and even taste the wonders of God.

February 16

REMEMBER

Saint Brigit of Ireland (c. 452–c. 524), believed to have been converted by Saint Patrick, became the abbess of Kildare Monastery, the only monastery in Ireland that included men and women. A cross made of dried reeds bears her name and in Ireland symbolizes hospitality. Credited with many miracles, Brigit is the patron saint of poets.

READ

Psalm 25:6-10

PONDER

Learning to follow the paths of the Lord requires an awareness of the times we have strayed from doing what is right and good. "Forgive the many times I have walked away from You choosing to walk alone" (v. 7, PFP). Not only do we need forgiveness for the sins of our youth, but we need forgiveness for all those times we have turned our back on God. The psalmist asks God to "remember me" (v. 7), not all the wrongs, sins, and faults. The psalmist counts on God's steadfast love, which abounds in forgiveness. To move from sin to right living, the psalmist counts on God's instruction and guidance. "You are honest and merciful, and you teach sinners how to follow your path" (v. 8, CEV).

PRAYER/PRACTICE

Saint Brigit was known for her acts of compassion and generosity. Today try the following activity:

> As you encounter other people, whether face-to-face, or by phone or letter [or e-mail], think of the light of God surrounding them. Try to become aware of the hurt, bewildered, or anxious "child" within the other. Inwardly reach out and greet each person's inner child. If you feel in any way drained or threatened by the presence of the other, picture or think of Christ, the Healer, standing between you and the other, nurturing the other as well as protecting you.[4]

Carry this awareness of God with you throughout the day, and look for opportunities to perform many acts of compassion and generosity.

February 17

REMEMBER

Janani Luwum (1924–1977), the Anglican archbishop of Uganda, was killed by Idi Amin during his reign of terror.

READ

Psalm 25:11-22

PONDER

General Amin accused Archbishop Luwum of plotting an uprising against him and of storing weapons. The accusations were false, and the archbishop would not sign the confession Amin demanded. Witnesses said that General Amin, angered by Luwum's refusal, flew into a rage when the archbishop began to pray, and Amin shot the archbishop. Perhaps the archbishop remembered the words of this psalm: "Consider how many are my foes, and with what violent hatred they hate me. O guard my life, and deliver me. . . . May integrity and uprightness preserve me, for I wait for you" (vv. 19-21).

In the face of danger, we can pray to the Lord, who hears and may deliver us from the situation or out of the situation into a place beyond tears and pain.

PRAYER/PRACTICE

Throughout this month we have been developing ways to deepen awareness of the Spirit of God around us. We set up markers in each day to call us to prayer and awareness. We looked at the ordinary moments and activities of life as ways to increase our sensitivity to wonder, grace, beauty—as opportunities to see the fingerprints of God.

Today look back on the suggestions for practicing the presence of God. Take time to still your mind and body with your breath prayer; then review your practice and give thanks for how your days have changed.

February 18

REMEMBER

Toni Morrison (b. 1931) and Audre Lorde (1934–1992), African American writers and poets born this day.

READ

Psalm 26

PONDER

If you have ever been falsely accused, you will find a companion in this psalm of lament. The author makes a case for his innocence and asks God to prove and test his mind and heart (v. 2). Life is not always fair, and the psalmist turns to God for help.

This psalm suggests elements of a temple ritual for forgiveness, one that includes cleansing of the hands, a procession, and singing songs of thanksgiving in the sanctuary. The psalmist commits to participating in the ritual and presenting his case before the congregation. The author trusts God and the community of faith to bring vindication and to affirm a life of integrity.

PRAYER/PRACTICE

Water has many layers of meaning. It can mean the cleansing of a hot bath or simply a refreshing splash on a hot day. Water quenches thirst and irrigates a field. Rain and snow refresh the earth. Water flows in a river, laps the ocean shore, tumbles down a waterfall.

Today remain aware of all the times you touch or see water. Pay attention to your need for cleansing, your need to be filled, your need for renewal. Every time you touch or see water, let it serve as a call to prayer, an experience of thanksgiving, a moment of delight.

February 19

REMEMBER

Fra Angelico (c. 1395–1455) combined life as a monk and as an accomplished painter in Florence, Italy. He became known as the patron saint of artists.

READ

Psalm 27:1-6

PONDER

Perhaps worshipers recited these first verses of Psalm 27 in the morning at the Temple. The psalmist exudes a sense of confidence and delight in God, who brings light and salvation to life. "Whom shall I fear?" (v. 1). No doubt there will be troubles, even an army of foes (v. 3) or an inner cloud of doubts and fears, but the psalmist brims with confidence. God remains the stronghold. The psalmist prays to be able to carry throughout the day the sense of God's presence experienced that day, perhaps even that morning "in the house of the LORD" (v. 4). The melodies of praise, the beauty of the Temple, and the assurance of God's presence power the confidence and eloquence of the psalmist.

PRAYER/PRACTICE

Journaling is another practice that can greatly aid our spiritual journey. In contrast to a diary, a journal focuses less on details and more on feelings and reflections in response to the day's events. The journal can help one carry on a dialogue with God, using the action of writing to express thoughts and concerns, hopes and dreams, even complaints and questions. Like the Psalms themselves, the journal directs conversation to God, conversation filled with all the ambiguities, frustrations, and successes of life. "Journaling can be a significant tool in deepening our spiritual lives because by its nature it leads us to further revelation of who we are and who God is in our lives."[5]

Today, try naming your fears and turning them over to God. After each group of fears, you might write, "The LORD is my light and my salvation; whom [or what] shall I fear?" (v. 1).

February 20

REMEMBER

Hagar the Egyptian (B.C.E.) bore Abraham a son, only to end up banished with her child to the desert. In spite of this experience, she saw God and possessed hope (Gen. 16:1-15; 21:1-21).

READ

Psalm 27:7-12

PONDER

Perhaps you have heard a parent say to a child, "Look at me." Communication often becomes challenging when we cannot see another person's face and watch his or her eyes and expressions. The Hebrews feared that God would turn away or hide God's face from them. If God no longer looked at them, that could mean God was angry, no longer cared, or no longer watched over them. So the psalmist pleads, "Do not hide your face. . . . Do not cast me off, do not forsake me" (v. 9). Even in the midst of pleading and crying for God to stay in contact, words of assurance weave their way into the prayer: "Even if my father and mother should desert me, you will take care of me" (v. 10, CEV). Think about your own life and how your longing for God's guidance interweaves with signs of God's direction.

PRAYER/PRACTICE

Many people find it helpful to have a separate book for their journal. Some choose a binder they can add pages to; others use a bound book with blank pages. Still others keep their journal on a computer. Choose whatever method works for you. I like an unlined book and often use a special pen to write or draw.

Many ways to journal exist, and helpful books giving suggestions abound. (See Appendix A.) As a beginning way to journal, reflect on the day's events. Use some of these questions in your journaling: When and how did you experience God's presence? When were you most aware of God's presence as light or joy, peace or comfort? When were you moved to offer thanks or to cry for help?

February 21

REMEMBER

Malcolm X (1925–1965), an African American liberation leader, writer, and prominent Muslim, advocated black power in the 1960s. He was assassinated in New York City.

READ

Psalm 27:13-14

PONDER

The psalm ends with two verses of strong confidence. "I believe I will see the goodness of the Lord while I am still living" (v. 13, AP). Despite the enemies and the betrayals mentioned in the previous verse, the psalmist remains confident that God still works for good and will make a difference in this lifetime. We too can have such confidence; we can wait and let our hearts take courage, for God will see us through every situation. This is not lazy waiting but active belief, strong trust, and heartfelt conviction that God intends good even in times of trial. God will prevail, so "take courage" (v. 14). You might commit to heart these two confident verses.

PRAYER/PRACTICE

Today try journaling in response to scripture. As you reflect on Psalm 27, list all the places you find the goodness of God in your life. Or reflect on some of your worries and troubles and then answer them by writing verse 14: "Wait for the LORD; be strong, and let your heart take courage." You may need to write this verse many times in response to your fears and concerns.

Many stories of Jesus provide a word or phrase that can prompt one to journal—for example, "Do you want to be made well?" (John 5:6) and "Who is your neighbor?" (Luke 10:36, AP).

In your reading of scripture, pay attention to words and phrases that seem to hold special meaning for you. Write about the promptings in your soul.

February 22

REMEMBER

Hans and Sophie Scholl (d. 1943), students armed with Christian conviction and an illegal mimeograph machine, published leaflets denouncing Hitler. Calling their group the White Rose, they stirred the conscience of German people, incurred the wrath of the Gestapo, and were killed on February 22.

READ

Psalm 28

PONDER

"You give strength to your people, LORD" (v. 8a, CEV). Several university students hoped to remind the German people that God did not condone evil and that, in their view, Hitler was the power of evil. Their leaflets and street signs shocked the Nazi leaders, who thought all Germans backed their schemes. Hans and Sophie and other members of the White Rose aimed to be a voice of conscience, a Christian witness, and a hidden encouragement to citizens to resist Hitler's evil however they could. Surely the students were buoyed by the words of scripture, "You [LORD] are my strong shield, and I trust you completely" (v. 7a, CEV).

PRAYER/PRACTICE

Reading the newspaper or watching the news can bring you into awareness of the world around you and give you much to journal about. Journaling helps you name feelings and overcome numbness about tragedies and disasters in the news. It allows you to enter into dialogue with God about starving children, senseless acts of violence, the gap between the rich and the poor, and the suffering of people after earthquake, hurricane, or fire. The Psalms give us a language for dialogue with God, for they provide models of complaints, laments, questions, pleas, and thanksgivings.

What world issue has caught your attention? Turn to God in your journal and describe your thoughts and feelings. Take time to listen in silence after your writing.

February 23

REMEMBER

Saint Polycarp (c. 70–c. 155), a disciple of John the Evangelist, an early bishop of the church, and one of the most important Christian leaders in Asia, died a martyr's death.

READ

Psalm 29:1-4

PONDER

This psalm, sometimes known as the "Song of Seven Thunders," describes the voice of God as thunder over all of creation. The psalm calls all of heaven and all humanity to praise God for the glories and splendor of creation. Sometimes we experience God in the "still small voice" (1 Kings 19:12, AP), in the deep sounds of silence. But other times we hear and see God in the crash of ocean surf or the thunderous boom of a mighty storm. We see the majesty of God in glorious sunsets. In the wildness and expansiveness of nature, we sense God's power and sovereignty and respond with awe and worship.

PRAYER/PRACTICE

Your journal provides a good place to write thoughts and prayers. Today I invite you to write a prayer about some storm you have experienced. Perhaps as a child you felt frightened by strong winds or by the loud, terrifying sound of thunder. Or, like the naturalist John Muir, you may have been thrilled and awed by a lightning storm that lit up the sky, so you braved getting wet and a little scared in order to watch the magnificent storm. You may also want to write about an inner storm that shook your faith, a time of doubt or despair, a time you needed the power and strength of God.

February 24

REMEMBER

Someone who broke down barriers between people.

READ

Psalm 29:5-11

PONDER

As a child I was both a little afraid of and mightily impressed by the summer thunder and lightning storms that roared across Michigan. Sometimes I ran outside to look; at other times I hid in the basement, daring only a little peek out the window.

The psalmist sees the power of storms as a metaphor for the voice of God. When God speaks, the winds howl and the lightning flashes—an impressive display from an awesome God. These verses do not describe a tame and domesticated God but a Being who is big and mighty and, above all, worthy of praise. Praise the awesome God, Creator of the universe, who speaks in lightning and yet blesses all people with peace.

PRAYER/PRACTICE

Journaling can offer a way to remember not only the day's events but also the past. Today, continue to journal about storms in your life, from childhood memories to the present moment. Do you recall certain storms and the feelings they evoked in you? Do you see any patterns of response? Have you felt the presence of God, been thankful for family and friends, been mindful of the needs of others?

Use your journal to prayerfully reflect on your experience of thunder, lightning, earthquakes, floods, fires, tornadoes, and other kinds of storms. If the memory of storms disturbs you, remember that Christ is our assurance, our peace, the One who quiets the storms (Mark 4:39).

February 25

REMEMBER

Esther (B.C.E.), a Hebrew woman who became queen of Persia, risked her life to save her people. Her cousin Mordecai supported and challenged her by reminding her, "Perhaps you are where you are for such a time as this" (Esther 4:14, AP).

READ

The book of Esther

PONDER

The Bible teems with wonderful stories packed with intrigue and plots, twists and turns, defeats and triumphs. The story of Esther is one of the hidden gems, with a strong woman lead, an evil plot, and a dangerous decision that could lead to life or death. When Esther learns of the decree to kill all the Jews, she fears approaching the king, for no one could go to the king without being called. Mordecai reminds her that she cannot hide her Jewishness in the palace, that her silence would spell doom for the Jews. Knowing she faces death if the king takes offense at her approach, Esther plots and fasts for a different outcome. Her beauty and offering of delicious food soften the king, and he orders that the gallows be used for his jealous, greedy advisor Haman rather than for Esther's cousin.

PRAYER/PRACTICE

God calls for you and me to actively address the hurts of the world, opposing injustices done to any people and speaking out for good. In your journal, reflect on current world problems. Think about Mordecai's reminder that keeping silent may do great harm and that God may have called you to act in such a time as this.

Journal about ways you and your faith community actively participate in resisting evil and doing good. Write about at least one concrete action you can take to combat injustice. Pray to be courageous and wise like Esther.

February 26

REMEMBER

God sometimes speaks through images and dreams. Read about Peter's dream in Acts 10, which led him to minister to Gentiles.

READ

Psalm 30:1-5

PONDER

Have you ever felt so sick you thought death was imminent? Such is the experience of the psalmist, who felt on the verge of falling into the pit of nothingness. Carroll Stuhlmueller explains: "Israel at this time had no clear belief in life after death. In fact, to preserve her religion from the polytheistic excesses of other religions which multiplied gods and goddesses in the realm of the dead and usually reserved immortality for kings and nobility, Israel flatly denied all this, but had nothing positive to put in its place."[6]

With great thankfulness, the psalmist reminds us, "Weeping may linger for the night, but joy comes with the morning" (v. 5).

PRAYER/PRACTICE

The Psalms contain such wonderful phrases that name our experience. We know about weeping in the night. In your journal recall times of sadness, times of illness, times when tears soaked your pillow, times when grief or depression seemed unending. Then write about how you experienced joy, how the long night turned into morning light, how you found the courage to sing praises and give thanks to God. Commit verse 5 to memory: "Weeping may linger for the night, but joy comes with the morning."

February 27

Julia Ward Howe (1819–1910), a poet and writer, advocated the abolition of slavery and fought for women's suffrage. One of her best known poems is "The Battle Hymn of the Republic." She also issued the first call for a day to honor mothers (see May 12).

READ

Psalm 30:6-10

PONDER

Two moods dominate these verses. The first mood, self-assured, full of confidence and swagger, borders on arrogance. "When things were going great I crowed, 'I've got it made. I'm God's favorite. . . . king of the mountain" (vv. 6-7, THE MESSAGE).

The second mood turns to God, pleading for help. Here exists no complacency, no forgetting God in times of trouble. "Hear, O LORD, and be gracious to me! O LORD, be my helper!" (v. 10). Just in case God needs an extra reason to help, the psalmist reminds God that dead people can't praise God. The underlying assumption suggests that the psalmist will lead the chorus of praise after God responds to the cry for help.

PRAYER/PRACTICE

When life goes well, we tend to forget God, to overlook who and what has supported, guided, helped, and loved us. Flora Wuellner suggests giving thanks for our bodies, often neglected and unappreciated:

> Occasionally through the day, give a loving thought to your bodily parts which are being used: your eyes, hands, feet, arms, legs, brain. They are your good friends who work with you. . . . Listen to any signals your body sends you of stress or tension. At these times, . . . relax your breathing, picture or just think of God's healing breath and light flowing through your body like a warm, renewing river.[7]

Practice this kind of awareness a couple of times through the day. Touch, massage, and relax the hard-working parts of your body.

February 28

REMEMBER

The Campaign for Nuclear Disarmament began in Great Britain in 1958 and created what we now know as the peace symbol.

READ

Psalm 30:11-12

PONDER

As we open ourselves to God in prayer, changes begin. Mourning turns into dancing. Anger transforms into favor. Weeping gives way to joy. Grim sackcloth becomes a bright new robe. The psalmist gives us a language of praise and thanks that we can share with others and direct to God. The psalmist stirs our joy and enthusiasm and encourages us not to be silent but rather to boldly sing, exuberantly dance, and joyously celebrate what God has done and will continue to do.

PRAYER/PRACTICE

Today pray the following prayer, adding your own words of praise:

> Amazing God, you have placed joy in my soul, dancing in my toes, and a song in my heart. You turn mourning into dancing. You desire gladness to flow like a mighty river and healing to extend from shore to shore. You gave the world Jesus, who laughed and healed, who lifts me up and invites me to walk the good path and trust in a Love stronger than death.

February 29

REMEMBER

Anyone born on this leap-year date.

READ

Your favorite psalm

PONDER

This year you have one extra day. Draw closer to God on this gift of a day. Ponder surprising gifts in your life, such as an unexpected letter, a phone call, a check, or an offer of help that came at just the right time. God's gifts often arrive in the guise of surprise. Anonymity becomes one of God's most endearing surprises.

PRAYER/PRACTICE

If possible, do not go to work or school today. Try to make this day different in some way. Can you take the day as a spiritual growth retreat? Could you spend an extra hour praying, reading, and journaling? Could you participate in an outdoor activity and enjoy God's gift of nature? Could you organize an event at your church to celebrate this extra day with God? Think of people you would like to celebrate this day with, people who could join you in prayer, dancing, silence, and singing. Make this a special day to spend with God.

March

As frozen ground thaws, gentle God,
also soften my hard attitudes and melt my cold heart.
Ready me for new life.
Tender my soul for the arrival of spring.
Let Easter happen in me and all around me.
Warm my expectations
and make me ready for what you have prepared
as I deepen my prayer and my walk with you. Amen.

March 1

REMEMBER

George Herbert (1593–1633), an Anglican priest and poet, wrote about religious themes. His poetry, published after his death, established him as one of England's finest poets.

READ

Psalm 31:1-8

PONDER

We know of this psalm from the New Testament, for Luke 23:46 records that Jesus prayed part of it from the cross: "Into your hands I commend my spirit" (v. 5). The psalm overflows with a supreme confidence, an abundance of images in the faithful God who is "indeed my rock and my fortress" (v. 3). Even in times of despair, God's presence delivers, rescues, guides, and redeems. No wonder Jesus found this psalm comforting and reassuring on the cross. The psalmist invites us to praise God for steadfast love, for delivering us from trouble, and for placing us not in cramped, narrow confines but in the freedom and openness of a "broad place" (v. 8).

PRAYER/PRACTICE

One monastic community I know adapts verses from this psalm as part of its night prayer: "Into your hands O God, I commend my spirit. You have redeemed me, Lord God of truth." The community sings this verse at the end of prayer, and whenever I visit there the verse brings comfort as I place myself into God's hands for the night. Our loving God neither slumbers nor sleeps but keeps watch over us. As you begin this month, I invite you to develop a prayer to use at bedtime. Consider incorporating Psalm 31:5, placing yourself into God's care and protection for the night.

March 2

March is Women's History Month. Think of women who have helped you grow in faith. Also remember Theodor Seuss Geisel (1904–1991), who wrote and illustrated wild, funny, and poignant children's books under the name of Dr. Seuss.

READ

Psalm 31:9-13

PONDER

Though sometimes we consider our burdens unique and our distress unusual, we are not the only ones with problems. The psalmist boldly and graphically lays a basketful of complaints before God: "My life is spent with sorrow, . . . my strength fails . . . my bones waste away" (v. 10). Such a frank and honest dialogue with God gives us permission to choose exaggerated, colorful language to spell out our complaints. As the old hymn states, "Take it to the Lord in prayer!" Trust that God will hear.

PRAYER/PRACTICE

This month we will spend time practicing *lectio divina*. The Latin phrase literally means "divine or holy reading." Originally it referred to contemplative study of the Bible, and that will be your main focus, but you can use the process with any book that brings you closer to God.

Lectio divina is a slow, thoughtful, prayerful reading and reflection on a portion of scripture. The number of verses or chapters read becomes less important than letting the words and images connect your heart to God's heart.

Prepare for *lectio divina* by praying this prayer:

Loving God, open me to hearing your Word addressed to me, touching my hurts, nudging my dreams, guiding my steps. Amen.

March 3

REMEMBER

Katharine Drexel (1858–1955), from a wealthy American family, used her inheritance to fund 145 Catholic missions, twelve schools for Native Americans, and fifty schools for black students. She also established a new religious community, Sisters of the Blessed Sacrament.

READ

Psalm 31:14-18

PONDER

Katharine Drexel endowed schools on Indian reservations with her inheritance, but more needed to be done. During a private audience with Pope Leo XIII, Drexel begged him to send priests to serve the Indians. He reportedly said, "Why don't *you* become a missionary?" At first she dismissed the pope's suggestion, but she grew to understand that not only was she to use her wealth for God but her whole life belonged to God. Drexel understood the truth of verses 14-15: "You are my God. My times are in your hand."

PRAYER/PRACTICE

Slow reading goes against the grain of our high-speed, fast-paced culture where computers and satellite television dominate. Yet *lectio* offers the gift of time, an attentive and focused time, to deepen our relationship with God. In preparation for divine reading, settle into a time and space of inner and outer quiet. Set aside a place where you will not be interrupted, where you can be open to God's word for you. You might say your breath prayer several times to usher you into the silence.

Tomorrow we will look at the first of the four stages of *lectio divina*. For today, sit quietly and repeat the line from Psalm 31, "My times are in your hand."

March 4

REMEMBER

Jeannette Rankin (1880–1973), from Montana and an outspoken critic of war and violence, became the first woman elected to the U.S. House of Representatives in 1917.

READ

Psalm 31:19-24

PONDER

This psalm weaves complaint and plea into a strong message to God. Yet mixed into the petition are words of confidence and trust in a mighty God who hears and rescues. The psalm builds toward a strong conclusion filled with blessing and encouragement for the whole community. "Blessed be the Beloved, Who has wondrously shown steadfast love to me when I was beset by an army of fear" (v. 21, PFP). "Be strong, and let your heart take courage, all you who wait for the LORD" (v. 24). Lament and tears, which began the psalm, give way to final words of celebration and hope. God hears and cares. "Blessed be the LORD" (v. 21).

PRAYER/PRACTICE

The first stage of *lectio divina* focuses on reading (*lectio*). Read a small portion of scripture slowly and attentively. A single story from the Gospels (not necessarily a whole chapter) or a short psalm works best. Try Mark 6:45-52, Matthew 17:14-21, or Psalm 30. You may read aloud or silently. Reread and listen with your heart for any word or phrase that calls to you, leaps out at you, or lodges itself in your memory. Put your name in the story or hear the words as addressed to you. Listen for a word from God for you this day.

In your prayer time, slowly repeat Psalm 31:24: "Be strong, and let your heart take courage, all you who wait for the LORD."

March 5

REMEMBER

Karl Rahner (1904–1984), one of the foremost Catholic theologians of the twentieth century, added wisdom and theological insights at the Second Vatican Council in 1962.

READ

Psalm 32:1-5

PONDER

When we hold our sins inside, trying to ignore the wrong we have said, done, or thought, it can affect our whole being. The psalmist knew the experience of keeping silent and how the body "wasted away" (v. 3). "Then I acknowledged my sin to you . . . and you forgave the guilt of my sin" (v. 5). This humble confession marks the theme of the penitential psalms, of which this is the second.

This passage invites us to see clearly our need to confess and states the promise of God's forgiveness. God delights in forgiving and seeks to restore our lives. When we receive God's forgiveness, we become the people spoken of in verse 1: "Happy are those whose transgression is forgiven, whose sin is covered."

PRAYER/PRACTICE

The second stage in *lectio divina* focuses on *meditatio,* a Latin word usually translated as "meditation." Having read the chosen passage slowly, we now meditate or ruminate, as a cow chews its cud, on the word or phrase that speaks to us. We allow it to interact with our thoughts, hopes, memories. We repeat the word and look at it from different angles, letting it touch and affect our thoughts.

Today choose a passage of scripture (perhaps the one you used yesterday) and begin your two-step process of reading and meditating on the passage. You may choose today's psalm or a new passage from the Gospels, for example, Luke 8:22-25 or John 5:1-9.

March 6

REMEMBER

Jean-Pierre de Caussade (1675–1751), an author and spiritual director, wrote that the path to holiness lies in the performance of everyday tasks. His writing focused on how individual lives become the living texts of the Holy Spirit.

READ

Psalm 32:6-11

PONDER

Most of us would not respond well to being called a mule (or something worse). The psalmist paints a negative image of mules, claiming they carry on as stubborn, stupid, wild, and unruly animals. The psalmist invites us to not be like mules. Be wise, learn from past mistakes, the poet urges. Follow God's gentle guidance and sure leading. "I shall instruct you and teach you the way to go; I shall not take my eyes off you" (v. 8, NJB). Thus the psalmist pushes us to a deeper trust in God and invites us to shout for joy, rejoice, and be glad. The message rings clear: Evil and wickedness bring grief, while trusting in God brings love.

PRAYER/PRACTICE

The third stage in *lectio* focuses on *oratio,* a Latin word usually translated as "prayer." In this stage, I invite you to take the passage you have been meditating upon and use it to begin a conversation, a prayer, with God. Enter into dialogue with God, who wants to be close to you and wants to open up the meaning of this word or phrase for you. Is the word one of blessing or challenge? Allow God to use the word to touch or heal, to instruct or transform you. Let the word descend from your mind to your heart.

Today, add this third step of prayer to your practice of *lectio divina* with one of the passages you have been reading.

March 7

REMEMBER

Saints Perpetua and Felicity (d. 203) were early Christian martyrs; Perpetua's diary gives one of the oldest accounts of a martyr's suffering. These young Christian women with children lived a life of obedience to God.

READ

Psalm 33:1-5

PONDER

We had no songbooks, no words projected onto a screen. Only a young man playing a couple of used conga drums and three teenagers with tambourines led the music. But we praised God with songs and instruments in that little Cuban church. We sang new and old songs in a language that was not my native tongue. The experience filled me with joy. The music and worship simply captivated and invigorated all who came to pray. We all praised God, for God is truthful and can be trusted. "[God] loves justice and fairness, and . . . is kind to everyone everywhere on earth" (v. 5, CEV). Praise God with drums and tambourines; the Lover of truth and justice fills the earth with love.

PRAYER/PRACTICE

The fourth stage of *lectio* turns us toward *contemplatio,* a Latin word meaning "contemplation." After you meditate on the word or phrase from scripture and then use the word as the beginning of dialogue in prayer, *contemplatio* suggests that you simply rest in the presence of God. Let go of trying to figure out anything or come up with some life-changing meaning. Let go of all words and images and simply be; let God hold you. God has called you to rest in openness, to abide in this moment. Abide without words, images, concerns.

Add this stage of *lectio* to the passage you have been praying.

March 8

REMEMBER

International Women's Day. Also remember Saint John of God (1495–1550), a former soldier who experienced conversion at age forty and began ministering to the poor and sick. He founded a hospital in Spain.

READ

Psalm 33:6-9

PONDER

We have grown jaded, too accustomed to hearing people (often politicians) make promises they do not intend to keep or making statements they do not mean. This psalm stands in marked contrast to such separation of word and deed, for God speaks and the heavens are created; God speaks and the world is created. As God's creations, indeed, created in God's image, our words and deeds should be congruent, reflecting our Maker. We may not create the stars with our spoken word, but we should at least not turn out the light of hope for another person with untruthful speech.

PRAYER/PRACTICE

One of my teachers in spirituality says we should add another stage to the practice of *lectio divina.* She would add *incarnatio,* meaning we should listen in the silence for any word or deed we should incarnate into our lives. Is there some action God wants you to take? In the silence, God may bid you to witness to some truth, speak a word of challenge or comfort, take up a cause for justice, practice a hidden kindness. In this way you enflesh God's word, enact God's truth into your life and deeds. The Incarnation happens anew.

As you have prayed with the Psalms or a Gospel passage, have you sensed something you should do or be? Make a commitment to carry out God's bidding.

March 9

REMEMBER

Saint Frances of Rome (1384–1440), born to an affluent family and married to a wealthy man, cared for the needy. She often disguised herself in simple clothes and left her palace home to care for the sick and distribute goods to the poor.

READ

Psalm 33:10-17

PONDER

The psalmist senses that God not only created humanity, "fashions the hearts of them all" (v. 15), but also God watches over and "observes all their deeds" (v. 15). God must see the kindness of such persons as Frances of Rome, who felt so called to care for the poor that she left her royal palace robes and dressed in simple dresses and veils to visit the sick and distribute goods to the poor. Even when she and her sister-in-law were discovered and ridiculed, she persuaded her husband to let her continue as long as she did not neglect her duties at home. In recent times, Mother Teresa of Calcutta lived a simple life of service and compassion that evoked remembrances and comparisons to Frances of Rome.

PRAYER/PRACTICE

You have been taught how to read for information. In *lectio*, however, you read for insight, letting the Word of God shape and transform. *Lectio* nurtures a contemplative intellect, a mind not filled with facts but rather a mind connected to the heart of God, seeking to live in harmony with God's desire for creation. *Lectio* presents the self to God with sheer receptivity, open to what God may reveal. A friend gently reminded me that one may not always receive insight or direction, so above all, one should give thanks for the gift of being in God's presence.

Today, take time to practice *lectio, meditatio, oratio, contemplatio,* and *incarnatio* with a portion of scripture. You might choose Luke 24:13-35 or Matthew 9:18-26.

March 10

REMEMBER

Harriet Tubman (c. 1820–1913) worked tirelessly as an abolitionist and a "conductor" on the Underground Railroad, leading many groups of slaves to freedom.

READ

Psalm 33:18-22

PONDER

That the religion of the slaveholder, which was used falsely to justify slavery and was forced on slaves, should still emerge as a gospel of freedom and liberation presents evidence of an amazing grace and a redeeming God. "Our soul waits for the LORD; . . . our help and shield"(v. 20). Harriet Tubman waited and trusted for the right moment to escape from slavery in Maryland. Traveling at night and following the North Star, she arrived in the free state of Pennsylvania. Though Tubman was free, no one welcomed her to the land of freedom. She felt like a stranger in a strange land, but freedom tasted and felt so good that she wanted to share it with many others. She promised herself to make a home in the North, and with God's help, she would go and bring the captives to freedom. Over the next twelve years, Tubman made nineteen trips back to guide people along the Underground Railroad. She was called the Moses of her people.

PRAYER/PRACTICE

I invite you this wonderful day to remember your breath prayer and take some extra time in quiet prayer to remember people who have helped you in your spiritual journey. Who has guided you and brought you to new understanding, new depths, new freedom? Who has risked loving and caring for you? Who has offered to lead you through the darkness? Give thanks for those who have been "Moses" to you, and give thanks for people like Harriet Tubman who trusted that God would help them and use them to make the world a better place.

March 11

REMEMBER

Saint Maximilian (274–295), an early Christian martyr, refused to serve in the Roman army, thus becoming one of the first Christian conscientious objectors. He lived out his beliefs that he could not give allegiance to anyone but God and that he should not kill or do evil.

READ

Psalm 34:1-3

PONDER

How do we begin prayer? Sometimes we simply cry, "Help!" But most often we begin with praise and adoration. The psalmist says, "I will bless the LORD at all times; . . . praise shall continually be in my mouth" (v. 1). We experience the presence of God in the signs of spring, in the song of the robin, in the warmth of the sun, in the splash of rain. We experience the love of God in answered prayer, in a supportive community, in a time of worship, in a sense of peace in the midst of difficulty. So we gather others with us and pray, "Let us exalt and celebrate God's name together" (v. 3, AP). Whether as individuals or as a community, we begin prayer by blessing, praising, and thanking God.

PRAYER/PRACTICE

These next few days we will explore and practice praying for others, a kind of prayer frequently known as intercession. Jesus instructed his friends to "pray for those who persecute you" (Matt. 5:44). Paul began many of his letters by saying, "I remember you always in my prayers" (Rom. 1:9). James wrote about praying for the sick and said, "The prayer of faith will save the sick, and the Lord will raise them up; and anyone who has committed sins will be forgiven. Therefore . . . pray for one another" (James 5:15-16). Scripture abounds with accounts of prayer for others. We stand in a long line of intercessors.

You may begin the practice of intercession by simply naming persons and situations that concern you. Make no specific request; simply trust that placing them before God is a genuine act of faith and prayer. Who and what do you want to place before God this day?

March 12

REMEMBER

Rutilio Grande (1928–1977), an El Salvadoran priest, encouraged the church to minister to the poor. His death prompted newly appointed Archbishop Romero to speak out against government-sanctioned violence and to advocate the church's caring for the oppressed.

READ

Psalm 34:4-6

PONDER

"This poor soul cried, and was heard by the LORD, and was saved from every trouble" (v. 6). The poor have long cried to God; later in this psalm we find the testimony that God draws near to the brokenhearted and crushed (v. 18). In the 1970s, Christians, led by the Roman Catholic Church, made a serious attempt to address the plight of the poor in Central and South America. A new theology of liberation developed in which oppressors were confronted and the poor organized. Those who benefited from keeping the poor enslaved—often an unholy alliance of the rich, the government, and the military—fought back and targeted religious leaders. The death of Father Grande became the first of many in El Salvador, and it would be some time before the last part of verse 6, "was saved from every trouble," was carried out.

PRAYER/PRACTICE

Intercessory prayers often go hand in hand with action to address problems. In times of injustice and social oppression, when the gap between the rich and the poor widens, prayers of intercession for change become linked with letter-writing campaigns, marches and sit-ins, and the creation of alternative models.

Today lift up to God a situation of pain or hurt in the world. Pray for leaders who could make a difference. Pray for people who are hurt, oppressed, and ignored. Pray for those whose actions contribute to the pain. Pray for the church to involve itself as an agent of change, a voice of reconciliation, and a partner in healing.

March 13

REMEMBER

Jane Frances de Chantal (1572–1641) became a nun after her husband was killed. She founded the Order of the Visitation of Holy Mary in France. Working with her mentor and spiritual friend Francis de Sales, she established eighty convents in thirty years.

READ

Psalm 34:7-10

PONDER

Verse 8, "O taste and see that the LORD is good," has long been associated with the Eucharist, or Holy Communion. The entire psalm combines the presence of God with compassion for the poor. When we come to the Communion table, we taste the goodness of God, but we also remember that God's love extends to all. The Eucharist gives a foretaste of the heavenly banquet that will include the poor, the sick, the foreigner, and the hungry—those whom Jesus calls "the least of these" (Matt. 25:40). Whenever we eat the holy meal, we unite with all Christians, near and far, and promise to live and work to bring that heavenly banquet closer to earth even as we pray, "Your kingdom come, Your will be done, on earth as it is in heaven" (Matt. 6:10).

PRAYER/PRACTICE

One friend keeps a boxful of cards on her kitchen table. Each card contains a name and often a prayer request. My friend keeps her promise when she says, "I will pray for you." The cards become part of her prayer each morning, intercessions for specific and current situations. As the need becomes more distant, she moves some cards to a weekly section. I was touched to discover that my card remained in her box, though we had not seen each other in years and the prayer request seemed outdated. I asked her to continue praying for me—to keep my card in her intercession box—and gave her a new request.

Create your own intercession box or make a list of people and situations needing prayer. The act of writing cards or names and prayer requests can become part of the intercessory prayer.

March 14

REMEMBER

Fannie Lou Hamer (1917–1977), a daughter of sharecroppers, led the effort during the civil rights movement to register blacks to vote. She became known as the Prophet of Freedom.

READ

Psalm 34:11-14

PONDER

Practical advice pours forth from these verses. If you want a long life, "Keep your tongue from evil, and your lips from speaking deceit. Depart from evil, and do good; seek peace and pursue it" (vv. 13-14). Jesus and other spiritual teachers recognize the need to watch what we say. Words do hurt and harm. Once spoken, words cannot be taken back. But it is not enough to refrain from doing wrong or speaking evil; we must do good and actively seek peace and justice. Many stories of people who battled evil and did good in the face of great obstacles came out of the civil rights movement. Fannie Lou Hamer's struggle to register voters and to change unjust laws remains one of those powerful, justice-producing stories.

PRAYER/PRACTICE

Intercession enlarges your world. Perhaps you become so focused on your own needs and problems that you forget God carries the whole world in mind and heart and rejoices when you participate in making it better. Intercession links you with God's compassion for the oppressed, the sick, the forgotten. Your voice and prayer unite with countless others. Prisoners who have been adopted by Amnesty International say it makes a difference to know that they are not forgotten.

Is there some part of the world, some problem outside your circle of family and friends, for which you might become an intercessor?

March 15

REMEMBER

Ruth (B.C.E.) crossed national and religious boundaries as she moved with her mother-in-law, Naomi, from Moab to Israel.

READ

The book of Ruth

PONDER

Ruth often serves as a model for covenant relationships. "Where you go, I will go; where you lodge, I will lodge; your people shall be my people, and your God my God" (Ruth 1:16). When two people speak those words to each other, a bond of unity and commitment forms. The words provide a good foundation for the challenges that will inevitably arise in the relationship.

Ruth also models a willingness to break down barriers between different nations and cultures. This foreign woman becomes part of the genealogical tradition that brings us David and Jesus. God welcomes the courage and faithfulness of this stranger, and indeed God welcomes all to come and dwell in the house of the Lord.

PRAYER/PRACTICE

In her insightful book *Soul Feast,* Marjorie Thompson asks, "How can I ask in simple trust for a gift to be granted, and at the same time yield up my will to God?"[1] That question expresses the tension we often feel in our intercessory prayers. We want to ask boldly, yet we often temper our requests and protect our disappointments by adding the biblical tagline "if it be your will."

Thompson suggests that we continually seek God's will and approach God with gratitude. "Here is the posture from which we can ask that abundant grace be given those we pray for. We can be confident that grace will be given in a way that best expresses God's loving purpose, with which we are united."[2] We can believe that God always works for good even if the answer takes longer and takes a different shape from what we first prayed for. Continue in your prayers of intercession.

March 16

REMEMBER

Saint David of Wales (520–589) founded monasteries known for their extreme simplicity and charity.

READ

Psalm 34:15-18

PONDER

Though we do not have any of the original music of the Psalms, we do know that they were intended to be sung (even danced), and we have recovered that tradition by setting the Psalms to music. In the monastic tradition, one line often appeared as a response or refrain. This line, set to music, helped the monks learn and memorize the individual psalms.

I would create a strong tune for verse 18, "The LORD is near to the brokenhearted, and saves the crushed in spirit." The theme of this verse permeates the entire Psalter; it is an amazing affirmation of faith in God who hears and saves. God hears the cries of the poor. Blessed be the God of justice, who comforts the suffering and gives hope to those in despair.

PRAYER/PRACTICE

Does intercession work? Some would say that God already knows the need, so why bother God? Others say intercession becomes too human-centered if we think that by increasing the number of people praying we will change God's mind or affect the outcome.

Our belief that God desires our prayers and uses them in working for good in the world forms the basis for intercession. In intercessory prayer, you place your intentions before God and seek to align your desires with God's will. The more you open to God in prayer, the more God shapes your life and your prayer. Always when you pray for another, you trust God to do good and to work as God is able in the situation.

Sometimes in intercessions for others, you may find that you are the one who changes, becoming more open, more at peace, more ready to grow. Has this been your experience? Write about your experience with intercession in your journal.

March 17

REMEMBER

Saint Patrick (c. 389–c. 461), kidnapped by Irish pirates and taken from Britain to Ireland, escaped from slavery and became a priest. When he returned to Ireland to convert the nation, he baptized thousands and ordained hundreds of priests. According to legends, Patrick drove all snakes out of Ireland and gave the shamrock religious significance.

READ

Psalm 34:19-22

PONDER

"Many are the afflictions of the righteous, but the LORD rescues them from them all" (v. 19). Sometimes God seems to take a long time to perform the rescue. Kidnapped from England and sold into slavery in Ireland, Patrick had to wait six years before he could escape. He went home a changed person, now a man of faith who went on to study for the priesthood, much to the surprise of his family. In his dreams he heard the call to go back to Ireland, not to seek revenge but to preach the gospel. For thirty years he preached, established churches, baptized thousands, and changed the course of the nation. The legends about him may stretch the truth, but there is no doubt that Patrick lived as a remarkable servant of Christ.

PRAYER/PRACTICE

If Patrick at first prayed for revenge on his captors, his intercession changed from anger and bitterness to reconciliation and conversion. When we pray for our enemies, God may help us see them in a new way, perhaps as part of God's own family.

Create a photo collage of people and situations that you include in your prayers. Sometimes putting a face with a prayer opens us to a new level of compassion. You may realize that your enemy belongs to a loving and worried parent. You may find that the oppressor carries an unhealed wound. You may realize that the one you have trouble praying for is still God's child, still loved by God. Create your photo collage and use it in your prayer time.

March 18

REMEMBER

Ann Lee (1736–1784) joined the Shaking Quakers (known as Shakers) in England and, when persecuted, led a small group to emigrate to the United States. The Shakers were pacifists, emotional in worship, and creators of elegant and economical furniture.

READ

Psalm 35:1-10

PONDER

Sometimes we feel all alone in the battles we wage. We get no support from friends; we may even experience their opposition. The tasks ahead appear to be growing larger, the battles more difficult, and we feel like sinking into self-pity. The psalmist knows our experience and reminds us to pray. "Contend, O LORD, with those who contend with me; fight against those who fight against me!" (v. 1). Or, as another version puts it, "Pray on my behalf" (v. 1, PFP).

The poet reminds us to not rely solely on our efforts but to call on God, to see God going before us, praying for us, speaking for us, guiding us. We do not stand alone as we seek deliverance from our troubles and victories over our enemies.

PRAYER/PRACTICE

Intercession joins our prayers with God's ongoing prayer for all of creation. God continually seeks to love and be in relationship with all persons. When we pray for another, we link our prayers with God's everlasting compassion. Douglas Steere, a wise Quaker writer, ponders whether our prayers might help another over the threshold of belief, might "tip the balance."[3] In the mystery of prayer, God can use our openness, our intercession, to increase the interconnectedness of life. Today as you pray for others, let God shape and align your prayer for God's good purpose. Know that as you pray for God's will to be done in the life of another, you also open yourself to praying for God's will to be done in you.

March 19

REMEMBER

Joseph (first century), the earthly father of Jesus, provided for and protected the Holy Family. On this day we remember him for his care and nurture. Also remember Sacajawea (c. 1786–1812), a Shoshone Indian guide, who helped Lewis and Clark explore the Northwest.

READ

Psalm 35:11-18

PONDER

When illness struck friends, the psalmist prayed and fasted for their health. But when the psalmist became sick or merely stumbled, friends laughed with glee, rejoiced over the misfortunes, "impiously mocked" (v. 16), and kept their distance. Instead of the problem evoking compassion, it created hostility. "They repay me evil for good" (v. 12), writes the psalmist in disbelief and hurt. In the face of such attacks, the psalmist turns to God. "Rescue me from their ravages, my life from the lions!" (v. 17). When we feel like the lions have camped on our doorstep, the times call for prayer.

PRAYER/PRACTICE

A New Testament image of intercession occurs in the story of the four friends who carry their paralyzed friend to Jesus but find the crowd too big to allow them to enter the house. They go up on the flat roof, dig through the layers, and lower their friend on a mat through the opening. Jesus, impressed by their efforts and their faith, says to the paralytic, "Stand up, take your mat and go to your home" (Mark 2:11).

Imagine carrying someone you care about to Jesus. Who goes with you? Do any obstacles stand in your way? Whom do you see on the mat? What does Jesus say to the person? How does the person respond? Could you visualize yourself on the mat? What part of you needs healing? Try this visualization of intercession today. Also, today, give thanks for people like Joseph and Sacajawea whose care and guidance form a prayer of intercession for you.

March 20

REMEMBER

The spring equinox balances the hours of light and darkness.

READ

Psalm 35:19-28

PONDER

"Yahweh, do not stay silent; Lord, do not stand aloof from me. Up, awake, to my defence [sic]. . . . In your saving justice give judgement [*sic*] for me, Yahweh my God, and do not let them gloat over me" (vv. 22-24, NJB). The psalmist implores God not to give the troublemakers, the evildoers, the last word. Expressing confidence in God's ability to respond and to act for justice, the psalm ends with affirmation and assurance: "Then my tongue shall tell of your righteousness and of your praise all day long" (v. 28).

In the death and resurrection of Jesus, death does not have the last word. Thanks be to God, who does not remain silent and does not allow evil to have the last word!

PRAYER/PRACTICE

Intercession is not just a solitary practice. When a community of faith gathers for worship and lifts up names of people and situations needing prayer, the community engages in corporate intercession. Corporate intercession also occurs when people participate in a prayer vigil organized around a particular need. Consider gathering with several others to pray for a situation where evil seems to have the last word. Do you know of a place of violence, tension, or disaster you can lift up in prayer? You might use some of the visualization practices from these past few days. Each person present could offer a spoken prayer followed by silence and visualization. Remember to close by affirming God's ability to bring justice, to have the last word. Also, on this equinox, seek balance in your life and in the world.

March 21

Johann Sebastian Bach (1685–1750), a German church organist and composer, wrote many of his works for the church, including almost three hundred sacred cantatas.

READ

Psalm 36

PONDER

The description of the wicked in Psalm 36 still seems accurate today. Evildoers give no thought to God; they concern themselves only with their power and fame, use secret accounts and well-paid lawyers to hide their evil deeds, and plot takeovers and deals while on their beds or cell phones.

In contrast, the upright "finds shelter in the shadow of your wings. You give your guests a feast in your house, and you serve a tasty drink that flows like a river" (vv. 7-8, CEV). The psalmist knows God's steadfast love offers the better way, so the words of praise soar: "Your love, Lord, lights up the sky, your faithfulness shapes the clouds. Your integrity towers like a mountain, your justice plunges deeper than the sea. Lord, you graciously hold all of life. How exquisite your tender mercy!" (vv. 5-7, AP).

PRAYER/PRACTICE

On the birthday of Johann Sebastian Bach, remember that music can lift us into sacred space. Bach, an accomplished organist, sought in his music to inspire praise and devotion. He knew the Bible, immersed himself in the Psalms, and expressed his faith by ending many of his compositions with the initials *S.D.G.* The letters represented Latin words that translate as "To God alone the glory."

Today reflect on the importance of music in your life. Recall favorite hymns or church songs you know by heart. What music do you listen to or play when you want to enter sacred space? Listen to some music of Bach today.

March 22

REMEMBER

Alfred North Whitehead (1861–1947), an English philosopher, sought to integrate religion and science by suggesting that both God and nature remain in process. God's nature is love, and God draws all toward love. Whitehead's writings became the foundation of process theology.

READ

Psalm 37:1-4

PONDER

Walter Brueggemann says that most psalms fall into three large categories: *psalms of orientation*, where all the world seems fine; *psalms of disorientation*, where life is hard, painful, and unjust; and *psalms of new orientation* (reorientation), where despite all the difficulty, God works to restore, renew, and rebuild each day and life.[4]

We call Psalm 37 a psalm of orientation. "Don't worry about the wicked; take it easy; they will fade. Just trust and everyone will get the desires of his or her heart" (vv. 1-4, AP). The psalm may not speak to the tragedies in our life, but it reminds us to trust in God and do good regardless.

PRAYER/PRACTICE

Our intercessions for others may take on a more active nature. I invite you to think about and begin to practice simple acts of kindness and compassion as an expression of your intercession. We can embody our prayer for others and for the world through our deeds of care and acts of kindness.

I invite you to try occasionally to do a hidden kindness, an unexpected act that cannot be repaid or would be hard to repay. Can you send a card to someone in need without signing it? Can you make an anonymous donation to some group, perhaps on behalf of someone? Can you arrange for a meal to be delivered to a person unable to get out? Look for ways to be creative and surprising, yet act with humility and grace.

March 23

REMEMBER

Deborah (B.C.E.), a wise judge in the Hebrew Scriptures, guided the nation of Israel before the people asked for and received a king.

READ

The story of Deborah in Judges 4–5

PONDER

Some think that the only poetry in the Bible resides in the Psalms, but delightful verses weave their way throughout the Bible, verses that would often be set to music. The Song of Deborah, hidden in Judges chapter 5, remembers Deborah's leadership in poetic form. It recounts the victory of the Israelites over the Canaanites. It testifies to the prophetic wisdom of one of the quiet women leaders of the Bible. In a patriarchal culture, God used a woman to help free the people; God lifted up the contribution of a wise woman. Give thanks for this hidden song, for its inclusion in scripture, and for another saint worth remembering and singing about.

PRAYER/PRACTICE

My Quaker friends speak of receiving a "leading." As you deepen your prayer life, you may find that a person or situation comes to mind during your prayer time. You may feel led to call someone. You may feel beckoned to speak up for the lost and forgotten. You may feel called to join a demonstration for human rights or to address your city council. All these would be a leading from the Spirit, an opportunity to live out your prayer, to express God's concern for all people, especially the ignored or forgotten. Take time in your prayer today to listen for a leading. Is there someone God wants you to contact or something God wants you to do? Act on this leading as your prayer of intercession.

March 24

REMEMBER

Oscar Romero (1917–1980), a conservative Catholic bishop, became an outspoken and progressive archbishop, championing the poor and oppressed in El Salvador. Gunmen murdered him while he said Mass the day after calling for the military to stop the repression.

READ

Psalm 37:5-13

PONDER

When someone commits his or her life to God, the road ahead contains no guarantees where that person will end up. Oscar Romero, a timid, conventional minister chosen to lead the church in El Salvador, underwent a transformation when he presided over the funeral of his friend Father Rutilio Grande (Mar. 12) and began to see the violence of the government and military against the poor. "A church that does not unite itself to the poor in order to denounce from the place of the poor the injustice committed against them is not truly the Church of Jesus Christ. . . . We either believe in a God of life, or we serve the idols of death."[5] Romero's strong words earned him the enmity of the country's leaders and even other church leaders, but he courageously sought to serve as a voice for the voiceless. Perhaps he meditated on the words of promise from Psalm 37, "For the wicked shall be cut off, but those who wait for the LORD shall inherit the land" (v. 9).

PRAYER/PRACTICE

Taking a stand for justice lives out our intercession for the needs of the world and becomes a way to live out our belief that God takes special interest in the poor, the forgotten, the foreigner. God cares because often the world does not care for all God's people. Find a way today to write about some world issue, speak up about an injustice, or contribute to some organization working for justice and peace. I invite you to learn more about Oscar Romero, a courageous contemporary voice in the struggle for the poor. The movie *Romero* depicts some of the struggle that went on in Central America. (See Appendix A.)

March 25

REMEMBER

The Feast of the Annunciation of the Lord, celebrated today, commemorates the angel Gabriel's announcement to Mary that she would bear a son, the Savior of the world.

READ

Psalm 37:14-22

PONDER

In the long run, justice wins over evil, and goodness brings its own reward. The psalmist paints this view in these verses that see wicked schemes coming back to hurt the originators (v. 15) and abundance coming to cover the table of the blameless in the days of famine (v. 19). Generosity defines the character of the righteous. "The wicked borrow, and do not pay back, but the righteous are generous and keep giving" (v. 21). Generosity flows from belief in a caring and providing God. Paul wrote, "God is able to provide you with every blessing in abundance, so that by always having enough of everything, you may share abundantly in every good work" (2 Cor. 9:8).

PRAYER/PRACTICE

One of the simple and wise teachings in Buddhism describes the deeds or acts one can do that cost nothing. A good and generous person will seek to extend these seven offerings: "a compassionate eye, a smiling face, loving words, physical service, a warm heart, a seat, and lodging."[6]

Write down these seven offerings so that you can put them into practice. Today look for ways you might offer one or more of these seven gifts to others. Can you think of other acts of kindness that cost nothing? Ask God to give you guidance and courage in enacting these prayers of intercession.

March 26

REMEMBER

Amos (eighth century B.C.E.) called the nation Israel back to justice. His prophetic voice confronted the people with their proud words yet dismal deeds: [God says] "I take no delight in your solemn assemblies. . . . But let justice roll down like waters" (Amos 5: 21, 24).

READ

Psalm 37:23-33

PONDER

Like a toddler's first steps, walking through our rough-and-tumble world can be difficult. Temptations overflow, inviting us to make a quick buck or to become an instant millionaire. Calls abound to try this pleasure or buy this product that will solve all our problems. Yet, "if you do what the Lord wants, God will steady each step you take. God will hold your hand, and if you stumble, you still won't fall" (vv. 23-24, AP).

We do not walk alone. We have the words of scripture as guidance for our journey. The wisdom of the Christian tradition blesses us and illumines our path. Through worship, prayer, and reading, we seek to incorporate the law of God in our hearts (v. 31). If we stumble, God helps us not to fall or helps us get back up.

PRAYER/PRACTICE

The psalmist, now old (v. 25), looks back on the journey of faith and notes the generosity of the righteous. Older persons can offer a lasting gift to the young by reading to them. The simple act of reading or telling Bible stories to a child can function as intercession; we all can do this act of service and bless future generations. I invite you to read or tell stories to your children or to the children of your faith community. Many wonderful children's Bible storybooks line the shelves of bookstores. (See Appendix A for suggestions.)

March 27

REMEMBER

Meister Eckhart (1260–1329), mystic and writer, stressed the path of self-emptying and taught that God could be found if one looked for God, whether in church or not.

READ

Psalm 37:34-40

PONDER

The psalmist invites us to look around and see that the wicked have vanished and the righteous are still standing. In the end, crime does not pay. Or to put it in a more positive light, "There is a future for the [person] of peace" (v. 37, NIV). Despite the fear and violence on some city streets, despite ongoing tensions in the Middle East, despite a growing gap between rich and poor, the future belongs to the peacemakers. Despite companies moving to get cheaper labor, despite lotteries and gambling spreading across the United States, the future belongs to the peacemakers. Matthew 5:5 says, "Blessed are the meek, for they will inherit the earth." God sees the big picture and works for good over the long haul.

PRAYER/PRACTICE

Do you know someone who is sick or in prison? Can you assist in a soup kitchen or food pantry? Is a bill that addresses the needs of the poor pending in your state legislature or in Congress, and will you write your representatives? Will you lend a helping hand to a neighbor who can no longer drive or get out? Can you give supplies or help to a shelter for the homeless or for abused persons? Could you volunteer to help build a Habitat for Humanity house? Find a way to put your intercession for the poor and hungry into practice.

March 28

REMEMBER

Toyohiko Kagawa (1888–1960), a Japanese writer and activist, was disinherited by his parents after he became a Christian but went on to minister to the poor, found the first Japanese labor union, oppose war, and support missionaries.

READ

Psalm 38:1-14

PONDER

Ancient peoples often thought that God sent illness; that belief seems evident in this third of seven penitential psalms. Rather than claiming goodness or innocence as in the lament psalms, the psalmist openly confesses all misdeeds and problems. We know that God does not send or desire illness for any of creation. We know that we play a role in our health and that much mystery remains as to why some people get sick and others get well. Whatever the particular malady of the psalmist, it becomes the occasion for prayer and for confession, which is good news for anyone who wants to get well.

PRAYER/PRACTICE

In your journal, I invite you to review the first spiritual practice of this month, *lectio divina*. Have you been able to incorporate some meditation on scripture into your daily prayer routine? Do you find yourself reading and meditating more slowly on the psalm passages for each day? Do you find yourself led into times of contemplation more easily? Do you have a group of friends who might want to do this kind of scripture reading together? What additional commitments would you like to make regarding *lectio divina*?

March 29

REMEMBER

John Donne (1572–1631), an Anglican priest, poet, and pastor, served as dean of Saint Paul's Cathedral in London. His vivid poetry captured the attention of people near and far.

READ

Psalm 38:15-22

PONDER

We tend to blame others for our problems. We fault the parents. We blame our genes. We accuse the school or complain about a certain teacher. The fault lies outside of our responsibility. We make good excuses for why a particular trial was not our fault. But the psalmist, with almost brutal honesty, looks within: "I confess my iniquity; I am sorry for my sin" (v. 18). The psalmist takes responsibility for mistakes and pleads for God to come with haste, to bring salvation. Even in the midst of troubles, the psalmist displays a healthy pattern of personal responsibility, honest confession, and turning to seek God's help.

PRAYER/PRACTICE

Today I invite you to journal about this month's suggestions for practicing intercession. Keep a list or a box of names of people or situations to pray for. Use your imagination to place people before God. Enlarge your intercession to include situations or people around the world. Complete some acts of kindness; take part in ministry to the poor. Seek to align your concerns with God's will for all of creation. Name the ways intercession has become part of your prayer life.

March 30

REMEMBER

Sister Thea Bowman (1937–1990), an African American Franciscan nun, did not blend into dominant culture but used spirituals, story-telling, and preaching to confront a European-dominated Roman Catholic Church and to reach out to new people.

READ

Psalm 39:1-6

PONDER

Some life experiences force us to question the meaning of existence. The psalmist has experienced some serious misfortune. All efforts to be silent, patient, and not complain have finally burst, and the psalmist questions God about the meaning of life, the length of one's days, and the meaning behind suffering. Finally, the psalmist concludes, "Surely everyone stands as a mere breath. Surely everyone goes about like a shadow" (vv. 5-6).

Job also questions God, and so do many people with serious illness. Thea Bowman put it this way, "When I first found out I had cancer, I didn't know what to pray for. I didn't know if I should pray for healing or life or death. Then I found peace in praying for what my folks call 'God's perfect will.' As it evolved, my prayer has become, 'Lord, let me live until I die.' By that I mean I want to live, love, and serve fully until death comes. . . . How long really doesn't matter."[7]

PRAYER/PRACTICE

Journal your responses to questions about the meaning of life and the length of our days. Reflect on any misfortunes you have experienced that caused you to doubt the presence of God. Can you trust God for each day, no matter how many or how few days remain? Can you voice your complaints and then wait calmly for God's reply? Can you pray like Sister Thea, "I want to live, love, and serve fully until I die"?

March 31

REMEMBER

Cesar Chavez (1927–1993), a farmworker born this day, used his faith and the principles of nonviolence to organize and lead a union of farmworkers. He called for justice, higher wages, and better working conditions for the poor.

READ

Psalm 39:7-13

PONDER

From questions about the meaning of life, the psalmist turns again to God. "And now, O Lord, what do I wait for? My hope is in you" (v. 7). Answers may not emerge clearly, but we know where our hope rests.

Cesar Chavez remained hopeful and faithful even in the face of opposition. "When we are really honest with ourselves we must admit that our lives are all that really belong to us. So it is how we use our lives that determines what kind of men [persons] we are. It is my deepest belief that only by giving our lives do we find life," he wrote.[8]

PRAYER/PRACTICE

Today I invite you to journal about your reflections on this month's suggestions for serving and practicing compassion and kindness. Have your interactions with others, especially with the poor or the service workers you encountered, been marked with greater kindness and respect? Have you been able to do some hidden acts of kindness? Can you make this a monthly practice? Cesar Chavez provides a good example of one who put his faith into practice, who lived out Christ's compassion by organizing some of the most exploited workers in the United States. Learn more about Cesar Chavez, and see if farmworkers need your help today.

April

God of openness and new life,
in this Easter season,
remove me from the tombs of doubt and despair,
turn me from dead ends and shattered dreams,
and lead me to new hope and a bright tomorrow.
Walk with me down uncharted roads and ordinary paths,
always leading me to a deeper trust
and more faithful service.
I open my heart to your Easter joy. Amen.

April 1

REMEMBER

"This is the day upon which we are reminded of what we are on the other three hundred and sixty-four." Mark Twain's words about April Fool's Day invite us to laugh a little. Be a fool for Christ.

READ

Psalm 40:1-8

PONDER

These verses contain strong descriptions of God. "God bent down to hear my cry. God drew me up from the pit, out of the miry bog. God put a new song in my mouth, a new song of praise" (vv. 1-3, AP). The psalmist gives thanks for God's saving and rock-solid action and believes that many will come to know and put their trust in God. Inviting us to turn from following the lies of the proud and from seeking false gods, the poet urges us to proclaim God's deeds and sing God's praise. God desires our singing and our praise, not our sacrifices and burnt offerings (v. 6).

PRAYER/PRACTICE

Music has long been seen as a bridge between heaven and earth. In singing, playing, or listening to music, one can sense a larger universe, a divine reality. Virtually every religious tradition sings, and the variety is endless: Gregorian chant, Byzantine polyphony, hymns, Islamic calls to prayer, gospel music, shape-note singing, requiems, cantatas, and praise songs.

Think of the first times you experienced singing as a prayer. What songs can you recall? What music leads you into prayer? How do you sing your prayers? Give thanks for the songs God has given you.

April 2

REMEMBER

Carlo Carretto (1910–1988), an Italian contemplative, wrote letters from the desert that introduced people to the rich tradition of desert spirituality. He returned to Italy, taught, wrote, and combined a life of prayer with a passion for social justice.

READ

Psalm 40:9-17

PONDER

Carlo Carretto left a busy life in Italy to live in the Saharan desert of Algeria. The solitary time did not remove him completely from public life. His book *Letters from the Desert* echoes the psalmist, "I have spoken of your faithfulness and your salvation; I have not concealed your steadfast love and your faithfulness from the great congregation" (v. 10). Carretto's joy-filled spirituality; his commitment to poverty, nonviolence, and the simple life; and his instructions about living a holy and contemplative life in the midst of whatever "desert" people experienced touched the hearts and minds of contemporary and urban people searching for a deeper relationship with God.

PRAYER/PRACTICE

Music can encourage one's commitment to compassion. Spirituals gave hope to a people forced to be slaves. The spirituals told of freedom; "Steal Away to Jesus," "Oh, Freedom," and "Follow the Drinking Gourd" referred to more than just heaven. During the civil rights movement and opposition to the Vietnam War, music again played a part in motivating and encouraging marchers and workers for a new order of life. I still cannot sing "We Shall Overcome" without recalling marching for peace in Washington, D. C., in the 1970s.

What songs encourage your faithfulness to God's call for justice and freedom? What songs do you associate with struggles for freedom and justice?

April 3

REMEMBER

Moses (B.C.E.) grew up in Egypt, experienced God's call from a burning bush, and responded by leading the Hebrew people from slavery to freedom. Moses conversed with God on Mount Sinai and received the Ten Commandments.

READ

Psalm 41:1-3

PONDER

Care for the poor flows as a major stream in the Psalms. Indeed throughout all of scripture, concern for the poor testifies to and mirrors our love for God. As we care for "the least of these"—the forgotten, the sick, and the homeless—we attest to the depth of our love and the breadth of our compassion. We align ourselves with the very intentions of God, who delivers, protects, keeps alive, and sustains them (vv. 1-3). As we take up the cause of compassion, we follow in the footsteps of Moses, who led the captives to freedom.

PRAYER/PRACTICE

Joyce Rupp composed a Blessing of Compassion[1] that I invite you to use for the next two days. You can enact the blessing with a partner as a leader reads the words or as one person reads them to the other, or you can pray the blessing for yourself.

1. *Touching the forehead*—May you approach all other beings with Christlike compassion, observing them with kindness. May you let go of all harsh judgments.

2. *Touching the ears*—May you be aware of the suffering of those around you, and of all those in the cosmos. May your ears be open to hear their cries of distress.

3. *Touching the mouth*—May you have the courage and wisdom to speak up for those who are wronged, to be a voice for those who suffer from injustice of any form.

April 4

REMEMBER

Martin Luther King Jr. (1929–1968), the central leader in the U.S. civil rights movement, was assassinated in Memphis, Tennessee, while lending support to striking sanitation workers.

READ

Psalm 41:4-13

PONDER

Steeped in the prophets' justice message and Jesus' radical, nonviolent love, Martin Luther King Jr. preached a strong message of hope and freedom. Using biblical images and advocating nonviolent resistance to discrimination, he captivated a nation and pushed it to change its ways. King's nonviolent, spiritual marches faced angry mobs, fire hoses, and police brutality and yet took the higher moral ground. His death robbed the world of a dynamic, prophetic voice for all people.

Psalm 41 ends with a doxology, marking the end of the first grouping, or book, of Psalms. The five books, many scholars believe, correspond to the first five books of the Hebrew Scriptures.

PRAYER/PRACTICE

I invite you to continue with the Blessing of Compassion.[2]

4. *Touching the hands*—May you be open to receive from others when you are in need. May you be ready to give when someone needs to receive your gifts.

5. *Touching the heart*—May you be willing to meet your own suffering. May you do so with deep compassion for yourself.

6. *Touching the feet*—May your faith give you strength when you stand beneath the cross of another.

7. *Embracing (hugging) the other person (whisper in his or her ear)*—May you always know the shelter of God when you are hurting and in pain. May you trust this Compassionate Being to protect you and to comfort you. May you be at peace.

April 5

REMEMBER

Pandita Ramabai (1858–1922), an Indian Christian and reformer, became known as a mother of modern India.

READ

Psalm 42:1-5

PONDER

In a wonderful, poetic metaphor, the psalmist compares thirst for God to a deer longing for flowing streams. The image evokes not only a gracefulness but also a deep longing—to be in the house of the Lord, to see the face of God. When we experience sadness and feel distant from God, we long to feel the closeness of God. God has placed this longing in us, and the longing is accompanied by a firm hope in God, our source of help.

PRAYER/PRACTICE

The Psalms have inspired a large collection of church music. I usually play religious music as I eat breakfast; often I choose a recording of the Psalms. Many monastic communities, contemporary writers, and musicians have either set the Psalms to music or used images from the Psalms in new songs. Listening to this music in the morning helps me start the day feeling less frantic, and it keeps me from filling my mind with disturbing images from the morning's news. It also places the Psalms in my mind and heart for the day.

I invite you to enjoy recorded music of the Psalms. See Appendix A for suggestions.

April 6

REMEMBER

Hadewijch of Brabant, a thirteenth-century mystic, wrote letters stressing the value of prayer, works of mercy, a life of simplicity, and following the love of Christ.

READ

Psalm 42:6-11

PONDER

At times in life, a certain verse or refrain often comes to mind, serving as an anchor when the storms of life rage. It serves as a lamppost when darkness threatens to overtake us. Psalms 42 and 43 repeat the same refrain three times: "Why are you cast down, O my soul, and why are you disquieted within me? Hope in God; for I shall again praise . . . my help and my God" (vv. 5, 11). Life may give us many reasons to feel cast down, but help and hope persist. Our hope rests upon God. In times of trials, the refrain bears repeating: "Why are you cast down? . . . Hope in God . . . my help and my God."

PRAYER/PRACTICE

Songs can also serve as anchors in troubled times. The simple act of humming a tune can turn a dark day into a day filled with radiant light. Recalling a hymn or song can set our toes to tapping and our lips to singing. Martin Luther King Jr. found great encouragement in the song "Precious Lord." The image of God taking us by the hand and leading us through stormy times to a healing light offered great comfort and hope to Dr. King in the struggle for civil rights.

Make a list of songs that give you hope in the midst of threatening shadows. What songs encourage your faith and discipleship? What music anchors your soul in the midst of windy and troubling storms? What singers lift your spirits? Sing or hum your music throughout the day.

April 7

REMEMBER

André Trocmé (1901–1971), a Protestant pastor in a small French village, Le Chambon, organized the townspeople so they could offer haven to thousands of Jewish refugees from Nazi Germany.

READ

Psalm 43

PONDER

Perhaps André Trocmé took literally the idea that God is our refuge (v. 2), and if we are sheltered by God, then we should extend that shelter to others in times of need. The story of Le Chambon, like *Schindler's List,* glimmers like a small ray of human goodness in the face of great human evil. Pastor Trocmé taught his church to live out the Beatitudes and to practice loving one's neighbor. The town and surrounding farms protected an estimated twenty-five hundred Jews. Again we hear the refrain, "Hope in God . . . my help and my God" (v. 5).

PRAYER/PRACTICE

Music touches the emotions. Some songs make us sad. Others set our feet to dancing. Some music makes our spirits soar to the heavens. When we cannot find the words for our prayers, sometimes music can help us express our feelings. Some pray best by using their fingers on a keyboard or other instrument. What music helps you sing your praise? What music expresses your deepest longing for God? What music soothes your sadness? What music takes you to the heavens? What music sings of resurrection? What music fills you with courage? Reflect and write in your journal about music in your life.

April 8

REMEMBER

Dietrich Bonhoeffer (1906–1945), a Lutheran pastor and teacher, revealed the ethical dilemmas of faith in hard times and called for a faith that makes sense to the suffering. His alleged involvement in a plot to kill Hitler landed him in a concentration camp. He continued to write and struggle with remaining faithful to God until his death by hanging.

READ

Psalm 44:1-8

PONDER

The Hebrew people lived with a memory of what God had done in the past. They remembered and celebrated the Exodus from slavery in Egypt. "In God we have boasted continually, and we will give thanks to your name forever" (v. 8). Their memory of God's deeds in the past helped them when current times proved difficult and painful.

Remember signs of hope and promise from the past. Many have learned from Dietrich Bonhoeffer's writings that faith can be costly, that grace is not cheap, and that we need to understand and view history from the perspective of the outcast and the powerless.

PRAYER/PRACTICE

Singing together constitutes a form of communal prayer. In chant and choral singing, the goal is not to sing the loudest but to blend in making a glorious sound. Though I am not a great singer, someone invited me to participate in a "toning circle." The leader, who had a fine voice, started a tone, and everyone in the circle joined in. A beautiful sound emerged that included my quiet tone and astounded me. Some tones continued for several minutes, with the music never ending but shifting and floating as people took breaths at different times. Then we all stopped as if on some hidden cue but more on the sense that it felt right to end. This week, find some time to sing along with a choir, congregation, CD, or radio station. Blend your voice in communal prayer.

April 9

REMEMBER

Paul Robeson (1898–1976), an African American singer and actor, became an early proponent of black liberation.

READ

Psalm 44:9-16

PONDER

God's past deeds on Israel's behalf stand in painful contrast to the nation's plight now that it has been invaded. "You have made us like sheep for slaughter, and have scattered us among the nations" (v. 11). "You have made us . . . a laughingstock among the peoples" (v. 14). Like Job, the people cry out for answers. This is not one of the psalms where everything is right with the world. Our gift from this psalm is good company and feisty language we can use to complain to God when there seems to be no answer for why racism, violence, greed, hunger, and despair still run rampant in the world.

PRAYER/PRACTICE

Meditate on this poem by Rumi. What message does it hold for you?

> God picks up the reed-flute world and blows.
> Each note is a need coming through one of us,
> a passion, a longing-pain.
> Remember the lips
> where the wind-breath originated,
> and let your note be clear.
> Don't try to end it.
> *Be your note.*
> I'll show you how it's enough.
>
> Go up on the roof at night
> in this city of the soul.
>
> Let *everyone* climb on their roofs
> and sing their notes!
> Sing loud![3]

April 10

REMEMBER

William Booth (1829–1912), a British evangelist, founded the Salvation Army, known for its brass bands, uniforms, and care of the poor.

READ

Psalm 44:17-26

PONDER

Does anger or a desperate prayer erupt in the last four verses? "Rouse yourself! Why do you sleep, O Lord? Awake, do not cast us off forever! Why do you hide your face? . . . Rise up, come to our help" (vv. 23-24, 26). Do we genuinely turn to God only in desperate times? Have we ever dared to use such strong language with God? Do even the faithful need reminders that they do not control their destiny? Perhaps this psalm finally finds an answer in Jesus, where God's amazing resurrection transforms the worst event imaginable.

PRAYER/PRACTICE

When I served a small church in Manchester, England, we had a brass band. Though the band members were not professional musicians and their style of music was not my favorite, the band still ranked as an important ministry of the church because neighborhood kids comprised most of the band. These young lads could be a terror, even at practice, but when the band played in worship services, their joyful sound helped us praise God.

Give thanks for a time when music helped you worship. Add that thankful memory to your journal.

April 11

REMEMBER

Pierre Teilhard de Chardin (1881–1955), a French scientist, mystic, and Jesuit, wrote extensively and argued that God participated in the evolutionary process. In his devotional writing he perceived the face of the divine in all of creation.

READ

Psalm 45

PONDER

A royal wedding forms the occasion for this psalm, and the whole community celebrates the love of the king and queen. The beloved king rules with equity, loves righteousness, and hates wickedness (vv. 6-7). The beautiful queen, led in a joyous procession, goes to meet the king. Hope for the relationship and for future generations prevails. This love song stands in sharp contrast to the last lament and reminds us that all of life serves as an opening for prayer.

Early Christians saw in this psalm the marriage of Christ and the church and the hope that the throne of God would endure forever.

PRAYER/PRACTICE

I invite you to move from considering music in your prayer life to looking at ways the body prays without words. In Christian thought, the mind, body, and spirit are one. At times we cannot find the words we want for prayer—though the Psalms certainly help us push the edges of language.

Even when we cannot find words, the body still may be able to pray. We may find a posture that feels right, a dance that emerges, or a gesture that expresses our prayer. For the next few days we will consider ways the body may pray.

Jesus not only used words but also touched people. He touched eyes, ears, and mouths, and he knew when someone touched him. Today pay attention to how you touch others. Can your touch communicate openness, comfort, peace, blessing? Be mindful of others' boundaries and need for space. Ask for permission to touch or hug them. Offer respect and reverence.

April 12

REMEMBER

Carl Jung (1875–1961), a psychologist and philosopher, focused on myths, archetypes, and the collective unconscious. Also remember the resurrection of Jesus, which Christians usually celebrate in April.

READ

Psalm 46:1-7

PONDER

I have lived through several earthquakes. I have seen storms that pounded and destroyed houses along the ocean shore. These natural disasters are fearful, awesome events that increase anxiety and create chaos in a community. Scripture reminds us with a strong assurance, though, that no matter what happens, "God is our refuge and strength, a very present help in trouble" (v. 1). God provides our security in an unstable and shaky world; this truth may account for the rise in church attendance during times of calamity.

When we dwell in the "city of God"—when we live in right relationship with God and remain present in the community of faith—we experience a stability that holds us fast in the midst of the roaring and shaking.

PRAYER/PRACTICE

Different postures exist for prayer, and each one seems to enable different moods of prayer. Today I invite you to try praying as you lie facedown on the floor. The prostrate posture evokes humility, obedience, and even confession. Such a posture recognizes the awesomeness of God and the frailty and weakness of humankind.

As you try this posture, what feelings emerge in your prayer? How do you experience God? What gift do you receive from God through this prayer posture? How can you incorporate this posture into your regular prayer life?

April 13

REMEMBER

James (first century), together with his brother John, fishermen known as the "sons of thunder," were some of Jesus' closest disciples. Popular tradition suggests that James took the gospel to Spain. He was the first of the twelve apostles to be martyred.

READ

Psalm 46:8-11

PONDER

In our anxious world, "Be still, and know that I am God!" (v. 10). In our noisy communities, "Be still, and know that I am God." In hospital waiting rooms and disaster shelters, "Be still, and know that I am God!" In the midst of war, peace negotiations, or economic decisions, "Be still, and know that I am God!" This refrain resides at the heart of prayer and meditation. It recognizes that we are not God; we do not control the universe or even our lives. God makes wars cease and causes nations to pay attention to a Higher Power, to the One exalted among nations. Allow the verse to dwell in your heart: "Be still, and know that I am God!"

PRAYER/PRACTICE

The posture of kneeling for prayer occurs in many churches. In some churches, congregants kneel frequently during the liturgy; in others, worshipers kneel only occasionally, such as when receiving Communion. Some individuals find a prayer bench or cushion provides a comfortable, supported way to kneel.

Today try kneeling for your time of prayer. What emotions does this posture evoke? Do you discover a sense of humility? Do you find kneeling to be a posture of rest and gentle yielding? Can you sense a spirit of prayer in the very act of kneeling? Record your experience in your journal.

April 14

REMEMBER

Anne Sullivan Macy (1866–1936) taught sign language to Helen Keller, who was blind and deaf, and she accompanied Helen when she became an articulate and passionate champion for persons with disabilities. The movie *The Miracle Worker* recounts her difficulties and breakthrough in teaching Helen.

READ

Psalm 47

PONDER

If we read and practice the truths of this psalm, we have no excuse for boring worship. Enthusiasm and joy permeate the psalm and the experience of worship. People sing; they even shout and clap their hands. Trumpets blow and praise erupts, for God is awesome. God reigns over all the earth and rules over all the nations (vv. 2, 7, 8). In our praise of God in worship, sometimes we should pull out all the stops—let our praises soar and the trumpets raise the roof.

Many churches use this psalm to celebrate Jesus' ascension into heaven. "God has gone up with a shout, the LORD with the sound of a trumpet" (v. 5).

PRAYER/PRACTICE

The posture most associated with praise is standing. When good news triumphs, when joy overflows, when gladness makes its home in us, we cannot sit still. We leap for joy, skip with delight, jump with excitement, raise our hands, stand on tiptoe, and shout at the top of our lungs.

Today stand to read this psalm aloud. Read it with a strong voice as you offer thanksgiving for God's deeds in your life. Stand with your head tilted back and your hands extended as you praise God. You might even find your feet want to dance a little. Carry this mood of praise with you throughout the day.

April 15

REMEMBER

Damien of Molokai (1840–1899), a Belgian priest, ministered among lepers on the Hawaiian island of Molokai. He died of leprosy on this day.

READ

Psalm 48

PONDER

Israel built the temple in Jerusalem on the highest point, Mount Zion. The Hebrews believed that God watched over and protected God's people from that mountain. Even foreign kings and armies (v. 5) took to flight when they beheld the mighty fortress of Jerusalem with the temple at the center. The people stood in awe of God's steadfast love and guidance.

When we read about people like Father Damien, we feel the same sense of awe, for surely God must have been present with Damien as he ministered to lepers in a place where no one else would even go.

PRAYER/PRACTICE

Sitting, the most common prayer posture, usually provides support for our backs, a resting place for our uncrossed feet, and a lap in which to lay our hands. Some individuals sit on a pillow on the floor, while others prefer yoga positions to keep upright and alert. Sitting quietly in a relaxed position, perhaps with palms up, expresses openness and receptivity. Mary sat at Jesus' feet and opened her heart as she listened to his teaching. When Jesus went to Zacchaeus's house and sat at the table, the dialogue convinced Zacchaeus to change his ways.

For most of us, sitting in a chair provides a comfortable way to relax and remain attentive for our time of prayer. Today sit quietly, letting the chair or bench or floor hold you, and use your breath prayer. In your journal write reflections about this posture of prayer. Imagine sitting in the presence of Jesus.

April 16

REMEMBER

Jonah (B.C.E.) found out that God's care for the people of Nineveh exceeded his own reluctance to do God's work. His story reveals that even big fish cooperate with God.

READ

Psalm 49:1-12

PONDER

"Hear this, all you peoples; give ear, all inhabitants of the world, both low and high, rich and poor together" (vv. 1-2). Wealth, though useful in human exchange, becomes useless in dealing with God and powerless in fending off death. Death, the great leveler, does not respect money, wisdom, age, or beauty. "We see that wise people die, and so do stupid fools. Then their money is left for someone else" (v. 10, CEV).

Hear this, Jonah: God's compassion extends to all people, whether you like them or not. God's call to serve can be avoided for a while, but God persists, and all nature conspires to do God's will.

PRAYER/PRACTICE

Bowing is a brief prayer gesture not as common in Western Christian practice as in Eastern cultures, which incorporate bowing in both ordinary greeting and in services of worship. Genuflecting (touching the knee to or near the ground), bowing, and profound bowing (lowering the top of the body to an almost horizontal position) all indicate honor or respect in worship or in greeting. Some cultures understand the bow to imply, "The spirit in me greets the spirit in you."

Today try to incorporate brief or slight bows as you meet or greet other persons. Intend your movement to be one of gentle respect. As you begin your prayer time, bow before God. In bowing you might place your hands, palms together, in front of your chest. Know that God's spirit greets your spirit.

April 17

REMEMBER

Georgia Harkness (1891–1979), a theologian and hymn writer, worked for the inclusion of women in all of church life.

READ

Psalm 49:13-20

PONDER

The popular expression "You can't take it with you" finds its roots in this psalm. "When they [the rich] die they will carry nothing away; their wealth will not go down after them" (v. 17). Even though relatives or followers construct elaborate tombstones, marble monuments, or stunning pyramids, the ancient wisdom still bears repeating: "You can't take it with you."

For most of the Hebrew Scriptures, no belief in the afterlife existed. Yet in the immediate centuries before Christ, a notion of some kind of retribution for the faithful began to emerge. Verse 15 hints at this developing thought. Not until the establishment of Christianity did a new view of life beyond death become central.

PRAYER/PRACTICE

I invite you to pray or sing this powerful text by Georgia Harkness:

> Hope of the world, thou Christ of great compassion,
> speak to our fearful hearts by conflict rent.
> Save us, thy people, from consuming passion,
> who by our own false hopes and aims are spent.

> . . . .

> Hope of the world, afoot on dusty highways,
> showing to wandering souls the path of light,
> walk thou beside us lest the tempting byways
> lure us away from thee to endless night.

April 18

REMEMBER

Leonardo da Vinci (1452–1519), a Florentine artist, was one of the most important artists of the Italian Renaissance. A multitalented person, he not only was a gifted painter and sculptor but also an architect, engineer, inventor, and scientist. Da Vinci's paintings depicted many religious subjects, including the Last Supper and John the Baptist.

READ

Psalm 50:1-15

PONDER

Our actions, deeds, and decisions matter. We are accountable to one another in the community of faith and accountable to God, who at times calls us to accountability. "My people, I am God! Israel, I am your God. Listen to my charges against you" (v. 7, CEV). God indicts Israel for her public worship, which included daily sacrifices of animals. The indictments focus on external religious performances. Our worship may equally be judged. "I am God Most High! The only sacrifice I want is for you to be thankful and to keep your word" (v. 14, CEV). If we offer praise, if we care for the forgotten, if we know our dependence on God, then God says, "Call on me in the day of trouble; I will deliver you, and you shall glorify me" (v. 15).

PRAYER/PRACTICE

Each morning I do some basic stretches. Over the years, most of the stretches have become a prayer as I associate a scripture verse or prayer phrase with the motion. As I lie on my back and draw my knees to my chest, I say, "Draw me close to you, O God." As I rotate my ankles, I name the fruits of the Spirit from Galatians 5. As I stand and turn to the right, then to the left, I say, "All around me be peace, all around me be joy" (or whatever other qualities I need for the day). Instead of counting forty sit-ups, I name forty family members, friends, and world situations (from a list) as I lift them in prayer. If you have a stretching or exercise routine, determine ways you could make it a time of prayer.

April 19

REMEMBER

Saint Bernadette (1844–1879), a young French girl, believed that the Virgin Mary appeared to her in Lourdes, France, which has become a holy site and place of pilgrimage. Also remember the Oklahoma City bombing that occurred on this date in 1995, killing 168 people, including nineteen children.

READ

Psalm 50:16-23

PONDER

God clearly and directly judges the wicked in this psalm. "I rebuke you, and lay the charge before you" (v. 21). The list of charges reads like an indictment against contemporary people: hypocrisy, arrogance, stealing, adultery, deceit, slander. God threatens to cut off the wicked, to no longer befriend them. "Mark this, then, you who forget God, or I will tear you apart, and there will be no one to deliver" (v. 22).

Occasionally, and sometimes more often, we need a strong reminder of what God holds against us, as well as the assurance that God desires not our destruction but our salvation if we will turn from our evil ways.

PRAYER/PRACTICE

Walking not only offers a way to exercise but also a way to pray. Take a walk today, and focus on your breathing. The miracle of breath connects us to the One who gave us breath. Remain aware of the world around you. Develop prayers of thanks or blessing for what you see— the trees, the birds, the sky, the sidewalks, the flowers, the dogs. As you walk, feel your body moving gracefully through God's creation, and give thanks for the way your body works and moves. You may carry persons in your heart, a way of walking your intercession. Invite God to fill you with joy and peace. Today, walk in the awareness that God goes with you, breathes in you.

April 20

REMEMBER

Käthe Kollwitz (1867–1945), a German artist, depicted the sorrow of war, the struggles and suffering of the poor, and the experience of women. Her lithographs often portray women protecting, sheltering, and nurturing children.

READ

Psalm 51:1-9

PONDER

This psalm, the fourth of seven penitential psalms, tenderly and poignantly admits error and sin. Not only has the author offended others, but because of the psalmist's connection with God, the sin appears as an affront to God. "Against you, you alone, have I sinned, and done what is evil in your sight" (v. 4). At the same time, a steady confidence remains in God's mercy—a mercy that washes away the stain of error and blots out the mistakes of the past. The first two verses set the tone of the psalm and are often repeated in the worship life of the church: "Have mercy on me, O God, according to your steadfast love; according to your abundant mercy blot out my transgression. Wash me thoroughly from my iniquity, and cleanse me from my sin" (vv. 1-2).

PRAYER/PRACTICE

I invite you to try this prayer stretch, which is not only good in the morning but also during the day when energy wanes. Stand with your arms by your sides. (You can do this sitting if standing is not possible.) Slowly raise your arms from your sides until they are over your head, turning your palms to face each other. Bring your palms close together, yet not touching, and open them as if making a large vessel to hold something. Look up and imagine God pouring light, joy, and peace into your vessel, your chalice. Then turn your imaginary chalice to pour the gifts of God over your head, shoulders, and body. Let your hands circle around until they both rest on your heart. The gifts of God, poured out all around you, now reside in you. I usually do this stretch three times to remind me of the Trinity.

April 21

REMEMBER

Saint Anselm (1033–1109), a major theologian and archbishop of Canterbury, wrote insightfully on the meaning of the Incarnation.

READ

Psalm 51:10-14

PONDER

This beautiful psalm, often used on Ash Wednesday, ushers the faith community into a time of repentance. It deserves a place in our daily life of prayer. The psalm moves from heartfelt confession to honest petition and asks for enough wisdom to teach God's way of forgiveness. We ask God to create in us "a clean heart . . . a new and right spirit" (v. 10). We ask God to restore our joy and strengthen our will. We pray that our sin will not keep us away from God's Spirit. We trust in God's forgiveness, and we promise to live and teach God's way and to sing God's praises.

PRAYER/PRACTICE

Today I invite you to try a forgiveness dance. Dancing offers another way to pray without words, to let our bodies express what we feel. People who feel self-conscious about dancing in public often find that creating their own dance in a private space becomes a wonderful way to pray. Others, like King David, dance their joy and praise comfortably in the presence of the community of faith (2 Sam. 6:5). Today many sacred dance troupes create dances for worship celebrations.

I invite you, in whatever way you choose, wherever you choose, to dance your sense of God's forgiveness. You might read portions from Psalm 51 and then close your eyes and let your body dance what it feels like to have a clean heart, a new spirit, and to have joy restored. Closing your eyes may help you to be less critical of your dance. Dance your prayer.

April 22

REMEMBER

Earth Day, celebrated in the United States on this day, began in 1970 to encourage care and preservation of God's creation.

READ

Psalm 51:15-19

PONDER

The psalmist declares that God does not want more sacrifices, more burnt offerings, more empty phrases, more good intentions. God desires "a broken spirit; a broken and contrite heart" (v. 17). God desires our friendship, our humble estimation of ourselves, a sense of our unworthiness, a sense of our blessedness in God's boundless mercy. After admitting our sin and receiving a clean slate, we praise God. Tears of penitence change into tears of gladness, and we know we belong to an amazing, loving God. "My mouth will declare your praise" (v. 15).

PRAYER/PRACTICE

In your prayer time on this Earth Day, praise God for the wonders of creation. You can create your own prayer or pray these words:

> God of wonder and delight, you created stars sparkling in a dark sky, sunrises and sunsets that take my breath away, whales and dolphins that dance along the ocean shore, hawks that soar and lizards that scoot. May I never lose the sense of mystery; may I never grow tired of smelling a rose or looking at the heavens.

> Wondrous God of creation, keep me aware of my sacred connection to the earth and sky, and help me to walk lightly on the planet, forever cherishing the circle of life. Amen.

See if there is an Earth Day event or celebration to join. Do something good for the earth.

April 23

REMEMBER

Saint George (third century), soldier and patron saint of England, converted many to Christianity. According to legend, he killed an evil dragon.

READ

Psalm 52

PONDER

Almost all students at some time feel tempted to cheat. Some even boast of cheating and never getting caught; they view cheating as a way to get ahead. Cheating is just one way to do evil and to trust in one's own cleverness rather than to trust in the God of all life. "Why do you boast, O mighty one, of mischief? . . . You love evil more than good, and lying more than speaking the truth. . . . But God will break you down forever" (vv. 1, 3, 5). Our cheating, our wealth, our lies, our ignoring God will not save us. The choice becomes clear: Do we want to be like an uprooted tree or like "a green olive tree in the house of God"? (v. 8).

PRAYER/PRACTICE

Simple gestures can enhance our prayer time. The gesture of placing palms together in front of the chest has long been associated with prayer. Folding our hands in prayer may bring back childhood memories of being taught to pray with our heads bowed and hands folded. Placing our hands on our head may remind us of our baptism. Sitting with our hands in our lap, palms open and up, often indicates readiness to receive. Making the sign of the cross, though uncommon in some Protestant churches, is a gesture common throughout the world that can remind us of the threefold nature of God. To make the sign of the cross, touch the forehead, the middle of the chest, the left shoulder, and then the right shoulder. I invite you to add one of these gestures to your prayer today and incorporate movement into your prayer life.

April 24

REMEMBER

A Sunday school teacher who not only taught but also lived the gospel of Jesus.

READ

Psalm 53

PONDER

An absence of belief in God within us contributes to an absence of goodness among us. "Fools say in their hearts, 'There is no God.' They are corrupt, . . . there is no one who does good" (v. 1). Wise people know God exists and cares what happens to people, God desires justice and compassion, and God establishes consequences for evildoers. The fools and the wicked, looking for the quick and easy profit, pay no heed to God. They "refuse to pray" (v. 4, CEV). But the wise have hope; they believe that God will restore the fortunes of the good, and they will celebrate.

Compare Psalm 53 with Psalm 14.

PRAYER/PRACTICE

Other religious traditions have practices related to movement and prayer. I learned a way of walking from a Roman Catholic priest who had spent a long time in Japan and led a group of us in a walking meditation. He instructed us to take off our shoes (a good gesture in itself, reminding us that we are on holy ground; see Exodus 3) and to walk slowly, very slowly in a circle.

Try this exercise during your prayer time. Remove your shoes and walk slowly in a circle. Remain aware of the movement of slowly lifting one foot, slowly shifting balance, and slowly placing the foot down as the other foot begins the same slow, meditative journey. You can do this meditative walk in any space, indoors or outdoors, and whether alone or in a group. Stay aware of your breathing, your balance, your body. God has given you a blessed body.

April 25

REMEMBER

John Mark (first century), cousin of Barnabas, accompanied Paul on his first missionary journey. His short book, the Gospel of Mark, is believed to be the first Gospel written.

READ

Psalm 54

PONDER

"Save me" (v. 1) is one of the oldest, shortest, and most common prayers. Variations of these words permeate the lament psalms, which contain powerful, direct appeals to God to address a current problem. The psalmist assumes and believes that God will hear and respond, and then the person or community will sing or shout thanks and praise. This psalm and the next three form a group of individual laments. In this psalm, the author appeals to God and voices a strong complaint; the last four verses proclaim trust in God who is the "upholder of my life" (v. 4) and offers thanks to God who "has delivered me from every trouble" (v. 7). In the lament psalms, "Save me" is transformed into another short prayer, "Thank you."

PRAYER/PRACTICE

Native Americans can teach us a great deal about prayer and movement. Many tribes developed a way to pray in each of the four compass directions. They associate colors, winds, and meanings with each direction. An individual or a community can simply face the direction and pray with words or in silence.

Today I invite you to face north as you pray. North, the place of cold, reminds us of the harsh winds of winter. The purifying and cleansing winds cause the leaves to fall and the earth to rest and renew. The Lakota Indians equate the color red with this direction for strength, endurance, and patience to face the storms of life. Other tribes use the color white for the white snow of winter and the bright moon of night. You might pray for cleansing wind in your life or for strength to face tough times.

April 26

REMEMBER

William Stringfellow (1928–1985), a lawyer, author, and social critic, sought to call America's attention to the radical implications of love and justice in the Gospels.

READ

Psalm 55:1-11

PONDER

Two contemporary themes emerge in this ancient psalm. One concerns our tendency to run away from problems. "O that I had wings like a dove! I would fly away and be at rest" (v. 6). When conflicts or problems emerge, some of us do anything to escape. We hope in our absence the problem will just disappear. The psalmist knows this tendency well but also knows that God often calls us to involve ourselves in the change, the new possibility.

The second theme points to trouble in the city. In our age, William Stringfellow worked among the poor in Harlem, New York, and called the nation to a new morality and a new social witness. Yet today "oppression and fraud" still run rampant in the "market place" (v. 11).

PRAYER/PRACTICE

Today I invite you in your prayer time to face the east, where the sun comes up and light spreads over the whole earth. This direction focuses on new beginnings and new understandings, the start of a brand new day. Many Native American tribes choose yellow as the color for this direction. As you face east, turning toward the dawn, ask God for wisdom for the new day, for illumination of all the situations awaiting you, and for your face to radiate God's light to all you meet. Let the dawning light bring you energy, fill you with boldness, and empower you with hope. Morning has broken, revealing a new day to thank God and to pray for God's guidance and wisdom.

April 27

REMEMBER

In South Africa's first all-race election in 1994, Nelson Mandela, after years in prison, was elected as the first African president, signaling the end of racial apartheid.

READ

Psalm 55:12-23

PONDER

Perhaps Nelson Mandela prayed some of the lament psalms while imprisoned for years on an island off South Africa. "Morning, noon, and night you hear my concerns and my complaints. I am attacked from all sides, but you will rescue me unharmed by the battle" (vv. 17-18, CEV). The battle in which Mandela engaged was the struggle against apartheid, a philosophy and system of government that treated blacks and mixed-race citizens of South Africa as lower-class persons, discriminating against them because of color. International pressure, church protests, economic boycotts, and the prophetic voices of leaders like Nelson Mandela turned the tide against the evil of apartheid. "Give your burden, your tears to God, who will be your support" (v. 22, AP).

PRAYER/PRACTICE

Today I invite you to face south. Native Americans associate south with the warm and gentle breezes of summer. South, the direction for warmth and growth, focuses on the sun at its highest point in the sky and summer as the time of planting and growing. The Lakota choose the color white for this direction, while other tribes often use green. As you face south, offer a prayer of thanks for the goodness of the earth and its abundance of food. Pray for wise use of the earth's resources, that all creation might live in harmony. Pray that you will also remain open to new growth and that your heart and mind will align with the Creator's. Feel the warmth of God's love and blessing.

April 28

REMEMBER

Oskar Schindler (1908–1974), a German industrialist, employed and protected Jewish workers in his plant in Poland, saving the lives of over a thousand Jews.

READ

Psalm 56

PONDER

The word *trample* in verse 2 calls to mind the Nazi war machine that trampled nations, annihilated the opposition, and killed millions of Jews. Verse 8 acknowledges that God hears the prayers of the faithful: "You have kept count of my tossings; put my tears in your bottle." God raises up persons like Oskar Schindler, an unlikely person who nevertheless turned a profitable factory into a place of protection for Jews in Poland. He used his money and influence to save the lives of his workers, even at great risk to himself. In the 1960s the nation of Israel declared him a "Righteous Gentile." "For you have delivered my soul from death, and my feet from falling, so that I may walk before God in the light of life" (v. 13).

PRAYER/PRACTICE

Today I invite you to face west. The sun goes down in the west, ending the day. This direction represents the end of life, a place of introspection and letting go. Most Native American tribes choose black to represent west, though a few tribes choose red. Thunder and rain come from this direction, so the west reminds us of water, rivers, lakes, and streams. As you face west, thank God for the gift of water, for we cannot live without it. As the day ends and darkness covers the earth, pray that you will be able to reflect on the gifts of the day, confess the words and deeds of which you are ashamed, and trust in the cleansing and renewing power of water and God's amazing grace. This direction also becomes important if you contemplate a change in direction or face an ending. Breathe deeply as you contemplate the west.

April 29

REMEMBER

Saint Catherine of Siena (1347–1380), a Dominican mystic, devoted her life to prayer, service, and bringing reform and reconciliation to the papacy and the Roman Catholic Church. She influenced popes, wrote a series of letters in a book called *The Dialogue,* and cared for the poor in a time when women usually stayed at home.

READ

Psalm 57

PONDER

The psalmist employs the images of lions, nets, and deep pits to describe the current state of affairs. However, the images amount to nothing compared to "God Most High" (v. 2). Using one of the feminine images for God in scripture, the psalmist describes taking refuge under God's wings much like baby birds gather under the mother bird's wing. We can rest in God's embrace "until the destroying storms pass by" (v. 1). Confident of God's steadfast love and faithfulness, the psalmist ends this lament with praise that extends to the heavens and covers the whole earth, praise that even awakens the dawn!

PRAYER/PRACTICE

Some Native American traditions not only pray in the four compass directions but also include up and down, representing the sky and the earth. As you pray in the four directions, your path can shape a cross. Imagine a circle with each of the four directions as points on the circle. The center, where east and west intersect with north and south, is a holy place. As you stand in the center, look up to the blue sky and then down to the earth below, which the color green symbolized for Native Americans. Today's psalm calls us to look up and praise the God who is above all, over all. I invite you to stand outside in the center of a circle and extend your hands and your gaze to the heavens. Let your words or songs of praise arise and float to the heavens.

April 30

REMEMBER

Philip Berrigan (1923–2002), an ex–Roman Catholic priest, protested the deployment of nuclear weapons, which he labeled a curse against God, humanity, and the earth. Active in protesting the Vietnam War with his brother, Father Daniel Berrigan, he served time in prison for participation in nonviolent resistance.

READ

Psalm 58

PONDER

This psalm, which addresses false leaders and unjust judges, includes some of the most violent images in scripture. Withering language implores God to act and reveals the psalmist's anguish and outrage. Even though the psalmist feels burning anger, Hebrew tradition says that vengeance belongs to God (Deut. 32:35). In the end, the psalmist believes God will strike the wicked and reward the just. From the perspective of the New Testament, we know that Jesus revealed a God more intent on salvation than on vengeance, more filled with mercy than with judgment. Still, this angry psalm lets us know that we can pray our strongest feelings to God and leave them with God so that we don't become vengeful.

PRAYER/PRACTICE

Consider now the last direction, looking down to the green earth. I invite you to give thanks for the ground upon which you stand, even if it is not a beautiful green lawn. I invite you to praise God for earth, for rich soil and sandy deserts. We live upon this common ground that supports life in all its shapes and forms. Native Americans often call it Mother Earth. The earth provides a home for us and all creatures. Bend down and touch the earth; feel its moistness; smell its aroma; let it flow through your fingers. I invite you in some way to bless the earth and offer your prayer of thanks.

May

Come, Spirit, breath of God,
breathe new life into me.
Blow away the cobwebs in my mind;
clear away the debris in my soul.
Bring healing to my wounds and comfort to my grief.
Refresh my spirit, set my feet to dancing,
and set my heart ablaze.
Wind of God, touch my life
and open me to your direction. Amen.

May 1

REMEMBER

Today is International Workers' Day and the Feast of Saint Joseph the Worker. Also, Celtic Christians celebrate this day as Beltane, a day of light marking the midway point between the spring equinox and the summer solstice.

READ

Psalm 59:1-7

PONDER

God intended work to be useful, productive, satisfying. After all, God worked for six days, and "God saw that it was good" (Gen. 1:12). But the opposite of good work happens in this psalm. "Deliver me from those who work evil" (v. 2). David, to whom the psalm is attributed, knows of no fault or error on his part, but others are actively working against him, "howling like dogs and prowling about the city" (v. 6). Their involvement in such mischief and destructiveness would cause us to say they have too much time on their hands. The psalmist looks to God for deliverance from the evildoers.

PRAYER/PRACTICE

On this International Workers' Day, I invite you to reflect on the work of your hands and the common work of the world. Try writing a prayer about work, or offer this prayer to God.

> Great and glorious God, you have given us holy hands—hands to hold a hurt child and embrace a lonely friend, hands to till the soil and make a bed, hands to create art and prepare a delicious meal, hands to mold steel and to photograph a rose. You have given us holy hands. Help us to honor and cherish the work of our hands, and, generous God, may all receive just reward for their work. Amen.

May 2

REMEMBER

Thomas à Kempis (1380–1471), priest and author, wrote the popular book *The Imitation of Christ,* which has been translated into more languages than any other book except the Bible. It stresses personal piety over learning and the inner life over active service.

READ

Psalm 59:8-17

PONDER

"O my strength, I will watch for you. . . . O my strength, I will sing praises to you" (vv. 9, 17). Twice in this psalm, the psalmist calls God "my strength." In contrast to the evildoers, God is so strong that God can laugh at their attempts to control and dominate. Laughter can provide perspective. Who do we think we are, compared to God? The psalmist has confidence that God will deal with the wicked, who howl and prowl like hungry dogs, and that God will provide a strong fortress and secure place from which the psalmist can sing, "O my strength, I will sing praises to you" (v. 17).

PRAYER/PRACTICE

For the next few days I invite you to consider gratitude as a spiritual practice. Gratitude expresses both an inner state of mind and an outward way of life. It guards us against taking life for granted, thinking we deserve more or are entitled to what we have. Gratitude counters and tames greedy thoughts and unhealthy comparisons. As a spiritual practice, gratitude helps us recognize that all life flows as a gift from our generous God.

Today consciously say thank you throughout your day—to other people, to your family, to God. Express your thanks for the good in your life and for challenges as well.

May 3

REMEMBER

James (first century), an apostle known as James the Less, the son of Alphaeus, may have been "the Lord's brother" (Gal. 1:19). He may also be the James who became the first bishop of Jerusalem and authored the epistle of James.

READ

Psalm 60

PONDER

This James would certainly qualify as a "lesser" disciple during Jesus' time. He must have quietly been formed and nurtured in the way of Jesus, for after the Resurrection he became one of the leaders of the growing church. James expressed his concern for the issues of the day in a letter. He warned against showing favor to the rich and upheld the link between faith and works, between hearing and doing the Word. He warned against loose tongues, boasting, and judging. James instructed Christians to pray and care for the suffering. His short letter, full of practical advice for being the church, bears reading again. James reminds us that though one may be quiet for a time, the call to leadership may come at any time.

The psalm for this day prays for God's help after a defeat in battle.

PRAYER/PRACTICE

I often keep a gratitude list. Each day I write one thing for which I am grateful. The key to developing a grateful spirit is not to repeat any item on the list. After about three or four weeks, I have mentioned all the usual good things around me: my family (one person at a time, of course), the birds, the flowers, last night's dinner, my friends, and so on. Keeping a list for months or years sharpens one's senses to look for opportunities and things for which to give thanks.

Today I invite you to keep a gratitude list. Set aside a page in your journal, and write one thing to thank God for this day. Keep up the practice each day of this month (and longer), and try not to repeat any gratitude listed.

May 4

REMEMBER

In 1970 four Kent State University students were killed on this date as they protested the Vietnam War.

READ

Psalm 61

PONDER

"Lead me to the rock that is higher than I" (v. 2). When the storms of life rage, we long to go to higher ground. Higher ground not only provides safety and protection, but it also gives a place of perspective. We can view our problems in new light. Memorize this wonderful refrain to call forth in difficult days.

"Let me . . . find refuge under the shelter of your wings" (v. 4). When Jesus looked over Jerusalem during his last days, he said he wished he could gather her like "a hen gathers her brood under her wings" (Matt. 23:37). Countless mothers and fathers felt a similar longing to protect their sons and daughters who fought in Vietnam or protested in the United States. The longing for shelter and for peace deepened after the shooting of four college students by the National Guard, resulting in an outcry to stop the killing at home and overseas.

PRAYER/PRACTICE

In his book *How to Want What You Have: Discovering the Magic and Grandeur of Ordinary Existence,* Timothy Miller suggests creating a gratitude game where one person chooses an unremarkable object in the immediate area and searches for ways it might evoke gratitude. You can play this game with others, challenging them to name a gratitude in response to the item selected. Select the most common, ordinary, and undistinguished objects and see if they can lead a person to give thanks to God.

Today for your gratitude list, add an unremarkable item that still causes you to be grateful.

May 5

REMEMBER

Cinco de Mayo commemorates the 1862 defeat of French forces at Puebla, Mexico. Remember Hispanic friends this day and their struggles for freedom in our global village.

READ

Psalm 62:1-7

PONDER

Often the lament psalms name an external situation or experience as the enemy from which the psalmist needs to be saved. The lament psalms can also encourage us to confront the enemies within us that keep us from fully living in God's grace. In *Psalms for Praying*, Nan C. Merrill names fear as a major enemy: "Yet, how long will fear rule my life, holding me in its grip like a trembling child, a dark and lonely grave? Fear keeps me from living fully, from sharing my gifts; it takes pleasure in imprisoning my soul. Fear pretends to comfort, so long has it dwelled within me; truly, it is my enemy" (vv. 3-4, PFP). Against such fear the psalmist cries, "For God alone my soul waits; in silence I wait, for all my hope is in God" (v. 5, AP).

PRAYER/PRACTICE

Many religious traditions encourage the use of short blessing prayers as a way of acknowledging the Creator. Some Jewish traditions set a goal of saying one hundred blessing prayers each day. For example, "Blessed are you, God our Creator, who has given us this refreshing rain." "Blessed are you, God our God, who has blessed us with the song of the robin." "Blessed are you, amazing God, who kept me from falling when I stumbled." Even today, traditional blessing prayers form a significant part of the ritual of Passover, which commemorates the Hebrews' deliverance from slavery.

Create your own pattern for a blessing prayer, and try to say many prayers today. Don't forget to add to your gratitude list.

May 6

REMEMBER

Henry David Thoreau (1817–1862), a naturalist, author, and social critic, wrote *Walden*, a book encouraging a return to a simpler and more harmonious relationship with nature. His essay "On the Duty of Civil Disobedience" influenced Tolstoy, Gandhi, and Martin Luther King Jr.

READ

Psalm 62:8-12

PONDER

The theme of God as refuge echoes through this passage. Like the desert mothers and fathers who left civilized areas for the deserts of Egypt and Syria during the third, fourth, and fifth centuries, Thoreau left the city to live in the wilderness by Walden Pond, near Concord, Massachusetts. "I went to the woods because I wished to live deliberately, to front only the essential facts of life, and see if I could not learn what it had to teach, and not, when I came to die, discover that I had not lived,"[1] he wrote. The wisdom and insights Thoreau gained from those two years continue to inform and guide us to live more harmoniously with God's creation and to be truer to our inner wisdom.

PRAYER/PRACTICE

Pray this prayer or compose your own to thank God for the wonder and beauty of creation:

> O Mystery, hidden in the stars, rooted in the trees, deeper than our knowing. O Mystery, pulsing through our veins and every mountain stream. O Mystery, bringing us to our knees in worship, filling our eyes with tears, breaking our hearts with the sorrow of the earth. O Mystery, ablaze in sunsets, and shining like the moon. O Mystery, calling forth a reverence for that which you have created. O Mystery, God beyond our names and greater than our certainty or our doubts. O Mystery, how wonderful you are, and holy is this day and this ground upon which we stand.

Add to your gratitude list.

May 7

REMEMBER

Holocaust Memorial Day, whose date is determined each year by the Jewish lunar calendar, honors the six million Jews killed between 1933–1945.

READ

Psalm 63:1-4

PONDER

Our yearning for God is as deep as our thirst for water in a dry land; this longing is rooted deep in our hearts. "O God, you are my God, I seek you, my soul thirsts for you" (v. 1). As Saint Augustine said, "Our hearts are restless until they rest in You [God]."[2] We are filled with desire for God, for we know that God's "love is better than life" (v. 3). This extreme statement acknowledges that life without God is empty, thirsty. But we have confidence that God will respond to our longing. God longs for us just as we long for God. The meeting between us and God is so wonderful, "So I will bless you [God] as long as I live; I will lift up my hands and call on your name" (v. 4). Does this psalm speak to your yearnings for God?

PRAYER/PRACTICE

I encourage you to "count your blessings," as one old hymn puts it. Today I invite you to find a symbol, a picture, or an object that reminds you of some blessing. It may be a photograph of people, a rock from a mountaintop experience, a candle, or a gift from a special friend. Place the object on your dining room table, desk, or altar as a visual reminder of your blessing. The visual stimulus will encourage you to give thanks and remain aware of the surprising ways God works in your life.

Add to your gratitude list.

May 8

REMEMBER

Philip (first century), one of the original twelve apostles, brought people to Jesus (see John 1:45-46; 12:21).

READ

Psalm 63:5-11

PONDER

In the monastic tradition, certain psalms were read or sung at particular times of the day. Psalm 63, usually sung in one of the morning services, implies a restful night, a night of prayer followed by joy, praise, and affirmation in the morning. "For you [God] have been my help, and in the shadow of your wings I sing for joy" (v. 7). It calls to mind the line from Psalm 30, "Joy comes with the morning" (v. 5). Praising God in the morning conditions one to praise God all day long. "I sing for joy" (v. 7). Furthermore, God's right hand, the symbol of strength, remains with you, supporting you throughout the day (v. 8).

PRAYER/PRACTICE

Today I invite you to try a gratitude dance. Last month you looked at ways the body prays without words. Think of some item, experience, or person for which you are grateful. Then, with your eyes closed (if that helps free your dance), express your thanks with your body. Remember David's joyful dance as the ark of the covenant was brought into Jerusalem (2 Sam. 6:14-15). Let your dance reflect or take the shape of your object of gratitude.

Add to your gratitude list again this day.

May 9

REMEMBER

Peter Maurin (1877–1949) cofounded the Catholic Worker movement (with Dorothy Day, Nov. 29) in New York, which published a newspaper, ran a soup kitchen/hospitality house, and set up a communal farm. He challenged the church to act with more compassion and deeper justice.

READ

Psalm 64

PONDER

Evil done in secret still counts as evil. In Psalm 64, God sees what is being plotted, knows about the arrows, ambushes, and snares. The psalmist declares that God will foil the evil planned and safely guard the just.

Peter Maurin saw what the institutions of government and church did not do to help the poor, and he called them to task for hiding behind excuses, bureaucracy, and inadequate programs. Maurin thought the church had covered up the radical love of Jesus, which could change society. In the Catholic Worker movement, he sought to stir the church and to create, in a small way, a model of the new world of compassion.

PRAYER/PRACTICE

Prophets, ancient and modern, call and challenge all people to live out the radical love of Jesus. Find out whether a Catholic Worker group exists near you. I worked in one of their soup kitchens. Their commitment to feed the poor and to change the uncaring bureaucracy that fosters poverty challenged me. Write your own prayer of compassion, or use this one:

> Compassionate God, you see me as I am. There is no place to hide
> from you. You know my reluctance to follow Christ's way of care and
> service; you know I prefer to care from a distance. Challenge me and
> teach me the kind of servanthood that is a joy, not a burden. Teach me
> a way of care that is humble, not proud. Take away my excuses and use
> me to show your compassionate care for the poor and needy. Amen.

May 10

REMEMBER

Karl Barth (1886–1968), a pastor, theologian, teacher, and writer, helped author the Barmen Declaration that shaped the Confessing Church, an organization of Christians in Germany who resisted Hitler.

READ

Psalm 65:1-8

PONDER

This psalm begins with praise, a refreshing change from the series of laments. Praise God because God answers prayers. For all those who wonder if prayer works, the psalmist wholeheartedly answers in the affirmative, "O you who answer prayer!" (v. 2). Notice the exclamation point.

"All humanity must come to you with its sinful deeds. Our faults overwhelm us, but you blot them out" (vv. 2-3, NJB). Praise God because God forgives sins, gets rid of them once and for all, and brings salvation and hope. Praise God because God created the mountains, calms the seas, and blesses us with morning light and evening rest. Praise God and "shout for joy" (v. 8).

PRAYER/PRACTICE

Gratitude not only engenders private reflection but also provides an opportunity to verbally and publicly express our thanks. By sending appreciative notes, letters, and e-mails, we touch others' lives and create ripples of smiles and gratitude. A note to a former teacher or Sunday school teacher could brighten his or her entire day. A note to the mail carrier, grocery clerk, or another service provider lets that person know you notice and appreciate his or her work. Write a letter, card, or e-mail today to thank someone for being in your life and for his or her deeds of kindness and compassion. Add to your gratitude list.

May 11

REMEMBER

The Old Testament book of Job tells of Job's struggles with suffering, his friends' rationalizations, and God's wisdom. Job experiences the mystery and suffering of life and learns that only God sees and knows the full meaning and redeems us from complaint and disaster.

READ

Psalm 65:9-13

PONDER

Praise continues in these verses with thankfulness for the rains that watered the fields just in time and produced a wonderful harvest. Imagine the farmers, the people of the land, singing to God, giving thanks for God's goodness, rejoicing at the abundant harvest and the growing flocks. Stretch your imagination and hear the meadows and valleys "shout and sing together for joy" (v. 13). Listen for the chorus of music in the hills and trees, in the fields and forests.

PRAYER/PRACTICE

Joyce Rupp suggests a contemplative walk as a way to express gratitude and greet a new day. This walking prayer consists of seven steps that can be done alone or with a group. You can change the attributes.

> My (our) first step is that of *gratitude* . . . for the gift of another fresh day of life.
> My (our) second step is that of *love* . . . for the Holy One and for all of my dear ones.
> My third step is that of *hope* . . . for the possibility of growth in each moment.
> My fourth step is that of *compassion* . . . for all of creation and our deep connection.
> My fifth step is that of *generosity* . . . for all that shall be asked of me this day.
> My sixth step is that of *laughter* . . . for the joys that will refresh my heart.
> My seventh step is that of *patience* . . . for the difficult challenges that may arise.[3]

May 12

REMEMBER

Mother's Day is celebrated in the United States on the second Sunday of May. In 1872 Julia Ward Howe worked to establish a Mother's Day for Peace to honor peace, motherhood, and womanhood. In 1907 Anna M. Jarvis initiated a letter-writing campaign to get Mother's Day declared a national holiday. The first national observance of Mother's Day was in 1914.

READ

Psalm 66:1-12

PONDER

The psalmist invites all the earth to sing praises to an awesome God, then enumerates God's deeds, pivotal events that provided opportunity for the Hebrews to deepen their trust in God. "Come and see what God has done," the psalmist says, recalling how God led the Hebrews to freedom through the Red Sea and brought them to the Promised Land through the Jordan River. Though the Hebrews experienced many trials and hardships, the psalmist reminds them that God has "brought us out to a spacious place" (v. 12). What songs of thanksgiving would you sing for the ways God has led you?

PRAYER/PRACTICE

On or near Mother's Day, write a letter to your mother or create a prayer of thanks. These words may help get you started.

> God of all life, I am grateful to be remembered in a mother's heart and carried in a father's prayer. I am blessed by hours of care, seasons of love, moments of play, and times of patience that brought me through many years and many tears. Loving God, even as I recognize that my parents were less than perfect, I give you thanks that some of your love got through to me and blessed me. Amen.

May 13

REMEMBER

Julian of Norwich (1342–1416), an English laywoman, wrote down her mystical revelations in the book *Showings*. She was an anchoress (someone who lived in a dwelling attached to the church) and spiritual guide who used feminine images for God. Because of Jesus' Passion, she could say, "All will be well, and all will be well, and every kind of thing will be well."[4]

READ

Psalm 66:13-20

PONDER

The communal hymn of praise now becomes a solo song of thanksgiving. "All who worship God, come here and listen; I will tell you everything God has done for me" (v. 16, CEV). Perhaps Julian of Norwich voiced such a song. Living in a small building attached to the church in Norwich, England, she talked with many about her revelations, about the compassion and love of God, and about how persons could live a more holy life. From her witness, we receive encouragement in the art and practice of spiritual direction. From her position as an anchoress, we learn to value people in faith communities who live the life of prayer for the whole community.

PRAYER/PRACTICE

During the next few days, I invite you to review and practice various ways of contemplation and meditation. Meditation can be understood as a mental martial arts practice. Our minds are so active that we need discipline to focus our thoughts on God. Trying to resist mundane thoughts or unholy thoughts usually keeps our focus on them. We do better to acknowledge the distractions and let them fly away.

Today remember the importance of focusing on your breathing. Count your breaths from one to four, then from four back down to one. Focus your mind on counting as you gently and slowly breathe. Remember to use your belly breathing. Try to do this for five minutes.

Add to your gratitude list as well.

May 14

REMEMBER

Matthias (first century), selected as an apostle by drawing lots, replaced Judas in the group of Jesus' twelve disciples. According to early Christian legend he served as the first missionary to Palestine; some traditions say he was a missionary to Cappadocia or Ethiopia.

READ

Psalm 67

PONDER

The opening of the psalm echoes the priestly blessing in Numbers 6:24-25, "May God be gracious to us and bless us. May God's face shine on us" (v. 1, AP). Two faces of God clearly emerge in this psalm of thanksgiving. God is judge and guide of the nations, ruling with justice and equity (v. 4), and God is the Creator who blesses the earth with bountiful harvests (vv. 6-7). Not only does Israel celebrate these actions of God, but she becomes a model of praise so that all the nations will know God's saving power and join in the chorus of praise. Do we let others know of God's blessings?

PRAYER/PRACTICE

Most meditative practices employ a word or image to focus the mind. Today find an object you can use to focus your thoughts, an object from nature if possible. Hold or observe the object and concentrate on its feel, smell, and appearance from different angles.

Next, choose three observations that struck you most strongly, that surprised you or came back to your mind repeatedly. How do these observations make you think about life, relationships, work, and God?

Next, choose one of the observations that resonates with you (or choose any of the observations if none has a strong pull) and ask, "What word of God does this observation hold for me?" Can you take some action or make some decision to bring this observation into reality in your life? Set the object in a visible place for the next few days. Give thanks to God for whatever this meditation prompted.

May 15

REMEMBER

Saint Isidore the Farmer (1070–1130), a humble farmer, wrote nothing and founded no monastery, yet he lived a life blessed with signs, wonders, and great charity that touched the people around him.

READ

Psalm 68:1-6

PONDER

God takes the initiative in routing evildoers and in becoming parent to orphans and protector of widows, two of the most vulnerable groups of people in Jewish culture. "God makes homes for the homeless, leads prisoners to freedom" (v. 6, THE MESSAGE).

Such compassion resided in a humble farmer in Spain. Isidore assisted those poorer than himself; he frequently received the hungry and the foreign traveler at his table. Amazingly, his deeds became known, and the Roman Catholic Church made him an honored saint in 1622. God knows and remembers your simple deeds of kindness.

PRAYER/PRACTICE

In many traditions, especially the Eastern Orthodox tradition, looking at paintings or pictures is a common way of meditation. While Western Christianity focuses on listening and speaking to God, in the Orthodox tradition, gazing becomes a prime path for drawing close to the heart of God. A person gazes at an icon—a special, ritually painted picture of Jesus, Mary, or the saints. The stylized painting does not try for realism but attempts to create an image that becomes a window into the reality of the divine. One gazes at the icon and discovers a connection between one's soul and the soul of God. The paintings intend to take the viewer to the inner room of prayer.

Find an icon or other religious picture and spend a few moments gazing at it. Do not stare or strain your eyes, but keep your eyes relaxed as you patiently and prayerfully let the picture focus your meditation.

May 16

REMEMBER

Saint Brendan of Clonfert (sixth century) founded many monasteries in Ireland. Legend has it that he crossed the Atlantic in a curragh, a small boat made of skins. Thus he became the patron saint of sailors.

READ

Psalm 68:7-10

PONDER

Thankfulness for God's presence in the past weaves its way into this psalm of praise. In the Hebrews' forty-year sojourn in the wilderness, God went before the people. "The earth quaked, the heavens poured down rain. . . . Rain in abundance" (vv. 8-9). God spoke from the thundering mountain and provided for the needs of the people and their flocks. The trials and grumblings of life in the desert recede into the shadows, for in hindsight, God's goodness becomes the dominant theme. Recall how God has led you through times of struggle to a new place or new land.

PRAYER/PRACTICE

Nature provides a wonderful place for meditation. Rather than bringing an object or picture inside to focus your meditation, try going outside and observing. Choose one object on which to focus your attention. It may be as big as a tree or mountain or as small as a bumblebee or ant. Watch and observe as you did with the object on May 14. What do you see—colors, shape, and texture? What observations do you make that relate to life? What might God be saying to you in one of the observations? As always, pay attention to your breathing; open your eyes and heart and listen for the word of the Creator in the splendor of creation.

Remember your gratitude list.

May 17

REMEMBER

Marian Wright Edelman (b. 1939) advocates the well-being of all children through political action, writing, and speaking. The first black woman admitted to the Mississippi Bar, Edelman now focuses on America's children as president of the Children's Defense Fund.

READ

Psalm 68:11-20

PONDER

The exact historical references may be lost to us, but the psalm now refers to the conquest of the Promised Land (vv. 11-14) and the settling of Jerusalem (vv. 15-20). Through all these events the presence of God abides in strength. "Blessed be the Lord, who daily bears us up; God is our salvation" (v. 19). These words of praise and blessing bring comfort and strength for the Israelites and for us. Daily God journeys with us, bears us up, and keeps us alive. Daily we sing our praises. Daily we proclaim, "Blessed be the Lord."

PRAYER/PRACTICE

Gazing at a candle is another meditative practice that many have found helpful. For Christians the candle symbolizes the light of Christ. It also symbolizes warmth, life, and unleashed power. How amazing that one candle can chase away the darkness. Fire is one of the four basic elements, along with water, air, and earth. Candles come in all sizes, shapes, and fragrances. You may purchase or make a candle especially for your times of meditation. Many people sit in a favorite chair and light a candle for their time of meditation. Today light a candle and focus your attention on it. Let it lead you into the quiet and into the presence of God. Christ is the Light of the world (John 8:12) and your life.

Add to your gratitude list.

May 18

Remember

Origen (186–c. 253), a great theologian of the early Greek Church, strongly encouraged biblical study and interpretation.

Read

Psalm 68:21-27

Ponder

After graphic descriptions of crushing the enemy (vv. 21-23), the psalm lifts up a mighty procession led by the king, singers, musicians, and dancers. Possibly the ark of the covenant, the chest containing the two stone tablets that God gave Moses on Mount Sinai, headed this great procession of praise. Oh, that our worship would be as joyous and exuberant as the Hebrews' celebration of God's presence and victory.

Prayer/Practice

Some meditative practices are ends in themselves, while others intend to become the doorway into contemplation, a wordless, imageless dwelling with God. Desmond Tutu wrote: "Our relationship with God is a love affair and ultimately the greatest joy is just to be with the Beloved, to drink in the beauty of the Beloved in a silence that will become ever more wordless and imageless—the silence of just being together."[5]

Today remember your breath prayer (see Jan. 8) and use your prayer to still the mind and open you to the silence of communing with the Beloved.

May 19

REMEMBER

Amelia Earhart (1897–1937), an adventurous and courageous woman, in 1932 became the first woman to fly solo across the Atlantic. On a round-the-world flight in 1937, her plane disappeared.

READ

Psalm 68:28-35

PONDER

The psalm ends with a vision of all the nations coming to worship God in Jerusalem. Some nations may need to see evidence of God's strength to be encouraged to come: "Show your strength, O God, as you have done for us before" (v. 28). Some rulers will respond to the majesty of creation: "Now sing praises to God! Every kingdom on earth, sing to the Lord! Praise the one who rides across the ancient skies; . . . speaks with a mighty voice" (vv. 32-33, CEV).

Perhaps Amelia Earhart sensed some of the grandeur of the heavens as she flew; perhaps she had a sense of the One who rides the clouds. Take some time to look up at the heavens today and think of courageous women and times you acted courageously in your own life.

PRAYER/PRACTICE

Centering prayer (see Jan. 13) is another form of meditation that leads to imageless prayer, often known as contemplation. As Jane Redmont says, "Contemplation is a gift. Contemplative prayer is a practice."[6] We practice these forms of meditation and contemplation in order to dwell at one with God. In centering prayer you sit in prayer using a sacred word to focus your thoughts. The sacred word expresses your intention to be in God's presence and to remain open to God's bidding. A short, one- or two-syllable word works best. As other thoughts come into your mind, return gently to the sacred word. The sacred word functions as an anchor to the divine while boats of mental traffic float by. Try to spend fifteen to twenty minutes in centering prayer.

May 20

REMEMBER

The Celtic Church recognized three forms of martyrdom: *red*—death for Christ's sake; *green*—controlling desires through fasting, hard work, or penance; and *white*—exile from home and family.

READ

Psalm 69:1-8

PONDER

This powerful lament is one of the most frequently quoted psalms in the New Testament. It echoes Jeremiah, Jesus, and all the innocent who suffer at the hands of others. The psalm graphically describes the need for help: "The waters have come up to my neck. . . . there is no foothold. . . . I am weary with my crying" (vv. 1-3). It exaggerates: "More in number than the hairs of my head are those who hate me without cause" (v. 4). It confesses: "My sins, O God, are not hidden from you; you know how foolish I have been" (v. 5, GNT). It worries: "Do not let those who hope in you be put to shame because of me" (v. 6). All these moods occur in the first eight verses.

PRAYER/PRACTICE

Music can gently still the mind for meditation and contemplation. Sometimes I use my breath prayer to focus my breathing and quiet my mind. Other times I repeat a line from a song or hymn as a refrain several times. I usually sing it silently until I have focused on all the words. It is amazing how my mind can wander even while singing a short refrain. Sometimes I create my own tunes for prayers and scripture verses. Celtic prayers lend themselves to simple harmonic phrasing, and their picturesque language is easy to remember. Music from the Taizé Community is also wonderfully meditative. I listen for music that resides easily in the heart and memorably in the mind.

May 21

Jessica Powers (1905–1988), a mystic, farmer, and Carmelite nun, is best known for her poetry.

READ

Psalm 69:9-15

PONDER

Zeal for the house of prayer caused Jesus to chase out the money changers and merchants (Matt. 21:12-13). Zeal for the Temple and passion for God's cause also consumes the psalmist and becomes an affront to others. Despite being gossiped about and made the brunt of drinking songs, the psalmist possesses an abiding hope: "At an acceptable time, O God, in the abundance of your steadfast love, answer me . . . rescue me from sinking in the mire" (Ps. 69:13-14). Think about your own zeal for God, and your abiding trust in God's saving power in the face of harassment and opposition.

PRAYER/PRACTICE

Any type of contemplative prayer, like centering prayer, is not easy. Listen to these words from the book *The Cloud of Unknowing* by an unknown fourteenth-century author:

> Lift your heart up to the Lord, with a gentle stirring of love desiring him for his own sake and not for his gifts. Center all your attention and desire on him and let this be the sole concern of your mind and heart.

> . . . in the beginning it is usual to feel nothing but a kind of darkness about your mind, or as it were, *a cloud of unknowing.* You will seem to know nothing and to feel nothing except a naked intent toward God in the depths of your being. . . . learn to be at home in this darkness.[7]

Practice centering prayer today, and add to your gratitude list.

May 22

REMEMBER

Israel ben Eliezer (c. 1700–1760), known as the Ba'al Shem Tov (Hebrew for "Master of the Good Name"), founded Jewish Hasidism, a mysticism of the everyday, in eastern Europe. He taught his followers to find the divine spark in everything and to live with a spirit of joy.

READ

Psalm 69:16-29

PONDER

The insults, the rejection, and the vinegar the psalmist had to drink remind us of the last days and hours of Jesus. The psalmist's anger may be too strong for us, yet for people in concentration camps or ghetto slums who choose to voice a prayer, their anger might be as strong as verses 22-28. Once again, the psalmist expresses anger to God, who can handle our fears and our anger and who continually works for good and seeks justice. If we tried to take revenge into our own hands, it would be a pretty bloodied world. It would be much better if we had some of the joy of the Ba'al Shem Tov, who taught his followers to live responsibly with a joyful holiness.

PRAYER/PRACTICE

John Main, an English Benedictine monk, teaches a form of meditation (called Christian meditation) similar to centering prayer. A teacher in this tradition gives these guidelines:

> Sit down. Sit still and upright. Close your eyes lightly. Sit relaxed but alert. Silently, interiorly begin to say a single word. We recommend the prayer-word "Maranatha" [which means "come, Lord"]. Recite it as four syllables of equal length. Listen to it as you say it, gently but continuously. Do not think or imagine anything—spiritual or otherwise. If thoughts and images come, these are distractions at the time of meditation, so keep returning to simply saying the word. Meditate each morning and evening for between twenty and thirty minutes.[8]

I invite you to try Christian meditation today.

May 23

REMEMBER

Daniel (B.C.E.), a faithful follower of Yahweh, an interpreter of dreams, and a survivor of a fiery furnace and the lions' den, understood the cost of obedience to God in the face of empires and governments that demand unquestioned patriotism and allegiance.

READ

Psalm 69:30-36

PONDER

The climax of the lament psalms usually occurs in the final verses, a song of praise. The psalmist moves through hardship, anger, and despair to a place of thanksgiving. Many scholars believe that after the complaint was made in the liturgy of the worship service, a priest would read an account of God helping the people. Some biblical scholars believe that wherever the word *selah* appears in the lament psalms, it signals a time for the reading about God's faithfulness. After the reading, the lament concluded with words of praise and thanksgiving. In Psalm 69 the praise moves from the individual, "I will praise the name of God with a song" (v. 30), to include the nation as well, "For God will save Zion and rebuild the cities of Judah" (v. 35). Think of a time you made it through a period of suffering to end in glorious song.

PRAYER/PRACTICE

The practice of meditation and contemplation aims at developing an awareness of God. Non-Christian religions of the East often call this awareness "mindfulness," a way of living that remains conscious of one's breathing, conscious of being in the present moment, and awake to the divine in all of reality. Thich Nhat Hanh, a Buddhist monk and teacher, uses the term *mindfulness* to refer to keeping one's consciousness alive to the present reality. With practice, one experiences existence as "a miraculous and mysterious reality. People usually consider walking on water or in thin air a miracle. But I think the real miracle is not to walk either on water or in thin air, but to walk on earth."[9]

Try to bring such mindfulness to all your activities today.

May 24

REMEMBER

Aldersgate Day (1738) commemorates the day John Wesley, founder of the Methodist movement, experienced an inner, heartwarming conversion that propelled him to begin a revival, which led to the formation of a new denomination in England. Wesley's conversion happened in a small chapel on Aldersgate Street in London.

READ

Psalm 70

PONDER

In the eighteenth century John Wesley and his brother Charles initiated a religious renewal in England that swept over to America and became one of the largest Protestant churches in the United States. The Wesleys taught an inner piety that expressed itself in personal disciplines and social compassion. They organized small groups of believers and guided them into a more mature Christian life. Music, open-air preaching, and care for the needy became hallmarks of this growing group of Christians.

Today's psalm repeats Psalm 40:13-17. Verse 1, "O LORD, make haste to help me!" traditionally opens some monastic prayer services and remains a wonderful prayer line to memorize.

PRAYER/PRACTICE

Charles Wesley's hymns hold a firm place in many churches' musical traditions, regardless of whether they are United Methodist. Try singing one of Wesley's hymns today:

> O for a thousand tongues to sing my great Redeemer's praise,
> the glories of my God and King, the triumphs of his grace!
> . . . .
> Jesus! the name that charms our fears, that bids our sorrows cease;
> 'tis music in the sinner's ears, 'tis life, and health, and peace.[10]

Charles Wesley also wrote "Come, Thou Long-Expected Jesus," "Hark! the Herald Angels Sing," "Christ the Lord Is Risen Today," "A Charge to Keep I Have," and "Love Divine, All Loves Excelling."

May 25

REMEMBER

Rahab (B.C.E.), a Canaanite prostitute, hid and protected Israelite spies just before the siege of Jericho. She is one of five women listed in the genealogy of Jesus in Matthew 1:5.

READ

Joshua 2

PONDER

Rahab seems an unlikely person to include on any list of biblical saints and heroes, yet scripture remembers her for her good work and her crafty lies that kept the spies of Joshua hidden from her own nation's leaders. James remarks that she stands as a witness to faith needing works for salvation (James 2:25-26). Rahab chose to follow the God of the Israelites and trusted in the spies' promise that she would be saved when the city fell to the Israelite army. God used this outsider, and Rahab is remembered as one of God's servants because of her deeds and her faith.

PRAYER/PRACTICE

Meditation and contemplation require us to befriend silence, for listening and attentiveness reside at the heart of this kind of prayer. Meditation and contemplation invite us to make silence our companion, to feel comfortable in sitting in silence, to trust in a holy presence who permeates the quiet. Quakers teach us a lot about silence and prayer, for they believe that God most often chooses the avenue of silence to speak to us. We befriend silence so that we might hear the voice of God. The practices we have been reviewing give us some tools to deepen our experience of silence and listening.

Today choose your breath prayer or your sacred word from centering prayer as a tool to hold you gently in the silence. Try to dwell in God's presence for fifteen to twenty minutes.

Remember to add to your gratitude list.

May 26

REMEMBER

Saint Philip Neri (1515–1595), a Roman Catholic priest, sought to reinvigorate the church by bringing together groups of clergy and laypersons to discuss spiritual themes and to live lives of compassion. The small groups, called oratorians, opened clergy to the wisdom of the unordained, a novel approach in the sixteenth century.

READ

Psalm 71:1-16

PONDER

Old age can be both a glorious and a worrisome time. The psalmist looks back, praying not to be cast off or forgotten as strength fails (v. 9), praying that accusers "be put to shame and consumed" (v. 13), and promising to hope in God continually and to praise God more and more (v. 14). Though growing old often evokes a list of regrets, the psalmist expresses an underlying confidence in God, who remains "a rock of refuge, a strong fortress" (v. 3). Do you sense a long line of hope and confidence extending from your birth to the present moment? Can you sing with the psalmist, "I will never give up hope or stop praising you" (v. 14, CEV)?

PRAYER/PRACTICE

Find a new object for meditation and review the questions suggested on May 14. Observe the object. Choose three observations about the object that speak about life and relationships. Choose one observation as a focus for your prayer. Slow down your breathing. Enjoy the silence. Revel in the touch and the feel of your object. Thank God for this part of creation that opens you to a deeper awareness of the blessings and wonder of a loving God. If possible, invite some others, both lay and clergy, to participate in the meditation with an object. Provide several objects and allow seven to ten minutes for each section of the meditation. Invite brief sharing after each section with a longer time of sharing at the end.

Remember to add to your gratitude list.

May 27

REMEMBER

Pentecost celebrates the coming of the Holy Spirit to the disciples fifty days after Easter. This movable feast depends on when Easter falls. Many Christians wear red on this day to commemorate the tongues like fire that descended upon the followers of Jesus (Acts 2).

READ

Psalm 71:17-24

PONDER

Though some may die young and often in a tragic way, God intended and planned for people to get "old . . . and gray" (v. 18). A long life provides much material for praise, many occasions for thanksgiving, and lots of stories of God's faithfulness to pass on "to all the generations to come" (v. 18). We hope that in our later years we will be able to say, "I will praise you, God, for your faithful friendship. I will play the lyre and harp for you. . . . I will sing your praises with joy, sing with my whole heart of how you saved me" (vv. 22-23, AP). Even if we cannot play an instrument or sing, may we find ways to praise God all our days.

PRAYER/PRACTICE

Visit an older person today if possible, or call someone on the phone. Find a way to thank God for the friendship and blessings of the older people you know. Offer a prayer of gratitude. Use these words to get you started.

> Most gracious God, thank you for my older friends. Though their eyes grow dim, they bring the wisdom of insight. Though their words may be softer and their voices weaker, older persons can still laugh and delight in telling old tales. Though bones ache and bodies become bent, still a spirit of dancing remains. Most gracious God, may I praise you all my days in many ways. Amen.

May 28

REMEMBER

Walker Percy (1916–1990) wrote novels shaped by his Christian understanding of the meaning and destiny of human existence.

READ

Psalm 72:1-14

PONDER

This psalm, the last in book 2 of the Psalms, unveils a majestic prayer of intercession for the king. Justice ranks high on the list of important tasks for the king. Prosperity, commonly ranked high and experienced as wonderful, pales as a measure of successful ruling. God looks at and judges a king and government by the way they care for the poor and needy (vv. 12-13). The language used is so hopeful and some of the Israelite kings were so lacking that this psalm has often reminded people to look to its fulfillment in the King of kings, Jesus the Christ. How well does our government "defend the cause of the poor" and "give deliverance to the needy" (v. 4)?

PRAYER/PRACTICE

Silence loosens us from ordinary perceptions and attitudes. It nudges open a fresh look at life and attunes us to see, hear, and think differently. Today try to find some little spaces of silence. Turn off the car radio or CD player as you drive. Pay little attention to the noise of the traffic around you. Observe a minute of silence before you begin your work or after you park your car. Turn off the TV or music at your house for a while. Walk the dog in silence. Aim for several short periods of silence during the day in addition to your time of meditation or contemplation.

May 29

REMEMBER

G. K. Chesterton (1874–1936), a witty and humorous English author and social critic, wrote frequently as an apologist, defending the Christian faith.

READ

Psalm 72:15-20

PONDER

The psalmist invites us to pray for the king. "May prayer be made for him continually and blessings invoked for him all day long" (v. 15). This verse reminds us that all government leaders need to be remembered in prayer. Is there a time in your Sunday worship service to remember political leaders and social reformers? Some of those prayers can be in the form of letters expressing our concerns to our president and congressional representatives. Have you written or called a leader about a social issue or personal concern? We need to help our leaders know that care for the "poor and those who have no helper . . . the weak and the needy" (vv. 12-13) forms a critical and essential part of our government's task.

PRAYER/PRACTICE

For several years, our family invited others to our house during the holidays to sign a letter to world leaders. Our family would think of who in the world needed a word of encouragement, who was doing something for world peace or meeting the needs of the poor. We would write a brief note and then invite our guests to sign their names or add their notes of encouragement. We received many replies of gratitude from around the world. Try writing a prayer of encouragement to a local, state, or national leader. Offer a prayer for a world leader and all those trying to create a more just and compassionate world.

May 30

REMEMBER

Saint Joan of Arc (1412–1431), a young French woman, heard voices that gave her a mission to save France. Compelled by this strong inner conviction, she became a military leader who engendered support from the masses and incited anger in church leaders and politicians, who condemned her as a heretic and burned her at the stake.

READ

Psalm 73:1-9

PONDER

The psalmist reflects on a question that still disturbs us today. If the wicked are healthy, successful, and prosperous; and good people suffer and struggle, why be good? The psalmist admits to being envious, almost slipping and stumbling with the arrogant and wicked who even "set their mouths against heaven" (v. 9). The temptations are slick and well-packaged. Who can resist a chance to win big money in the lottery? Who does not want to be an instant millionaire? It looks so easy and so inviting. We will hear the rest of the debate from the psalmist over the next few days.

PRAYER/PRACTICE

Joan of Arc, a contemplative and an activist, heard voices that propelled her into battle. She refused to compromise her conscience even when standing before the highest civil and religious authorities.

Often in times of meditation or contemplation, we may receive a bidding, a call to action or service. Usually our mission is not as big as saving France, as in Joan's case, but still we can hear a call to be faithful to God's desire. Reflect on your prayer life and recall any "voices" or nudges, or calls to act or respond. How have you been faithful to God's call? Add to your gratitude list.

May 31

REMEMBER

The traditional Feast Day of the Visitation of Mary to Elizabeth.

READ

Luke 1:39-56

PONDER

This day does not commemorate a saint but a meeting between two important women in the life of Jesus. Mary takes the initiative to visit Elizabeth, who is farther along in her pregnancy. Wise Elizabeth confirms that Mary's baby will be special, and Mary begins to see her role in the unfolding of God's intervention into human history. Mary's song of praise remains one of the most subversive of all New Testament texts, as it links Jesus with a special compassion for the poor and oppressed and reveals a willingness to turn the existing order upside down. The last shall be first; the lowly shall be lifted up; the hungry shall be fed. Two women begin to sense what this birth could mean for the world. Perhaps every birth has the potential to bring about new signs of hope and possibility.

PRAYER/PRACTICE

Review your gratitude list today. Do you find any surprises? Have your eyes opened to see gratitude all around? Has your heart enlarged with thanksgiving? Try keeping your gratitude list for another month.

I invite you, like Mary, to write your own song of praise, your own "Magnificat." Begin with these words: "My soul magnifies the Lord, and my spirit rejoices in God my Savior, for God has . . ." Write how God has blessed you this year.

June

Summer God, you dance in on golden sunbeams.
Like soil that must be plowed or turned over,
so I must prepare to receive your warmth and
the planting of your message in my heart.
Open me to receiving the seed of hope
and the promise of growth.
Plant your Spirit deep within me
and make my life fruitful and bountiful. Amen.

June 1

REMEMBER

Saint Justin (c. 100–c. 165), a philosopher and early Christian martyr, wrote some of the first descriptions of early church worship and baptism.

READ

Psalm 73:10-20

PONDER

"Such are the wicked; always at ease, they increase in riches" (v. 12). In the face of temptation, the psalmist proclaims the foolishness and vanity of trying to remain honest and clean when the wicked lead such a good life. Yet the psalm takes a new turn on one small word—*until* (v. 17). In essence, the psalmist says, "I almost gave in until I went into the sanctuary." Or in modern vernacular, "I almost made the deal until I sat in silence and prayed." "I almost cheated until I envisioned the outcome." The psalmist received a revelation in the holy place: The wicked are on "slippery places" (v. 18) filled with terror and fear, ready to fall to ruin. Beware of the temptations of power and wealth; their treasures do not last.

PRAYER/PRACTICE

One summer I traveled to Canada for a wilderness retreat. After a long drive to the park, we piled into four-wheel drive trucks that would haul us and our gear to the camping spot high in the park. Cathedral Lakes, an awesome place of beauty, became our home for the next week. Each morning after breakfast, I met with a spiritual director, talked about my prayer life and spiritual journey, and made plans for hiking or exploring that day. The evenings brought time for sharing the day's adventures with the group, an evening meal, and worship. The only agenda for the retreat was to spend time with God. I hiked and prayed a lot.

Think about incorporating time with God in your summer agenda. What would you plan?

June 2

REMEMBER

Anthony de Mello (1932–1987), an Indian Jesuit, infused his writings and retreats with stories and parables from many traditions. He encouraged people to wake up to the divine presence in their midst.

READ

Psalm 73:21-28

PONDER

The psalmist looks back on the amazing journey from faith to doubt and back to faith. "I was stupid and ignorant; I was like a brute beast toward you. Nevertheless I am continually with you; you hold my right hand. You guide me with your counsel" (vv. 22-24). Here the psalmist uses another transition word, *nevertheless*. Instead of slipping in with the arrogant, proud, and wealthy, the psalmist discovers God's nearness and strength. Nothing on earth could be better than that (v. 25). The psalmist sends a clear reminder, "It is good to be near God" (v. 28). Otherwise we make stupid, unwise decisions.

PRAYER/PRACTICE

Anthony de Mello collected stories from many traditions and invited people on his retreats to practice *lectio divina* (see March) with them. One of his stories follows; read it slowly and meditate on it.

> The disciples were full of questions about God.
> Said the master, "God is the Unknown and the Unknowable. Every statement about him, every answer to your questions, is a distortion of the truth."
> The disciples were bewildered. "Then why do you speak about him at all?"
> "Why does the bird sing?" said the master.

De Mello then adds, "Not because it has a statement, but because it has a song." So let the song and the stories awaken something in the heart beyond all knowledge.[1]

What stories awaken your soul and shape your life?

June 3

REMEMBER

Pope John XXIII (1881–1963) called together Roman Catholic leaders and observers from other denominations for an ecumenical council (Vatican II) to update the policies of the Catholic Church and to increase dialogue between the church and the modern world.

READ

Psalm 74:1-11

PONDER

The fall of Jerusalem and the destruction of the Temple in 587 B.C.E., significant historical events in the life of the Israelites, lie behind this lament. In the face of his nation's collapse, the psalmist questions why God has done nothing (v. 11). "God, don't you remember your sheep? Don't you remember Mount Zion where you came to dwell? "(vv. 1-2, AP).

A pastor friend from Germany recalls how the Nazis came into the church, removed the cross and other sacred objects, and displayed the Nazi flag in the sanctuary. "Your foes have roared within your holy place; they set up their emblems there" (v. 4). My friend understands this psalm in a personal way; to this day it bothers him to see flags in church.

PRAYER/PRACTICE

Pope John XXIII believed that the church needed to open its windows and let in some fresh air. What "fresh air" do you need this summer? Summer often provides time for retreats, vacations, travels. To what or where might God be calling you? For the next several days I invite you to explore the idea of spiritual retreats—special times set apart for prayer, renewal, and silence. A retreat gives time to restore balance to our lives, to reflect on where we have been, and to listen to where God might be calling. It also allows us to pay attention to parts of ourselves we often neglect, like prayer and solitude, rest, and spending time in nature. Which of your summer plans provides space for spiritual renewal?

June 4

REMEMBER

Saint Kevin (seventh century), considered a patron saint of Dublin, founded the abbey of Glendalough in Ireland. According to one story, a blackbird built a nest and laid an egg in Kevin's outstretched hand while he engaged in a long prayer—a wonderful tale of stillness and receptivity.

READ

Psalm 74:12-23

PONDER

The psalmist urges God to remember—remember subduing the sea monsters (v. 13); remember establishing day and night (v. 16); remember creating the seasons (v. 17). After reminding God of God's great activity and power in the past, the writer pleads with God to do something about enemies in the holy place. "Rise up, O God" (v. 22). We share in this lament every time we pray for Christians and other religious groups persecuted for their beliefs. We pray and trust that God still acts through people raising their voices of concern and addressing the problems of division. "God, you have ruled from the beginning, working for salvation in every land"(v. 12, AP).

PRAYER/PRACTICE

"In the morning, while it was still very dark, he got up and went out to a deserted place, and there he prayed" (Mark 1:35). Jesus knew the value of solitude for prayer. A retreat sets apart time for God. Most likely you desire to spend more time in prayer, to step back from the frantic pace of a busy life. You face many demands and feel the conflicting pulls of family, vocation, church, and social responsibilities. Sometimes daily life keeps you too busy to stop and look for the movements of the Spirit. Retreats give space to look back and sort out your identity and God's callings in the midst of life. They allow you to draw a deep breath and remember who and whose you are. Recall a retreat you have attended, and if possible, schedule a retreat for this summer.

June 5

REMEMBER

Saint Boniface (c. 675–754), an English monk, played an instrumental role in converting Germany to Christianity. In a dramatic confrontation with people who worshiped trees, Boniface chopped down a tree sacred to the pagans and did not die, which led to many conversions.

READ

Psalm 75

PONDER

The image of the cup occurs in scripture again and again. The cup in Jesus' hand can symbolize his suffering and death, or it can represent blessing at the table of communion and fellowship. The cup in this psalm, like the one in Isaiah 51:17, reveals a cup of God's anger. The wicked, who try to lift up their horn—to show their power and promote themselves—will end up drinking the cup of God's anger and facing the judgment of God, who turns the tables by lifting up the righteous even as the wicked descend to a lower level. Our task remains to trust that God still works to bring about this reversal; we can continually rejoice and sing praises to God (v. 9).

PRAYER/PRACTICE

A retreat not only provides a good time to look back with reverence and thanksgiving but also a time to open oneself to the amazing love, forgiveness, power, and direction of God. I remember a time on retreat when I complained to God about the church I served. In the middle of the complaint, I felt God's presence reassuring me that I was not alone, that God loved me, and that God was sending me back "down the hill" to love the people. This retreat reaffirmed my vocation, cleared up some doubts, and straightened out my priorities. The time away, with plenty of rest on the first couple of days, opened me to receive the blessing and insights I needed to carry on in ministry. In the silence, away from the blaring noises of daily life, I heard the still small voice of God.

Recall a time you felt God's blessing or assurance of love. Continue making plans for a retreat.

June 6

REMEMBER

Kateri Tekakwitha (1656–1680), the first Native American woman to be called Blessed by the Catholic Church, came from the Mohawk tribe in New York. She converted to Christianity and spent her last three years teaching and caring for the sick in a mission near Montreal.

READ

Psalm 76

PONDER

Some unknown victory of Israel over its foes lies behind this psalm. In our day, when we hope to avoid war because of its lethal power and nuclear capabilities, this psalm still carries a word of challenge. God passionately seeks to "save all the oppressed of the earth" (v. 9). God desires that all people have shelter and food, receive fair pay for work, and enjoy the goodness of creation. God desires that we share God's righteous indignation and let our hearts be stirred to love, our thoughts turned into pleas for justice, and our intentions shaped into acts of compassion.

PRAYER/PRACTICE

Most retreat centers locate themselves at the edges of civilization, somewhat removed from the noise, bright lights, and temptations of a seductive culture that wants to fill all our time with activity. A desert place, a mountain retreat, a hidden ranch—any place where the stars can be seen, the air breathed, and the silence heard—becomes a good place for a retreat. A good retreat place helps you sense the nearness of God, a thinning of the "veil" between heaven and earth. I like places where I can spend time in God's creation—taking long walks, sitting beside a stream, looking up at the stars, stretching toward the sun. These places of "green pastures and still waters"—these holy places— "restore the soul" (Ps. 23).

Spend time outside today if possible. Continue to plan for a summer retreat; get a list of retreat centers from Retreats International. (See Appendix A.)

June 7

REMEMBER

Wendell Berry (b. 1934) lives out a passionate concern for the land as a farmer; as a writer, he calls us to accountability for harming the earth. As a poet, he explores the mystery and harmony of solitude, beauty, and creation, encouraging us to practice resurrection every day.

READ

Psalm 77:1-10

PONDER

Wendell Berry's essays echo the power and despair of the Hebrew laments, decrying the rape of nature, the dependence on machines (even computers), and the neglect of the rhythms and seasons of the year. Today's poetic, melancholy lament psalm touches the core of despair. Sleepless nights, a sense of abandonment by God, and a deep grief penetrate this psalm. Here is a psalm we can pray in hard times, in times of distress, in times when we have no words but groans and cries. Even at those times, God receives our prayer. God welcomes even our most unacceptable prayer. God hears, and God will not let despair or death have the last word. We have the Resurrection as the final answer.

PRAYER/PRACTICE

In one of his poems, Wendell Berry writes about "the peace of wild things."[2] When the world's trouble invades your soul and disturbs your sleep, seek out the peace of wild things. When you worry about the future for your children, go dwell where the squirrels run. Sit beside a stream where herons feed. Look at the sky and at fragrant flowers where the hummingbirds fly. Let go of worry and fear, and rest in God's gift of creation. Seek the healing, renewing powers of places where the wild creatures dwell.

Where do you go to find your despair healed? Where are your places of rest? Where do you go to lift your sagging spirits?

June 8

REMEMBER

Mary Harris (Mother) Jones (c. 1837–1930) impacted the American labor scene as a forceful, compassionate, and picturesque organizer. After losing her husband and children to an epidemic, she became "mother" to thousands of poor workers whom she helped organize.

READ

Psalm 77:11-20

PONDER

The despair and self-pity in this psalm begin to lessen as the psalmist remembers the deeds of God, especially during the Exodus. If God could provide strong leadership in that desperate time, then hopefully God will lead the people again. The God of the Exodus and of Easter testifies to a God of hope and promise. We may not know when or how God will act, so we must believe and surrender ourselves and our concerns to the God who hears and acts, often in surprising ways. "With your strong arm you redeemed your people" (v. 15).

PRAYER/PRACTICE

Various kinds of retreats abound. One option is an individual or private retreat in which the retreatant sets the agenda and structure. The retreat may involve twenty-four hours of silence and fasting. Or it can mean spending several days at a retreat center that offers regularly scheduled worship services and mealtimes but leaves the rest of the time unscheduled. One may decide to take a book to read, do some journaling, and spend long times in silence and prayer. A private retreat provides time to rest—from sound, from obligations, from labor. It allows time to listen to God, to befriend the silence and let God speak, touch, and heal. When I choose an individual retreat, I look for a place with a worshiping community so I can join others in prayer and yet spend most of my time on my own. I usually require a day of rest before I can pay attention during the silences.

Recall a special time away by yourself on a retreat. What kind of retreat are you planning?

June 9

REMEMBER

Saint Columba (521–597), an Irish monk, founded an abbey on the island of Iona, off the coast of Scotland. Today the monastery houses the Iona Community, an ecumenical group devoted to peace and reconciliation and known for its music and worship.

READ

Psalm 78:1-8

PONDER

Whether communicated orally, in writing, or through film, a good story thrills and delights. It can bring laughter, tears, inspiration, or insight—and often a touch of each. The psalmist reminds us and encourages us to pass on the stories of faith, "the glorious deeds of the LORD" (v. 4). The church should give teachers and storytellers a prominent place to inspire the young to "set their hope in God" (v. 7). We who have experienced God's grace have an invitation and an obligation to share what we know.

PRAYER/PRACTICE

A special kind of a retreat involves making a pilgrimage to a sacred place where others have found God's presence. I traveled to the island of Iona on one pilgrimage; the beauty, the history, and the ongoing witness of Christians on that remote island deeply moved me. Worship services in the old chapel, with its thick walls and history of centuries of prayer and song, evoked an unusual sense of the holy. As I walked the path around the island and heard the stories of Columba, I felt connected to God, to the amazing pilgrims who had gone before me to carry the message of God's love.

Recall a pilgrimage you have made, or plan to make a religious pilgrimage. Look for a book about Celtic Christianity, or seek information on monasteries and retreat centers. (See Appendix A.)

June 10

REMEMBER

Through their small-group meetings, Twelve Steps to recovery, and other resources, Alcoholics Anonymous, founded in 1935, gives hope to millions dealing with addiction to alcohol and other substances.

READ

Psalm 78:9-31

PONDER

Even if we lost most of the Hebrew Scriptures except for the Psalms, we would still have much of the story of God and the Israelites. The Psalms preserved history for the Hebrew people. In today's passage we revisit the Exodus, the dramatic escape of the Israelites from Egypt through the sea; the wandering in the desert; and the complaining about lack of water and food. God was with them, providing water from the rock, manna from heaven, and birds from the air. Still the people complained. The familiar story happens even today, as people test God, complain to God, and possess incredibly short memories about God's wonderful deeds in the past.

PRAYER/PRACTICE

A group retreat, in which an established group decides to go away together, offers another retreat option. Usually a leader guides the group through the retreat theme. Most retreats usually offer unstructured times as well as times of presentation, conversation, and worship. Going away together can increase the bonds of friendship as well as provide time for spiritual renewal.

Or individuals may choose to go to a program offered by a retreat center. They may attend because of the presenter, the program topic, or the reputation of the retreat center. The presenter guides, directs, and structures the time and content of the retreat.

Learn about retreat centers in your area and what programs they offer. See if others in your church may be interested in planning or attending a spiritual growth retreat.

June 11

REMEMBER

Barnabas (first century), one of the earliest missionaries in the church, introduced Paul to the Jerusalem community before joining him in the work of bringing the news of Jesus Christ to the Gentiles.

READ

Psalm 78:32-55

PONDER

It is a wonder that God did not give up on the Israelites, for they continually complained, disappointed God, and carried on with their sinful ways. "Yet God, in compassion and mercy, forgave their sin, did not destroy them, but held back anger and wrath" (v. 38, AP). "God remembered that they were made of flesh, and were like a wind that blows once and then dies down" (v. 39, CEV).

It is also a wonder God does not give up on us. But God abounds with compassion. Our hope does not lie in our own goodness but in God's great compassion and forgiveness.

PRAYER/PRACTICE

Still another retreat option is the individual directed retreat. On this kind of retreat, you ask to be guided by someone at a retreat center. This usually takes the form of meeting once or twice a day with a spiritual director who listens and responds to what you experience on the retreat. The spiritual director may make suggestions for prayer, journaling, or reading but keeps the focus on supporting, encouraging, clarifying, and sometimes challenging your journey with God. The retreatant usually determines the structure and content of the retreat, but the spiritual guide may help give some shape to the days as the Spirit leads. If you are looking for this kind of retreat, check with a retreat center to see if they have spiritual directors available.

Take some extra time today to breathe deeply and to discern the kind of retreat you would like to participate in this summer or this year. Remember your breath prayer.

June 12

REMEMBER

Anne Frank (1929–1945), teenage author of a diary, described the life of her Jewish family as they hid from the Nazis in Amsterdam. "In spite of everything I still believe that people are really good at heart," she wrote.[3] She died in a concentration camp after her family was betrayed. Her diary testifies to hope in the midst of darkness.

READ

Psalm 78:56-72

PONDER

This part of the historical psalm recounts more of the Israelites' failures. After reaching Canaan, the Israelites once again worshiped idols; God became incensed and abandoned the people for a time (Ps. 78:59). The Philistines captured the ark of the covenant, the symbol of God's presence with the Hebrews (see the story in 1 Sam. 4). Trouble resided in the land until God "awoke as from sleep" and "put . . . adversaries to rout" (Ps. 78:65-66). The psalm ends on a hopeful note, with David chosen as the new leader for Israel. Once again God provides hope for a rebellious and forgetful people. Whether through new leaders or hidden diaries, God lifts up hope.

PRAYER/PRACTICE

This hymn expresses the purpose of retreats and invites us to plan for the quiet center that can be found on a retreat:

> Come and find the quiet center in the crowded life we lead,
> Find the room for hope to enter, find the frame where we are freed:
> Clear the chaos and the clutter, clear our eyes that we can see
> All the things that really matter, be at peace, and simply be.

June 13

REMEMBER

Saint Anthony of Padua (1195–1231), a Franciscan preacher, lived a life of service and friendship to the poor.

READ

Psalm 79

PONDER

In 587 B.C.E. King Nebuchadnezzar and his Babylonian army attacked Jerusalem, destroyed the Temple, and deported the Israelites to Babylon. Such a calamity gave rise to this community lament: "How long, O LORD? Will you be angry forever?" (v. 5). The psalmist acknowledges some of the nation's sins but voices an even greater plea for God to punish those who have ignored God and devoured the city. "Let us and the other nations see you take revenge for your servants who died a violent death" (v. 10, CEV). The Hebrews expressed their lament in strong language and trusted that God would respond. The lament psalms teach us to take our strong feelings to God rather than using weapons of destruction to express our anger.

PRAYER/PRACTICE

As wonderful as a retreat may be, it is not a place to stay. You go on a retreat to spend time with God, discover your identity, reorder priorities, gain new perspective, look back with gratitude, and look forward with hope. You withdraw from your ordinary routines but always with the intention to return—hopefully transformed, renewed, and refreshed. A danger exists in retreats if you become tempted to stay, or think God can be found only on the mountaintop or by the gentle stream, or see retreats primarily as quiet time to plan, organize, and gain information. A retreat really serves as time for soul work, for putting yourself in the presence of the awesome and challenging God, and for receiving your instructions for continuing on the path of Christ.

How have you changed as a result of attending a retreat? What balance do you need between work, family, social, civic, and church responsibilities and times of retreat?

June 14

REMEMBER

Gerard Manley Hopkins (1844–1889), an English Jesuit and poet, wrote poetry using vivid language to address God and the human condition. Christendom considers Hopkins one of the great devotional writers of the nineteenth century.

READ

Psalm 80:1-7

PONDER

Twice the refrain gets repeated, "Restore us, O God of hosts; let your face shine, that we may be saved" (vv. 3, 7). In the days before streetlights, neon signs, and fluorescent tubes, light was a powerful symbol. Light came from God, and when God was displeased, it seemed as if God turned away and the light ceased to shine. The defeat of the northern tribes by the Assyrians provides the historical background to this psalm. The devastating defeat brought on a time of darkness and tears. Such times cause us to turn to God in prayer, saying, "God, bring us back, let your face shine on us and we shall be safe" (v. 3, NJB).

PRAYER/PRACTICE

Native Americans experience a retreat called a vision quest. In the vision quest, a person goes to a place set apart in the wilderness, usually a mountaintop or hilltop, for a time of prayer, fasting, and discernment. The person spends several days alone, without food, and generally spends most of the time in the center of a circle. Prayers to the four directions and to the earth and the heavens form a major part of the prayer time. (See Apr. 25–30.) Prayer and fasting in the nature setting provide an environment of openness without external distractions so that the person may hear the voice of God, receive a vision, or deepen gratitude for life.

June 15

REMEMBER

John Howard Griffin (1920–1980) wrote an eye-opening book, *Black Like Me,* describing his life in the South after dyeing his skin black so he could see and experience racism. Griffin also wrote a biography of the monk Thomas Merton (Dec. 10).

READ

Psalm 80:8-19

PONDER

After the Exodus from captivity in Egypt, the nation of Israel became a strong vine that spread to the sea. The psalmist witnesses how the vine has been chopped down and enemies now feed on it (vv. 12, 16). Once again the cry goes out to God: "Turn to us, Almighty God! Look down from heaven at us; come and save your people! Come and save this grapevine that you planted, this young vine you made grow so strong!" (vv. 14-15, GNT).

This psalm offers hope and strength after a difficult time in life, not only for the nation but also for the church. We can ask God to make us a fruitful vine once again, bringing sweetness, healing, and joy to a hurting world.

PRAYER/PRACTICE

In describing a directed retreat, I mentioned a spiritual director. For the next few days I invite you to look at this tradition and practice.

Spiritual direction, akin to the teacher-student relationship, seeks to help another in practicing the spiritual life. Throughout Christian history, people have sought others for guidance, encouragement, and even challenge to deepen their spiritual journey. One-on-one guidance, often modeled after the desert fathers and mothers in Egypt from the third to sixth centuries, offers advice, counsel, and wisdom to those who come seeking insight for their relationship with God.

Think of persons who have helped you on your spiritual journey. Name them and offer God a prayer of thanks.

June 16

REMEMBER

On this day in 1976, black students in Soweto, South Africa, led a demonstration to protest the apartheid government's ruling that classes were to be taught in Afrikaans—the language of the oppressors. Hundreds of Soweto residents, including children, were killed when police opened fire on the demonstration.

READ

Psalm 81

PONDER

Trumpets, harps, and songs call people to worship in this psalm and in our churches. We gather to praise God, to "shout for joy" (v. 1) as God bids us to do. But we also gather to listen to God's Word. God has done so much for us, rescued us from distress (v. 7), but we ungratefully have short memories and turn to other gods. God longs for us to listen and obey (v. 13). God wants to feed us the finest wheat (v. 16), and at the Lord's table we now commune. Bring out the trumpets and songs for the feast!

PRAYER/PRACTICE

"Spiritual direction concerns the movement of our entire lives in and toward God," writes Kathleen Fischer.[4] In *Soul Feast,* Marjorie Thompson describes five responsibilities of a spiritual guide:

1. A spiritual guide listens to us. . . .
2. A spiritual guide helps us to notice . . . the grace of God in everyday life. . . .
3. A spiritual guide helps us to respond to God with greater freedom. . . .
4. A spiritual guide points us to practical disciplines of spiritual growth. . . .
5. A spiritual guide will love us and pray for us.[5]

Do you find yourself wishing for this kind of listening presence in your life? If you have a spiritual guide, give thanks. If you do not, pray for openness and God's leadership in finding a spiritual guide.

June 17

REMEMBER

John Wesley (1703–1791), an Anglican priest, and his brother Charles founded the Methodist movement. Wesley combined a personal life of devotion with social witness and viewed the entire world as his parish. Deeply ecumenical and open-minded, he wrote, "Though we cannot think alike, may we not love alike?"[6] He advocated small accountability groups as a means of encouraging spiritual formation.

READ

Psalm 82

PONDER

In scripture the word *gods* often describes earthly judges and rulers. In this psalm God takes these leaders to court and holds them accountable for injustice and favoring the wicked, probably those who had money to influence the decision (v. 2). God desires justice for the weak and oppressed, the lowly and destitute, the orphans and the poor (vv. 3-4). The church lives and serves faithfully when it follows God's intentions and cares for the afflicted and the powerless.

PRAYER/PRACTICE

John Wesley encouraged the spiritual growth of his followers by placing them in small groups. In their meetings, group members read scripture and supported one another through prayer, counsel, and financial offerings. Many people today participate in small groups as a way of spiritual guidance. In a group spiritual direction meeting, one participant describes God's activity in his or her life; the others listen and sometimes respond. The leader sometimes notes common threads in the experiences shared and suggests a way to close the gathering. The leader models acceptance and listening so sharing may happen without fear of being corrected or put down. The leader reminds the group to listen for the Spirit, the real guide in the group.

Recall an experience in a group where you sensed God's grace supporting, encouraging, and blessing each one in the group. Can you find a group near you in which you can participate?

June 18

REMEMBER

Joshua (B.C.E.), whose name means "The Lord is salvation," succeeded Moses and led the Israelites into the Promised Land.

READ

Psalm 83

PONDER

Enemies can be internal or external. This psalm names the nations surrounding Israel, the ones that oppose her, as the enemies. The psalmist pleads with God not to be silent or inactive toward these enemies but rather to soundly defeat them and shame them. God did this in the past, and God can do it again! Though we may strongly plead for God to change violence and hatred, to defeat greed and oppression, sometimes it seems that God takes awhile to respond. We may feel forsaken, but still we pray and trust that God continually works for good for those who trust in God (Rom. 8:28).

PRAYER/PRACTICE

Eugene Peterson describes how he was drawn to spiritual direction:

> My sense of need was vague and unfocused. It had, though, to do with my development in prayer and my growth in faith. . . . I began to pray for someone who would guide me in the essential, formative parts of my life: my sense of God, my practice of prayer, my understanding of grace. I wanted someone who would take my life of prayer and my pilgrimage with Christ as seriously (or more seriously) than I did, who was capable of shutting up long enough to hear the distinct uniqueness of my spirituality, and who had enough disciplined restraint not to impose an outside form on me.[7]

What qualities should you look for in a spiritual guide? Someone with a mature faith, experience in the ways of prayer, and the ability to listen deeply and to take you seriously. Consider how important it is to you to have someone from your own tradition and whether you prefer male or female. Pray that God will lead you to the right person.

June 19

REMEMBER

June 19 (known as Juneteenth) celebrates the emancipation of black slaves in 1865. It honors the day slaves in Texas heard they were free— two months after the end of the Civil War.

READ

Psalm 84:1-7

PONDER

Do you look forward to going to church for worship? Can you sense the longing and delight of the Israelites as they processed to the glorious temple of God? For the Israelites, the Temple was *the* place where the presence of God abided and could be seen and felt. "Happy are those who live in your house, ever singing your praise" (v. 4). As you read this psalm, substitute the name of your church or place of worship every time the psalmist refers to the house of the Lord. Imagine yourself filling with joy (v. 2) and going from strength to strength (v. 7) as you attend your worship service.

PRAYER/PRACTICE

In contrast to counseling and therapy, spiritual direction does not focus on solving problems. Though both spiritual guidance and therapy seek to help people, they have different goals and questions. Spiritual direction focuses on seeing the hints and whispers of God in all the circumstances of life. "A spiritual director may work with the same raw material (as a therapist), but his or her focus is on helping the client find God's hand or wishes in the client's life."[8]

As you seek a spiritual director, continue to pray that God will lead you to the right person. It may be someone you already know, or God may lead you to ask for names at a retreat center or from a list of spiritual directors (see Appendix A). Arrange an initial meeting, and share your hopes for direction. After the meeting, reflect and pray to see whether this is the right relationship for you.

June 20

REMEMBER

Father's Day is celebrated in the United States on the third Sunday of June. Give thanks for the love and care of fathers.

READ

Psalm 84:8-12

PONDER

Give thanks for the time you spend in worship, "for a day in [God's] courts is better than a thousand elsewhere" (v. 10). Give thanks for greeters and ushers at church who carry on the joy of being "a door-keeper in the house of . . . God" (v. 10). Give thanks for families where God's love has a human face. Be joyful as you walk with integrity with your God (v. 11).

PRAYER/PRACTICE

I moved to another state, away from a person who had been my spiritual guide for nearly a year while I was on sabbatical. I wrote her several times about my new work, and her return letters showed me the gift of spiritual guidance from a distance. She responded to my news about starting a new program in spiritual formation with these words:

> Will you let me know as you go along what . . . directions open up in your inward and outward life as a result? I suspect your greatest teacher will continue to be your own life with its ups and downs, its dry periods and oases. There is something very moving about that. It is so easy to talk of all the grand theories of spirituality. Yet our lives often take us to another reality. That other reality shatters the idol we constantly rebuild of a life full of great experiences of God. Those experiences are sometimes given. But I sometimes think the opposite experiences are the most important because they bring us out of dependence on our mastery of the spiritual life and throw us in all our frailty toward growing dependence on God, not "growth" in the spiritual life.[9]

Who has written letters that provide guidance for you?

June 21

REMEMBER

Summer solstice in the Northern Hemisphere celebrates the day with the most hours of sunlight. Soak up some sunlight and rejoice in the warmth of the Creator.

READ

Psalm 85:1-7

PONDER

Many scholars believe the Hebrews' return from captivity in Babylon provides the context for this psalm. The Israelites have come back to the land (v. 1), but so many difficulties lie in restoring the land and in fighting off enemies, the people wonder if God might still be angry with them (v. 5). Once again they pray to God, "Revive us. Kindle our joy. Show us mercy" (vv. 6-7, AP). This prayer merits repeating whenever our practices of obedience get stiff, whenever our enthusiasm wanes, whenever our compassion becomes fatigued: Revive us, O God, with the fresh winds of the Spirit, and let the joy of Jesus infuse the depths of our being.

PRAYER/PRACTICE

Do people bring questions about prayer to you? Do you feel a calling to accompany people as they deepen their spiritual journey? Or do you feel a little uneasy about "directing" another person? Here are some thoughts about preparing for a ministry of spiritual guidance.

If people seek you out, trust that they and God see some quality in you that helps others. Begin to cultivate an attitude of humility, trusting that God will be with you as you guide others. Search out centers of training and read books to better prepare you for this ministry of holy listening. Deepen your practice of prayer so that God dwells as a close companion. Familiarize yourself with scripture, especially the Psalms, for they will be a valuable resource for this ministry of guidance. Practice your listening skills and learn how to be a nonanxious presence. Pray for openness to whomever God sends your way.

Today practice seeing Christ in every person you meet.

June 22

REMEMBER

Thomas More (1478–1535), a lawyer and lord chancellor to King Henry VIII, did not side with the king on breaking with the church in Rome.

READ

Psalm 85:8-13

PONDER

In this psalm God addresses the people's hope and plea that the rebuilding of the land might go better. God speaks peace to the faithful who open their hearts (v. 8) and promises that "salvation is at hand" (v. 9). The psalmist eloquently describes God's promise of a new period of growth and harmony. "Love and faithfulness will meet; justice and peace will kiss; faithfulness will spring up from the ground, and justice will lean down from heaven" (vv. 10-11, AP).

In our day we carry these memorable images and work toward and pray for a world community where love and faithfulness will meet and justice and peace will kiss.

PRAYER/PRACTICE

When I moved to a new state and looked for a new spiritual director, I set up initial meetings with three different people, all wonderful directors. One lived too far away. Another said he was too much like me (we were the same personality type, according to Myers-Briggs) and might not be able to challenge me enough. I ended up choosing the third person because she prayed for me. She listened to the journey of my life and at the end of our time, she gently lifted my life up to God. It felt like being cradled in God's arms and provided me with a deep blessing. At the end of each of our meetings over the next six years, she prayed for me, my family, my ministry, my concerns. She lifted me into the arms of God, and her prayers touched my life deeply.

Who prays for you? Who carries you to God's heart? Give thanks for those people, and ask your spiritual guide to pray for you.

June 23

REMEMBER

Martha (first century), the sister of Mary and Lazarus, showed hospitality to Jesus and modeled the ministry of humble service. Her faith caused her to be one of the first to say, "I believe that you are the Messiah, the Son of God, the one coming into the world" (John 11:27).

READ

Psalm 86

PONDER

Like musical groups that put out a "best of" CD or tape, this psalm selects many verses and ideas from earlier psalms. It reads like a familiar poem, weaving deeply moving pleas for help with wonderful testimonies of thanksgiving. If you feel needy this day, use verse 1, 3, 6, 7, 14, or 16 to guide your prayer. If you feel grateful, full of thanksgiving, use verse 5, 13, or 15 to begin your prayer. Perhaps verse 11 sums up all the petitions: "Teach me your way, O LORD, that I may walk in your truth; give me an undivided heart to revere your name." Pray that you may have an undivided heart, a heart filled with one desire: to walk in the way of God's truth.

PRAYER/PRACTICE

Spiritual direction is an art, an oral, heartfelt, handed-on tradition. Though it is important to study the art of spiritual direction, to take classes in becoming a director, and to attend seminars and discussions, one best learns spiritual direction by experiencing the gift of direction. Every good spiritual director receives spiritual direction. Much of what I know and do in spiritual direction comes from being shaped and guided by wonderful people, my directors. I count them among my saints, and I believe those who have died still watch over me.

Today I invite you to give thanks for those saints who shaped, guided, loved, and challenged you to be a living disciple of Jesus Christ.

June 24

REMEMBER

Mary (first century), the sister of Martha and Lazarus, modeled the contemplative life that dwells in every person. Jesus affirmed her right to sit at his feet, thus opening the door for women to become students and followers—to move beyond their traditional role of serving.

READ

Psalm 87

PONDER

This psalm not only describes the vision of all nations turning toward Jerusalem, the "city of God" (v. 3), but it also prophetically points toward the church universal, or the celestial new Jerusalem. Nan C. Merrill chooses this last image for her paraphrase. "In the heavenly realm stands the City of Light; the Beloved welcomes all who come to its gate, all who have surrendered themselves to Love. . . . Among those who enter are the humble and kind, those who reflect peace and radiate integrity, those who have faced darkness with Love by their side. Prepare yourselves for the City of Light, all you who hear; for the Most High reigns there in glory. Your name is written in the holy register. . . . Those who live by the Spirit of Love will know joy and harmony in the everlasting Dance of the Cosmos!" (Ps. 87, PFP).

PRAYER/PRACTICE

Margaret Guenther, an Episcopal priest, spiritual director, and author, uses fresh images for spiritual direction. She describes direction as a ministry of hospitality in which the spiritual director becomes a host or innkeeper offering a welcoming, safe place for the guest to lay down burdens, clean up, and rest. The host puts aside personal needs to attend to the needs of the guest. He or she prepares for each person who comes, creates a comfortable and sheltered space, and invites the guest to sit awhile and tell his or her story. The host remains fully available to the guest yet knows when the visit is over.[10]

Who serves as an innkeeper for you, creating a welcoming space and sitting to listen to your story?

June 25

REMEMBER

Sadhu Sundar Singh (1889–1929), an Indian mystic, dressed as a holy man (in saffron robe and turban) and devoted his life to traveling as a pilgrim. Using parables to teach about Jesus, he carried the gospel to Nepal and Tibet.

READ

Psalm 88

PONDER

Usually lament psalms conclude by expressing confidence that God hears, responds, and merits praise. This lament has no such ending— no praise, only darkness. Psalm 88 exists for our darkest times, for times of utter despair, for times when death seems close and friends abandon us. It expresses our prayer when we are in the pit and the waves are up to our neck (vv. 6-7).

Yet even in the midst of desolation, we can pray. "Every day I call on you, O LORD" (v. 9). We can also complain to God. "Is your steadfast love declared in the grave?" (v. 11). "Why do you hide your face from me?" (v. 14). Though God makes no response in this psalm, the rest of scripture reveals that darkness and death do not have the last word.

PRAYER/PRACTICE

Margaret Guenther uses midwifery as another image for spiritual direction. As midwife the director remains present with the person throughout the process of giving birth to something new. Waiting, caring, and praying are essential because the process may be long and challenging. The director as midwife knows when to assist, how to hold, and when to interpret but also knows that the new creation is the directee's responsibility. The midwife, wise yet gentle, knows when to push and move ahead and when to refrain from pushing or trying too hard. The director as midwife shows loving detachment, great solidarity, and joins in the celebration of the new.[11]

Who has assisted you in birthing a new creation in your spiritual life? Thank God for the presence of these persons in your life.

June 26

REMEMBER

Kathleen Norris, a contemporary poet and author, wrote about her move from the city to a rural area, which prompted a discovery of a spiritual geography and a new openness to God.

READ

Psalm 89:1-4

PONDER

God's steadfast love and faithfulness form the theme for many songs of praise. These two strengths of God become the dominant chords, the strong melody in this psalm. Look back upon your life with all its ups and downs, hesitant steps, and nagging doubts. How has God demonstrated steady love and care? Name as many instances as possible of God's faithfulness on your pilgrim journey. What song of praise comes to your lips as you remember and give thanks? Perhaps you could write a song detailing how God has remained with you on your journey and letting all generations know of God's steadfast love and faithfulness.

PRAYER/PRACTICE

The spiritual director and directee decide together on the frequency and length of meetings (I usually meet my directees once a month for an hour or more), as well as the structure of the meeting, including how to begin and how to end. They set a time to evaluate the relationship. Marjorie Thompson suggests that the directee ask these evaluative questions: "Is this relationship helping me to grow in my way of understanding and relating to God? Is it helping me to connect my life and my faith? . . . Am I quite comfortable with my guide? Do I expect to be able to open up more and more freely, or is there something disturbing me?"[12] Use these questions to reflect on your experience of direction.

June 27

REMEMBER

Helen Keller (1880–1968), an author, lecturer, and advocate for persons with disabilities, turned her blindness into action and achievement, a witness to overcoming great obstacles.

READ

Psalm 89:5-18

PONDER

These verses form a glorious hymn to God, the creator and ruler of the seas, the heavens, and the earth. Even if at times chaotic powers like disasters and storms, symbolized by Rahab the sea monster, should erupt, God will subdue and silence them (v. 10). So the people gather for worship and offer a shout of joy (v. 15) as they celebrate God's acts of creation. "The heavens and the earth belong to you. And so does the world with all its people because you created them and everything else" (vv. 11-12, CEV). "The Right and Justice are the roots of your rule; Love and Truth are its fruits. Blessed are the people who know the passwords of praise, who shout on parade in the presence of GOD" (vv. 14-15, THE MESSAGE). Blessed and happy, we can join in "the festal shout" (v. 15).

PRAYER/PRACTICE

Sometimes the preaching, worship, and program life of the church seem sufficient for your growth in faith. Sometimes books feed your spiritual life. Sometimes small groups and the special friendship of a few serve to guide your spiritual journey. Yet times of transition or crises, times of uncertainty and doubt, or experiences of awe or darkness may awaken in you a yearning for someone to serve as a wise and faithful guide for your journey. Such persons, a precious grace in your life, extend God's blessings to you in a tangible and personal way. Give thanks for the rediscovery of the art and tradition of spiritual guidance as a part of the ministries of the wider church.

Call, write, or e-mail someone who does spiritual direction and thank that person for his or her ministry.

June 28

REMEMBER

Saint Irenaeus (c. 130–200), a second-century theologian, wrote against Gnostic, dualist beliefs that the spirit was more important than the body.

READ

Psalm 89:19-37

PONDER

The king of Israel symbolized God's presence among the people, and King David gave the clearest witness to the mighty presence of God. Chosen, anointed, and endowed, David carries out God's will on the earth, even over the waters of the sea (v. 25). God makes a covenant of faithfulness to all who follow in David's footsteps. Even if David's children abandon God's ways (and they do), God promises not to violate the covenant (vv. 30–34).

God has also made a covenant with us, to be our God. God remains faithful even when we wander off the path and venture after the gods of success, fame, wealth. God sent Jesus, a descendant of David, to remind us of the covenant and to bring us back to the heart of God.

PRAYER/PRACTICE

Revisit the practice of journaling, introduced in February, and write about your experience in spiritual direction if you have a spiritual guide, or write about whether you feel drawn to begin such a relationship.

With whom would you feel comfortable talking about your prayer life? Who has guided and helped you already in your spiritual life? Who helps you hear the voice of God? To whom would you turn for counsel in making a major decision about your vocation as a follower of Christ? Who listens to you with deep compassion?

June 29

REMEMBER

Peter (first century), a bold, outspoken, and very human apostle of Jesus, became a rock as a leader of the early church. Despite his denial of Jesus, he helped pave the way for ministry to the Gentiles.

READ

Psalm 89:38-48

PONDER

Though the psalmist makes no concrete historical reference, this part of the psalm seems to recall the time when the Babylonians destroyed the walls of Jerusalem and deported the king. The psalm has suddenly shifted. The covenant made to David, praised as glorious and unending in verses 19-37, now appears broken and renounced (v. 39). Once again with faith tested, the psalmist raises a lament, "How long, O LORD? Will you hide yourself forever?" (v. 46).

Gladness and sadness weave their way in our lives. Through all our experiences we turn to God in prayer, offering our praises and our laments. As the Andraé Crouch song says:

> Through it all,
> Through it all,
> Oh I've learned to trust in Jesus,
> I've learned to trust in God.
> Through it all,
> Through it all,
> Oh I've learned to depend on His Word.

© Copyright 1971. Renewed 1999 by Manna Music, Inc., 35255 Brooten Road, Pacific City, OR 97135. All rights reserved. Used by permission. (ASCAP)

PRAYER/PRACTICE

In honor of Peter, reach out to someone unlike you. As you meet people today, smile and greet them, perhaps with a small bow, to honor the spirit residing in each person. Strive this day to do a hidden kindness for someone, or write a note to someone who works to create understanding between different ethnic or religious groups.

June 30

REMEMBER

Paul (first century) moved from persecuting Christians to become Christianity's strongest missionary. He shaped the expanding mission of the church by opening its doors to Gentiles. His three missionary trips planted churches; his letters encouraged these churches and continue to encourage us today.

READ

Psalm 89:49-52

PONDER

The covenant seems broken—the promised line of kings descending from David disappears. Only a question remains: "Lord, where is your steadfast love of old, which by your faithfulness you swore to David?" (v. 49). The psalm began by praising God's love and faithfulness, but now only doubt and questions remain. "At this point, all that religion can do is to keep asking and thereby to keep the people in the presence of an absent God."[13]

Though the psalm ends with questions, the editors of the Psalms added verse 52 as the conclusion to book 3 of the Psalter to remind us that God goes beyond our questions and will raise us to praise: "Blessed be the LORD forever. Amen and Amen."

PRAYER/PRACTICE

In honor of Paul, write a letter today the old-fashioned way, with pen or pencil, to encourage someone in his or her walk with God. Take time to think of what you wish to say. Write about what gives you hope, about your faith and the spiritual practices that shape your life and give it meaning, about blessings you have received, and about God's amazing grace. Offer God's comfort, peace, and strength for whatever situations the person faces. Say a prayer over the letter, and perhaps draw a small cross at the top of the letter to symbolize your prayer. Send the letter with your love and prayers, asking God to bless the recipient.

July

Bountiful God, you fill the earth with beauty,
painting breathtaking sunsets and
splashing colors into bouquets of flowers.
Let me bloom this month.
Let my life bring light and color into your world.
Let me shine for you, play for you, delight in you.
Open me to the miracles of summer,
the flowering of praise,
the sunshine of song. Amen.

July 1

Georgia O'Keeffe (1887–1986), an American artist known for her portrayal of flowers, revealed colors and sights often missed in her large closeups of poppies, iris, and other flowers. She also painted landscapes of the U.S. Southwest, which became her adopted home.

READ

Psalm 90:1-2

PONDER

The fourth book of the Psalms begins with a glorious affirmation of God: "You have been our dwelling place in all generations" (v. 1). We, and everyone before us, have found a haven, a home, a resting place in God. Home remains a positive image for most people, a place of shelter, love, and nurture. Home is where we learn our name, learn to talk, sense our responsibility, learn our story. The psalmist clearly intends and evokes positive feelings in the use of the appealing language of childbirth, "brought forth . . . formed" (v. 2). God created the world. God shaped and formed humanity through all time and for all generations. God invites us to discover our true home, abiding in our Creator's heart.

PRAYER/PRACTICE

Artists help you see in a new way. Georgia O'Keeffe transformed ordinary flowers and wilderness landscapes into huge flowers and stark landscapes. Her paintings encourage viewers to take a closer look at objects they might normally pass by without noticing.

At one retreat I attended, our leader brought a large book of Georgia O'Keeffe flower paintings. She played a recording of gentle music and invited us to immerse ourselves in receiving beauty. The music and pictures soothed my weary soul. I saw flowers in a new way. I marveled at the depth and beauty at the center of each flower. I let the colors enrich me and smiled at the boldness of O'Keefe's work. I felt renewed and given new sight.

What artist helps you see and touches your spirit?

July 2

REMEMBER

The fourteenth-century author of *The Cloud of Unknowing*, an unknown English mystical writer, lifted up the contemplative life and encouraged the abandoning of all images and concepts of the divine.

READ

Psalm 90:3-6

PONDER

Compared to God, human life seems brief, like "tender grass that sprouts and grows in the morning but dries up by evening" (vv. 5-6, CEV). In the grand sweep of existence, one person's life span appears short, and death comes all too quickly. The psalmist helps us maintain a sense of perspective without overexaggerating our importance or diminishing our worth.

If tempted to despair about our brief existence, we can recall Jesus' admonition that worry cannot add a single hour to our life span (Luke 12:25), and we can remember that Jesus came that we might have abundant life (John 10:10). Knowing that our life is brief can compel us to make each day count, to fill each day with joy and service, and to acknowledge that all our days belong to God.

PRAYER/PRACTICE

For the next few days I invite you to look at prayer with and for children. You may be tempted to skip these reflections if you do not have children at home, but I hope you recognize that children have much to teach us about prayer. Children comprise our faith communities, extended families, and friendship networks, and Jesus encouraged us to become like children (Matt. 18:3). Adapt and use the suggestions to fit your situation and encourage your growth in prayer.

Today remember the many ways you learned patterns of prayer at home. Perhaps you watched your parents say grace before a meal or you prayed together at bedtime. Maybe you lit candles for Advent and read scripture during Lent in preparation for Easter. Give thanks for parents and others who helped you on your journey of faith.

July 3

REMEMBER

Thomas (first century), the disciple of Jesus remembered as "Doubting Thomas," exclaimed, "My Lord and my God!" (John 20:28). Believed to be the first missionary to India, Thomas suffered martyrdom there.

READ

Psalm 90:7-10

PONDER

Who lives with integrity? Who has no regrets? "You [God] see clearly all our sins in the piercing light of your presence. All our days wither beneath your glance, our lives disappear like a sigh" (vv. 8-9, AP). The psalmist looks back over life and feels humbled, grieved, and distraught by the errors, sins, and troubles. We know, however, that God's anger remains tempered by mercy and forgiveness. God's anger exists as disappointment; God's forgiveness brings renewal. God prunes and reproves so that we might be more productive and more faithful. Acknowledging our sins becomes the first step to receiving God's forgiveness. Acknowledging the brevity and hardship of life gives impetus to seek God's guidance.

PRAYER/PRACTICE

Faith is often caught as much as taught. Children catch a spiritual life as families pray together, celebrate the church seasons, read the Bible, develop rituals for special occasions, attend church, practice compassion, and honor differences. You cannot give or impose faith on children, but you can share faith with them. The church becomes an extended community that supports parents and children in their quest for faith.

Remember and give thanks for the ways your family shared Bible stories as you were growing up. Think of the Bibles in your current home. Does your family use them? Do children have their own Bibles? When does your family read the Bible? (For a questionnaire that helps families review their spiritual practices, see Appendix A.)

July 4

REMEMBER

Mark Twain (1835–1910), an American author and satirist, helped the United States see its national life more clearly. Give thanks for the Declaration of Independence signed on this day.

READ

Psalm 90:11-12

PONDER

Every precious day counts. In the opening verses of today's passage, the psalmist contrasts God's greatness with human limitations. But rather than despairing over the enormous gap, the psalmist asks God to teach the way to make use of every day and so to gain a heart of wisdom. Out of disparity comes a prayer of longing and hope: "Teach us to use wisely all the time we have" (v. 12, CEV).

I invite you to pray the following prayer, attributed to Richard of Chichester in the thirteenth century:

> Day by day, dear Lord, of Thee three things I pray:
> to see Thee more clearly,
> love Thee more dearly,
> follow Thee more nearly, day by day.[1]

PRAYER/PRACTICE

One Fourth of July, I penned these words for a worship gathering:

> From shore to shore
> Let God's praise be sung.
> From mountain highs to valleys low
> Let the echo of praise resound.
> From the mouths of children and the prayers of saints
> Let thanksgivings abound.

Invite your family to join in writing a prayer for this Fourth of July. Consider a time to lift up the contributions of many different nationalities in creating a nation.

July 5

REMEMBER

Georges Bernanos (1888–1948), a French novelist, wrote *The Diary of a Country Priest,* the story of a young preacher's humble ministry.

READ

Psalm 90:13-17

PONDER

"How long?" This frequent refrain from the Psalms still echoes in prayers today. How long before the poor are fed? How long will *cancer* and *AIDS* be words that send fear into our hearts? How long will fighting continue in the Middle East? How long before we accept people of different races, socioeconomic levels, religions, and sexual orientations?

The psalmist asks God to "Make our future as happy as our past was sad" (v. 15, JB). That request still resounds in prayers today.

Psalm 90 ends with a prayer for the ordinary tasks of each day, "Let the loveliness of our Lord, our God, rest on us, confirming the work that we do. Oh, yes. Affirm the work that we do!" (v. 17, THE MESSAGE). Give thanks for your hands and the tasks they will do today.

PRAYER/PRACTICE

Mealtimes provide opportunities for prayer at home. A prayer before eating acknowledges the bounty of the Creator who provides food for us to eat. Many families and individuals speak a memorized blessing. Others hold hands and offer silent prayers. Still other families pray spontaneous prayers, often as simple as everyone naming something for which he or she thanks God. Families may rotate the responsibility for leading the prayer, fully involving children.

Memorized prayers can be simple: "God is great. God is good. Let us thank God for our food. Amen." They can be sung, as in the Johnny Appleseed Grace: "Oh, the Lord is good to me and so I thank the Lord / For giving me the things I need, / the sun and the rain and the apple seed. / Oh, the Lord is good to me."

See Appendix A for books containing table graces and other prayers.

July 6

REMEMBER

Jan Hus (1372–1415), a Czech priest, reformer, and martyr, advocated a spirituality for laypeople through deeper knowledge of scripture.

READ

Psalm 91:1-6

PONDER

Trouble comes in all shapes and sizes; evil wears many disguises. Yet God's love and protection remains broad and varied, strong and true. God is a refuge and fortress to which we can go for protection (v. 2). God will cover us as an eagle protects her young (vv. 3-4). Resting beneath God's wings is a powerful image of warmth and security, of a mother's strength and caring. This psalm provides a nighttime prayer: "I will not fear the shadows of the night, nor the confusion that comes by day, Nor the dreams that awaken me from sleep, nor the daily changes that life brings" (vv. 5-6, PFP). As you let this assurance of God's protection enfold you, you might pray: "Almighty God: . . . grant that I may be more expectant of your protective care than fearful of the dangers of evil."[2]

PRAYER/PRACTICE

Our family created a prayer with motions.

> Loving Jesus, be our holy guest. *(Pretend to open a door.)*
> Our morning joy, our evening rest. *(Raise one arm in an arc like the sun going up and then going down.)*
> And with this food to us impart *(Reach out hands over the food to bless it; then bring the hands to the mouth.)*
> Justice and peace to every heart. *(Draw the letter J in the air; then move your hands like a peaceful flowing river, finally bringing them to rest on your heart.)*

Try praying this prayer at mealtime, or create your own prayer. Consider using motions.

July 7

REMEMBER

Ludwig van Beethoven (1770–1827), a German composer, battled hearing loss but still composed ten symphonies. His music, including an arrangement of the glorious "Ode to Joy," echoes through choirs and instruments in thousands of churches.

READ

Psalm 91:7-13

PONDER

The killing of thousands of Jews in the gas chambers in World War II, the assassinations of leaders like Gandhi and Martin Luther King Jr., and the terrorist attacks that toppled the World Trade Center towers raise doubts about the protection promised in this psalm. Where were the guardian angels? Where was the safe dwelling place?

A literal reading of the psalm seems to indicate that the faithful will not suffer any more trouble. However, an awareness of the use of metaphor in this psalm reminds the faithful that God and the angels will be present in times of peril. Though we walk among those who roar like an lion or strike like an adder, God abides with us.

PRAYER/PRACTICE

Singing provides a wonderful way to help children learn to pray. The doxology used in many churches can be sung before a meal.

> Praise God, from whom all blessings flow;
> Praise God, all creatures here below;
> Praise God above, ye heavenly host:
> Creator, Christ, and Holy Ghost. Amen.[3]

Songs like "Jesus Loves Me" and "Jesus Loves the Little Children" contain great truths. If you have children, be sure to include songs that teach spiritual truths in the music you provide for your children.

Give thanks for music in your life. If possible, listen to a recording of Beethoven's music today.

July 8

REMEMBER

Jean Vanier (b. 1928), a Canadian Christian and author, founded L'Arche in 1964 in France. L'Arche provides a home for developmentally disabled and able-bodied persons living together in community. Today more than 120 L'Arche communities exist in thirty countries.

READ

Psalm 91:14-16

PONDER

God makes promises and keeps them. If we love God and acknowledge God as our ruler, God will deliver and protect us (v. 14). God will answer, accompany, rescue, and honor (v. 15). God will give a long life to the faithful and will save them (v. 16).

Our responsibility as faithful persons is to continually seek God, to surrender our need to control, and to pray always. We turn our lives toward God and trust that God works in our lives and in the world.

Jean Vanier left a successful naval and academic career to answer God's call to form a new kind of Christian community based on the Beatitudes. This community would bring persons who were mentally and developmentally disabled into a living relationship with able-bodied caregivers. The psalmist invites a turning toward the One who births new creations, who rescues the disabled from neglect.

PRAYER/PRACTICE

"In probably every culture and period of history, a shared meal has symbolized solidarity, peace, mutual trust, and joyful friendliness."[4] Whether the shared meal occurs when a child invites a friend for peanut-butter-and-jelly sandwiches; or when disabled persons eat at the same table as able-bodied ones at L'Arche; or when U.S. President Jimmy Carter invited Anwar Sadat and Menachem Begin to Camp David, Maryland, to talk about peace; the fellowship and sharing that happen at a table constitute another blessing from God.

Give thanks for people who have shared a meal with you. Recall meals when the conversation and food became a feast of delight.

July 9

REMEMBER

Theophan the Recluse (1815–1894), a Russian Orthodox bishop and author, taught the need to pray with the heart and not just the mind. He encouraged and led the way in promoting use of the Jesus Prayer.

READ

Psalm 92:1-4

PONDER

Some peak religious experience, some moment of deliverance lies behind this psalm of praise and thanksgiving. Though we do not know the reason for the psalmist's gratitude, we can join in the exuberant chorus. It is right and good to give thanks continually to God in prayer, to praise God with songs and all kinds of instruments, to begin each morning with praise on our lips, and to end each day by thanking God. We find delight in cooperating with the work of God and in celebrating all of God's good gifts. This psalm teaches us to give thanks all through the day and to rest in praise all through the night.

PRAYER/PRACTICE

The tradition of blessing prayers (May 5) may have started with blessing a meal. Biblical people realized their daily dependence on God for food and began their meals by blessing God for God's bountiful kindness. Typically the prayer began, "Blessed are you, O Lord our God, King of the universe, who brings forth bread from the earth."

At one retreat center I visit, the group not only says a blessing before the meal but also afterward. When everyone finishes eating, all stand, push their chairs in toward the table, and one leader prays. I cannot remember the exact words, but they may form another blessing prayer: "Blessed is God of whose bounty we have partaken. Blessed be God through whose goodness we live."[5]

Today, either by yourself or with your family, add a postmeal blessing. Begin with "Blessed are you, O Lord our God. . . ."

July 10

REMEMBER

Mary McLeod Bethune (1875–1955), the daughter of slaves, became an educator who founded an institute for girls at a time when few places existed for African American girls to further their education. She served as president of Bethune-Cookman College and as a special advisor to Franklin D. Roosevelt on the problems of minority groups.

READ

Psalm 92:5-11

PONDER

If we have eyes to see, God's wonders and works abound everywhere. Such an awareness of God's presence looks deeply into the ordinary and discovers "how great are your works, O LORD" (v. 5). The fools, the ignorant, the busy, the arrogant, and the wicked cannot see or understand the holy in the midst of the ordinary. Those after a quick dollar, instant success, and the fast track will wither away like grass (v. 7), but the faithful ones, the visionaries, see the depths of God's thoughts and deeds. The faithful remain strong and receive God's oil of blessing (v. 10). They witness the downfall of the wicked. This psalm encourages us to stay close to God.

PRAYER/PRACTICE

Another natural time for family prayer occurs at bedtime. For some children, the night appears filled with fearsome darkness and monsters under the bed. Older children and adults may experience nightmares. Prayer at night provides an opportunity to deepen trust in God, who watches through the night. Psalm 4:8 offers a calming bedtime reminder: "I will both lie down and sleep in peace; for you alone, O LORD, make me lie down in safety."

Our family created a simple melody for these words:

Keep us, God, as we wake and guard us as we sleep.
So may we wake with Christ and take our rest in peace.

What pattern of prayer do you observe at bedtime?

July 11

REMEMBER

Saint Benedict (480–550), one of the most important figures in church life, established a Rule for community life that has principally guided Western monasticism for over fifteen hundred years. His Rule encouraged humility, obedience, and stability.

READ

Psalm 92:12-15

PONDER

The psalmist compares the righteous person to a tree, and the Hebrews did not regard any tree more highly than the cedar of Lebanon. The mighty cedars seemed to reach to the heavens, and their large diameter provided beautiful wood for the temple in Jerusalem. Just as a tree planted by the water will always be green (v. 14), a person rooted in God's love will produce deeds of compassion and acts of kindness. A person planted in worship and prayer still produces fruit in old age and remains filled with sap, which could be understood as the wild, creative joy of the Holy Spirit. May the sap of God's spirit and love flow in us all the days of our lives.

PRAYER/PRACTICE

Bedtime prayers can be learned or spontaneous. Many families use this traditional bedtime prayer: "Now I lay me down to sleep. I pray the Lord my soul to keep. If I should die before I wake, I pray the Lord my soul to take." For some parents, this prayer speaks too explicitly about death. For others, it becomes a testimony of faith that in living or dying, we belong to God.

Many families use bedtime prayers as an opportunity for blessing and intercession. A child may begin a time of spontaneous prayer with "God bless . . ." Relatives, friends, and often surprising others (people and things!) get included in the blessing prayers. Or a parent may invite the child to remember people or situations that need God's care. "God, please take care of . . ."

Take time to offer blessings or intercessions today.

July 12

REMEMBER

Saint Veronica (first century), according to legend, wiped the face of Christ with her veil as he carried his cross to Calvary, and her veil miraculously retained the imprint of his face.

READ

Psalm 93

PONDER

The psalmist uses imaginative language to proclaim that God, supreme as king, rules the world. The Creator, robed in majesty, sits upon a throne. Though the world dwells securely under the guidance of the strong ruler, at the same time, it receives continuous threats. Often our days encompass a mixture of God's peaceful assurance that all is well with our worry that problems and disasters will soon overwhelm us. We make it through our crazy days by holding on to God's decrees (v. 5) and trusting in God's guidance.

PRAYER/PRACTICE

In *Prayers for the Domestic Church*, Edward Hays offers a pattern for night prayer. Try this pattern, inserting your needs and others'.

> My Lord, Beloved Source of All That Is,
> I bow before You as I come to the end of my day. . . .
> I thank You for all the sun-touched gifts of this day.
> *Pause for silent reflection*
> I ask Your mercy for the times, this day, when I have forgotten to be
>   kind and compassionate.
> I am sorry for the times when I have rushed through the mystery of
>   life, blind to the needs of others or to the beauties of creation. . . .
> *Period of silent prayer or meditation*
> My Lord and God, . . . I praise and adore You. . . .Wrapped in grati-
>   tude, I now place before You my personal needs: _____
>   (as well as the needs of others: _____).
> Lord of the Day and Night, of Life and Death,
> I place myself into Your holy hands.[6]

July 13

REMEMBER

Michelangelo (1475–1564) expressed his artistic talents as a sculptor, painter, architect, and poet. The subjects for his works included the story of creation and Mary receiving the body of Christ from the cross.

READ

Psalm 94:1-11

PONDER

Truly a Renaissance man, Michelangelo employed a variety of artistic methods to reveal traces of God in stone and to show the face of God in colors and forms. He revealed the mark of the Creator by showing the beauty of the human body. He helped us see and appreciate God's world.

Likewise, this psalm helps us see not the good that we do, but the arrogance and wickedness of our ways when we oppress the widow, the foreigner, and the orphan (v. 6). We are foolish if we think God does not know, see, or hear what we think, do, or say.

PRAYER/PRACTICE

I find comfort and peace in praying prayers from the Celtic tradition. The community of Christians at Iona, Scotland, has kept alive some deeply poetic and wonderfully creative prayers that come from people who celebrated the essential goodness of all created life. The early Celtic Christians lived close to the earth and surrounded by the sea. This nighttime prayer comes from Iona:

> O Christ, you are a bright flame before me.
> You are a guiding star above me.
> You are the light and love I see in others' eyes.
> Keep me, O Christ, in a love that is tender.
> Keep me, O Christ, in a love that is true.
> Keep me, O Christ, in a love that is strong
> Tonight, tomorrow, and always.[7]

What prayers from other faith traditions do you incorporate into your prayers?

July 14

REMEMBER

George MacDonald (1824–1905), a Scottish clergyman, novelist, and poet, wrote fantasy books that still amaze children and adults today.

READ

Psalm 94:12-15

PONDER

Childhood experiences of punishment often give a negative tone to the word *discipline,* yet the psalmist welcomes the discipline of God (v. 12). In this context, discipline exists as the instruction, correction, and guidance of a loving God. Discipline provides training to live a life marked by charity and joy, confident that God will sustain us in times of trouble (v. 13), will remember our names and our community (v. 14), and will bring the wicked to justice and bring peace to the honest (v. 15). Because God cares so much for us, God seeks to guide and teach us and even sent the best teacher (Jesus) to show us how to live a happy, disciplined life.

PRAYER/PRACTICE

Pray the following prayer for your children or for children you know:

> God of the young and old, I offer this prayer for the children in my life: I pray that you will grant them full and joyous days, filled with wonder at things both grand and small, filled with times of silence and awe and times of exuberance and laughter. Show them the joy of sharing, the blessings of giving, and the satisfaction of serving. May they know comfort for their tears, assurance in their sadness, and hope in their disappointments. Guide them to a deeper faith in you, and may my words and deeds reflect your grace and forgiveness that they may be led to know you and believe in you. God of life, let them know not only the stories about Jesus but also the love of Jesus. Protect them in your grace and sustain them with your Spirit that in all their days, they may rejoice and dance in your presence. Amen.

July 15

REMEMBER

Saint Bonaventure (1221–1274), known as the second founder of the Franciscans, balanced the radical freedom of Saint Francis of Assisi with the need for rules and order in a new community.

READ

Psalm 94:16-23

PONDER

These ancient verses speak to our contemporary times, for we fight many of our struggles for justice and fairness against those who "contrive mischief by statute" (v. 20). Congressional bills often favor one group over another, often favor the rich over the poor, authorize cutting down old-growth forests in favor of oil exploration, or cut funding for education in favor of keeping funds for missile defense systems. The psalmist asks, "Who stands up for me against evildoers?" (v. 16).

Standing up for justice is not easy, yet the psalmist affirms, "When I felt my feet slipping, you came with your love and kept me steady. And when I was burdened with worries, you comforted me and made me feel secure" (vv. 18-19, CEV). God, our stronghold and refuge, will bring justice, so we must continue to seek justice.

PRAYER/PRACTICE

The seasons of the church year provide another opportunity for prayer and worship in the home. Many families prepare for the birth of Christ by creating Advent wreaths. The wreaths, made from evergreens and placed on a wood, metal, or Styrofoam circle, hold four candles to mark the four weeks until Christmas. Prayers, readings, and songs become part of each night's ritual of lighting the Advent candles. Many families also set up nativity scenes that show Mary, Joseph, shepherds, angels, animals, and kings. In these ways and with other decorations, the house and hopefully the heart prepares to receive the birth of Christ.

Even in July, think about ways you prepare for Christmas. How would you like to prepare differently this year? How can you involve children?

July 16

REMEMBER

Bartolomé de Las Casas (1484–1566), a Roman Catholic priest, opposed the mistreatment of the native peoples in the Americas and saw in their suffering the death of Christ repeated again and again.

READ

Psalm 95:1-5

PONDER

Some psalms focus more on individual prayer and reflection, while others clearly call for a community response. The verses of this psalm have often been used to call faith communities together for worship. "O come, let us sing to the LORD; let us make a joyful noise to the rock of our salvation!" (v. 1).

In the temple in Jerusalem, the psalm was sung as the procession moved into the gates for worship. The crowd moved with sounds of instruments and singing. The people gathered to praise God, mighty Creator of everything low and all things above, ruler of the ocean depths and the sky above, maker of the earth and everything that moves. These verses are just as valid for worship today.

PRAYER/PRACTICE

Home remains a place to learn about and commemorate the life of Jesus. During Epiphany, our family hangs stars around the house and puts several sets of Magi and camels on tables. We display pictures of people from other countries as a reminder that the Light of the world has come for all. During Lent we count down the weeks to Easter by lighting candles and saying prayers. For Easter one year, we fashioned a tomb out of clay and put a candle inside. Each night we rolled away the stone, lit the candle, and told where we saw light or new life happening that day. At Eastertime we display butterflies around the house as symbols of new life. On Pentecost, we wear red to church, display doves around the house, and put a red tablecloth on the table.

How do you celebrate the church seasons in your home? How are the house and your prayers different?

July 17

REMEMBER

Isaac Penington (1616–1679) joined George Fox and the early Quakers in England and became one of the leaders of the new movement. He wrote eloquently about mysticism and the divine presence within each person.

READ

Psalm 95:6-11

PONDER

Scholars believe this psalm may have been used as worshipers moved through the courtyards of the temple in Jerusalem. The procession sang praise before entering the Gentiles' courtyard, and then again as they passed through the gate to the women's court, bowing and kneeling in the presence of "the LORD, our Maker" (v. 6). Often in contemporary worship services, after a time of praise, there is time for confession, a way of bowing, kneeling, and acknowledging our humanness and our mistakes in the presence of the Good Shepherd.

The subsequent verses sound like the scripture and sermon of the day, reminding the people of a time during the Exodus when the Israelites complained about the lack of water (Exod. 17:1-7). The priest (or preacher in our time) warns the people against having hard hearts (v. 8) and encourages them to be obedient so that they may enter into God's rest (vv. 10-11). The psalm gives order to our worship and instructions for living faithful and obedient lives.

PRAYER/PRACTICE

A child looks at the world with wide, inquisitive eyes. All of creation teems with wonder. Bugs, flowers, lizards, and even dirt merit the child's time and attention. The simplest acts take on holy significance. To see the world through a child's eyes—to see newness and wonder everywhere, to not rush past the small and insignificant—can be a real spiritual discipline. Today remain aware of really seeing the world around you, of not hurrying past people or God's creation. Try to see the world afresh, filled with the grandeur of God. Record in your journal your sights and insights.

July 18

REMEMBER

Nelson Mandela (b. 1918), a leader in the struggle to overthrow the oppressive apartheid government in South Africa, endured many years in prison before becoming the first black president of South Africa.

READ

Psalm 96:1-6

PONDER

Sing God a new song, the psalmist says in verse 1. When Isaiah encouraged the exiles in Babylon to remain faithful because God would deliver them, he also said, "Sing to the LORD a new song" (Isa. 42:10). When the dictator of Chile was overthrown in the 1960s, the people sang a new song, and other Latin American countries hoping for liberation and justice developed their own *nuevo cancion* ("new song"). When hope abounds and God's justice draws near, the time arises for a new song, a song of salvation, a song of praise to tell of God's marvelous works among all the peoples (v. 4).

PRAYER/PRACTICE

Writer and parent Anne Broyles marched in a demonstration for peace in Central America. She walked with her children and later reflected on the experience: "I walked not only for myself and my convictions; I walked also as the parent of a three-year-old daughter and an infant son. I walked because I wanted my children to begin to realize that God's power can transform the bleakest situation, even the most evil of deeds. . . . I shared with each of my children my faith that God is ultimately in charge of the world."[8]

Many activities can be done with children and youth to develop their concern for the world and to encourage them to work for justice and peace for everyone. All ages can participate in making signs for demonstrations; recycling bottles, cans, and paper; writing letters to Congress; and praying for peace. Compassion knows no age limit and forms an important part of putting one's faith into action. (See Appendix A.)

July 19

REMEMBER

The Seneca Falls Convention, on July 19–20, 1848, in Seneca Falls, New York, launched the women's suffrage movement in the United States— the struggle for equal rights for women, especially the right to vote.

READ

Psalm 96:7-13

PONDER

Many ancient people feared the coming of their gods, but the Jews welcomed the coming of the Lord, because God will set the world aright and restore the nations to order. Not only do the people look forward to God's appearance, but also the heavens exude gladness, the earth rejoices, the seas roar, and even the trees sing for joy at the coming of the Lord (vv. 11-13). Worship in the sanctuary, with the community's songs of praise and offerings of service, seems to combine with all of creation in proclaiming that God rules and will bring justice: "Let's hear it from Sky, with Earth joining in, and a huge round of applause from Sea" (v. 11, THE MESSAGE).

PRAYER/PRACTICE

Most parents realize they hold their children only for a short time. Wise parents try to give children roots in family, faith, and community traditions. They seek to encourage their children's independence and sense of adventure, all the while hoping their offspring do not experience too many skinned knees, broken hearts, or disappointed dreams. Loving parents stand in the background, saying, "Go for it," "Try again," and "We love you." They place their children in God's hands, trusting that God will go with them into every future.

What prayer do you pray for your children or for the children of the world? How can you support parents in their quest to give children roots and wings? What legislation concerning children or parents needs support on this day when we remember women working for full participation in community life?

July 20

REMEMBER

Lao-tzu (sixth century B.C.E.), a Chinese philosopher considered the founder of Taoism, presumably wrote the religious teachings and wise thoughts of the *Tao-te Ching*.

READ

Psalm 97:1-9

PONDER

Clouds, earthquakes, lightning, and blazing skies, some of the climactic and sensational images from this psalm, spoke to the Hebrews of God's majesty and power. Dramatic sights in creation may have helped them recall the fiery pillar that led the Israelites out of Egypt or the smoke and clouds that hid Moses as he received the Ten Commandments. Remembering those pivotal events in their history and seeing the grandeur of God in creation helps them know that idolaters are bragging fools, worshiping nothing but useless idols, empty gods (v. 7). God will not only rule the universe but will also bring about justice and freedom from captivity. Once again, God reigns; God rules creation and all peoples, so let the farthest known lands be glad (v. 1). God rules.

PRAYER/PRACTICE

Buddhist monk Thich Nhat Hanh describes children as "a bell of mindfulness, reminding us how wonderful life is." As a way of encouraging young people to respond positively to life, society, and the earth, Nhat Hanh teaches a simple breath prayer to use while walking: With every inhalation, say, "Oui, oui, oui" ("Yes, yes, yes"); with every exhalation, say, "Merci, merci, merci" ("Thanks, thanks, thanks").[9]

Today, if possible, take a walk with a child. Pay attention to the child's pace and adjust yours as needed. Listen to the child and try to see the world through his or her eyes. Or take a walk by yourself and practice the above breath prayer. Try speaking the French words.

July 21

REMEMBER

Albert Luthuli (1898–1967), a leader in the African National Congress, which fought against apartheid and for freedom in South Africa, reminded people that Christianity included all people—not just whites.

READ

Psalm 97:10-12

PONDER

"Light dawns for the righteous, and joy for the upright in heart" (v. 11). Light and joy arise as the companions of those who struggle for justice. The fight against apartheid in South Africa was led by people of integrity and faith who carried light and joy in the midst of the darkness of oppression. "God loves those who hate evil; God protects and keeps safe their faithful lives and breaks the hold of the wicked" (v. 10, AP). Justice may take awhile to achieve; it may involve a long struggle or a difficult journey, but as long as we keep up the hope and the effort and let God's light and joy permeate our lives, God faithfully will bring a new and just day.

PRAYER/PRACTICE

Family events and occasions provide opportunities to pray. When a baby is born, blessings and prayers can be said after the birth and when the baby arrives home. Birthdays offer a time to pray a special blessing for the child and the new year. House blessings and room blessings can help a family transition into a new space. New pets or the death of a beloved pet often call forth rituals and prayers. Anniversaries of baptisms can be celebrated by lighting the child's baptismal candle (many churches give a candle to individuals as a reminder of their baptism). The beginning of the school year invites a time for a special blessing for learning and growth. When anger or hurt has occurred in a home, families can participate in a prayer for forgiveness or a liturgy for reconciliation to bring back God's harmony.

Look at your calendar. What coming occasions provide opportunity for celebration, prayers, and blessings?

July 22

REMEMBER

Mary Magdalene (first century), an early follower of Jesus, carried the Easter message from the tomb to the disciples: "I have seen the Lord" (John 20:18).

READ

John 20:1-18

PONDER

The Gospels include some surprising saints. In a time when women were seen but not heard, when pious male Jews would cross to the other side of the street to avoid contact with a woman, Jesus amazingly included women among his closest followers. Luke 8:2 describes Mary Magdalene as one from whom Christ had cast seven demons. In the accounts of the Resurrection, she holds a central place as one of the women who go to anoint the body of Jesus and then as the one who mistakes Jesus for the gardener. Though her eyes were bleary from tears, her heart could see, and she bore witness to the Resurrection.

Mary Magdalene is the patron saint of those who have loved much and have been forgiven much. She provides a model for women sharing the good news.

PRAYER/PRACTICE

Children and adults love stories. Children need to know the stories of people of faith. The Bible "rocks" with exciting adventures like the stories of Jonah, Moses and the Exodus, Joshua, Queen Esther, King David, and the prophet Elijah. Scripture also contains many stories of transformation; Mary Magdalene and Paul are just two examples of how God can work changes in the hearts of women and men. In addition to the biblical accounts, stories of the saints—amazing men and women, ancient and new—show and teach courage and faithfulness. You can find books about many saints mentioned in *Openings*. See Appendix A (books about saints are listed throughout), and look in the biography section at the library or your favorite bookstore.

July 23

REMEMBER

Saint John Cassian (360–433), one of the desert fathers, wrote that the desert practices are not for self-denial but become the tools for moving to deeper love—the goal of the ascetic life.

READ

Psalm 98

PONDER

As with Psalm 96, the psalmist again wants to sing a new song to commemorate the release of the captives from Babylon. This new song recognizes the new exodus, for again God has heard the cries of the people and led the people home from exile. "All the ends of the earth have seen the victory of our God" (v. 3).

This psalm gives us a glimpse into the music at worship services in ancient times: The lyre, trumpets, and horns accompany the new song, with voices and instruments all making a joyful noise to the Lord (vv. 5-6). The whole earth celebrates the coming of the Lord.

PRAYER/PRACTICE

Summer provides a break from the normal routines of work and school. As I was growing up, my family alternated kinds of vacations. One summer we would rent a cabin on a lake and enjoy swimming, boating, playing games, working puzzles, and exploring communities near the lake. The next summer we would take a traveling vacation and stay in motels as we visited distant geographical areas. Vacations provide time for deepening relationships, but they also provide times of spiritual renewal. Some people choose to spend their vacation at a retreat center. Often they select a center with a totally different environment from their home and one that offers courses of study and time for relaxation and recreation. Families can choose special family weeks at some retreat centers.

Imagine taking a vacation with God. Where would you go? What would you do?

July 24

REMEMBER

Ammon Hennacy (1893–1970) converted to Christianity while in prison for refusing to register for the draft. He found a revolutionary Jesus who worked to change each heart. He worked with Dorothy Day at the New York Catholic Worker and constantly advocated for peace.

READ

Psalm 99

PONDER

Scholars place this psalm as the last in a group known as the kingship of Yahweh psalms, or the enthronement psalms (Pss. 93, 95–99). The psalmist proclaims God as ruler on high, creator of the universe, great and exalted over all people, holy and just (vv. 2-4). God's love, forgiveness, and compassion inspire all of creation to worship (v. 5). Yet, at the same time, we tremble (v. 1) at the awesome power, the holy mystery, the infinite wisdom of God. We live and worship in the balance, awed by God's holiness and power and welcomed by God's compassion, justice, and forgiveness.

PRAYER/PRACTICE

Vacations provide an opportunity to visit other countries and explore other cultures. God created an immense and colorful variety of people and cultures. "God looked at all creation and saw that it was good—very good" (Gen. 1:31, AP). Before traveling to other countries, we would be wise to learn about their cultures so that we can visit with sensitivity, respect, and awareness. Some organizations, like Servas (see Appendix A), encourage travelers to stay in the homes of ordinary people of the host country. Such people-to-people visits build friendships and bridges of understanding. You might wish to make a retreat in a new country, whether it be attending an ashram in India or staying with the Taizé Community in France. Living with and praying with people in other countries can deepen the sense of oneness.

Remember a visit to a holy place in another country, or plan to make a pilgrimage to a religious center in the near future.

July 25

Remember

Walter Rauschenbusch (1861–1918), the foremost preacher and pastor of the social gospel movement, believed that the kingdom of God was not just for heaven but for every society on earth.

Read

Psalm 100

Ponder

This psalm implies a processional as people entered the gates of the Temple (v. 4). It remains one of the most popular psalms for worship, used often at morning prayer in monastic communities and as a call to worship in churches. The psalm urges us to praise, sing, worship, thank, and bless. It reminds us that we have much for which to be grateful. God made us, loves us, and forgives us. Our response is to make a joyful noise, worship with gladness, sing joyously, give thanks, and bless God's name (vv. 1, 2, 4)—and we can do all of this with even more enthusiasm because we know of God's great love for us in Jesus.

Prayer/Practice

Summer affords a good time to practice sabbath. The traditional meaning of sabbath comes from the creation story in Genesis, where God finished the work of creation and, on the seventh day, rested (Gen. 2:3). The Ten Commandments also speak to observance of sabbath: "Remember the sabbath day, and keep it holy" (Exod. 20:8). Scripture encourages and blesses a day of rest. For Jews, sabbath lasted from Friday sunset until Saturday sunset. Sabbath granted a day for prayer, worship, reflection, and no work (or minimal work in some traditions). It was truly for rest. Amazing. Despite only a five-day work week, most non-Jews in America do not rest. Weekends furnish time for catching up, shopping, doing household tasks, and family activities, and perhaps a hour for worship. Conversations about sabbath challenge one to create sacred space, holy moments, and days and periods of blessed rest.

Where do you find sabbaths in your life now?

July 26

REMEMBER

Saints Joachim and Anne (first century) are the names tradition has given to the parents of Mary, the mother of Jesus.

READ

Psalm 101

PONDER

This psalm portrays a leader, perhaps the king, reflecting on how the leader will serve God faithfully in personal and professional lives. "I refuse to be corrupt or to take part in anything crooked, and I won't be dishonest or deceitful" (vv. 3-4, CEV). The leader's household shall be a place of integrity. In the professional role, the leader seeks to rid the land of evil—to cleanse the city of God.

Historians say that George Washington prayed this psalm when he accepted command of the American forces in the Revolutionary War. The psalm supplies wisdom and counsel for all leaders. It invites probing and honest reflection on how we cultivate good qualities in our personal and professional lives and root out selfish pride, the haughty look, the arrogant heart (v. 5), and crafty deception.

PRAYER/PRACTICE

Rabbi Abraham Joshua Heschel wrote:

> Six days a week we wrestle with the world, wringing profit from the earth; on the Sabbath we especially care for the seed of eternity planted in the soul. The world has our hands, but our soul belongs to Someone Else.
>
> Six days a week we seek to dominate the world, on the seventh we try to dominate the self. Sabbath [is] a day of detachment from things, instruments and practical affairs as well as of attachment to the spirit.[10]

How much time in your day or week do you devote to sabbath rest and renewal? How do you care for the "seed of eternity" planted in your soul?

July 27

REMEMBER

Mechtild of Magdeburg (c. 1210–c. 1285), a German mystic, belonged to a community of mystics called the Beguines, most of them laywomen, who devoted themselves to prayer and to serving the poor.

READ

Psalm 102:1-17

PONDER

This, the fifth penitential psalm, expresses poignant pleas to God to hear the psalmist's distress and respond. The language sounds poetic and imaginative: "I am like a lonely bird on the housetop" (v. 7). "I eat ashes like bread, and mingle tears with my drink" (v. 9). "I wither away like grass" (v. 11). When we search for the right words in prayer, the Psalms have much to teach us and can supply us with a language.

Woven in this personal complaint rests a lament for the plight of Zion, which historically could refer to the exile and the destruction of Jerusalem. The psalmist speaks for individuals and the nation, express-ing grief and praying to God, "Let my cry come to you. Do not hide your face from me in the day of my distress" (vv. 1-2). When have the nation's problems and your distress flowed like one prayer?

PRAYER/PRACTICE

Though sabbath usually implies resting one day a week, we can move toward recovering sabbath by practicing smaller moments of sabbath each day. I call them *sabbath breaths.* They happen when you pause to honor the divine presence, the Holy Mystery, during the day—when you see a sunset and thank God, when you notice an eagle in flight and watch in awe, when you breathe in the fragrance of a fresh loaf of bread and let out a holy sigh. Activities such as walking, gardening, or playing with pets help take you out of the noise and stress of commerce. Moments of stillness, moments of awareness of God's creation, can restore the balance intended in keeping a sabbath rhythm to our lives. Take some sabbath breaths today.

July 28

REMEMBER

Stanley Rother (1935–1981), an Oklahoma farm boy turned priest, lived among the Tzutuhil Indians in Guatemala. He believed the church should be among the poor and was killed during the time of government oppression of the poor.

READ

Psalm 102:18-28

PONDER

In the midst of personal and national grief, the psalmist voices the word of hope, the promise of new life for the individual and for the nation. God looks down from on high "to hear the groans of the prisoners, to set free those who were doomed to die" (v. 20). Perhaps Stanley Rother was familiar with this psalm, its plea for justice, its awareness of grief and a shortened number of days (v. 23), and its promise of hope that all the oppressed shall gather together to worship and serve the Lord (v. 22).

PRAYER/PRACTICE

Sometimes on my morning walks, I sense my need for a longer time to spend with God, and then I know the short prayer walk must yield to a sabbath day or longer. I examine my schedule and plan a day when I can go to a retreat center. I look for a place with some green space where I can be outside and receive the blessings of creation. I look for a place with a worshiping community so that I may join with others in offering praise. I rest, quiet my mind, pray my breath prayer, walk, and spend time in meditation. I may take a spiritual book to read, but I try not to take work. I want silence and space so I can *be* more and do less. In my best years, I have taken a sabbath day each month. I seem a long way from taking a sabbath day each week.

When have you taken a sabbath day? When might you schedule one?

July 29

REMEMBER

Vincent van Gogh (1853–1890) expressed his compassion for suffering humanity through his art. He described his desire to "paint in men and women something of that quality of eternity which was symbolized formerly by a halo." His letters to his brother Theo reveal his passion for life.

READ

Psalm 103:1-5

PONDER

Other psalms praise God for creation, goodness, and beauty, but Psalm 103 acclaims God's compassion. This psalm nurtures the soul, caresses the heart, and evokes praise. It is a good psalm to commit to memory so that we do not forget that God forgives our sins, heals our illnesses, and redeems us from the fear of death (vv. 3-4). God "crowns you with faithful love and tenderness; he contents you with good things all your life, renews your youth like an eagle's" (vv. 4-5, NJB). We can let these words cascade over us when friends hurt us, our bodies fail us, fears overtake us, and schedules overwhelm us. God soars with us, renewing our strength like that of an eagle.

When the Hebrews said, "Bless the Lord," they meant, "Proclaim the greatness of God." This psalm gives plenty of reasons to bless the Lord.

PRAYER/PRACTICE

Just as nature can open us to the holy in our midst, so can art. One way to spend a sabbath day is visiting an art museum. Art museums usually offer quiet spaces that enable visitors to see with their inner eyes. Most museums encourage a slow, lingering pace, far from the places of worry and hurry, so you may encounter the holy. They provide a way to step out of business as usual into a contemplative space, set apart from the busy world.

Schedule a time when you can leisurely visit an art museum, especially one with van Gogh paintings. Look at a book of his paintings and read his letters to his brother Theo.

July 30

REMEMBER

William Wilberforce (1759–1833), an English evangelical Christian, devoted his parliamentary career to abolishing slavery.

READ

Psalm 103:6-18

PONDER

"The LORD is merciful and gracious, slow to anger and abounding in steadfast love" (v. 8). These often-repeated words first occurred in God's message to Moses after the Exodus (Exod. 34:6-7). They describe a God unlike any other gods. The other verses in this psalm add to the picture. God works justice for the oppressed (v. 6), removes our sins far, far away (vv. 11-12), and acts as compassionate and tender as a parent with a child (v. 13). This God indeed is like no other gods.

Many look to this passage for sustenance and confirmation that God desires justice, defends the oppressed, and remains steadfast in pursuing a new reign of compassion.

PRAYER/PRACTICE

Each year, I try to schedule one or two sabbath renewal times of three days or more. Often I am so tired from everyday life that I require a day to catch up on sleep before I am even ready to pray. It is hard to pray if weariness consumes one's thoughts and sleep overwhelms one's prayers. Three days allow time for the body to shift rhythms, the mind to slow down, and the spirit to open up. A deep resting in the embrace of God emerges—resting from creating, from working, from thinking, from economic concerns and relationship troubles. Sabbath time helps you take care of your soul, restore balance, and enjoy God.

Did you plan a retreat in June, or do you still need encouragement to set aside time for a longer sabbath with God?

July 31

REMEMBER

Saint Ignatius of Loyola (1491–1556) founded the Society of Jesus, commonly known as the Jesuits. His book *Spiritual Exercises* gives wise instructions for spiritual formation, using guided meditations and images. His writings also provide an orderly process for discernment questions and vocational issues.

READ

Psalm 103:19-22

PONDER

The psalm ends with the tender and compassionate God of the early verses uniting with the majestic and great God who rules over all. The whole world is invited to join in praising God: the angels, all peoples who do God's will, all of creation, and the psalmist too. The psalm echoes with the refrain, "Bless the LORD, O my soul" (v. 22). Perhaps this verse can become a refrain for you as you inhale and exhale. It will instill a spirit of gratitude and adoration in your prayer and in your often hectic journey through life. "Bless the Lord, O my soul."

PRAYER/PRACTICE

Barbara Troxell wrote that sabbath has three themes that weave into the practice of taking time for God. Sabbath is a time for contemplation, for resting in awareness of God, and silence and solitude become key components of this rest. Second, sabbath is "a time of companionship, of renewal with others . . . , keeping company with those who are dear to us and those with whom we reach out in hospitality.[11] Third, sabbath time provides for compassion, for restoration and reconciliation with a wounded society and a bruised creation. The Bible speaks of giving the earth a sabbath, of letting the land rest for a year every seven years (Exod. 23:10-11), and every fifty years, of celebrating a year of jubilee by giving land back to all the families and addressing inequalities (Lev. 25). Our times of rest can include caring for creation and for those in need. How are you weaving the three threads of sabbath into your life and spiritual practices?

August

Warming God, as the fruit and grain ripen
in your sunshine and showers,
so may I grow in love and compassion.
Ripen my sense of justice for all people,
especially the poor.
Deepen my gratitude for friends and family
who teach me to delight in each day.
Fill me with the joy of being fully awake
to your miracles all around me and within me. Amen.

August 1

REMEMBER

Sarah (B.C.E.), beloved wife of Abraham, laughed when God said she would bear a child in her old age. Their son, Isaac, became a leader of the chosen people.

READ

Genesis 18:1-15; 21:1-7

PONDER

God works in unusual and surprising ways. Some might respond to God's proposals by laughing. Sarah did. She laughed because she thought human limitations defined the actions of God. "Is anything too wonderful for the LORD?" God reminded her (Gen. 18:14).

Our scientific mind-set is both a blessing and a curse. We know many facts and figures and have acquired much knowledge that has advanced human existence, yet too often we close our minds to mystery, wonder, and surprise.

Genesis 18 also refers to the importance of hospitality. You never know when you might entertain messengers from God.

PRAYER/PRACTICE

The movie *Patch Adams* tells the story of a medical student who believes that humor belongs in a doctor's bag of treatments. The dean and some teachers of the medical school did not agree with Patch's use of humor, but patients laughed, the hospital staff smiled, and the children in the cancer ward responded to him and handled their treatment better. The doctors finally had to admit that health and healing connect to humor, laughter, and attitude in often mysterious and surprising ways. God and healing move beyond scientific limitations.

As you begin a new month, pray for God to kindle in you a new sense of joy, an openness to surprise, and a healthy dose of laughter.

August 2

REMEMBER

James Baldwin (1924–1987), an African American author born on this day, explored race relations in America in his novels and wove religious themes into marvelous stories.

READ

Psalm 104:1-4

PONDER

As children, many of us enjoyed lying on the grass, looking up at the clouds, and telling what animal or other object various cloud shapes resembled. As adults, we may no longer lie on the grass in such leisurely pursuits. But the psalmist must have spent time gazing at the sky before penning this magnificent psalm about the Creator of the universe. The sun, clouds, wind, and storms all serve as glorious pictures of the divine Creator. The psalmist expresses these images in fine poetry. This pearl of the Psalter contains lines that sing and soar, taking prayer to new heights of praise. "You make the clouds your chariot, you ride on the wings of the wind" (v. 3). After praying this psalm, we will never look at clouds the same way; we will see in wind and storms the grandeur and greatness of God.

PRAYER/PRACTICE

Summer offers a good time to reacquaint ourselves with play and laughter. Most of us don't play or laugh enough. We stay too busy, too serious, or too self-conscious to let ourselves enter into the mystery of abandonment in play. Frederic and Mary Ann Brussat write:

> Play is the exuberant expression of our being. It is at the heart of our creativity, our sexuality, and our most carefree moments of devotion. It helps us live with absurdity, paradox, and mystery. It feeds our joy and wonder. It keeps our search for meaning down to earth.[1]

This summer, experiment with different ways of playing. Try new activities; visit new places; do something spontaneous. Leave work early. Wear a funny hat. Read the comics. Sing a silly song. Laugh!

August 3

Flannery O'Connor (1925–1964), a Southern novelist, wrote from a Christian perspective. Her stories told how grace acted upon characters who often found themselves unable or unwilling to accept it.

READ

Psalm 104:5-9

PONDER

Infinity, a hard-to-grasp concept, provides an even more daunting challenge for meditation. Much of scientific inquiry occurs beyond our knowledge and remains difficult to articulate in poetry. Even creation seems unending, overwhelming, and baffling. But foundations and boundaries lead the psalmist to continue the psalm of praise. "You set the earth on its foundations" (v. 5). The earth remains solid and strong though we sorely test it with environmental pollution and nuclear explosions. "You set a boundary that they may not pass" (v. 9). The mountains and oceans have their place on the earth; the heights and depths of the earth are mapped in God's plan. The earth's boundaries tell us of the need for boundaries in our own lives, the need to let God's hand guide our lives.

PRAYER/PRACTICE

G. K. Chesterton said, "Angels can fly because they take themselves lightly." Who helps you laugh and play, to not take yourself too seriously? My children did this for me when they were young. I enjoyed building with blocks with them and reading story after story to them. I set aside my dislike of heights as we slid down slides and traversed jungle gyms. I laughed as they told "knock, knock" jokes and smiled as cake frosting got all over faces. I entered into their world, got out of my head, let go of worry, and felt better as a result.

If you have children or grandchildren, set aside time to play this summer. If you do not have children, visit a preschool or Sunday school class and offer to read stories. Visit the children's ward of a hospital. Offer to take neighborhood children to the ice cream store.

August 4

REMEMBER

Saint John Vianney (1786–1859), a French priest in a small village, had the remarkable ability to help people realize what obstructed their relationship with God. His insights amazed so many that extra trains were scheduled to carry people to his church for confession.

READ

Psalm 104:10-13

PONDER

Cactus plants dot the deserts of the southwestern United States with green. Even in those dry places, a little water sustains plants and animals. "You make springs gush forth in the valleys" (v. 10). After a rain in the desert, tiny flowers, bursts of color, often emerge from the desert sands.

God, the Creator, designed an earth that provides sustenance for animals and humans alike. "From the sky you send rain on the hills, and the earth is filled with your blessings" (v. 13, GNT). Enough nourishment exists for all. God the maker also exists as God the satisfier.

PRAYER/PRACTICE

I have creatively encouraged my playful side by experimenting with the arts. At one retreat I attended, the artist who led the retreat encouraged us to experiment, improvise, and have fun with monoprints. We painted watercolors on a table and then dragged, patted, or slid paper on top of the paint. Even we nonartist types could do this activity and have fun. The retreat leader showed us how to cut out a window in a piece of paper and slide it around the monoprint, revealing interesting sections of colors and patterns hidden in the whole smeared print. Many of us walked out of there with smiles on our faces and cutout art that we glued onto cards.

Consider setting aside some time to play with watercolors, finger paints, or clay. Hold a ball of clay in your hand, and listen for the shape it wants to be. Find a teacher who not only can help you learn skills but also believes that art helps reveal one's creativity, individuality, and spirituality.

August 5

REMEMBER

Saint Basil the Blessed (d. 1552), a well-known "fool for Christ" in the Russian Orthodox Church, wandered naked in the streets of Russia, praying and challenging both the pious and sinners. He even confronted Ivan the Terrible and escaped with his life.

READ

Psalm 104:14-23

PONDER

Tenderness exists in this majestic psalm of creation. The great God above cares for the cattle, waters the trees, and watches over the wild goats in the mountains and the young lions prowling at night. Humans, mentioned for the first time in verses 14-15, have food to enjoy, wine to gladden the heart, bread to strengthen the heart, and oil to make the face shine. People rise to work when the nighttime animals come in to rest. A sense of order, care, and provision permeates this psalm. God the Creator not only is great and powerful but also faithfully provides bountiful food and compassionate care. Let this truth soak into the marrow of your being: God cares for you and seeks to gladden your heart, strengthen your body, and make your face shine with love.

PRAYER/PRACTICE

Today read about, listen to, or view some of the great fools, the comedians of the airwaves or silver screen. Laughter is good for the soul, and many say it is also healing. Norman Cousins wrote a book about how watching old comedies facilitated his recovery. (See Appendix A.) I still enjoy watching old *I Love Lucy* and *Laugh-in* episodes. Our family watched *Bringing Up Baby*, *The Absent-Minded Professor*, and *What's Up, Doc?* many times, and the movies still make us laugh. Audiotapes of Jack Benny shows and the Smothers Brothers kept my son laughing many a night. Comedians can laugh at themselves, and they help us to not take ourselves and our all-important business too seriously.

Consider renting a comedy and letting yourself laugh a little or a lot.

August 6

REMEMBER

On this day in 1945, the dropping of the atomic bomb on the Japanese city of Hiroshima changed the thinking of the world, destroyed most of the city, and killed an estimated seventy to eighty thousand people.

READ

Psalm 104:24-30

PONDER

Perhaps Cecil Frances Alexander had Psalm 104 in mind when she wrote the words of this hymn: "All things bright and beautiful, /All creatures great and small, / All things wise and wonderful; / The Lord God made them all."[2]

The psalmist says that all things, great and small, look to God for food. All living things know their connection to the Creator. God's breath brings renewal. The Hebrew words for breath and spirit are the same. Our breathing connects us to the spirit of God and to all living things.

The church has long used verses 24-34 as the reading for Pentecost Sunday. When God pours out the Holy Spirit, we experience renewal, and so does the whole earth.

PRAYER/PRACTICE

Prayers for peace can take many forms. Sadako Saski, a young girl in Hiroshima, suffered radiation sickness after the dropping of the atomic bomb. She knew of a legend that said if a person folded one thousand paper cranes, he or she could be granted a wish. Sadako began folding cranes, first at home and then in the hospital. As she got sicker, her wish changed from a desire for her own healing to a desire for peace. Sadako did not finish the one thousand paper cranes, but at her memorial service, her school classmates folded the remaining cranes. Today a peace park in Hiroshima and a statue honor Sadako. Origami paper cranes, made by people all over the world, cover the statue. Each one carries a prayer for peace.

Add your own prayer for peace. If you know how, fold a paper crane as part of your prayer.

August 7

REMEMBER

Franz Jägerstätter (1907–1943), an Austrian peasant, was arrested and beheaded for refusing to serve in Hitler's army. His obedience to Christ won out over serving "on a train bound for hell," an image he had received in a dream.

READ

Psalm 104:31-35

PONDER

Our delight in praying this awesome psalm of creation is tempered by the awareness of human sin and pride (v. 35) that cause such destruction to the planet. In our ever-greedy desire to acquire and consume, we poison rivers, pollute the air, and contaminate the earth. We endanger the balance, destroy species of plants and animals, and foul the air we need for life.

Yet the psalm ends with a repeat of the first verse, "Bless the LORD, O my soul" (v. 35) and an additional word that echoes through our worship services today. The word appears for the first time in this psalm: *hallelujah,* which means "Praise the Lord!" May we enjoy, care for and preserve the goodness of creation. Hallelujah!

PRAYER/PRACTICE

For the next few days we will examine prayer and peace. The Hebrew word for peace, *shalom,* carries a sense of wholeness that dwells both internally and externally. Peace describes an inner state of well-being, centeredness, and calm. It also characterizes the way people should live together—in harmony, respect, and cooperation. One moves toward inner peace by meditation, prayer, and empathy. One moves toward a community of peace through peaceful means such as nonviolence, tolerance, and conflict resolution. The goals of inner peace and world peace join in God's desire for shalom. God's shalom permeates our inner being and our outer witness. Today, meditate on Jesus' words in John 14:27: "Peace I leave with you; my peace I give to you. . . . Do not let your hearts be troubled, and do not let them be afraid."

August 8

REMEMBER

Saint Dominic (1170–1221) founded a new community, the Order of Preachers, traveling Roman Catholic missionaries who spread the gospel. Today the preaching order is known as the Dominicans.

READ

Psalm 105:1-6

PONDER

The themes of praise, thanks, and remembering interweave in this historical psalm. Hindsight allows the Hebrew people to see the marvelous deeds of God. As they recall all Yahweh has done, the people offer praise and singing (v. 2).

The psalm also connects our needs and longing for God with God's actions toward humanity. In worship, our longing for God meets with celebration of all the ways God has been present in human history. We seek; God responds. We offer songs, thanks, and praise in worship.

PRAYER/PRACTICE

Author and teacher Henri Nouwen wrote that peace "starts every time we move out of the house of fear toward the house of love."[3] To live in the house of love means to be a person of prayer, to have the God of love as your center, to realize that your worth comes from God—not from the world's praise or blame. In the act of prayer, you let go of your hurts and wounds, your needs and desires, and discover the first love— God's announcement that you are precious, a beloved son or daughter of God. God loves you first, without any conditions. As you enter into and build your home in that love, you discover in prayer that "the one who loves you unconditionally loves all of humanity unconditionally, with that same all-embracing love. . . . therefore, when you enter into intimate communion with the God of the first love, you will find yourself in intimate communion with all the people of God."[4]

Today, in prayer, rest in God's embrace and use the phrase "God's peace" as your breath prayer.

August 9

REMEMBER

Saint Edith Stein (1891–1942), a Jew, atheist, and Catholic sister at various phases of her spiritual journey, opposed the Nazi treatment of Jews, was arrested as a Jewish Christian, and died at Auschwitz.

READ

Psalm 105:7-11

PONDER

Although elephants supposedly have good memories, no elephant could compare to God, who remembers divine covenants for a thousand generations (v. 8). God's faithfulness to promises looks even more remarkable when you consider all the times we have failed to uphold our side of the covenant. God promised to be with us, to be our God; yet like the Israelites we worshiped other gods many times. But God remembers the covenant and takes us back, sends us Jesus to teach us a better way, sends us the Spirit to help us each day. Oh, that our memories neared the depths and lengths of God's memory!

PRAYER/PRACTICE

As people of peace who live in the house of love, we need to resist our culture's fascination with violence, might, and death. Video games, TV shows, and movies are filled with images of combat and destruction. Some have suggested a new discipline of fasting from the violent images in entertainment as a method of noncooperation with evil.

Henri Nouwen urges us to pay attention to our language, which reveals our prejudices:

> The real violence starts in the way we speak about people, make assumptions about them, and decide that they are not like us. . . . As long as people keep buying into these words, it will not take much more for them to buy into the action that has to follow.[5]

God speaks the language of love and affirms life. In your prayer, ask God to show you where to resist the world's fascination with violence and death. Ask God to guide you in living with love and peace.

August 10

REMEMBER

In 1976 three Irish women—Betty Williams, Mairead Corrigan, and Ciaran McKeown—responded to the violence in Northern Ireland by organizing peace marches and forming an ecumenical group called Peace People.

READ

Psalm 105:12-25

PONDER

Someone has said that God writes straight on a crooked line. The story of Joseph looks like disaster in the beginning as jealous brothers sell him into slavery. But God turns the story into good as Joseph, the dream interpreter, released from prison, becomes the secretary of agriculture for Egypt. When famine strikes Israel, Jacob and his sons reluctantly travel to Egypt for food and receive surprising hospitality from the very one sold into slavery.

The psalmist retells Joseph's story to remind the people that God faithfully abides by the covenant even in times of famine. Reading this story reminds us that in times of trial, we can be "surprised, not by disaster, but by providence."[6]

PRAYER/PRACTICE

We do not live alone in the house of love. To be peacemakers, we need the support of others. We need a community that prays together and recognizes its dependency on God. We need people to challenge us and encourage us. A community can act as a limited mediator of God's unlimited hope and love.

"Community is the place of joy and celebration where we can say to one another, 'Be of good cheer: the Lord has overcome the world, the Lord has overcome the evil one. Do not be afraid.'"[7]

In what kind of community do you need to involve yourself to be a peacemaker? What communities already support your efforts in prayer and peacemaking? Give thanks to God and continue to meditate on being at peace in the house of love.

August 11

REMEMBER

Saint Clare of Assisi (1193–1253), a dear friend of Saint Francis, founded a community of women in Assisi, helped Francis rebuild the church, and devoted herself to poverty and service. We remember her community, the Poor Clares, for its dedication to the Franciscan ideal of joy in poverty.

READ

Psalm 105:26-36

PONDER

The story of God's faithfulness to the covenant continues by recalling how Moses and Aaron urged the pharaoh of Egypt to free the Israelite people from slavery. Convincing Pharaoh to release the Hebrews was no easy task. It took ordinary elements responding to God's will to convince the Egyptian ruler. The ten plagues, the ten court cases, the ten marches, the ten battles, the ten demonstrations constitute some of the ways God uses to free people from oppression. God hears the cries of the oppressed and works through leaders like Moses, Gandhi, Martin Luther King Jr., and Nelson Mandela to bring about a new taste of freedom.

PRAYER/PRACTICE

Sometimes simple things can encourage us the most. Often during times of quiet, I recall the words of a song for inspiration and encouragement. The song "Prayer for Peace" helps me visualize peace over and around me. Sometimes as I walk in the mornings, the words of "Let There Be Peace on Earth" ("and let it begin with me") come to mind and give me strength to take simple steps for peace.

What song strengthens you as a prayerful person committed to being one of Christ's peacemakers?

August 12

REMEMBER

William Blake (1757–1827), an English poet, artist, and visionary, was obsessed with Christ and the revolutionary aspects of Christianity. He wrote this poem: "To see a world in a grain of sand and a Heaven in a wild flower, / Hold Infinity in the palm of your hand / And Eternity in an hour."[8]

READ

Psalm 105:37-45

PONDER

The Exodus from Egypt comprises the final stanza in this litany of remembering God's faithfulness. God provided for the old and the young, and "there was no one among their tribes who stumbled" (v. 37). The psalm reveals a tender, compassionate God who fed the Israelites in the wilderness with food from heaven and released a stream from a rock so they would not be thirsty. "God remembered . . . and brought the people out in joy" (vv. 42-43, AP). As the Israelites sang this psalm of remembering, they took courage from it to remain faithful and obedient and to praise God.

PRAYER/PRACTICE

The previous night, a battle between two gangs had resulted in violence and bloodshed. The next day, a group of Christians gathered at the spot where the violence occurred. The group, comprised of clergy and laypeople from different churches and synagogues, gathered to pray for the injured, to pray for a lessening of violence, to pray for a window of hope, to pray for new jobs and more opportunities for young people to be listened to and valued. They lit candles and prayed for God to heal that space in the city and cleanse it from violence. They witnessed to a greater power at work in the world, to light that overcomes darkness. They enacted a small ritual of reclaiming the earth for God's purposes.

Are there places near you where destruction or violence have occurred? Perhaps you and a group could visit one of these spots to listen to the pain of the place and to offer prayer.

August 13

REMEMBER

Anne Morrow Lindbergh (1906–2001), an American writer, wrote about the need for solitude and freedom. She lived a very public life married to aviator Charles Lindbergh.

READ

Psalm 106:1-5

PONDER

Most worship services begin with acts of praise, spoken or sung or both. We begin worship by recognizing that God calls us together. We gather to thank and praise the One who gave us life. This awareness of God's love and compassion allows us to be honest about our sins and failures and to hope and trust in God's forgiveness and reconciliation. That worship pattern occurs in this psalm, which begins with praise and thanksgiving (vv. 1-2) but soon turns to confession of rebellion and faithlessness for the majority of the psalm (vv. 6-47).

Knowing that God is "slow to anger and abounding in steadfast love" (Ps. 103:8) enables us to confess our failure to keep God's covenant. Though our sins may be dark and many, Jesus promises forgiveness, and the prophet Isaiah says that "though your sins are like scarlet, they shall be like snow" (Isa. 1:18).

PRAYER/PRACTICE

Prayers for peace connect us to God's desire for peace. Create your own prayer for peace, or pray the Universal Peace Prayer:

> Lead me from death to life,
> from falsehood to truth.
> Lead me from despair to hope,
> from fear to trust.
> Lead me from hate to love,
> from war to peace.
> Let peace fill my heart, my world, my universe.
> Amen.[9]

August 14

REMEMBER

Saint Maximilian Kolbe (1894–1941), a Franciscan priest, sheltered thousands of Polish Jews and Christians. After his arrest, he performed hard labor at Auschwitz and volunteered to take the place of a man condemned to die.

READ

Psalm 106:6-12

PONDER

Many say that confession is good for the soul. Today's passage begins a lengthy confession by the Israelites, who remain out of sync with the faithfulness of God. "We and our ancestors have sinned" (v. 6). Way back in Egypt, they did not remember God's kind deeds but instead rebelled against God at the Red Sea (Exod. 14). Yet God saved them, rolling back the waters of the sea and letting the people pass through on dry land. The Egyptians, not so fortunate, died while pursuing the Hebrews. Then the Israelites believed God's promises and sang songs of praise (v. 12). At least for a while they sang their praises—until the next wave of doubt and faithlessness washed over them.

PRAYER/PRACTICE

Native Americans counsel that one should walk in another's moccasins before judging that person. Maximilian Kolbe took that advice one step further and literally stood in another's shoes until death. To be a person of peace requires a certain level of understanding and connection with other human beings. The wagon wheel serves as an appropriate metaphor for an increased sense of unity and peace. As persons on the rim of the wheel begin to pray, they draw closer to the center hub, which represents God. As they come closer to God, or move toward the center of God's love, they also draw closer to one another. In God's love, all find their home, their center. In God's love, we all share the same earth and walk in one another's moccasins.

Be mindful today of other cultures. Look for ways you can take the place of or stand in for someone in need.

August 15

REMEMBER

Susanna Wesley (1669–1742), the mother of nineteen children, including John and Charles Wesley, spent one hour per week with each child in religious instruction. She attended to her own spiritual growth by spending two hours a day in prayer and reflection.

READ

Psalm 106:13-23

PONDER

Soon after the Exodus, the Hebrews forgot God's deeds and began to rebel. Forgetfulness and rebellion often go hand in hand. Likewise, we forget to seek God's counsel (v. 13), turn to our greedy plans (v. 14), and start undermining the leadership of God's appointed (v. 16). Such forgetfulness and rebellion create a recipe for disaster, and the golden calf emerges from the ovens of foolish plans. In one of the great barbs of the Bible, the psalmist writes, "They exchanged the glory of God for the image of an ox that eats grass" (v. 20).

Scripture tells us that God is slow to anger, but that statement implies that God does get angry. The forgetfulness, idolatry, and rebellion of the people angered God. Moses, God's chosen one, "stood in the breach" (v. 23) and deflected God's wrath. Where are we called to "stand in the breach"?

PRAYER/PRACTICE

One spiritual practice I have adopted and adapted comes from the Buddhist tradition. Metta, or lovingkindness meditation, recognizes that peace begins in the depths of the heart.[10]

Begin by centering yourself in God's presence. Focus on the image of God's light filling and surrounding you. Then say this lovingkindness blessing for yourself.

> May I be at peace. May my heart always be open.
> May I awaken to the divine light deep within.
> May I be healed. May I be a source of healing for others.

August 16

REMEMBER

Catherine de Hueck Doherty (1896–1985), a Russian baroness who heard the call of Christ to serve the poor, founded Friendship House in Harlem and worked against segregation. She also founded Madonna House in Ontario, Canada, and wrote several books, including *Poustinia* (a Russian word for *desert*), which describes how to create a prayer space wherever one lives.

READ

Psalm 106:24-31

PONDER

Often we try to hide our sins or minimize them by saying, "No big deal," "I slipped," or "I made a mistake." The Psalms will have nothing of such timid, cautious confession. "They grumbled in their tents, and did not obey the voice of the LORD" (v. 25). The Hebrews took part in sacrificial parties at Moab, bowed down to the Baal of Peor, and became infected with plague. This unflattering story, which the Israelites probably would have liked to forget, remains in the litany of confession as a vivid reminder to choose the God of compassion and forgiveness.

PRAYER/PRACTICE

The second part of the lovingkindness meditation extends the prayer of blessing to others. Joan Borysenko writes, "It is not selfish to bless ourselves first, because if our heart remains closed we have nothing to give."[11]

As you focus on God's light filling and surrounding you, say the blessing for yourself. Then think of a loved one. See this person in as much detail as possible; imagine God's light and blessing surrounding him or her. Offer the lovingkindness blessing for your loved one:

> May you be at peace. May your heart always be open.
> May you awaken to the divine light deep within.
> May you be healed. May you be a source of healing for others.

Repeat this blessing for as many loved ones as you wish.

August 17

REMEMBER

Samuel Barber (1910–1981), an American composer, wrote the popular and meditative *Adagio for Strings*, Opus 11.

READ

Psalm 106:32-39

PONDER

The forty years of wandering in the desert and encountering other nations and religions presented a struggle and temptation for the Israelites. According to this confession, all too often they adopted unholy practices rather than share their experience of a liberating God. They adopted the savage practice of child sacrifice, pouring out "innocent blood, the blood of their sons and daughters, whom they sacrificed to the idols of Canaan" (v. 38). This passage reminds us not to build success or profit on the backs of children. Far too many children today work to enable their families to survive, and recently children have been used to fight in civil wars. We must form social policy with the care of children in mind.

PRAYER/PRACTICE

"You shall love your neighbor as yourself" (Matt. 22:39) does not instruct us to love only good or nice neighbors but all people. Some people are definitely harder to love than others. The third part of the prayer of lovingkindness extends blessings to difficult persons.

Again, begin by centering yourself in God's light. Pray the prayer of lovingkindness for yourself. Imagine God's light surrounding one or two loved ones, and repeat the blessing for them. Then visualize someone who troubles you as being surrounded by God's light, and offer the lovingkindness blessing for that person:

> May you be at peace. May your heart always be open.
> May you awaken to the divine light deep within.
> May you be healed. May you be a source of healing for others.

Pray this prayer whenever judgmental thoughts arise in you.

August 18

REMEMBER

Annie Dillard (b. 1945) writes books that open many to seeing God in the midst of the everyday world, especially in the natural world.

READ

Psalm 106:40-46

PONDER

The list of faithlessness in this psalm supplied more than enough reasons to kindle God's anger. Disgusted with the Israelites, God handed them over to nations that hated them, then allowed the foes to rule over Israel. Even then God helped the Hebrews, but still they acted rebellious and sinful. God had every right to give up on them, to let them suffer the consequences of their sin. "Nevertheless," verse 44 says, God cared. Nevertheless God remembered the covenant and "showed compassion according to the abundance of God's mercy and love" (v. 45, AP). *Nevertheless* connects our human sin with God's desire and commitment to our salvation; it becomes an important word at the end of this catalog of error.

PRAYER/PRACTICE

People in great need live in our world. We know of or read about poverty, hunger, abuse, tragedy. We respond with our social involvements, our financial gifts, our public witness. We can also respond with the prayer of lovingkindness.

Center yourself in God's light and pray the blessing for yourself, your loved ones, and for difficult persons. Now think of a person needing healing, comfort, or help. Or think of a group or situation important to your heart. Repeat the lovingkindness blessing for that person, group, or situation.

> May you be at peace. May your heart always be open.
> May you awaken to the divine light deep within.
> May you be healed. May you be a source of healing for others.

August 19

REMEMBER

Blaise Pascal (1623–1662), a mathematician, scientist, and defender of Christianity, wrote *Pensées*. This book invited people to find God through faith, which lies beyond the reach of human reason and is more persuasive than the external authority of the church or scripture.

READ

Psalm 106:47-48

PONDER

The psalm ends with a prayer of intercession: "Save us." Knowing our sin and error, we turn to God—but not in despair or ready to give up or wash our hands of any problem. We ask God to turn us around, forgive us, save us, gather us from places where we have strayed, and form us into a new community of praise and thanksgiving.

The last verse, considered the doxology for book 4 of the Psalter, offers a prayer of praise to God. A variety of doxologies exists in hymns and scriptures, giving us many ways to praise God for all eternity.

PRAYER/PRACTICE

The earth, with all of its people and creatures, stands in need of prayer. The abuse of its resources and the human propensity for violence call for a new vision of respect and preservation. It is time to deepen our prayer so that fear and anger do not rule our decision making.

Again, center yourself in God's presence. Pray the prayer of loving-kindness for yourself. Continue with any of the other steps of the blessing as you wish. Then imagine the earth, our marvelous planet, with all the two-legged and four-legged creatures, the fish that swim in the blue waters, and the birds that soar in the sky. Picture the world and offer this blessing:

> May there be peace on earth.
> May the hearts of all people be open to themselves and to each other.
> May all people awaken to the divine light deep within.
> May all creation be blessed and be a blessing to all that is.

August 20

REMEMBER

Bernard of Clairvaux (1090–1153), a French theologian and author, joined the Order of the Cistercians and founded a monastery in Clairvaux. He wrote several hymns and encouraged mystical prayer. Bernard also wrote about God's love that goes before us and is bigger than our love.

READ

Psalm 107:1-3

PONDER

Good news begs to be shared. If we like a restaurant or movie, we tell others. We can also tell about experiences of God's blessings. "Let the redeemed of the LORD say so" (v. 2). In other words, persons saved by God's amazing grace should tell their story. Testimony has gone out of favor in some churches because often the same people retold the same stories. Though the form may need to change, the telling of stories of God's love and blessing should always remain fresh and vital. God has never ceased working, the Spirit has not stopped blowing, and Christ did not stay in the tomb! Awake to the wonders and works of God and prepare yourself to share the good news, which is better than any award-winning movie.

PRAYER/PRACTICE

The prayer of lovingkindness recognizes that our lives interweave with the whole fabric of life. We began the circle of prayer with ourselves, and I like to end the lovingkindness prayer by repeating the opening blessing. I usually say the prayer in the morning, and by closing with the blessing for myself, I carry that peace throughout the day.

> May I be at peace. May my heart always be open.
> May I awaken to the divine light deep within.
> May I be healed. May I be a source of healing for others.

In this practice, we dedicate ourselves to living in God's shalom, a deep inner peace and an extension of God's peace to the world.

August 21

REMEMBER

Margaret Mead (1901–1978), an American anthropologist, writer, teacher, and committed activist, often testified on social issues before Congress. Mead viewed diversity as a resource, and she affirmed the possibility of learning from other societies, even primitive ones.

READ

Psalm 107:4-9

PONDER

Verses 4 through 32 demonstrate an orderly and masterful touch. These verses thank God for delivering the Hebrews from four ordeals they suffered because of their disobedience. The psalmist describes each of the four ordeals—wandering, imprisonment, illness, and experiencing storms—in four steps: the danger, the prayer, the deliverance, and an exhortation to praise God.

The wanderer in the desert appears hungry and thirsty. The wanderer in us prays for help, for a "straight way" (v. 7) to come home. God responds to our needs.

Mary, the mother of Jesus, knew this psalm, especially verse 9. In her song of praise when she visited her cousin Elizabeth, she prayed, "God gives the hungry good things to eat" (Luke 1:53, CEV).

PRAYER/PRACTICE

The practice of hospitality grows out of an open heart and can build a world of peace. Hospitality creates a welcoming space where another can enter and become a friend. It requires an open heart and a gracious spirit. The home does not have to be lavish, spotless, or perfect. The food does not have to be fancy or expensive. But the welcome must be genuine and from the heart.

The writer of Hebrews commends hospitality: "Do not neglect to show hospitality to strangers, for by doing that some have entertained angels without knowing it" (Heb. 13:2). Look at your summer calendar for a date and time you can invite some people over for a meal. Consider inviting people who may not be able to reciprocate.

August 22

REMEMBER

Jan Vermeer (1632–1675), a Dutch painter, mastered the use of color, light, and perspective. His subjects, painted in exquisite colors, frequently included persons busy with household tasks.

READ

Psalm 107:10-16

PONDER

The psalmist names imprisonment as the second ordeal the Hebrews faced. Prisoners must endure misery and confinement. At times we become imprisoned, though usually not literally. We get caught in despair, trapped by doubts, chained by resentments. We feel unable to move, controlled by darkness, with no future in sight. Our cry for help arises from the pit of our hopelessness, and our prayer of thanks for salvation then echoes off the dungeon walls. We praise God, who "shatters the door of bronze, and cuts in two the bars of iron" (v. 16).

Today is a good day to remember those in prison, literally and figuratively.

PRAYER/PRACTICE

In my travels to some countries, the hospitality I received overwhelmed me. I have eaten at tables spread with more food than the host family would normally eat all week. I have slept in beds vacated by parents or children so that I, the guest, could enjoy a good night's sleep. I have found gracious welcome in countries and homes that many Americans would consider poor. In fact, often the poor extend a more gracious welcome than affluent people, who sometimes worry about protecting their possessions. Gracious hospitality flows from belief in a gracious and providing God. Gracious hospitality believes that God's gifts exist not to be hoarded but shared.

Remember a time you received unexpected and gracious hospitality. Give thanks to God and pray for such a gracious and open heart.

August 23

REMEMBER

Simone Weil (1909–1943), a French philosopher, activist, and religious searcher, balanced a keen intellect with deep social compassion. Never baptized, she saw herself as a Christian outside the church. Yet she had mystical experiences of Christ and lived among the poor.

READ

Psalm 107:17-22

PONDER

Sickness, the third ordeal the Israelites pass through, arose because of their sinful ways (v. 17). God spoke a word and they experienced healing (v. 20). Jesus touched the blind, cured the lame, and healed the sick. Doctors prescribe medicine and perform surgery; chiropractors adjust spines; acupuncturists lessen pain; therapists listen to feelings; and people get well. God created many ways of healing body, mind, and spirit. God created us as whole persons, and healing takes place on different levels. God desires our wholeness and healing and yearns for our prayers and praise. Our Creator delights in the stories of our healing and rejoices in our songs of joy (v. 22).

PRAYER/PRACTICE

Hospitality can be a small, simple gesture. In my first parish, when I needed to think about a perplexing problem, I often went to a member's house to walk through the woods. As soon as I popped my head in the door and said I was going for a walk, the response came, "I'll put the kettle on for when you are done." At the end of my walk, I could look forward to a pot of tea, a plate of cookies, and a listening ear.

What simple gesture says that others are welcome in your home, office, or place of work? In what ways can you communicate, "I have been expecting you. I am glad you are here"?

August 24

REMEMBER

Bartholomew (first century), also known as Nathanael, was one of the twelve apostles and, according to tradition, preached in Asia Minor, India, and Armenia.

READ

Psalm 107:23-32

PONDER

Hints of the New Testament appear in this fourth ordeal of the Israelites. "God hushed the wind and stilled the mighty waves" (v. 29, AP). Reading that verse reminds us of Jesus calming the seas and soothing the disciples' fright (Mark 4:35-41). At times we, like confident sailors, think we have everything under control. The sea remains calm, the wind blows gently, the sky appears cloudless, and we sail masterfully. "But there are powers and forces over which cunning has no influence. Life has storms from which mere ingenuity cannot save us."[12] Life is not always a smooth sail but an adventure in which God remains our companion, guide, and the One who calms the mighty seas.

PRAYER/PRACTICE

Table fellowship played an important role in Jesus' ministry. He broke bread with rich and poor alike, which upset the Pharisees and others concerned about purity and social standing. Jesus clearly intended the good news for all; the new reign of God extended a new hospitality that could feed even five thousand. Transformations often happened at meals. Zacchaeus became a changed man after hosting a meal with Jesus (Luke 19:1-10). In the story of the prodigal son (Luke 15:23-24), the meal symbolized a celebration of new life. The breaking of bread at Emmaus (Luke 24:30-31) revealed the presence of Christ.

Choose a favorite table fellowship story from the Gospels. Imagine yourself as a character in the story. Read the story and discern whether a word about hospitality emerges for you.

August 25

REMEMBER

Anne Hutchinson (1591–1643), a Puritan, left England and worked for women's equality in the new Massachusetts Bay Colony. She started and led Bible study groups. Eventually branded a heretic, she was imprisoned for her beliefs.

READ

Psalm 107:33-38

PONDER

The structure of the psalm shifts from describing four ordeals to reflect on God's continuous and gracious care, which transforms "a desert into pools of water, a parched land into springs of water" (v. 35). This verse may allude to the experience of the Israelites upon returning from captivity and rebuilding the nation. However, where wickedness abounds and evil lurks, sometimes the opposite transformation happens. God may "turn rivers into deserts, flowing streams into scorched land, and fruitful fields into beds of salt" (vv. 33-34, CEV). These images seem all too relevant, since we know of rivers that have dried up and land that has been used up in our overfertilized, overindustrialized, ever-expanding economy. When we treat land and water with respect, we experience God's blessing.

PRAYER/PRACTICE

Our family has received blessings from participating in Servas, an international travel/host organization. We remain on a list of U.S. hosts willing to house people from other countries for up to two days. Over the years we have welcomed people from all over the world to our table. When we are asked to consider hosting someone, we check our calendar and ask ourselves whether we can create the time and space for new relationships. When we say yes, we have seldom been disappointed.

Consider joining Servas. Not only can you host people from around the world, but when you travel you can stay in the homes of Servas members and see the world through their eyes. (See Appendix A.)

August 26

REMEMBER

On this day in 1920, Congress ratified the Nineteenth Amendment to the U.S. Constitution, finally giving women the right to vote.

READ

Psalm 107:39-43

PONDER

Remembrance of times of exile probably forms the context of these final verses. God had allowed the Israelites, including their princes, to be carried off into exile, but God did not forget them. "God lifts up the poor and needy, shepherding them as a family of sheep" (v. 41, AP). God maintains a special concern for the poor and needy. The entire psalm testifies to a God who delivers those in trouble, a God who offers refuge and strength.

PRAYER/PRACTICE

Encounters with persons from other religious traditions offer another opportunity to extend hospitality. You might look for common beliefs among the religious traditions or practices. Examine ways each tradition worships and encourages spiritual disciplines, such as prayer. Approach someone of a different religious tradition with an open heart, ready to learn and dialogue. Rather than attempting to convert or threaten, hospitality practices welcoming and trusts that God remains present in the ongoing experience of encounter. You may even discover that interreligious dialogue deepens and challenges your faith.

Consider visiting the religious service of a faith community other than your own. Or organize an interreligious festival at your place of worship with panel discussions, art, worship, and food. See Appendix A for books and other suggestions.

August 27

REMEMBER

Saint Monica (323–387), the mother of Saint Augustine, devoted her years to seeing that Augustine became a Christian and nurturing this leader of the church.

READ

Psalm 108:1-6

PONDER

A joyous song of praise, accompanied by harp and lyre, begins this psalm. "I will awake the dawn" (v. 2). Instead of the dawn waking us, our joy, so expressive and uncontainable, supplies the energy for waking the dawn with song. What a wonderful line of poetry! The psalmist, prompted by a heightened awareness of God's steadfast love, higher than the heavens, and God's faithfulness, which reaches the clouds, pens a psalm of highest praise. No exaggeration appears too great for the poet. Oh, that our love and praise for God became a little excessive and that occasionally we might wake the dawn!

PRAYER/PRACTICE

"In my Father's house there are many dwelling places" (John 14:2). In his instructions to the disciples on the night before his death, Jesus used a wonderful image of hospitality: God's gracious welcome to a new home beyond time and death. A literal house may not await us in heaven, but the verse evokes a sense of warmth and hospitality. God has prepared a place for us; a table waits for us. God's love and welcome do not end with death. This is a hospitality beyond measure.

Today meditate on God's hospitality. Think about times you have experienced God's invitation to come in, sit down, rest, and renew. Think about times God's Word and God's table have fed you. Think about times God has welcomed you home after you wandered afar, drifted away. Meditate on this incredible hospitality of God that extends beyond death.

August 28

REMEMBER

Saint Augustine (354–430), the bishop of Hippo in North Africa and one of the leading theologians of Western thought, wrote the moving story of his conversion in his autobiography, *Confessions*. His other writings demonstrate a remarkable and persuasive defense of the Christian faith.

READ

Psalm 108:7-13

PONDER

Confidence in God's presence and help enables the psalmist to turn from praise to pleading for victory. The psalmist names nations that Israel conquered or held at bay. Though we may not recognize all the locations, they symbolize the powerful obstacles we face. Edom, with its rocky fortress city of Petra, carried the reputation of being unconquerable. The psalmist reminds us that what is impossible for humans is more than possible with God. For us, that incredible confidence in God does not concern wars and battles against nations as much as the problems of ordinary life.

PRAYER/PRACTICE

In March, we considered *lectio divina*, a contemplative way of reading scripture. Summer affords a good time for reading, perhaps differently than *lectio divina*.

Reading books on prayer, faith, and spirituality blesses us in unforeseen ways. Such holy reading lets us feast on the treasures of books meant to help us on the journey. We catch a glimpse into another's experience of prayer that may shed light on our practice. We learn of other people's struggles in faithfulness to God's command to make peace, to forgive, to share with the needy. We read to understand more about the life of Jesus, to more fully pray the Psalms, to meet Old Testament heroes.

This summer, read one book that deepens your spiritual journey. See Appendix A for suggestions.

August 29

REMEMBER

John the Baptist (first century), the cousin of Jesus, a prophet and voice in the wilderness, announced the coming of the Messiah and baptized Jesus. His death marked a turning point in Jesus' ministry.

READ

Psalm 109:1-5

PONDER

Once again we enter the world of lament. Here the psalmist raises a heartrending cry because of the verbal attacks hurled by friends. "They beset me with words of hate, and attack me without cause" (v. 3). Even though the psalmist prays for them, still they "reward me evil for good, and hatred for my love" (v. 5). The psalmist pleads for God not to be silent (v. 1).

For our most difficult times, the Psalms let us know that no language is too strong for God to hear. The poet may speak for us of our anger and despair. Always the confidence that God will hear and will respond prevails.

PRAYER/PRACTICE

Biographies can provide fascinating summer reading. Perhaps this book piqued your curiosity as it introduced you to a number of saints. The brief words about them only begin to inform you about the faith journeys of some remarkable and often ordinary women and men. Perhaps a particular historical period interests you, and reading about the saints from this period may open up that history. Maybe you found one person whose journey seems to mirror yours, and you wish to spend more time with that saint. Consider choosing a book about a saint for your summer reading. Look in a library for books on certain saints, or see Appendix A in this book.

August 30

REMEMBER

William Temple (1881–1944), archbishop of Canterbury, led the ecumenical movement and strongly advocated labor reform.

READ

Psalm 109:6-19

PONDER

Translators disagree on whether the psalmist spoke these verses of invective against accusers or, as the New Revised Standard Version suggests, others leveled this abuse against the psalmist. Either way, this passage contains a diatribe against a person, his or her family and children, the person's very existence. Modern readers may find it difficult to relate to the graphic, colorful, and condemning language. We are not to memorize or hold onto such angry words but rather to express them to God and release them into God's gracious and reconciling hands.

PRAYER/PRACTICE

Carefully chosen novels may qualify as holy reading. A well-chosen novel would be a step up from most "summer reads." A good story can both edify and entertain. Good novels have moved me to tears and laughter; they have challenged and enlightened my faith. The definition of a good novel may be much debated, but I look for books that wrestle with real issues from a moral, ethical, and sometimes outright religious perspective; that take me to a new country or a new experience; that tell a good story. See Appendix A for some of my favorites.

August 31

REMEMBER

Rainer Maria Rilke (1875–1926), perhaps the greatest lyric poet of modern Germany, infused his poetry with images of the divine.

READ

Psalm 109:20-31

PONDER

A change of mood occurs in the psalm. The psalmist puts aside angry thoughts and hurled insults and prays to God for deliverance (v. 21). "Help me, O LORD my God! Save me according to your steadfast love" (v. 26). Even if the curses continue, the psalmist knows that God's blessing determines the outcome of life (v. 28). Others' opinions do not compare with God's affirmation and blessing. The world may condemn, criticize, and belittle, but God "stands at the right hand of the needy, to save them from those who would condemn them to death" (v. 31). Once again, the lament, which pours out strong feelings, ends in a word of confidence in God. God hears, responds, and redeems.

PRAYER/PRACTICE

Consider poetry as another possibility for summer reading. Some lines of poetry are etched in my soul. "Be patient toward all that is unsolved in your heart. . . . try to love the questions themselves. . . . Live the questions now. Perhaps you will then gradually, without noticing it, live along some distant day into the answer."[13] *Threatened with Resurrection,* a book of prayers and poems about the struggle for justice in Central America, mocks those who think they can stop the dream of liberation with death.[14] When I feel discouraged, I remember these lines from Emily Dickinson: " 'Hope' is the thing with feathers / that perches in the soul / And sings the tune without words /And never stops—at all."[15]

What poetry do you remember? What poet(s) do you read?

September

God of the harvest, you have been growing
faith and discipline in me.
Harvest some of your work and enable me
to share your grace,
your compassion, your joy with others.
Let my words, my prayer, and my deeds
make a more blessed world.
Receive my praise and thanksgiving,
and keep me open to growing. Amen.

September 1

REMEMBER

Give thanks for and pray God's protection for children, many of whom return to school this month.

READ

Psalm 110

PONDER

The psalm, most likely composed for a coronation of a new king in the line of David, calls the ruler both king and priest. The ruler sits at God's right hand, the hand of power, and receives God's authority. Even when David's dynasty disappeared, this royal psalm gave the people hope that God would revive the kingdom of David. It comes as no surprise, then, that first-century Christians believed this psalm found fulfillment in the person of Jesus. Jesus the Messiah, the right hand of God, came as king to guide and rule life and acted as a priest, offering forgiveness, blessing, and healing. Jesus himself quoted this psalm in a conflict with the religious leaders over the nature of Messiah (Matt. 22:43-44).

PRAYER/PRACTICE

What memories do you hold of September—skipping rope on the blacktop? sitting in wooden desks arranged in rows? hearing the sound of chalk on the chalkboard? What childhood memories get stirred when a school bus passes or when you see a box of crayons? Some of my childhood remains in me, though I confess that anxious hurry has replaced skipping, seriousness has crowded out play, and complexity has drowned out simple wonder.

Offer a prayer for the school memories you still carry. You might begin, "Loving God, let a little wonder and joy flow in me this month. Let me be teachable and playful. Let there be a twinkle in my eye and a light in my soul. . . ."

September 2

REMEMBER

Elizabeth O'Connor (1921–1998), along with Gordon Cosby, shaped the Church of the Saviour in Washington, D.C., into a new vision of the church in mission. She wrote and interpreted the importance of a call to servanthood and community.

READ

Psalm 111

PONDER

Praise erupts not because we feel good, but because God is good. Praise rises as we focus on God's deeds, and in this psalm, the whole community gathers to publicly praise and give thanks for the faithfulness of God. In the Hebrew, each verse begins with a different letter of the Hebrew alphabet, forming an acrostic. That reminds me of a teacher giving an assignment to praise God using the twenty-six letters of the alphabet. The ideas may not flow nicely together, but the total list of thanksgiving can change a person and, as the psalmist notes, constitutes the beginning of wisdom (v. 10).

God's faithfulness to the covenant remains strong (v. 5), and God continues to show mercy (v. 4) and justice (v. 7). These great themes of the Psalms give rise again and again to songs of praise.

PRAYER/PRACTICE

For the next few days, I invite you to look at the spiritual practice of being a learner and valuing teachers. Teachers may be called by many names: sage, guide, master, instructor, elder, crone, rabbi, guru, priest, pastor. "They instruct directly and indirectly through stories, parables, koans, sermons, lectures, and personal example. They recommend readings in sacred texts, assign exercises and tasks to be accomplished, demonstrate devotional acts, and challenge us to reach the sacred fullness of our potential."[1] We learn from our teachers when we cultivate a spirit of openness and receptivity.

Today pray for openness to ways God might teach you. Pay attention to the wise teachers you encounter today.

September 3

REMEMBER

Saint Gregory the Great (540–604), the first monk to become a pope, encouraged monasticism, advocated taking the gospel to England, and promoted plainsong choral music, now known as Gregorian chant.

READ

Psalm 112

PONDER

This psalm paints a happy picture of those who center their life in God. Those who delight in God's commands will have descendants, be prosperous, and be generous. Contrast this with the wicked, who "gnash their teeth and melt away" (v. 10). Though other psalms let us know that goodness and happiness do not always come to the upright, this psalm appears notable for including generosity as a trademark of persons of integrity. "They have distributed freely, they have given to the poor; their righteousness endures forever" (v. 9). If we are concerned about leaving a lasting legacy in this world after we die, the psalm suggests our generosity will endure.

PRAYER/PRACTICE

Some of our spiritual teachers appear obvious: a Sunday school teacher who told Bible stories with flair and always gave everyone a hug and a kind word. A Bible teacher who opened up the historical background, cultural traditions, and multiple sources of the scriptures, which shook and challenged our childhood understandings but eventually laid groundwork for a deeper faith. An elder who taught us how to befriend silence and sit peacefully, expectantly, and faithfully in prayer. A minister who lifted the call to justice and led people into a new ministry of compassion. A book that opened the door to new understandings of spiritual disciplines. A friend whose experience with addictions shed new light on God's amazing grace.

Give thanks today for the teachers in your life who helped develop your faith. If possible, write some of them a word of thanks.

September 4

REMEMBER

Albert Schweitzer (1875–1965), a French humanitarian, theologian, philosopher, author, and music scholar, is best known for becoming a doctor and building a hospital in Lambaréné, an outpost in French Equatorial Africa. His reverence for life and care for all living beings earned him the Nobel Peace Prize in 1952.

READ

Psalm 113:1-4

PONDER

Psalm 113 begins a group of six psalms known as the Hallel (or praise psalms) because the Israelites sang them at festivals such as Passover, the Feast of Tabernacles, and the Feast of Weeks. They contain beautiful and memorable lines of praise. Quite possibly, Jesus prayed these psalms as he and the disciples gathered to celebrate the Passover meal. Imagine being in the upper room and singing these psalms.

"From the rising of the sun to its setting the name of the LORD is to be praised" (v. 3). Our daily experiences furnish the content for hymns of praise. Somewhere, somehow, every morning, praise should be on our lips. Somewhere in the middle of the day, we should praise God on high. Somewhere in the evening, when the sun is going down, praise should flow from our hearts. Hallelujah and "Blessed be the name of the LORD from this time on and forevermore" (v. 2).

PRAYER/PRACTICE

In the spiritual life we eventually learn that every experience and person serves as a teacher. We learn to see all the world as a classroom—whether in a small hospital in Lambaréné, or on the streets of Calcutta, or in a broken-down old church in Assisi, Italy. We develop eyes to see the footprints of God. We develop ears to hear whispers of the Holy Spirit. God as teacher appears in every situation. As we become receptive learners, nature becomes a book to be read and enjoyed. Animals become guides for living. Even negative experiences contain spiritual lessons. Pray today for openness to guidance from unexpected sources.

September 5

REMEMBER

Chief Crazy Horse (1842?–1877), a Sioux Indian leader, resisted white encroachment on Native American land in the Dakota Territory and was killed while in U.S. custody.

READ

Psalm 113:5-9

PONDER

This psalm gives two reasons to praise God. First, the great high God stoops down to human need, "raising the poor from the dust, lifting the weak and seating them among princes" (vv. 7-8, AP). This caring God enters into our despair and anguish, seeking to lift us up. "Who is like the LORD our God?" (v. 5).

Second, the great high God looks with favor upon childless women and blesses them with children (v. 9). Perhaps the psalmist had in mind Sarah giving birth to Isaac at an old age, but Jews of later times saw the verses as referring to Israel's deliverance from captivity. God works to bring about new life, freedom from captivity, and the joy of happy children. Indeed, "Who is like the LORD our God?"

PRAYER/PRACTICE

I have learned much about living from being with the suffering, even the dying. People seriously ill, permanently disabled, or slowly dying show a remarkable wisdom and thoughtful attitude toward life and death.

I played tennis against a friend who had lost an arm in a motorcycle accident. Missing one arm did not cause him to miss life. When my mother-in-law received a cancer diagnosis, she developed a breath prayer that testified to her faith and let us know she understood the prognosis and faced the future under God's care. She loved the Twenty-third Psalm, so her breath prayer became, "Loving Shepherd, guide me home."

Recall any lessons you have learned from those who have gone through great difficulty. Give thanks for those wise teachers.

September 6

REMEMBER

This Labor Day month, give thanks for workers who keep the food growing, the city glowing, and the highways moving. Give thanks for the work of your hands and of workers everywhere.

READ

Psalm 114

PONDER

Perhaps three moments in Israel's history stand behind this moving psalm. The Red Sea parted to let the Israelites pass through. Mount Sinai smoked and trembled when Moses talked with God. The Jordan River paused to let the Hebrews into the Promised Land. This psalm reminds us that all creation cooperates in the deliverance from slavery. Lightness and joy abound in this psalm, a wonderful psalm for a marching, dancing procession. Yet there remains a caution. "Tremble, O earth, at the presence of the LORD" (v. 7). We still need a healthy sense of awe and wonder even as we receive the grace to cross our Red Sea and to go through our Jordan River. We might even get to see mountains skip, walls tumble, and moons explored.

PRAYER/PRACTICE

Here are two exercises to develop your appreciation for teachers and your receptivity to learning:

1. Create a list of teachers as you envision a University of Life. You may want to invite others to help you select persons to teach prayer, scripture, and meditation. Who would teach music, art, and dance? Who would teach compassion and peace studies? Who would teach gratitude, journaling, and play?

2. At a gathering where people introduce themselves, instead of saying what they do or what church they belong to, have each person name his or her spiritual teachers—either someone living and personally known or a person from books or history. Whom would you name as your spiritual teachers?

September 7

REMEMBER

E. F. Schumacher (1911–1977), a British economist and scholar, wrote *Small Is Beautiful: Economics As If People Mattered*. Often called the father of appropriate technology, Schumacher championed aid that fit the rural nature of developing countries.

READ

Psalm 115:1-8

PONDER

The opening verse reveals a memorable gem of prayer: "Not to us, O LORD, not to us, but to your name give glory, for the sake of your steadfast love and your faithfulness" (v. 1). In a time of selfish preoccupation we humbly pray, "Not to us, O LORD, not to us, but to your name give glory."

Supreme confidence in God allows the psalmist to poke fun at other gods and idols. These gods are mute, blind, crippled, and deaf; so are the people who worship them. We could substitute gods of our own making: success, popularity, military might, wealth, power, privilege, pleasure, pride. The list forms a great crowd of pretenders that flows from the human mind. Are we also mute, blind, crippled, and deaf? Have we bowed down and worshiped the pretenders?

PRAYER/PRACTICE

Pride forms a major obstacle to learning. Pride appears as a know-it-all attitude. It keeps you from believing that another person or a particular situation can teach you anything. Pride isolates you with your own perceptions, your own knowledge, in your own limited world of experience. As Proverbs 16:18 states, "Pride goes before a fall."

Today concentrate on remaining open to teachers everywhere. Ask throughout the day, "What can I learn from you?" Keep that question in mind as you read, as you look at the sky or at a squirrel, as you interact with people. At bedtime review what you have learned and give thanks for a spirit of openness and receptivity. Ask God to keep your heart and mind open.

September 8

REMEMBER

Robert McAfee Brown (1920–2001), a teacher and author, brought liberation theology to the mainstream church and challenged Christians to be more socially active. He wrote about theology and global issues in a readable style.

READ

Psalm 115:9-18

PONDER

One senses how the Psalms guided and shaped worship in these next verses. Verses 9 to 11 sound like a wonderful antiphonal reading between priest and people. Verses 12 to 15 probably suggest a blessing the priest said to the people. "God will bless the house of Israel" (v. 12). The great psalm concludes with all the people singing verses 16-18 as praise to God. "We will bless the LORD" (v. 18). The worship experience invites the people to turn away from false idols, to trust in God, "their help and their shield" (v. 9), and to receive the blessings of an obedient people from the hand of a generous God.

PRAYER/PRACTICE

The sabbatical year that my family and I lived at Pendle Hill, a Quaker Center for Study and Contemplation, gave me many teachers from outside my own spiritual tradition. It provided a rich time of learning. I learned about the dark night of the soul from one teacher. I learned about humility from the dean who washed dishes with me every lunchtime. I learned about sustaining a life of social witness from the groundskeeper. I learned about trusting my own creativity from the pottery teacher. I learned to bake homemade bread for seventy people from the cook. I learned how to enter into silence and persevere from an elderly Quaker who took me under his wing and counsel. The Quakers furnished a rich year of many lessons from many teachers.

Remember a time in your life when a host of teachers surrounded you and you immersed yourself in a community of learning. Give thanks to God. Is it time to plan for such a learning experience?

September 9

REMEMBER

Saint Peter Claver (1581–1654), a Spanish Jesuit sent to Colombia, South America, ministered to African slaves despite opposition from business and civic authorities.

READ

Psalm 116:1-4

PONDER

The wooden idols the Israelites encountered in other religions had ears, but they could not hear. Not so with the God of the Israelites. This psalm of thanksgiving celebrates that God hears and cares. God not only speaks a world into being, but God also listens to the cries of our heart. We do not know whether illness or persecution put the psalmist in death's grip, but we do know that God's embrace brought about recovery.

The psalm begins like a love letter. Perhaps it is time for you to pen your own love letter to God, pouring out all your reasons to thank God.

PRAYER/PRACTICE

The Quaker teachers helped me understand the changing movements in the life of prayer. They described the first movement as involuntary. God takes the initiative in prayer, prompting your desire to pray. The first movement in prayer is not your own doing. God's initiative occurs all the time without your effort or even knowledge. Douglas Steere, Quaker writer and teacher, liked to say that God woos us, besieging us with love. Before you even start to pray, God places the yearning to pray deep within you. Before you even turn to seek God, God already seeks you, looks for you, prepares a welcome for you. The first movement of prayer invites you to quiet your restless searching and to simply abide in the love of God that has drawn you to this time of prayer.

In your prayer time, spend the first moments just resting in the awareness that God has been seeking you, wooing you, and drawing you to this time.

September 10

REMEMBER

Mother Teresa of Calcutta (1910–1997) cared for the destitute and dying of India and founded the Missionaries of Charity. Her life of service not only touched the poor but also touched and challenged the hearts of the whole world. Mother Teresa said, "We can do no great things—only small things with great love."[2]

READ

Psalm 116:5-11

PONDER

"The Lord protects the poor, lifting me when I was helpless" (v. 6, AP). Mother Teresa lived out the intention of this verse. She truly tried to be the hands and feet of Christ, ministering to the poor, elderly, and dying. Her deep spirituality, centered in adoration of God, expressed itself in service to others. I can imagine a sick or forgotten one looking up at Mother Teresa and quoting this psalm: "For you have delivered my soul from death, my eyes from tears, my feet from stumbling" (v. 8). When all our resources dwindle away, when even friends don't come through, God often appears in disguise, coming near in the touch of an unexpected saint.

PRAYER/PRACTICE

The second movement of prayer, according to Quaker teachers, is voluntary. You respond to God's initiative, choosing to turn toward God's love. Your prayer becomes a response to God's initiative. Douglas Steere says if God's love appears as a stream, you respond by rowing out into the flowing water. You place yourself where God can work in you and carry you to greater depths of prayer. This second movement of prayer requires setting aside time to pray and developing the practices of meditation, *lectio divina,* and other spiritual disciplines that open you to receiving God's grace and instruction.

Today use one of the spiritual disciplines you have practiced since beginning this book. Imagine rowing out into God's stream of love. What takes you to the center of the stream?

September 11

REMEMBER

Rembrandt van Rijn (1606–1669), a Dutch artist, painted many biblical themes, demonstrating mastery of shadow and light. Also remember persons affected by the September 11, 2001, terrorist attacks.

READ

Psalm 116:12-19

PONDER

In Hebrew culture, someone delivered from illness or persecution was expected to offer a public expression of thanks. The "cup of salvation" referenced in verse 13 likely refers to the wine offered in a religious ceremony of thanks. How do you express your thanks for all God's bounty to you? (v. 12). The Christian knows there is no way to repay God for the gift of salvation in Jesus Christ. However, we can offer our "cup of salvation" and "vows" in prayers and lives of gratitude, and in acts of kindness and service.

Perhaps verse 15 offers some comfort to the many who mourn on this day because of the 2001 terrorist attacks on the United States. "Precious in the sight of the LORD is the death of . . . faithful ones" (v. 15).

PRAYER/PRACTICE

The third movement in prayer shifts from voluntary to involuntary. Quakers call this experience "being prayed in." This kind of prayer affirms that God prays in you. Such prayer becomes less your effort and more God's grace. It occurs when you cease to be aware of rowing into the stream and let the stream carry you. You let go of the form of a spiritual discipline and trust God to hold you in a silent embrace. Mystics call this kind of prayer "union with God." It involves the mystery and grace of resting in wordless, imageless silence. We cannot make this kind of prayer happen; it is a gift.

Centering prayer and the breath prayer remain good preparations for this kind of resting in silence. Use them in your prayer time today. Remain faithful to the practice whether or not you experience the deep peace of God.

September 12

REMEMBER

Steve Biko (1946–1977), leader of the Black Consciousness movement in South Africa, spoke forcefully for liberation while Nelson Mandela and others were in prison. He died after a beating in prison.

READ

Psalm 117

PONDER

The shortest psalm in the entire Psalter appears packed with large inspiration. Martin Luther thought the whole book of Acts came to be written because of this psalm and its marching orders to spread the good news to all peoples and nations. Paul quoted verse 1 to open the mission of Christ to the Gentiles (Rom. 15:11). In the twentieth century, God's liberating word has traveled to such diverse locations as Montgomery, Alabama; Nicaragua; and South Africa; bringing dignity and worth to all people, regardless of race, economic status, or social standing.

The psalm also provides guidelines for meditation and response. It guides your thoughts and prayers to God's "steadfast love and faithfulness" (v. 2). As you remember blessings you have received, as you acknowledge God's presence in your life, as you journey to a joyful response, you proclaim, "Praise the LORD!" (v. 2).

PRAYER/PRACTICE

The fourth movement in prayer returns to a voluntary action. In the silence, in the depths of prayer, God may and often does speak to you. God may have a task for you to do. The Quakers call these strong impressions "the biddings of God." God may speak to your heart, inviting you to speak out against injustice, like Steve Biko. God may whisper, asking you to care for the dying, like Mother Teresa. Your biddings may be simpler, like calling a friend, visiting someone in the hospital, writing a congressperson. Still, the last movement of prayer urges you to prepare to act, to carry on God's work toward the new community of love.

In the silence of your prayer, listen for the biddings of God.

September 13

REMEMBER

Dante Alighieri (1265–1321), an Italian poet best known for *The Divine Comedy*, tells the story of a pilgrimage from hell to purgatory and finally to paradise.

READ

Psalm 118:1-4

PONDER

This is the last of the "Hallel" or praise psalms used at Jewish festivals. Likely the community sang this psalm in procession, with the opening verses sung antiphonally and the people responding in a chorus to the priest or leader. The refrain, "God's steadfast love endures forever" (v. 1, AP), could be added to any song of praise or experience of blessing. It is challenging to continue singing this refrain in the midst of troublesome experiences. Could Dante sing the refrain through hell and purgatory? You might try copying the refrain onto a card and singing it throughout your day. Can you see God's love at work in all the situations of life?

PRAYER/PRACTICE

Teachers can help you face the obstacles encountered in prayer. It should come as no surprise that most people will experience a difficulty or inability to pray at some time or many times in their spiritual journey. At these times you may feel like God no longer responds or resides near, or you feel restless, distracted, or absent during your time of prayer. You no longer feel connected to God. My Quaker friends would say you apparently have trouble rowing into the stream of God's love. Maybe you can't even find the boat!

When you cannot pray, the first step includes taking time to try to discern what is happening. Spiritual directors and trusted teachers can offer clarity and counsel at such times. For the next few days I invite you to look at obstacles in prayer and ways to remain faithful.

In your prayer time, name some obstacles you have experienced in prayer and what helped you overcome or work through them.

September 14

REMEMBER

In 1963 a bomb thrown into Sixteenth Street Baptist Church in Birmingham, Alabama, killed four black children—Addie Mae Collins, Carole Robertson, Cynthia Wesley, and Denise McNair. Martin Luther King Jr. delivered the eulogy for these children, who became known as the martyrs of Birmingham.

READ

Psalm 118:5-14

PONDER

The civil rights movement in the United States entailed a painful struggle toward freedom and justice. Out of distress and prejudice, a cry for hope rose to God. Despite opposition and resistance, the movement expressed hope, not fear. "What can mortals do to me?" (v. 6). Though marching in the face of angry mobs, fire hoses, and police dogs, demonstrators could recall, "The LORD is on my side to help me; I shall look in triumph on those who hate me" (v. 7). It was better for the marchers to trust God and the company of the nonviolent than to trust in the promised but often lacking help of "mortals and princes" (vv. 8-9) in the form of soldiers or officers. Even though the death of the four girls tragically occurred, "so that I was falling" (v. 13), God appeared, offering "strength and . . . might" (v. 14). The Psalms remain amazingly relevant and provide hope for people struggling for freedom. God hears the cries of the poor.

PRAYER/PRACTICE

Exhaustion is a chief obstacle to prayer. Most people do not realize their weariness until they have time to sleep and find themselves sleeping many hours. Though the workweek may have shortened, we often pack our weekends so full that we have no time for rest and renewal, no sabbath time. If you have trouble focusing in prayer, fatigue may be the reason. You may need to sleep in, rest more, shorten your prayer time for a while, or even find a different time for prayer. This may be a good day to take a nap or look at restructuring your calendar.

September 15

REMEMBER

Saint Catherine of Genoa (1447–1510), a mystic and author of several spiritual classics, devoted her life to caring for the sick.

READ

Psalm 118:15-18

PONDER

The whole nation joined in reciting this psalm of thanksgiving during the Jewish festivals. It reminded the Israelites to look back at trials, sorrows, and defeats and discover that though "the LORD has punished me severely, . . . God did not give me over to death" (v. 18, AP). This psalm reminds me of the adage, "That which does not kill us makes us stronger." Despite all the ordeals, despite death and defeat knocking at the door, "I shall live, and recount the deeds of the LORD" (v. 17). The entire community joins in the praise, singing glad songs and recalling the mighty right hand of God.

PRAYER/PRACTICE

Transitions and life changes can greatly affect your prayer life. Changing jobs or schools, starting a new relationship, adding to the family, discovering an illness, contemplating retirement, or expecting the death of a loved one—all these situations can impede prayer. Children's routines or lack of routines can affect your ability to carve out quality time for prayer. Anxiety over your work or relationships can disrupt your prayer. Sadness and grief sap your energy and seep into your prayer. Talking about these life changes with a spiritual guide or friend can help you recognize what is going on and encourage you to treat yourself more gently. You may also learn to reframe the life change into more of an opportunity and less of a difficulty. Talking over the transition with God in prayer may also help you see the way ahead.

What transitions or life changes are you going through right now, and how do they affect your prayer life? Have you talked to a spiritual director? Have you prayed about your concerns?

September 16

REMEMBER

James "Guadalupe" Carney (1924–1983), an American Jesuit priest, lived with the poor and served as chaplain to resistance fighters in Honduras.

READ

Psalm 118:19-20

PONDER

The Christian faith remains characterized by openness and invitation. Here as the procession of pilgrims stands at the gates of the Temple, the psalmist reminds the people that they will enter the house of God, a sacred place for the just and humble. The Temple exists as a place to give thanks, to seek a right relationship with God. Once people know and understand about sacred space, then the doors will open. Periodically, we need the reminder that though all people are invited, we need to go to church to restore our relationship and give thanks.

PRAYER/PRACTICE

Distractions may hinder prayer. We can control certain interruptions like telephones, radios, cell phones, and pagers. When we cannot control noise from the outside world, often the best practice is to acknowledge and accept the sound, then return to prayer by using your breath prayer or sacred word. Internal distractions, sometimes described as "monkeys jumping around in banana trees" or "bees buzzing around," can offer a greater challenge. Minds may race to other matters, fill with words and images, remember things to do, or recall past mistakes. Again, gently use your simple word or prayer to bring you back to center, to your prayer.

Persistent thoughts may indicate an unhealed wound, a call from God you may be trying to dodge, or a need for confession or action. A Jewish tradition sees distractions in prayer as "blemished deeds in our lives that push their way into the time of prayer in expectation of the blessing that is to come."[3] What distractions need your blessing? Name the distractions in your prayer life, and ask God to help you stay faithful.

September 17

REMEMBER

Saint Hildegard of Bingen (1098–1179), abbess and founder of a Benedictine community, touched many lives through her multiple talents as an author, preacher, and prophet; musician and composer; poet and artist; doctor and pharmacist. She celebrated the goodness of creation and spoke of the "greening power" of God.

READ

Psalm 118:21-25

PONDER

The Hebrew people most likely prayed this psalm at the end of the Passover meal. Israel knew it had once been rejected and exiled, but now the nation knew restoration, had become a "cornerstone" of new possibility, and thanked God, who made all this possible. The psalmist describes their journey from exile to freedom as "marvelous in our eyes" (vv. 22-23). When Christians read this psalm, they think of Jesus as the new cornerstone, since he referred to verses 22-23 in Matthew 21:42. Jesus may have sung this psalm before going out to Gethsemane. The cornerstone that the world discarded, rejected, and did not recognize became the way to new life.

PRAYER/PRACTICE

Sometimes when your faith wavers and God seems far away, you may wonder if you should change how you pray. Jane Redmont suggests:

> Try faithfulness first. You will not know for a while whether it is the right path. You will not find out unless you take the path itself. After a time, it may become clear that faithfulness to your prayer practice or routine is not helping your relationship with God, that the routine itself is getting in the way of prayer. If that is the case, try a change in routine, or a new way of praying.[4]

At other times, you may need to just be present in prayer, speaking and listening to God, and trusting that God works, even if you do not feel it. Thank God for your experiences of prayer, including this moment.

September 18

REMEMBER

Dag Hammarskjöld (1905–1961), secretary general of the United Nations, displayed a sensitive and spiritual wisdom in leading the United Nations. His journal, *Markings,* published after his death, shares the story of a man of faith as well as a public servant.

READ

Psalm 118:26-27

PONDER

The procession now approaches the center of the Temple, the altar in the inner court. On this joyous occasion the people wave branches and praise God. Again, as we read the psalm, we see from a New Testament perspective. We think of Passion/Palm Sunday, where the people waved branches as Jesus entered Jerusalem and shouted the words of this psalm: "Blessed is the one who comes in the name of the LORD" (v. 26).

The two processions culminate in praise and worship, proceeding toward the altar in the Temple or the Communion table in Christian churches. This psalm brings all the experiences of the journey to the celebration of worship. "God, . . . Create a readiness to receive from you and a faithfulness to respond to you, so that all you give in love and all we bring in praise may be fire on your altar. Amen."[5]

PRAYER/PRACTICE

Sometimes obstacles arise in prayer because of a lack of commitment to persevere. You may not set a time to pray and therefore other activities crowd out your prayer time. You may keep experimenting with different ways of prayer but find no pattern you wish to practice. You may claim an interest in prayer but demonstrate no serious devotion. You lack the discipline to show up faithfully and consistently and wonder why prayer does not seem to work. Comedian Woody Allen once remarked, "Eighty percent of life is just showing up."

Ask God for the strength to show up for prayer, or thank God for the grace that you have been able to show up for prayer.

September 19

REMEMBER

Huston Smith, a contemporary scholar, writes and teaches about the value of knowing and appreciating the world's religions. He would revel in the Celtic wisdom that teaches that three candles illumine every darkness: truth, nature, and knowledge.

READ

Psalm 118:28-29

PONDER

This marvelous psalm ends with the leader inviting the whole community to join in thanking and praising God for God's goodness and steadfast love. The psalm has acted as a pilgrimage—recalling anguishing distress and painful captivity, calling and pleading for God's help, and singing songs of victory, not defeat. The psalmist describes the people bringing all the experiences of life to the place of worship. The more we know of God, the more reason we have to offer praise. The more our knowledge increases, the more our thanksgiving develops. All of life elicits and evokes our praise.

PRAYER/PRACTICE

Your image of God may hinder your prayer. I have counseled persons who found praying difficult because they saw God as a stern judge, critical and demanding. Because they did not view God as offering warmth, welcome, or delight, they had little desire to spend time in prayer. Still others find it hard to pray because of anger over world situations or frustration and discouragement with the institutional church. Where is God in the midst of the hurt and pain? Why has the church sometimes caused hurt and pain? Why has the church fostered judgment and hatred instead of mercy and love?

The Psalms provide a good antidote to such obstacles in prayer because they depict God as a tender shepherd, a strong refuge, and a soaring eagle. They give you words to pray your anger at injustice and laments to name your hurt. Write a lament today about some injustice. Or make a list of images or titles of God. To which images or titles do you respond?

September 20

REMEMBER

Henri Nouwen (1932–1996), a Dutch-born Catholic priest, became a popular and influential spiritual writer. His books invite readers to deeper intimacy with Jesus and to solidarity with the poor and wounded.

READ

Psalm 119:1-8

PONDER

The longest psalm, also the longest chapter in the Bible, begins with a word that permeates the psalm: *Happy*. The focus of joy is the law, specifically the first five books of the Hebrew Scriptures and more generally, Israel's relationship to God. The psalm appears remarkably structured. Except for seven verses, every verse contains a synonym for law—commandments, decrees, precepts, judgments, and so forth. The psalm has twenty-two stanzas; in each stanza all eight lines begin with the same letter of the Hebrew alphabet. The order of the psalm leads to a prayer for God's help in living a life of praise.

PRAYER/PRACTICE

Even writers and teachers of prayer experience difficulties in prayer. In the journal of his last year, Henri Nouwen wrote:

> The truth is that I do not feel much, if anything, when I pray. . . . None of my five senses is being touched. . . .Whereas for a long time the Spirit acted so clearly through my flesh, now I feel nothing. I have lived with the expectation that prayer would become easier as I grow older and closer to death. But the opposite seems to be happening. . . .
>
> Maybe part of this darkness and dryness is the result of my overactivity. As I grow older I become busier and spend less and less time in prayer. . . . Maybe the time has come to let go of my prayer, my effort to be close to God, my way of being in communion with the Divine, and to allow the Spirit of God to blow freely in me.[6]

In what ways do Nouwen's words connect with your experiences? In your journal, write about your current prayer life.

September 21

REMEMBER

Saint Matthew (first century) left behind his occupation as a tax collector and became one of Jesus' disciples.

READ

Psalm 119:9-16

PONDER

God's way to walk through life, revealed through the scriptures, provides an ample guide for keeping young people's lives pure (v. 9). The wisdom of God advocates not hard rules to be kept or limitations to be endured but pathways that lead to joy. Children not only need rules, but they also need a hand to hold on the path. Further, the psalmist suggests treasuring God's Word in our hearts so we may not sin against God (v. 11). Jeremiah echoes the same thought when through him God decrees that the covenant will be written on human hearts so they won't forget (Jer. 31:33). If God's words reside in our hearts, it will be easy to "delight in your statutes; I will not forget your word" (v. 16).

PRAYER/PRACTICE

In prayer, the call comes to surrender to the God who loves us, yet many find relinquishing control difficult. We may try to control the outcomes of our prayers, defining how and when God should respond. We may spend more time talking to God than listening or fear what we might discover in prayer. "When we pray, we encounter not only God but also our own truth, the brokenness of our human condition."[7]

Prayer may not always bring you peace; at times prayer may become a furnace of transformation. You can carry to God in prayer your need to control and your fear of facing your wounds and sins. Because God is merciful and full of compassion, you can let go of your fears and anxieties and enter more deeply into prayer. Thomas R. Kelly suggests, "Begin where you are. Obey *now*. Use what little obedience you are capable of, even if it be like a grain of mustard seed. . . . Live this present moment . . . in utter, utter submission and openness toward [God]."[8]

September 22

REMEMBER

The autumn equinox blesses us with a day of balance for the entire world as everyone experiences twelve hours of sunlight and twelve hours of darkness.

READ

Psalm 119:17-24

PONDER

Imagine writing 176 verses about any topic, never mind starting each stanza with a different letter! Appreciate how the psalmist must have entered into a deep and personal relationship with God to be filled with such a creative mind and poetic spirit.

In this stanza, there exists deep longing to know and obey the commandments. "My soul is consumed with longing for your ordinances at all times" (v. 20). The psalmist prays, "open my eyes" (v. 18), desiring to be more attentive to the words of guidance, to treat them as valued counselors (v. 24). We most often don't need another book, but rather, better vision to see in the Hebrew Scriptures and in the life of Jesus the way that leads to joy and peace. Our continual prayer remains, "Lord, help me see."

PRAYER/PRACTICE

One writer said he wanted to be so in touch with God's creation that he wanted to feel the tilt of the earth on the equinoxes. I don't know if that is possible, but on this equinox day, feel a connection with the divine Creator who blesses you with equal hours of light and darkness.

If possible, plan an autumn celebration. Decorate with autumn leaves of red, yellow, and gold. Invite others to talk with you about transitions, considering these questions: What is changing in your life? What do you need to release so that new life might grow? What are you gathering in to sustain you through the winter?

Begin a series of prayers with, "God of the day and God of the darkness. . . ." Consider saying a special prayer at sunrise and sunset, and give thanks to God for the balance in your life.

September 23

REMEMBER

Padre Pio (1887–1968), an Italian monk, bore wounds on his hands and feet like the wounds of Christ at his crucifixion and reportedly made remarkable prophecies and worked many miracles.

READ

Psalm 119:25-32

PONDER

Twice in this stanza, the psalmist uses the word *cling* (vv. 25, 31). This word conveys someone in trouble, reaching out to hold on for dear life. Other images come to mind. God remains the solid rock to which we cling, the strong hand to pull us out of despair. "When I told of my ways, you answered me" (v. 26). In times of trouble, the psalmist reminds us to cling to God and to God's promises.

Grief emerges as a second image in these verses. "My soul melts away for sorrow; strengthen me according to your word" (v. 28). In times of bereavement, the words of scripture become a great comfort. I do not believe I have ever done a funeral or memorial service without using the Twenty-third Psalm. God's words give strength and comfort, a very present help in times of need.

PRAYER/PRACTICE

Later in the book (Dec.) you will spend more time with the experience often called the "dark night of the soul," but since I have brought up the matter of praying through the obstacles in prayer, I should also note that sometimes these problems arise from a deep dryness or darkness that is not helped or changed by increased commitment or new patterns of prayer. The experience of God's absence—empty silence, inability to pray, the dark night—usually lasts longer and seems more uncomfortable than other difficulties in prayer. For now, remember that faithfulness is a key to praying in the darkness, that wise spiritual direction can be a valuable companion, and that rushing to fill the emptiness usually is counterproductive. If you are in the midst of a dark night, read the entries for December 14 and following.

September 24

REMEMBER

Douglas Steere (1901–1995), a Quaker writer, teacher, and ecumenical pioneer, participated in Vatican II as an observer. He remained active in relief work after World War II but left his greatest mark as one who helped people get to know God.

READ

Psalm 119:33-40

PONDER

The image of teaching appears in this stanza. "Teach me, O LORD, the way of your statutes . . ." (v. 33); "Give me understanding, that I may keep your law and observe it with my whole heart" (v. 34). People thirst for knowledge and wisdom. Of all the subjects we can study, none yields greater importance than learning God's ways, learning that God loved us first, learning that Christ came to save us, and learning that God's love remains stronger than death. The psalmist adds, "Give me the desire to obey your laws rather than to get rich. Keep me from paying attention to what is worthless; be good to me, as you have promised" (vv. 36-37, GNT). We can study other subjects, like riches and vanities, but they will not lead to God.

PRAYER/PRACTICE

In her book *Soul Feast,* Marjorie Thompson describes prayer as communication and as communion.[9] Prayer as communication involves a two-way street: speaking and listening. Much of the challenge in prayer concerns developing the art of listening. Thompson suggests that we practice listening to God in the words of scripture; in the glories and mysteries of creation; in the words of others; in the up-and-down circumstances of our lives; in our dreams; and in the words, images, and dialogues in our journals.[10] Indeed, we can view most of life as a message from God, for nothing appears so insignificant, so small, that God cannot use it or be found at its center.

What ways of listening to God have you found most helpful? Give thanks to God and be extra attentive to listening for God today.

September 25

REMEMBER

Saint Aidan (d. 651), an Irish monk of Iona known for his learning, preaching, and kindness to the poor, founded the monastery on the holy island of Lindisfarne.

READ

Psalm 119:41-48

PONDER

The disciples wondered if they would ever be able to speak like Jesus—from a centered, fearless place. Jesus promised the Spirit would guide them into truth (John 16:13). The psalmist likewise focuses on speech. "Then I shall have an answer for those who taunt me, for I trust in your word" (v. 42). "I will also speak of your decrees before kings, and shall not be put to shame" (v. 46). God's truth and law give us confidence to deal with those who dislike us and those who tower over us. We stand firm because we know God's precepts; we meditate on God's commandments; and we love the One who promises to be with us in our words and deeds.

PRAYER/PRACTICE

Speaking to God in prayer requires "speaking from the heart with unreserved honesty."[11] The Psalms reveal that feelings of anger, praise, despair, and hatred can be expressed to God in prayer.

A simple acronym, ACTS, can remind us of elements to include in prayer: Adoration, Confession, Thanksgiving, and Supplication. I prefer to use five fingers to remember an order in my prayers: the thumb represents adoration; the index finger, thanksgiving; the middle finger, confession; the ring finger, intercession; and the little finger, petition. The little finger reminds me that my wants or needs do not occupy the central or strongest part of my prayer. Spending time on the other four elements of prayer keeps my own petitions in proper perspective.

Try using your five fingers as you speak to God. The "five-finger prayer" also proves helpful for children who are beginning to pray and adults who struggle with praying in public.

September 26

REMEMBER

Jeremiah (B.C.E.), one of the major prophets of the Hebrew Scriptures, called the southern kingdom of Judah to task for ignoring the poor and for disregarding God's covenant.

READ

Psalm 119:49-56

PONDER

The psalmist uses *promise* as a word for God's law. "This is my comfort in my distress, that your promise gives me life" (v. 50). We sometimes wish for a better life instead of fully relying on God's promises. Our wishes usually connect to human desires and short-term goals, whereas our lasting hopes remain centered in God's promises. God promises comfort in times of sorrow and distress, presence in the midst of loneliness, and joy that overcomes sadness.

This stanza of Psalm 119 invites us to sing our prayers. We don't often think about singing our country's constitution or our church's bylaws, but the psalmist shows no qualms about singing God's commandments: "Your statutes have been my songs" (v. 54).

PRAYER/PRACTICE

Prayer is not only communication but also communion with God. Marjorie Thompson describes communion as the "dimension of relationship that goes beyond words, images, or actions. Communion transcends the particularities of communication."[12]

Contemplation allows resting in God, gazing toward the One who loves us immeasurably, being present to the moment and unconscious of time. "In contemplation we move from communicating with God through speech to communing with God through the gaze of love. Words fall away, and the most palpable reality is being present to the lover of our souls."[13] Your breath prayer or sacred word of centering prayer can help you enter this time of communing with God. Today, after you center yourself with your word or phrase, let the word or image fade from consciousness and enter the place of union with God.

September 27

REMEMBER

Saint Vincent de Paul (1581–1660), a French priest, dedicated his ministry to the poor, trained priests (the Vincentians) to work with the poor, and founded hospitals and orphanages.

READ

Psalm 119:57-64

PONDER

Preacher Dwight L. Moody used to say that every Bible should be bound in shoe leather. This statement cleverly reminded Christians that God's Word is meant to be lived out in everyday life, on the streets, in the classroom, and in the office or factory. The psalmist concurs: "When I think of your ways, I turn my feet to your decrees; I hurry and do not delay to keep your commandments" (vv. 59-60).

Today as you walk, talk, shop, work, or study, carry God's commandments with you.

PRAYER/PRACTICE

Another way to enter contemplative prayer is what Marjorie Thompson calls the Prayer of Presence.[14]

Find a comfortable prayer posture, one that allows you to feel relaxed and alert. Breathe deeply. See yourself breathing in peace and breathing out tension.

Relax your mind. If any thoughts come to mind, give them to God and focus your attention on God's presence. Remain aware that divine love surrounds and upholds you. God breathes life into you with every breath. Rest in this holy presence—imagine yourself as a child resting in the lap of a loving parent, or see yourself floating on a cloud of pillows. Let God hold you in tender embrace; rest and soak up this love that holds you. Breathe deeply of this life-giving presence.

At the end of your prayer time, thank God for any gifts you received.

September 28

REMEMBER

Saint Wenceslaus (c. 907–929), a Christian king of Bohemia, encouraged his subjects to become Christian, built churches, and helped the poor. Recognized as a patron saint of the Czech Republic and Slovakia, Wenceslaus is memorialized in a well-known Christmas carol.

READ

Psalm 119:65-72

PONDER

Life has many paths. Some paths lead to dead ends. Others lead to suffering. The psalmist has taken a few of these divergent paths. "Before I was humbled I went astray" (v. 67). In humility, the psalmist admits to following a few paths that led away from God's commandments. But the psalmist can also look back and say, "It is good for me that I was humbled, so that I might learn your statutes" (v. 71). We know that setbacks can bring us from the wayward path back to God, that suffering can teach us a great deal, and that struggles can make us rely more on God. We do not ask for problems or suffering, only that whatever happens may draw us closer to God.

PRAYER/PRACTICE

In the life of prayer, you cultivate an open heart, ready to hear and receive from the bounty of God's grace. You cultivate an open spirit, ready to try different forms or experiences of prayer. You cultivate a persistence, which keeps you praying in all seasons and maintains a balance between speaking and listening, between communication and communion, between sabbath and action, between thanksgiving and petition, between confession and intercession.

Today look back over the last nine months of your prayer life. How have you nurtured an open heart? What new forms of prayer have you tried? How would you describe your current practice of prayer?

September 29

REMEMBER

Michael, Gabriel, and Raphael, three archangels mentioned by name in the Catholic Bible, served as God's messengers. Michael appears as the strong fighter/protector in Daniel and Revelation. Gabriel speaks to Zechariah and Mary in the Gospels. Raphael brings healing in the Book of Tobit.

READ

Psalm 119:73-80

PONDER

Someone once said, "We may be the only gospel some people read." This maxim reminds us that our lives reveal much about our faith. We pray that others may see something of God in our words and deeds, that Christ's light may shine in our speech and actions. The psalmist hopes that others will see and rejoice "because I have hoped in your word" (v. 74). "Let those who fear you turn to me, so that they may know your decrees" (v. 79). Perhaps as the psalmist gathered with others, a mutual upbuilding of the community occurred as they sought to know and live by God's commandments.

PRAYER/PRACTICE

Angels have become popular in recent years, a fact that either attracts or repels people on the spiritual journey. Some Christians are helped by knowing that angels have a long tradition in the church. On this angel/saint day, remember that Michael, associated with winter, embodies wisdom and love and helps when one needs insight and openness. Gabriel means "the strength of God." Associated with summer, Gabriel provides the strength to overcome fears and bring forth new life. Raphael means "healer of God" in Hebrew. Associated with autumn, Raphael furnishes the healing power to purge us of illusions that keep us from God and from realizing our potential. Uriel, though not mentioned in scripture, is traditionally viewed as the fourth archangel. His name in Hebrew means "God is my light," and he brings the gift of clarity.

September 30

REMEMBER

Saint Jerome (331–420), a monk and a scholar, first translated the scriptures from the original Greek into Latin.

READ

Psalm 119:81-88

PONDER

The language of lament dominates this stanza. Even though the psalmist has faithfully kept the commandments, nothing goes well for him. "My soul languishes for your salvation" (v. 81). "The arrogant have dug pitfalls for me" (v. 85). "I am persecuted without cause. . . . They have almost made an end of me on earth" (vv. 86-87). Still the psalmist turns to God for help (v. 86), keeps hoping in God's Word (v. 81), and does not forsake or desert God's precepts (v. 87).

Our lives can develop such a rhythm when the going becomes difficult. In the face of troubles we can say, "We have this trouble, but we also have God's promise." We can develop a ritual of "Yes, troubles exist, but God remains faithful." Its short version is a mantra, "Yes, but!"

PRAYER/PRACTICE

Thomas Merton once said, "The great thing is prayer. Prayer itself. If you want a life of prayer, the way to get it is by praying. . . . You start where you are and you deepen what you already have."[15]

Continue evaluating your prayer life. How have you grown in your practice and your dedication to prayer? What new forms of prayer would you like to deepen? What sabbath days have you scheduled on your calendar? When will you next meet with your spiritual director? Give thanks for what you already have!

October

Autumn God, the planet turns
and the earth signals a change.
Open me to the transitions I need to face in my own life.
Be with me in the letting go,
the saying good-bye
to habits, relationships, and plans
that stand in your way of growing.
Deepen my trust that as I let go,
like the falling leaves,
I will always fall into your embrace. Amen.

October 1

REMEMBER

Saint Thérèse of Lisieux (1873–1897), a French mystic and devotional writer, appealed to the pope for permission to enter the Carmelite monastery at age fifteen. Her autobiography, *The Story of a Soul,* simply recounts her experiences, good and bad, in the presence and love of God.

READ

Psalm 119:89-96

PONDER

Our continued reading of the longest psalm immerses us in the psalmist's deep reverence for the words of God. "I will never forget your precepts, for by them you have given me life. I am yours; save me, for I have sought your precepts" (vv. 93-94). The psalmist's life centers on following God's laws.

In the same way, Thérèse of Lisieux, in her brief life span, determined to live a holy life. An awareness of Christ's love filled her every moment, even as she did the simplest task or suffered the petty insults and injuries that come in life. She believed that offering the little things of life to God opened the way to holiness. Though Thérèse did nothing we would call extraordinary, her devotion to God in the midst of the ordinary continues to profoundly affect persons around the world.

PRAYER/PRACTICE

Can you sense the transition in seasons? The trees parade their colors, a last show of delight, a delicate falling dance before settling in for a time of rest and renewal. Perhaps you feel stripped of vibrant activity and growth and long to rest and renew, to reflect and review. The cooler weather and longer nights pull you inside to warmth and rest.

Try writing a prayer for autumn that expresses your sense of transitions and letting go. You might start and end with:

Autumn God, remind me again of the process of growing and changing. . . . Fill my life again with the harvest of your blessings, and let me sing songs of gratitude and thanksgiving. Amen.

October 2

REMEMBER

The pilgrim, a nineteenth-century Russian Orthodox wanderer, repeated the Jesus Prayer thousands of times a day until he understood the meaning of "pray without ceasing."

READ

Psalm 119:97-102

PONDER

Reading the Bible all our waking hours or praying on our knees all day is not what scripture intends when it encourages us to immerse ourselves in God's Word and to "pray without ceasing" (1 Thess. 5:17). The psalmist and the unnamed Russian pilgrim describe ways to carry out these important spiritual disciplines while living in the world. The psalmist meditated on God's Word throughout the day (v. 97). Most likely the psalmist memorized a portion of scripture and thought of it throughout the day; this is the practice of *lectio divina*, which you learned in March. The pilgrim's prayer consisted of a simple mantra, a short verse he prayed over and over as he breathed, walked, and talked on his journey throughout Russia. The saints and the psalmist invite you to chew and meditate on God's Word, like a cow chewing its cud, until it becomes a part of you. Such a practice will make you "wiser than [your] enemies" (v. 98).

PRAYER/PRACTICE

Today is a good day to revisit your practice of using short sentences, phrases, or single words for prayer. Many people still find the Jesus Prayer ("Lord Jesus Christ, Son of God, have mercy on me, a sinner") to be a gentle guide to prayer. It floats easily on an inhalation and exhalation. The breath prayer, which you explored in January, emerges from the Jesus Prayer.

Intentionally use the Jesus Prayer or your own breath prayer today.

October 3

REMEMBER

John Calvin (1509–1564), a French-Swiss Protestant reformer, theologian, and writer, sought to make Geneva a model Christian city. His writing and preaching led to the founding of the Presbyterian denomination.

READ

Psalm 119:103-4

PONDER

The Psalms teem with emotion—anger and despair, praise and thanksgiving, confidence and pride, humility and sadness. They stand out as a poet's delight, a marvel of verse and song. They also taste "sweet, sweeter than honey to my mouth!" (v. 103). God's words not only challenge us at times, but they also give pleasure and delight. The Psalms extend to us a banquet of joy, a feast of wisdom, a table of gladness. What words of the Psalms have you taken in with delight? What verses do you find yourself meditating upon? What images sustain you in difficult times? What verses give you understanding for your decisions? Give thanks to God for the sweetness of God's Word.

PRAYER/PRACTICE

You make decisions every day: what to wear, what to eat, what channel to watch. Most decisions are not earthshaking or life-changing. They fall into the realm of your everyday walk with God; they flow out of your values of following Jesus. At times, though, you face major choices, tough decisions, and you seek God's will and direction for your life. Discernment, the name given to this process of attending to God's voice, focuses on making decisions in the light of faith. Discernment can help you distinguish the true movement of the Holy Spirit from personal willfulness and social expectation. It does not pretend to be an exact science but rather a deepening trust in the mystery of God who desires that we listen and obey. As you look at the process of discernment, you might begin by praying this verse throughout the day: "If we live by the Spirit, let us also be guided by the Spirit" (Gal. 5:25).

October 4

REMEMBER

Saint Francis of Assisi (1182–1226), the son of a wealthy Italian cloth merchant, followed God's call to live a life of poverty, repair the church of San Damiano, and renew the spirit of compassion and simplicity in the whole church. He felt deep reverence for nature, lived a joyful and radical gospel of peace, founded the Franciscan Order (Friars Minor), and, according to tradition, created the first nativity representations.

READ

Psalm 119:105-12

PONDER

A contemporary songwriter has etched the words from this passage into my brain. I can sing verse 105 as a mantra: "Thy word is a lamp unto my feet and a light unto my path" (KJV). Though the stanzas of the song mention various difficulties, the refrain strongly reminds us that God's Word is a lamp, a light to show us the path.

Saint Francis took a different path from most of his contemporaries, becoming a poor beggar. Deeply rooted in God's Word, he humbly followed Jesus in a life of service, simplicity, and obedience. He challenged the well-to-do to a life of joyful compassion, and he encouraged warring nations to pursue a life of peace. His life encourages us to be instruments for peace, to let our lives proclaim the gospel.

PRAYER/PRACTICE

Scripture may not give you precise answers to specific questions, but it sheds light on your pathway and provides signposts when choices appear like a fork in the road. During times of discernment, you need to cultivate an awareness of biblical images and verses. Do certain verses come to mind as you ponder a decision? Do images from scripture emerge in your dreams or prayers? Do biblical characters and their decisions shed light on your path? These become important guides as you seek to make faithful decisions.

Today carry Psalm 119:105 in your mind and heart. Remain open to any other scripture verses or images that come to mind.

October 5

REMEMBER

Jonathan Edwards (1703–1758), an American Puritan theologian and fiery preacher, led the revival known as the Great Awakening. He taught that God's excellency, wisdom, and love was in everything.

READ

Psalm 119:113-20

PONDER

"I hate those who are not completely loyal to you, but I love your law" (v. 113, GNT). The psalmist is anything but timid in declaring a single-minded devotion to God's law, using strong words that we sometimes say too casually ("I hate rap music"; "I love chocolate"). Sometimes we act only curious or halfhearted in our approach to scripture and in following God's way. Thomas à Kempis wrote, "Our curiosity often hinders us in the reading of the Scriptures, when we want to understand and to discuss, when we should pass simply on. If you wish to absorb well, read with humility, simplicity and faith."[1] We need to read scripture with love, hope, and a single-minded devotion.

PRAYER/PRACTICE

Discernment rests on the belief that the living Christ leads all to the heart of God. God does not hide the purpose of life. Neither does God try to deceive us or to make life difficult but constantly seeks us and bids us to draw near. To enter the process of discernment implies a belief that God's will can be known. Perhaps a better translation of the Latin *voluntas* is "yearning" or "longing" rather than "will." What does God yearn for you? What yearning has awakened in you?

God's will is not some preestablished, rigid scheme beyond knowing but rather a longing that connects and interacts with your deepest feelings and desires. "In a discernment we look at ourselves—at our feelings, our values, our priorities—and try to uncover our deepest yearnings."[2]

Record in your journal some of your deepest yearnings. How might your longing be a response to God's initiative and prompting?

October 6

REMEMBER

John Woolman (1720–1772), an American Quaker, opposed slavery and war taxes and lived a life of simplicity and spirituality. His journal reveals how he lived out the radical demands of the gospel. Woolman's persistent testimony to the equality and dignity of every person led the Quakers to become the earliest religious group to oppose slavery.

READ

Psalm 119:121-28

PONDER

Verse 122 is one of seven verses in this psalm that does not contain the word *law* or a synonym for law. That note should not obscure a theme that is more prominent and more difficult for many North Americans (or the well-to-do in any society). The psalmist says, "Truly I love your commandments more than gold, more than fine gold" (v. 127). God's Word offers life, abundant life, but the allure of money tempts so strongly, vying for our highest allegiance. Yet God's law must shape our behavior and our spending.

John Woolman exemplifies someone guided by God's Word. When his successful business demanded more of his time, he cut back its growth to give him time to travel and speak about ending slavery and living at peace. He chose faithfulness to God over more gold.

PRAYER/PRACTICE

Discernment concerns making choices between two or more good possibilities. God usually works in and through our major covenants. Our choices usually connect with our God-given talents and abilities.

As you think about decisions you face, offer this prayer:

In your wisdom, God of freedom, you created a world where there are always choices. Then you gifted us with sight and sense to make good choices. When I am faced with a difficult decision, soften my anxiety, sharpen my insight, strengthen my commitment to listen to your nudges, and remind me to trust your way. Amen.

October 7

REMEMBER

Desmond Tutu (b. 1931), born this day, emerged as a leader of the anti-apartheid movement in South Africa. He led justice and reconciliation efforts between oppressors and victims after the fall of apartheid.

READ

Psalm 119:129-34

PONDER

"Keep my steps steady according to your promise" (v. 133). Archbishop Tutu appears small in stature, but he stands tall, faithfully and steadily speaking out against injustice and forging a new way of reconciliation. The long and painful struggle against apartheid caused many blacks to lose their lives. Yet many persisted in their opposition, taking steady steps toward justice according to God's desire for freedom and dignity for all of God's creation.

We keep our steps steady by reading and meditating on the Bible. As wonderful as the Bible is, it will not benefit us if we do not spend time with it. "The unfolding of your words gives light; it imparts understanding to the simple" (v. 130). Keep reading God's Word.

PRAYER/PRACTICE

In discernment, you not only consider your covenants and abilities, but you also listen for God's call in the needs of the world and in the concerns of your community. My decision to enter the ministry was shaped by friends who knew of my wrestling with the decision, who said, "You have gifts that the church and the world can use. The church needs what you have to offer."

As you consider choices of vocation, the discernment process includes these kinds of questions: Which choice will help me be more loving and contribute to a more loving and just world? How am I being called to greater servanthood? How do my gifts and abilities match the needs of the community? How is God speaking to me in the cries and concerns of the world? Reflect on your involvements as God's servant in the world. Read more about the life of Desmond Tutu.

October 8

REMEMBER

Penny Lernoux (1940–1989), an American journalist, described the struggle for liberation in Latin America from the vantage point of the church's work with the poor. Her writing showed the human face of hope in the midst of oppression.

READ

Psalm 119:135-36

PONDER

Compassion lies at the heart of the Christian faith. "My eyes shed streams of tears because your law is not kept" (v. 136). When injustice reigns in the world, when oppression tramples the poor, when those who speak out against wrong disappear in the night, somewhere a church (or many churches) weeps a pool of tears. When the Ten Commandments are ignored, parents dishonored, neighbors shot, or relationships violated, somewhere a river of tears flows. When individuals show indifference for the grace of God or the plight of the needy, a stream of tears flows to heaven. And God's grief joins our tears when war, greed, violence, hunger, prejudice, and environmental destruction scar the face of creation. "My eyes shed streams of tears because your law is not kept."

PRAYER/PRACTICE

Imagination provides one tool in the discernment process. Saint Ignatius (July 31) suggested exercises to use before a more formal and lengthy process. Imagine yourself on your deathbed. In this fantasy, ask yourself what decision you wish you had made at this particular time in your life. Or, imagine yourself before the judgment seat of God, who dearly loves you. From God's perspective, what choice would have been wisest? Another exercise is to imagine another facing the same decision. That person comes to you for counsel. What advice would you give in that situation?[3]

Try these imagination exercises for a decision that you face, or share them with a friend who faces a choice.

October 9

REMEMBER

The International Fellowship of Reconciliation was founded in 1919 in response to the horrors of war in Europe. Today branches of IFOR around the world build bridges of understanding between people and clear the paths to peace.

READ

Psalm 119:137-44

PONDER

An older friend of mine says, "I don't know what people do without God." She has seen a beloved daughter die in a car accident, endured many hospitalizations, and battled addictions. Yet she understands the psalmist: "Trouble and anguish have come upon me, but your commandments are my delight" (v. 143). God has seen her through many hard times. She knows the truth of verse 140: "Your promise is well tried." Her faith testifies to God's abiding presence, well tried and never failing. Centuries of testimony reveal that God's Word and God's love abide, endure, and offer hope and delight.

PRAYER/PRACTICE

Saint Ignatius developed a process of discernment that has stood the test of time. Gather the data. What does the decision involve, and what are your gifts and graces? Consider the negative or less attractive choice and try living for several days as if you have made that decision. Listen to your feelings and your body, and record your observations. After several days, try the other alternative and again notice how you feel when you live into this choice. Make a tentative decision and see if you sense God's peace. If not, try the other decision and see if God's peace resides there. If God's peace abides after either alternative, make the decision and give God thanks. If you feel no clear peace, consider postponing the decision. If a decision is needed, choose one and trust God for the future.[4]

Recall a time you felt God's consolation and peace after making a decision. Use this process for a decision you have to make.

October 10

REMEMBER

Mollie Rogers (1882–1955) pushed American Catholics to see that women could be involved in mission. She founded a new religious order, the Maryknoll Sisters, who lived not in a convent but went overseas to live with the poor.

READ

Psalm 119:145-52

PONDER

Dietrich Bonhoeffer wrote, "The early morning belongs to the Church of the risen Christ."[5] Christians have long encouraged one another to begin the day with words of praise and petition to God the Creator. "I rise before dawn and cry for help; I put my hope in your words" (v. 147). Monastic communities have traditionally used the Psalms in an early morning vigil, long before dawn in some monasteries. To begin the morning conscious of God, to offer words of praise, and to remind ourselves of the source of our hope centers each day and its activities in the heart of God. If morning begins on the holy path, we can confidently walk with God the whole day long.

PRAYER/PRACTICE

Making a decision may not prove difficult when one gets knocked to the ground, sees a light, and hears a voice, as happened with Paul (Acts 9). Such drama rarely occurs, though, so you must learn to look and listen for the nudges and whispers of God. God often speaks through unexpected events and persons. Many individuals have learned to pay attention to surprising hints that hold out a different way of seeing and being in the world. Discerning people listen for the "sound of sheer silence" (1 Kings 19:12), the still small voice of God, the subtle presence of God in everyday life.

Pay attention today to the unexpected, to the silences between the noise and clamor, to the surprises and delights of God.

October 11

Thich Nhat Hanh (b. 1926), a Vietnamese Buddhist monk, poet, and teacher, founded a school that encouraged Vietnamese youth to work nonviolently for peace in the midst of the Vietnam War. He continues to teach and write about peace and spirituality. His book *The Miracle of Mindfulness* serves as a contemporary guide to meditation.

READ

Psalm 119:153-60

PONDER

The way of mindfulness, as taught by Thich Nhat Hanh and other Buddhists, finds common threads in the psalmist's understanding of meditating on God's precepts. Our awareness of God and our mindfulness of the present moment links the divine with the ordinary. God's Word, when we receive it, love it, and meditate on it, offers guidance for the common experiences of life and wisdom to share with others. God's truth becomes lived out in our day-to-day interactions. God's decrees, read and digested, become part of the very fiber of our being and doing.

PRAYER/PRACTICE

United Methodists have contributed a pattern of reflection that has proven useful in discernment. The Wesleyan quadrilateral invites individuals and groups to reflect on four areas in making decisions: (1) What does *scripture* say about the decision you are facing? (2) What does *Christian tradition* say? Do you find precedents in church history, other religious communities, religious writings, or the lives of the saints? (3) What bearing does *experience* bring? How is the Spirit of God active now in people's experience? What is the testimony of those involved? (4) Is the decision *reasonable*? Does it make logical sense?

Use the quadrilateral to think through an issue or decision you are facing.

October 12

REMEMBER

Elizabeth Fry (1780–1845), an English Quaker, read the Bible to women prisoners, which led her to campaign for prison reform in Great Britain and abroad.

READ

Psalm 119:161-68

PONDER

"Seven times a day I praise you for your righteous ordinances" (v. 164). Perhaps the psalmist refers to specific times of prayer during the day, but many scholars believe that "seven times a day" may indicate many times a day or continual prayer. Memorizing verses and passages of scripture allows you to recall them throughout the day. "Great peace" comes to those who love and meditate on the precepts of God, an inner assurance of God's presence that keeps them from stumbling even though the road may be rough (v. 165). God's law not only is better than gold (v. 127), but it can withstand the persecutions and harassment of those in power (v. 161).

PRAYER/PRACTICE

The path of discernment builds on prayer patterns you already have practiced. Prayer is central to any discernment practice, but you may find real help for discernment through creating a special breath prayer for the decision you are facing. In a spirit of stillness and prayer, choose a name or image for God and then imagine God asking you what you want. Keep in mind your desire for clarity in your decision making. You might choose a phrase that focuses on deciding, such as: "Show me your way." "Give me your guidance." "Help me make a wise decision." "Let me see your path." "Be my light and guide." Your new breath prayer will help you remain attentive, focused on God and on the ways God speaks to you and seeks to guide you through the everyday happenstances of life.

Take time to develop a breath prayer for discernment.

October 13

REMEMBER

The Syrophoenician woman (first century) persuaded Jesus that even dogs eat crumbs off the table, so even Gentiles deserved God's care. Her persistence opened the door to ministry beyond the Jews.

READ

Psalm 119:169-72

PONDER

Like a grand symphony that moves toward a big finish, this powerful meditation on the law of God reaches a crescendo of praise. "My lips will pour forth praise. . . . My tongue will sing of your promise" (vv. 171-172). The repetition not only constitutes good poetry, but it emphasizes the importance of the thought. This long psalm examines God's commandments as one would a diamond, looking at all the different facets from different angles and finally summing it all up in a glorious song of praise. God's way, God's path, God's statutes, and God's commandments are right, just, and true (v. 172).

PRAYER/PRACTICE

Discernment is not typically a solitary practice. A spiritual director or some spiritual companions can help you pay attention and respond to God. Other people can urge you to do some inner work. What messages might God send through your dreams? Do they contain any recurring images, any vivid or intense pictures or dialogues? What messages does your body give as you think about the choice? Do you feel tense and edgy? Are you sleeping well? Do you feel an inner peace? One of my friends always asks if I am keeping a journal in times of decision making. Am I recording images and thoughts, dreams and insights? When I face a decision, I feel the need to ask others, especially my faith community, to pray for me. Though I ultimately have to make the decision, I turn to fellow travelers for help with overcoming blind spots and biases.

Pay attention today to any images that come from dreams or any messages from your body or encounters with others. Carry your journal with you, ready to listen and record.

October 14

REMEMBER

Guido of Arezzo (c. 992–1050), an Italian Benedictine monk, revolutionized music by adding two lines to the musical staff, thus developing a system that enabled people to sing a notated song correctly from the written page.

READ

Psalm 119:173-76

PONDER

I wish this psalm ended with a grand finale of praise. It would provide a fitting climax, a high point of adoration. But the psalmist knows that life goes on after a grand finale, and God's assistance will be needed for the next step, the next performance: "Let your hand be ready to help me" (v. 173). The psalmist recognizes the possibility of getting lost on the way: "I wander about like a lost sheep; so come and look for me, your servant" (v. 176, GNT). Thus the longest psalm ends on a somber note. We will always need God's guidance. Our praise will always mix with petition, asking for God's help, guidance, and protection even as we praise and thank God for blessings upon blessings. With true wisdom the psalmist prays (and maybe sings, even before the invention of the staff), "Let me live that I may praise you, and let your ordinances help me" (v. 175). This verse expresses a good prayer for us all.

PRAYER/PRACTICE

Making faithful decisions is not always easy. Often time pressures do not allow you to gather adequate data, reflect, and pray. The pressures of earning a living may inhibit thoughtful reflection. You may believe that you can't make good decisions, or you may distrust your own inner guidance. You may feel tempted to take someone's advice or to follow the same course you did last time if it worked out all right. You may distrust your ability to sort out God's voice from all the other competing and often conflicting voices around you. Recall and believe these words from James: "If any of you is lacking in wisdom, ask God, who gives to all generously and ungrudgingly, and it will be given you" (1:5).

October 15

REMEMBER

Saint Teresa of Avila (1515–1582), a Spanish mystic and religious reformer, founded seventeen convents, wrote able instructions to her community, and consequently served as a wise guide to prayer.

READ

Psalm 120

PONDER

This psalm begins a group of fifteen "Songs of Ascent," or pilgrimage psalms. Scholars can only surmise the origins of the name for this group of psalms. Some speculate that worshipers sang these psalms while standing on the Temple steps. Others believe that Jews returning from the Babylonian exile chanted them. Many scholars argue that pilgrims who came to the Temple for the great feasts sang these psalms.

The collection begins by expressing the anguish of being among those who hate peace and speak lies. We feel a kinship with the psalmist as we experience a culture of fear and violence, as we listen to leaders put a positive "spin" on falsehoods and troubles. Like the psalmist, we pray to God for help, for courage to speak the truth. We might even admit to joining the psalmist in calling for God to pay back the liars with a few arrows, giving them some of their own medicine (v. 4).

PRAYER/PRACTICE

Teresa of Avila uses the image of mansions to describe growth in prayer; we progress through a series of mansions, or rooms, on the way to spiritual union with God. She believed the test of spiritual growth was increased love for one's neighbor. Teresa also compares the life of prayer to a gardener watering a garden. We may draw water with a bucket from a well, use a mechanical means like a pulley or pump, channel a stream, or let the rain do the watering. Each of these methods moves away from depending on our efforts and toward letting God water our life of prayer. How hard are you working at prayer? In what ways do you feel the grace of God watering your spirit? What evidence do you find of growth in your love for others?

October 16

REMEMBER

Rigoberta Menchú (b. 1959), a Quiche Mayan Indian of Guatemala, won the Nobel Peace Prize in 1992 for her tireless and persistent work in resisting human rights abuses in her country.

READ

Psalm 121:1-4

PONDER

This psalm breathes tranquility and confidence. "My help comes from the LORD, who . . . will neither slumber nor sleep" (vv. 2, 4). Other religions had shrines and altars in the hills, but the pilgrim to Jerusalem looked beyond the mountains to the Creator, "who made heaven and earth"(v. 2). Looking to the high city of Jerusalem, the pilgrim found hope and help from the God who dwells with humankind. Regardless of shadows or lurking danger, God remained present, fully awake, and ever watchful to keep the pilgrim from stumbling. No wonder worshipers through the centuries have spoken this psalm, sung it joyously, and memorized it frequently.

PRAYER/PRACTICE

Marta Becket, a New York dancer and artist, once traveled out West and while driving through the Death Valley region of southern California had a flat tire. The only place to get it changed was a ghost town called Armagosa (now Death Valley Junction). As she waited for the tire to be repaired, Becket walked the mostly empty and lonely streets and discovered an old hotel and theater. Despite the buildings' dilapidated condition and boarded-up windows, she heard a call, "This place is begging for a life."[6] Not long afterward, she bought the place, fixed up the stage, painted an audience of faces on the walls, and started to give dance performances—at first to the faces and now, over thirty years later, to large crowds.

Sometimes in discernment, the call of a place reveals God's vision and your mission. What place calls to you?

October 17

REMEMBER

Jalal Al-Din Rumi (1207–1273), a Persian scholar and teacher, ranks as one of the greatest Sufi (the mystical tradition within the Muslim faith) poets. His mystical verses often describe a union with God.

READ

Psalm 121:5-8

PONDER

The poet's touch emerges in this beautiful psalm. In an economy of words, the psalmist encompasses day and night, near and far, present and future. Because all of life rests under God's protection, we can walk with assurance. We shall not be harmed during the day nor frightened at night (v. 6). God watches whether we travel short or great distances, and God will welcome us home. God sustains us, protects us, keeps us safe from evil. God will be with us in the future, always keeping our life under provident care and protection (vv. 7, 8). Even when life gets difficult, this psalm serves as a touchstone of assurance and confidence. Its poetry resides in our hearts.

PRAYER/PRACTICE

Like the poet Rumi, Anthony de Mello artfully used words in stories and sayings to invite people into deeper reflection. He encouraged people to plant a sentence or image in the heart and let it take root—in other words, give it time to reveal its truth rather than forcing it with mental strength or impatient waiting. De Mello wrote these statements that may prove useful in discernment:

> You do not have to change for God to love you.

> Be grateful for your sins. They are carriers of grace.

> Say goodbye to golden yesterdays—or your heart will never learn to love the present.[7]

If any of these thoughts appeal to you, meditate on it and give it time to speak to you.

October 18

REMEMBER

Luke (first century), a Gentile Christian and physician, authored the third Gospel and probably the book of Acts. His Gospel depicts a compassionate Jesus who shows concern for the poor and marginalized.

READ

Psalm 122:1-5

PONDER

King David made Jerusalem the capital of Israel. Jerusalem gleamed as a magnificent city, home to temporal rule and to the temple. A pilgrimage to Jerusalem for a festival was a grand and glorious occasion. The highlight was standing in and worshiping in the awesome house of the Lord. "I was glad when they said to me, 'Let us go to the house of the LORD!'" (v. 1). Oh, that people attending church today felt such joy. Pray for a recovery of gladness in going to worship. Pray for the place where you worship. Pray for those who lead, sing, and pray in your worship services.

PRAYER/PRACTICE

Not only individuals but also institutions, including churches, must make decisions. Acts 15 records the early Christians meeting as a council to decide about their mission to Gentiles. Discerning God's will for a church requires the same prayerful, reflective, listening stance as individual discernment. Many recent sources on discernment encourage churches to move from voting and strict adherence to *Robert's Rules of Order* to a consensus, discernment model. The discernment model in a church or institution invites people to set aside their personal agendas and focus on listening for God's will, God's desires for the group. It encourages communal listening and prayer, asking what God seeks rather than how big the cost and how many persons favor the endeavor. Consensus decision making looks for agreement and values dissent as a way to hear other persons' perception of God's will.

Reflect on groups in which you have participated that operate by consensus to seek God's will in their decision making.

October 19

REMEMBER

C. S. Lewis (1898–1963), an English professor, novelist, and Christian apologist, became one of the twentieth century's most published Christian writers.

READ

Psalm 122:6-9

PONDER

In the middle of this psalm, the poet shifts from talking about Jerusalem to speaking to and praying for Jerusalem: " 'Peace be within your walls, and security within your towers' "(v. 7). Because troubles still persist in Israel and Jerusalem, the imperative to pray for peace remains clear. Pray for peace, for God's shalom to reign in that holy land claimed by three great religions. For the sake of all peoples living there and for the sake of all the nations in the world, "I will say, 'Peace be within you' " (v. 8). Raise a prayer for the cities where we live as well as for Jerusalem. May peace abide among all peoples and dwell in the places where we live.

PRAYER/PRACTICE

Spiritual discernment by consensus takes time. The group needs to identify the issue (not all matters need to be discerned), gather data, and develop clarity about the guiding principles. The process invites mutual vulnerability and accountability. Each person seeks to shed pre-judgments and to let go of feelings or perceptions that get in the way of listening to God's will. Each person bears responsibility for sharing insights from scripture and from his or her own prayer life, and for remaining open to other ideas, options, paths. The entire group seeks to hear God's word in the midst of all the words spoken. A suggested proposal can be improved, clarified, and prayed about before inviting a decision. Consensus means that all group members consent or agree, or at least that those not fully in agreement do not feel strongly enough to oppose the decision.

Practice listening for the voice of God as you listen to others today.

October 20

REMEMBER

Jerzy Popieluszko (1947–1984) served as chaplain to the Solidarity reform movement in Poland and became a spokesperson for the church's involvement in the struggle for human liberation.

READ

Psalm 123

PONDER

People living in poverty and oppression know the sentiment of this psalm; they can relate to the longing for hope and mercy. Those who have known contempt and scorn (v. 4) hear the call to keep their eyes focused and hearts centered on the God of mercy. Many scholars think this psalm emerged after the Israelites returned from exile and discovered a neglected land and hostile neighbors who mocked and sneered at them. In the midst of discouragement and gloom, the people turn their eyes to God. The psalmist invites us to deepen our trust in God, the God of mercy and kindness.

PRAYER/PRACTICE

The Quakers developed the Clearness Committee in the seventeenth century to guide decisions because they had no pastors to "solve" their concerns. The Clearness Committee draws on individual and communal resources to make a decision. Parker Palmer explains:

> Behind the Clearness Committee is a simple but crucial conviction: *each of us has an inner teacher, a voice of truth, that offers the guidance and power we need to deal with our problems.* But that inner voice is often garbled by various kinds of inward and outward interference. The function of the Clearness Committee is not to give advice or "fix" people from the outside in, but to help people remove the interference so that they can discover their own wisdom from the inside out.[8]

Think of persons who can ask thoughtful questions and listen to "the delicate intersection of the human heart, with its desires and dreams, and the vast and silent mystery that is God."[9]

October 21

REMEMBER

Frederick Buechner (b. 1926), an American writer and clergyman, has written novels and nonfiction books about grace and redemption that give a refreshing glimpse into the contemporary life of faith.

READ

Psalm 124

PONDER

Look back over your life. If God had not been with you, would you have survived the trials and transitions, times of illness and grief, seasons of sadness, or occasions of disappointment? Read this psalm as part of your own story. The psalmist declares that God has seen the people through calamities and disasters: fires, flood waters, wild beasts, and snares. "If it had not been the LORD who was on our side" (v. 1), would we have made it? The clear affirmation of the psalm and the last verse echoes in countless worship services: "Our help is in the name of the LORD, who made heaven and earth" (v. 8).

PRAYER/PRACTICE

In the Quaker practice of discernment, the person seeking clearness, the focus person, first writes about the problem. The writing (or oral presentation, if the Clearness Committee happens at a retreat or conference where time is limited) should cover three areas: "a concise statement of the problem, a recounting of relevant background factors that may bear on the problem, and an exploration of any hunches the focus person may have about what's on the horizon regarding the problem."[10]

The focus person chooses five or six persons for the Clearness Committee, taking into account gender, age, and diversity. Above all, the persons should be trustworthy and prayerful. The committee schedules a meeting of up to three hours, knowing that another meeting may be needed. The generous amount of time provides ample space for a prayerful, reflective, listening pace.

Are you wrestling with a discernment question that a Clearness Committee could help reflect upon?

October 22

REMEMBER

Howard Thurman (1900–1981), dean of the chapel at Howard University, cofounded the Church for the Fellowship of All Peoples and wrote poetry, taught, and preached. He wrote many books with themes of spirituality and social justice.

READ

Psalm 125

PONDER

The mountains surrounding Jerusalem not only provided protection for the city but also became a metaphor for God's embrace of Jerusalem and her people (v. 2). Like the mountains encircling Jerusalem, God's care encircles people. But within the mountain's embrace lurks the possibility for trouble. "The wicked will not always rule over the land of the righteous; if they did, the righteous themselves might do evil" (v. 3, GNT). Whenever a repressive regime rules a nation, the temptation exists for faithful persons to give up hope, to profit along with everyone else, to do wrong. The psalmist again prays for the nation, prays for evildoers to be led away, and prays for peace (v. 5).

Give thanks for mountains. Whenever you see mountains, let them remind you of God's everlasting embrace.

PRAYER/PRACTICE

In a Clearness Committee, a facilitator opens and closes the meeting and invites participation from all. The committee may choose a secretary to make notes of questions and perhaps answers. The meeting begins with a centering silence, followed by the focus person's description of the problem. Committee members then follow one rule: They can ask only honest, open questions. "Nothing is allowed except . . . questions that will help the focus person remove the blocks to his or her inner truth."[11] The facilitator listens for questions that are disguised advice or judgment and may gently ask someone to rephrase a question or save it until a closing time of dialogue.

Practice forming questions that do not hide advice or analysis.

October 23

REMEMBER

Think of an artist, poet, or author who helps you draw closer to God. Today Greek and Russian Orthodox Churches remember James of Jerusalem (first century), who guided the early church and supported Paul in extending the Christian message to Gentiles without first requiring them to become Jews.

READ

Psalm 126:1-3

PONDER

Some things seem too good to be true. They appear like a dream. Did they really happen? The Israelites returned home. From slavery in Egypt. From captivity in Babylon. From many nations after they had been scattered following the fall of Jerusalem. The return to Jerusalem abounded with laughter and joy (v. 2). This psalm invites us to celebrate our homecomings—whenever we return to God from some spiritual captivity, whenever we learn to laugh and enjoy God after a time of depression and disappointment, whenever we rekindle hope and joy after grief or illness. "The LORD has done great things for us, and we rejoiced" (v. 3).

PRAYER/PRACTICE

In a Clearness Committee the focus person usually responds to questions as they arise. The most helpful questions center on the person as well as the problem and elicit feelings rather than just facts. Asking such open, unbiased questions takes thought and practice. The challenge remains to prayerfully search for questions that serve the focus person's needs. The focus person may decline to answer any question, keeping in mind the need to protect vulnerable feelings and guard appropriate privacy, yet desiring to place responses in the open where God and the committee can nurture them. A gentle pace of questions interspersed with silence facilitates deep reflection.

What is the best question someone has asked you? What question elicited a thoughtful, revealing response? Treasure that question.

October 24

REMEMBER

The United Nations, established in 1945 to build bridges of cooperation and understanding among nations, needs our support to continue
bringing nations together.

READ

Psalm 126:4-6

PONDER

Water remains essential for living. Nowhere is that fact more evident
than in desert areas. The psalmist prays that Israel may be restored like
the trenches (watercourses) in the Negeb desert (v. 4) after desert
storms. Thus water provides an abundant harvest. But water in the
form of tears also plays a role in restoring the decimated country. Hard
work, suffering, sweat, and tears become part of the sowing of new
hope, new lives, new crops. The desert rains from above blend with
tears and bring to blossom seeds that have lain dormant in the earth
and indeed in our own lives. May we become fields of joy, revived and
replenished by God's healing waters.

PRAYER/PRACTICE

Near the end of the time for the Clearness Committee, the facilitator
may ask the focus person if he or she wants to suspend the "questions
only" rule and invite committee members to mirror back what they
have heard and seen from the focus person. This is not time for the
committee to advise, tell off, or fix but instead an opportunity to affirm
and review what they heard. They should give the focus person opportunity to say, "Yes, that is me," or "No, that is not who I am or what I
meant to say."

In the final ten minutes of the time, the facilitator "should invite
members to celebrate and affirm the focus person and his or her
strengths. This is an important time, since the focus person has just
spent a couple of hours feeling vulnerable."[12]

Recall and give thanks for times when friends have gently listened
and guided you to make faithful decisions.

October 25

Fritz Eichenberg (1901–1990), a Quaker artist known as a master of wood engraving, illustrated many classics and provided religious engravings that graced the pages of the *Catholic Worker* newspaper.

READ

Psalm 127:1-2

PONDER

Do our plans prosper without God as partner? Do our families thrive, our studies succeed, or our marriages and relationships blossom without God as partner? If God does not inspire and bless our efforts, doing our best accomplishes nothing; we eat "the bread of anxious toil" (v. 2) but do not partake of the "bread of life"(John 6:35). This psalm gently but poignantly indicts our busy, driven culture and intense lives where we burn the candle at both ends and give little time or thought to God. It sets the stage for the words of Jesus: "Do not worry about your life, what you will eat or what you will drink, or . . . what you will wear. Strive first for the kingdom of God" (Matt. 6:25, 33). So, relax, partner with God in all your endeavors, and be blessed while you sleep, for you indeed rest as one of God's beloved children (v. 2).

PRAYER/PRACTICE

If you face a discernment time, a Clearness Committee can be a real gift. "We are simply to surround the focus person with quiet, loving space, resisting even the temptation to comfort or reassure or encourage this person, but simply being present to him or her with our attention and our questions and our care."[13] Even if the focus person does not instantly make a decision, the process keeps working and God uses the experience as part of revealing the next steps. The Clearness Committee, a moment in holy space and time, allows a small community of faith to serve as a channel of God's grace.

How can you make use of the Clearness Committee for yourself? Would you suggest it to your church or faith community?[14]

October 26

REMEMBER

Noah (B.C.E.) and his family remind us of the importance of obeying God. They served as a remnant to preserve the earth and live in harmony with God.

READ

Genesis 6:9–9:17

PONDER

People of all ages know the story of Noah and the ark. The image of animals walking two by two onto the ark especially captivates children. Scholars have long debated the facts or myths of this story, but for today, ponder Noah as one who intercedes for the world. He carries responsibility for and enacts concern for preserving the earth. Ponder God's displeasure with humanity's wickedness, injustice, and rape of the planet. Ponder as well God's covenant of care and the sign of the rainbow. We cooperate with God in caring for the earth and in shunning complacency and ignorance. We send out the dove of peace in hopes of finding new signs of care for the green earth.

PRAYER/PRACTICE

One of my friends was trying to discern whether to return to college to finish her degree. It seemed like a good direction to go, even though she was worried about how to finance her education. She asked God to give her a tangible sign of confirmation, such as a rainbow. The next two days it rained, but no rainbow appeared. She became a little angry at God for not confirming what seemed to be the right direction. Later a child brought her a bookmark he had made at church. The bookmark contained the verse "Do not be afraid," and the boy had glued on a rainbow as a decoration. My friend chuckled at the way God continues to guide and surprise her. God's direction can come in unexpected ways.

When have you asked God for a sign? Did you look for answers in unexpected places? If you received no confirmation, did you remain open to another decision? Read the story of Gideon and the fleece (Judg. 6:36-40).

October 27

REMEMBER

Harry Chapin (1942–1981), an American folk singer, devoted his concert proceeds and energy to ending world hunger. He wrote the music for a retelling of the life of Jesus in a modern musical, *Cotton Patch Gospel*.

READ

Psalm 127:3-5

PONDER

A bias toward sons existed in Hebrew culture. Sons provided protection from enemies, worked in the fields, took care of parents in old age, and defended the father's honor in the law courts or in transactions at the gates (v. 5). Unfortunately, the bias toward males continues in many cultures today. The deeper meaning of these verses lies in this inclusive translation: "Children are a blessing and a gift from the Lord" (v. 3, CEV). The birth of a child reigns as a moment of mystery, gift, and grace. In contrast to our "anxious toil" (v. 2), a child comes as a miraculous sign of God's blessing, a gift entrusted to parents. Happy are those who have children, and happy are those who adopt, love, and care for children.

PRAYER/PRACTICE

Are there ways to test the choices you make? How do you know if you have heard God rather than some false spirit or even the growling of your stomach? Having others participate with you in discernment can help. These questions may give you some guidance: Is the decision in harmony with scripture? Does it feel life-giving? Is the choice congruent with Christian tradition and practice, recognizing that tradition may broaden and deepen? Do you feel a sense of rightness, deep peace, lasting consolation? Does the choice lead you closer to God? Have you made the decision in freedom? Does the choice increase your ability to love and give of yourself; does it increase your compassion? Does the decision bring growth and maturity in discipleship, a growing sense of being God's beloved child? Do you feel God's blessing in the choice?

Which of these questions beckon your attention?

October 28

REMEMBER

Jude (first century), an apostle, probably wrote the letter of Jude. He remains the patron saint of lost causes and of hospitals.

READ

Psalm 128

PONDER

Perhaps the priest spoke this psalm to confer blessing on pilgrims before they returned to their homes. Since most of the travelers were men, the priest offered a blessing upon their work (v. 2), then on their wives and children (v. 3). The psalmist uses the grapevine and olive tree as images since they were common and vital to the life of the Hebrews. Imagine someone conferring a blessing on your work and your family. What words and images might that person use? Imagine offering a blessing to others in your family. The last two verses offer a threefold blessing: May you have a long life, may you have many grandchildren, and may your city know peace. Create your own threefold blessing for your family.

PRAYER/PRACTICE

Some decisions unfold, revealing themselves over time. If no deadline presses, can you let the decision open like a rose? Thomas Merton used the image of an apple ripening. Think about how an apple ripens—it just sits in the sun. A small green apple cannot ripen in one night by tightening all its muscles. Neither can it suddenly become large, red, ripe, and juicy by imagining great changes. Just as the red apple takes time to develop, so the birth of the true self and decisions take time. We must wait for God, remain awake, and trust in God's hidden action within us.

In your prayer time, envision an apple ripening or a flower unfolding. Can you trust God with your decision, your life, your becoming?

October 29

REMEMBER

Clarence Jordan (1912–1969), a Baptist preacher, founded Koinonia Farm in Georgia in 1942 as an interracial community where blacks and whites could live and work together in a spirit of partnership. Despite violent persecution, Jordan persisted in his vision of blacks and whites living in Christian community.

READ

Psalm 129

PONDER

Israel tells her story in this psalm. From her youth, from the days of slavery in Egypt when her people felt the whips of taskmasters, Israel has known suffering. Armies have frequently invaded the nation and carried the people to far-off places. So much history of oppression lies behind the first three verses, yet the story does not end there. God breaks the bonds of oppression (v. 4); the wicked do not prevail (v. 2). Instead of offering a prayer of thanksgiving for deliverance, the psalmist, fueled by memories of oppression, calls for God to punish Israel's enemies and to withhold blessing from them. In our prayers we can choose to pray for more patience in dealing with our suffering and for God's mercy to temper our anger.

PRAYER/PRACTICE

Clarence Jordan translated the Gospels of Matthew and John into a Southern setting and vernacular. Jesus, born in Gainesville, Georgia, to Mary Davidson, tramps around the South gathering disciples of all colors and upsetting the established powers. He gets lynched on Good Friday in Leesburg, Georgia, but three days later Jesus holds a big Easter Sunday victory party.

Imagine Jesus coming to your hometown. Where does he stay? With whom does he associate? Who becomes upset by what he does and says? Who gets thrown out of the church, who gets fed, and who gets healed? Watch the video *Cotton Patch Gospel* or read a book about Jesus in contemporary times. See Appendix A for suggestions.

October 30

REMEMBER

Fyodor Dostoyevsky (1821–1881), a Russian novelist, explored themes of grace, conversion, and salvation in such books as *Crime and Punishment* and *The Brothers Karamazov.*

READ

Psalm 130:1-4

PONDER

The sixth of seven penitential psalms, Psalm 130 probably began as an individual lament of someone in danger and despair but became the communal prayer of a sinful nation turning toward the love and mercy of God. Whatever depths we have experienced, whatever discouragement or despair we have tasted, we can still call on God. We can still lift up our prayer, "Out of the depths I cry to you, O LORD"(v. 1). If thoughts of our faults, mistakes, and sins weigh us down, we can still turn to God, for God stands ready to forgive. "There is no trouble so severe that it cuts a person off from God; there is no sin so powerful that it removes a person from the greater power of forgiveness."[15]

PRAYER/PRACTICE

Gratitude lies at the heart of the spiritual life. It offers an appropriate response to a time of discernment. Hopefully you feel peace about the decision made and desire to celebrate not only the decision but also God's grace and trust in you to choose the wisest course of action. You may wish to gather friends and family for a time of celebration. If you used a Clearness Committee, consider inviting committee members to the celebration. You might offer a prayer of gratitude like the following:

> Thank you, God of the journey, for you have been my guide; you have been my help; you have called me to this new path. Let me live every day in awareness of and gratitude for your direction. Help me believe that every decision to be made offers another opportunity to be blessed and to offer blessing to others. Amen.

October 31

REMEMBER

Today is Reformation Day, the anniversary of Martin Luther's posting Ninety-five Theses on the door of the church in Wittenberg, Germany.

READ

Psalm 130:5-6

PONDER

Captives wait for deliverance. Dry lands wait for water. Those afraid of the dark wait for the dawn. The sick wait for a good word from the doctor. The lost child waits for the parent to return. The soul waits for God, and the expectation of God's love and forgiveness remains greater than everything else for which we wait. We look for God more than those who watch for the morning (v. 6). Jesus instructed his followers to be vigilant in their waiting, "Therefore, keep awake—for you do not know when the master of the house will come" (Mark 13:35). God indeed has already come and will come again.

PRAYER/PRACTICE

Hearts ache when Christians see how their church or community fails to share Christ's love or be the compassionate hands of God. Out of passionate care for the church, Martin Luther sought to make it aware of some faults and to return the church to its high calling.

On this Reformation Day, think of your church community and ways it lives faithfully as the body of Christ. Perhaps you could make a list of ninety-five ways to improve the church and circle two to four items you would be willing to work on. Is there anyone in your faith community you could share the list with who would see it as positive suggestions rather than criticism? Ask God for a pure heart and wisdom to move ahead in creating strong, vibrant faith communities.

November

God of the changing seasons,
the winter trees stand naked,
graceful against a cold, crisp sky,
lines etched like lace, full of promise.
God of the changing seasons,
let me see the beauty in simple things
and hold me as I disencumber myself,
striving for a simplicity
that is graceful, joyous, and full of promise.
Open me to the wisdom that comes from maturity. Amen.

November 1

REMEMBER

Today is All Saints' Day. Give thanks for all those persons whose lives reflected the glory of God and shed light on your path, enabling you to walk with joy and serve with compassion.

READ

Psalm 130:7-8

PONDER

Author Mark Link sees similarities between a well-known piece of classical music and Psalm 130: "Tchaikovsky's *1812 Overture* celebrates Russia's victory over Napoleon's invading armies. It portrays this by having the Russian hymn gradually drown out the French national anthem. Something like this happens in Psalm 130. The psalmist's confidence in God's mercy gradually drowns out . . . fear of God's punishment."[1]

We have hope because "with the LORD there is steadfast love, and . . . great power to redeem" (v. 7). This hope overcomes our sins. Give thanks that the music of mercy sings the loudest and brings hope, joy, and forgiveness.

PRAYER/PRACTICE

This All Saints' Day, offer a prayer of thanks for those in your life who blessed, guided, and inspired your journey with Christ. Write your own prayer, or use these words to shape your prayer.

> Generous and gracious God, we give you thanks for those who have gone before us who now belong to the communion of saints. We thank you for ordinary persons with laughter in their eyes and kindness in their deeds. We thank you for common ones with compassionate hearts and listening ears. We thank you for holy ones who saw light in the midst of darkness and potential when others saw dead ends. We thank you for strong ones who remained faithful in times of crisis, who endured suffering yet remained joyous, who fought for justice when they could have chosen comfort. Help us walk in the shadow of the saints who go before us, now and always. Amen.

November 2

REMEMBER

John Muir (1838–1914), an early environmentalist, fought to preserve wilderness places, which for him exuded holiness and a connection to the divine.

READ

Psalm 131

PONDER

This psalm provides an antidote to the anxious striving and pressured acquiring that passes for success in our day. "I'm not conceited, Lord, and I don't waste my time on impossible schemes" (v. 1, CEV). This simple prayer soothes the rush and quiets the noise. "I have calmed and quieted my soul" (v. 2). Here resides a simplicity and humility that attracts us. Here lies an intimacy with God, as close as a child in its mother's arms. Here echoes the relationship Jesus offers, "I am gentle and humble in heart, and you will find rest for your souls" (Matt. 11:29). Here lives a prayer of trust in God's providence and an invitation to abandon pretense, pride, and pursuit and to rest in God's lap.

PRAYER/PRACTICE

This book has lifted up many saints for you to remember, some well-known and others new to you. This month provides a wonderful time to claim your own communion of saints. Think of persons you have known or read about in scripture, religion, history, or the arts—individuals who have inspired you to walk the path of Christ. Write their names on small pieces of paper. Try to come up with thirty saints, women and men, and place the pieces of paper in a bowl or cup. Keep the container of names visible, and each day during November, draw out a name and give thanks for the way this person has encouraged, challenged, or inspired you. You might also pray that you live his or her particular gift throughout the day. Families may also enjoy the practice of creating a "bowl of saints" and thanking God for these persons.[2]

November 3

REMEMBER

Saint Martin de Porres (1579–1639), son of a Spanish nobleman and a black freedwoman, was shunned by his father and excluded from the privileges of nobility because of his dark skin. He entered a Dominican monastery, gained a reputation for spiritual insight and healing, and exhibited concern for the poor, the slaves, and the mulattos in Peru.

READ

Psalm 132:1-10

PONDER

The beginning of the psalm reminds the pilgrims of David, who brought the ark of the covenant to Jerusalem after recovering it from the Philistines. David promised God that he would build a temple for the ark's resting place. Though David did not complete the task, his intention gained him great glory. As pilgrims journeyed to Jerusalem, they remembered the mighty procession, led by a dancing David, as the ark was brought to Jerusalem.

May we also know dancing and worship on our journeys. May we imitate Saint Martin and abound in acts of kindness and compassion, especially to people rejected by popular culture.

PRAYER/PRACTICE

Another ritual for remembering saints involves the use of candles. Gather family members or friends to remember and give thanks for saints. Provide plenty of candles. The saints often walked through darkness, giving us insight and courage for our own struggles. Invite each person to light a candle for a saint and briefly mention a characteristic of the saint that brings hope and light to his or her life. Take turns lighting candles and speaking about saints, giving everyone opportunity to participate and encouraging individuals to light more than one candle. Conclude by holding hands in a circle and praying or singing a song.

Though candle rituals are best done with a group, you may also do your own candle ritual on one day or light a candle each day as you name a different saint for every day of the month.

November 4

REMEMBER

Anthony Bloom (b. 1914), a Russian Orthodox archbishop and monk living in England, writes books on the spiritual life, inviting readers into a deeper life of prayer and a greater awareness of the Orthodox faith.

READ

Psalm 132:11-18

PONDER

The remainder of this psalm recalls two more great events in Israel's history: God's promise that David's descendants would inherit the throne and God's choice to reside in Jerusalem. The Christian church has long seen this psalm as pointing toward the Messiah as one of David's lineage. The "horn" (v. 17) symbolized strength, but the strength Jesus brought subverted power and domination. Jesus displayed the strength of love and forgiveness, of healing and blessing. Jesus transformed the military hero image of David by riding into Jerusalem not on a war horse but on a donkey. Jesus, the heir of David, still lives as a Prince of peace and servant of love.

PRAYER/PRACTICE

Revelation 7:9-14 describes the heavenly vision of John, who saw the saints before the throne of God in white robes worshiping, singing, and praising God. I invite you to imagine yourself seated in a large room. The doors open and saints in white robes begin to gather. A soft peace, serene joy, and sweet smell fill the room. The saints have gathered to present gifts to you. See one of them approaching you, offering a gift— a quality, attitude, or insight you need to live your life more faithfully. Another saint comes and extends a second gift. Imagine the saints in procession, giving you qualities, attitudes, and insights that will bless you and others. Receive as many gifts as you need for this stage of your life. Close this meditation by standing in the middle of the circle of saints, offering a prayer of thanks to God, and praying that you will always remember that you are surrounded by "so great a cloud of witnesses" (Heb. 12:1).

November 5

REMEMBER

Saint Hilda of Whitby (614–680) founded the double monastery (a monastery that housed men and women separately but united them for daily prayers) at Whitby, England, which hosted the Whitby Synod (664) to bring harmony between Celtic and Roman Christians.

READ

Psalm 133

PONDER

In a hot, dry country like Israel, people needed oil to soothe their faces in the blazing sun. In such a parched land, the dew or melting snow played an important role in watering the earth. Those two pleasant, important, and beneficial images—oil and water—express how unity feels. Unity refreshes and restores. Experiences of unity bless us and whet our appetite for more. We long for our places of worship to provide such community. We cannot but help think of Jesus' words, "Where two or three are gathered in my name, I am there among them" (Matt. 18:20).

PRAYER/PRACTICE

I invite you to rediscover the wisdom of Celtic saints. For Celtic Christians, the earth with its seasons points to the marvelous Creator who established the world and its people. The sights, sounds, and smells of the land shape Celtic spirituality. Though the influence of the Celtic rule and spirit diminished after the Whitby Synod, it has reemerged in the popularity of Celtic music, pilgrimages to holy places in Ireland and other islands, and in the writing, music, and prayers of the Iona Community. (See Appendix A for a suggested resource.) Today remember or read about some Celtic saints and legends. Saint Patrick (Mar. 17) and Saint Brigit (Feb. 16) are just two among a host of Celtic saints. Consider this word of truth from Celtic wisdom: There are three things that can ruin wisdom: ignorance, inaccurate knowledge, and forgetfulness.

November 6

REMEMBER

Little Sister Magdeleine of Jesus (1898–1989) founded the Little Sisters of Jesus in the desert of North Africa. Following the model of Charles de Foucauld (Dec. 1), the sisters live a life of simplicity and contemplative prayer as they serve among the very poor.

READ

Psalm 134

PONDER

This is the last of the Songs of Ascent. Some scholars believe pilgrims gathered in the Temple after the heat of the day to pray this evening psalm. They gathered to lift hands in prayer, to offer God blessing, and to receive blessing. Others think this psalm formed part of the farewell ceremony before pilgrims departed for home. The pilgrims extend blessing to God, proclaim God's goodness, and receive a blessing for their journey: "May the LORD, maker of heaven and earth, bless you from Zion" (v. 3). However the psalm is interpreted, common themes emerge. To bless God brings a blessing upon the people. Blessing exists as a central element of worship. To seek and bless God in the sanctuary prepares one to meet God everywhere, even on the journey toward home.

PRAYER/PRACTICE

Turn from reflecting on saints to consider your own faith journey. For the next few days I invite you to consider developing and claiming your own patterns and disciplines for spiritual growth. In Christian tradition this is known as developing a rule of life. A rule is a pattern of spiritual disciplines and attitudes that provides structure and direction for growth in holiness. "It is unlikely that we will deepen our relationship with God in a casual or haphazard manner. There will be a need for some intentional commitment and some reorganization in our own lives."[3] Growth in faith requires commitment, structure, and yes, discipline. Developing a rule of life moves you beyond good intentions into the arena of daily walking with God. Reflect on your daily practices of spiritual growth. You can count reading this book as one of your disciplines.

November 7

REMEMBER

Edward Hays, a contemporary Roman Catholic priest, artist, retreat director, and author, writes and illustrates stories, prayers, and spiritual reflections that reveal deep truths in unconventional and fresh ways.

READ

Psalm 135:1-4

PONDER

A thousand reasons exist to praise God. Praise erupts at the beginning of this psalm, and reasons for praise spill forth. "Praise the LORD; sing hymns, for God is good and gracious" (v. 3, AP). Goodness and mercy, clear attributes of God, evoke praise and singing. Lifting voices in song remains one of the chief ways we praise God. Singing together unites minds and hearts, breaths and voices—indeed the whole body—in praise. When we lack the talent or a community to join in song, we can still praise by praying the Psalms. They give voice to our praise.

PRAYER/PRACTICE

You can start developing a rule of life by choosing from this book some practices and disciplines to incorporate into your daily life. The behaviors, attitudes, disciplines, and practices you choose will become "routine, repeated, regular"[4] in your life of growing intimacy with God. Some people carry negative images of rules and discipline. You must remember that rules and discipline exist for guiding and training. Building a rule of life guides and supports your spiritual growth.

Your rule can be simple. Dorothy Day, cofounder of the Catholic Worker (Nov. 29), committed to daily practice the presence of God by reading the Bible, keeping a journal, receiving the Eucharist, and looking for the face of Christ in the poor and hungry she served every day.

How do you respond to setting a rule of life and developing spiritual disciplines? Journal about your excitement and your resistance.

November 8

Remember

Michel Quoist (1918–1997), a French priest and author, touched many with his popular books of prayer and diaries that addressed human longings for God and contemporary social realities.

Read

Psalm 135:5-7

Ponder

This psalm continues with more praise for God the Creator. I have seen a double rainbow over the desert in Arizona. I have caught huge snowflakes on my tongue in Michigan. I have walked through thick fog in England. I have seen sparkling fish swimming in and out of purple coral on the Great Barrier Reef. I have stared at constellations of twinkling stars in a clear blue winter sky in Alaska. I have climbed the mountain to see the sunrise over Machu Picchu in Peru. I have walked among giant sequoias and redwood trees in California. Each occasion and many more have stirred me to praise the Creator who continues creating. The whole world cannot hold all the wonders of God.

Prayer/Practice

Pope John XXIII (June 3) kept a journal, and some of the entries contain lists of rules he made for himself. They give insight into creating a disciplined life. He included these elements in his rule:

> Upon rising, fifteen minutes of silent prayer and fifteen minutes of spiritual reading.
>
> At bedtime, a general examination of conscience,* including time for confession. Identify issues for the next morning's prayer.
>
> Arrange the hours of the day to make this rule possible, and set aside time for prayer, recreation, study, and sleep.
>
> Make a habit of turning the mind to God in prayer.[5]

To which of these practices do you feel attracted? Consider incorporating it into your rule of life.

*See November 22 for a description of this practice.

November 9

REMEMBER

On this date in 1938, the Nazis unleashed a night of terror against Jews, burning synagogues, arresting Jews, and destroying Jewish-owned stores. This night, known as Kristallnacht, served as a prelude to the Holocaust, and little protest arose in Germany or abroad. For a positive remembrance, recall that in 1989 young people from East and West Germany led in dismantling the Berlin Wall.

READ

Psalm 135:8-14

PONDER

Countless reasons exist for praising God. God, the agent of history, shapes our story. God shows compassion to the needy and hears the cries of the oppressed. From the cries of the slaves in Egypt to the cries of the Jews on the night of November 9, 1938, God hears and responds. Forty years of wandering in the desert may be necessary, or many years may pass before walls of separation come down and hope emerges, but God persists and "will bring justice" (v. 14, CEV). Our God is a God of salvation who acts for good in our lives and in the world. "God gives justice, shows mercy, and attends to God's servants" (v. 14, AP). Praise God!

PRAYER/PRACTICE

How do you develop a rule of life? Begin by taking stock of your circumstances. What current commitments to family, work, and church affect your day? Your rule will take into account these commitments. Next consider what draws, beckons, attracts you. Review the practices mentioned in this book, and see if some of them call to you or seem a natural fit for you. Look for practices that challenge you. Perhaps God calls you to move beyond your comfort zone and stretch toward new growth. Perhaps you feel called to try some practice on the non-dominant side of your personality. Ask God in prayer to help you choose practices that both comfort and challenge you.

November 10

REMEMBER

Martin Luther (1483–1546), an Augustinian priest, sparked church reform by posting a list of Ninety-five Theses on the Wittenberg church door. His witness led to the founding of the Protestant Reformation and the Lutheran Church. Luther strongly advocated justification by faith alone and personal reading of the Bible.

READ

Psalm 135:15-18

PONDER

Idols made by human hands remain hollow gods. They may be pretty on the outside, lavishly covered in silver and gold (v. 15), but they exist without breath or life (v. 17) and evoke contempt and laughter. Yet idols still persist. People bow down before the silver screen and the golden bull of the stock market. We worship at the stadiums of sports and music concerts. We treat celebrities as if they carried a word from on high. Wealth, pleasure, and power have become the new trinity, begging for our allegiance and our trust. Martin Luther would post at least ninety-five theses on our church doors to name all the false gods we follow.

PRAYER/PRACTICE

As you continue to shape your rule of life, pay attention to these questions and suggestions. Aim for balance in your rule—balance between what feels easy and natural and what feels challenging; between personal and corporate practices; between quiet and active, mental and physical, firmly set and graciously flexible. Make realistic choices. Are you a morning or evening person? Be gentle in choosing and faithful in committing. Sticking with one discipline is better than feeling bad about not keeping five. Do you need to take on more or let go of some spiritual practices? Which spiritual disciplines fit best with your personality, your gifts and graces? Know that a rule requires a commitment of time and a plan for using the time.

November 11

REMEMBER

Saint Martin of Tours (c. 336–397) left the army to serve God and founded the first monasteries in France. Artists picture him tearing his cloak in half to share with a beggar.

READ

Psalm 135:19-21

PONDER

God desires, welcomes, and even requires praise from all of creation. The psalmist names three communities who constitute the leaders of praise. "House of Aaron" represents the priestly class. "House of Levi" represents the assistants, or Temple personnel. "House of Israel" represents all the people (vv. 19-20). The call to praise includes all people. Though society may separate persons because of heritage, occupation, gender, sexual orientation, or personality, when people gather for worship, they are to unite their voices in praise. Praising God becomes the unifying factor. Adoration of God, who abounds in grace and compassionately weaves history, joins all our differences into a chorus of praise.

PRAYER/PRACTICE

A rule of life should reflect some commitment to daily practices, keeping in mind the necessity for balance and flexibility. I believe that a rule should provide time for daily prayer—including praise, thanksgiving, confession, intercession, and petition—and ample time for silence, meditation, and contemplation. Reading scripture, particularly the Psalms, and other devotional resources like this book and those listed in Appendix A, becomes an important element of a daily rule. Journaling will help you record and notice the Spirit's prompting and nudging in your life. A time of reflection and self-examination, particularly in the evening, makes a positive contribution. (See Prayer/Practice entries, Nov. 19–30.) Finally, I hope that you give some attention to the body, whether in prayer postures, walking, exercising, or fasting.

Which of these practices are part of your rule?

November 12

REMEMBER

Søren Kierkegaard (1813–1855), a Danish theologian and philosopher, rejected Christianity as a system of ideas and challenged Christians to become true Christians in a so-called Christian nation.

READ

Psalm 136:1-9

PONDER

In Jewish tradition, this psalm was known as the Great Hallel. (*Hallel* is the Hebrew word for praise.) One of the psalms sung at the Passover feast, the Great Hallel exudes praise and jubilation. The psalmist's lines of praise expand images from the preceding psalm, beginning with creation and going on to recite the great history of the Israelites.

Growing up in the church, I thought only Protestants did responsive readings, but this psalm disputes that notion. It contains a wonderful refrain that the congregation or choir repeated as a response: "God's love never fails"(CEV).

PRAYER/PRACTICE

A rule of life includes more than just daily practices; it also includes weekly practices. The practice of weekly worship ranks as top priority. This corporate experience of fellowship and prayer with others provides a good balance to the more private and individual practices of each day. Many persons receive the Eucharist (Holy Communion) weekly as part of their rule, even if that means going outside their normal tradition. Participating in a weekly study/support/prayer group helps with accountability to disciplines. Involvement in mission or service projects might be a worthy goal—they can be as simple as recycling or visiting the sick, or involve others, such as serving at a soup kitchen or building a Habitat for Humanity house.

What weekly disciplines would you include in your rule?

November 13

REMEMBER

Frances Xavier Cabrini (1850–1917), an Italian American, founded the Missionary Sisters of the Sacred Heart. She became the first U.S. citizen canonized by the Catholic Church.

READ

Psalm 136:10-22

PONDER

Eugene Peterson writes, "History is a museum through which the praising person can stroll, finding down every corridor evidence of what God has done in judgment and deliverance."[6] The chorus of praise, "God's love never fails" (CEV), moves from thanking the Creator to praising God's action. The psalmist recalls how God freed the Hebrews from slavery in Egypt, led them through the Red Sea, and gave them the Promised Land. The poet praises God for overthrowing tyrant kings and rescuing the people from their enemies. We could add to the list people like Nero, Stalin, Hitler, and Idi Amin. We can also praise God for raising up missionaries like Frances Cabrini, who proved that women could do the hard task of working among poor immigrants.

PRAYER/PRACTICE

I include monthly, yearly, or episodic events in my rule. A monthly visit to my spiritual director forms an essential part of my rule. My daily pattern of prayer, reading, and journaling becomes the content for our conversations. Spiritual direction marvelously links personal disciplines with the corporate wisdom embodied in another person. I also include spiritual retreats as part of my rule. At times I have scheduled a day away every month. Ideally I also try to schedule two or three longer retreats during the year. Both monthly and yearly retreats nourish my soul. Longer service projects, done annually, could also become part of a personal rule.

What nondaily, nonweekly events would you claim as part of your rule? How do they help you move closer to God?

November 14

REMEMBER

Saint Gregory Palamas (c. 1296–1359), a monk and hermit of Mount Athos in Greece, taught the "hesychastic" way—an interior life of prayer based on praying the Jesus Prayer.

READ

Psalm 136:23-26

PONDER

"The memory of the good things we have experienced in life should be ever with us; the memory of what God has done for us, of his gifts to us, can be a constant source of encouragement."[7] The psalmist moves from specific events as occasions for praise to a trinity of theological truths: God remembers, God rescues, and God feeds. Prefiguring the prayer of Mary when she consents to be the handmaiden of God (Luke 1:48), the psalmist affirms "our low estate" but celebrates that God remembers and God rescues (vv. 23-24). We can most likely relate to the final reason for praise, thanking God for food. Twenty-six times this psalm reminds us to give thanks to God, yet we can probably think of even more reasons, for indeed God's steadfast love endures forever.

PRAYER/PRACTICE

Your own rule should be beginning to take shape. Marjorie Thompson suggests four guidelines to help you move into your commitments:

> 1) Persevere in practice: just as a tree cannot get rooted if it is continually transplanted, we cannot get rooted in the soil of God's love if we are constantly changing our practice. 2) Find support for your rule from at least two other persons of faith. . . . 3) Stay open to the Spirit with regard to possible revisions of your rule over time. Sometimes we need a mid-course correction, and sometimes our lives change enough to require a changed rule. 4) Finally, seek God's grace to be faithful to your practice. Grace is the ultimate key to spiritual growth.[8]

Look at your rule of life in light of these guidelines.

November 15

REMEMBER

Cardinal Joseph Bernardin (1928–1996), archbishop of Chicago, helped draft the U.S. Catholic bishops' pastoral letter on nuclear war and sought to combine piety with a consistent ethic of valuing all life. He waged a courageous battle against cancer that inspired many Americans.

READ

Psalm 137:1-6

PONDER

In 597 B.C.E. Nebuchadnezzar, king of Babylon, conquered Jerusalem and deported many of its inhabitants. Ten years later, a second mass deportation took place. For nearly seventy years the Israelites lived in exile, mourning, and weeping. The Hebrews' captors taunted them, begging them to sing one of the happy songs, the praise songs of Jerusalem (v. 3). Some scholars think the Hebrews never sang while in captivity. Others think they learned to sing as they discovered that God was not confined to Jerusalem but remained with them even in captivity. Perhaps we need to learn to sing new songs, to realize that God is not tied to one nation or one people. Still, this psalm poignantly and memorably expresses the longing for home, the yearning to escape from oppression, and the recalling of precious memories of God.

PRAYER/PRACTICE

If you haven't done so already, write down your rule of life. Include your daily, weekly, and yearly commitments. Putting something in writing tends to make it real. You may wish to develop a ritual and a blessing for the act of committing yourself to grow. Light a candle and invite God to bless you with faithfulness and persistence. Share your rule with another person, such as your spiritual director, your prayer partner, your prayer or covenant group. "Spouses and other family members should know enough of your rule to be able to encourage, or at least not interfere needlessly with, your practice."[9] Display your rule in a place where it can remind you of your commitments.

November 16

REMEMBER

Saint Gertrude the Great (1253–1302), a spiritual director and mystic at the monastery in Helfta, Germany, espoused a way of prayer that focused on the Sacred Heart of Jesus.

READ

Psalm 137:7-9

PONDER

The psalm shifts from weeping and self-pity to anger and violence. Pent-up feelings emerge, shocking us in their vehemence. We do not like to acknowledge such anger and darkness within ourselves. The Israelites, however, prayed their anger to God, for God was big enough to handle it and strong enough to deflect it.

In the closing verses of the psalm, the Israelites turn their anger toward their neighbors, the Edomites, who had rejoiced as the Babylonians destroyed Jerusalem (v. 7). They call for a standard form of revenge on the Babylonians (v. 9), though we stand appalled by such violence to children. Oh, that we were equally appalled by the violence that continues today, causing death to millions of children.

PRAYER/PRACTICE

Corporate rules exist in Christian tradition—attitudes and practices that guide groups in their common life. In the sixth century Saint Benedict (July 11) developed a rule for monks that shapes monastic communities to this day. Martin Luther King Jr. (Jan. 15) developed a rule to guide the nonviolent protests during the civil rights movement. Each demonstrator agreed (among other things) to meditate daily on the teachings of Jesus; to walk and talk in the manner of love; to pray daily to be used by God in order that all might be free; to refrain from violence of fist, tongue, or heart; and to seek to perform regular service for others and the world.[10]

Think of religious or faith groups (study or prayer groups) you belong to. Do they have any written or unwritten rules to guide you in spiritual progress? Consider adding their wisdom to your own rule.

November 17

REMEMBER

The Jesuit Martyrs of San Salvador—six Jesuit priests who taught at University of Central America—were murdered (along with their housekeeper and her daughter) by government troops for speaking out against the Salvadoran government's oppression of the poor.

READ

Psalm 138:1-3

PONDER

We do sit-ups for stomach and back muscles. We do push-ups for the arms and chest. We run or walk for our heart and lungs. We may even join a gym or club to keep us faithful. But what do we do for the soul?

I believe the psalmist had prayer and praise in mind when writing the words "you increased my strength of soul" (v. 3). Our souls grow stronger when we call on God in prayer (v. 3). Our souls expand when we stretch our lives in praise and thanksgiving. Our souls reach full capacity when we sing our praise (v. 1). Our souls become more powerful when they worship and connect with a community of faith. This may be a good day for soul exercises.

PRAYER/PRACTICE

I have long been interested in nongeographical communities that intentionally shape their life together and apart, often creating a corporate rule of life. In many of these communities, laypeople adopt particular practices in connection with a monastic community. These oblates have a parallel rule to the monks but maintain their current relationships and work. I belong to a group called SisBros whose corporate rule calls us to meet twice a year, to remember one another in a Monday liturgy, to give a tithe to our religious communities, and to give 2 percent of our income to SisBros to go toward projects involved in justice. When we meet in the summer and winter, we study, worship, and play together and encourage one another to live a more just and simple life.

Learn about nongeographical communities (see Appendix A) and see how they live out of a corporate rule.

November 18

REMEMBER

T. S. Eliot (1888–1965), a British poet, also served as a critic and drama-tist. Albert Camus (1913–1960), an author and Nobel laureate, witnessed to a public conscience and a common struggle for life against death.

READ

Psalm 138:4-6

PONDER

Many consider Psalm 138 to be a royal psalm, a psalm of praise the king prays for some unmentioned favor or victory. God's special favor to Israel gives reason for all the kings of surrounding nations to see the greatness of the God of Israel. Praise begets a public celebration, a glo-rious witness to the power of God. That power of God bends toward the lowly, the poor, the forgotten, the despised (v. 6). God's compassion reveals God's greatness. God's might brings hope to those Jesus calls "the least of these"—the hungry, the sick, the imprisoned, the naked. (See Matt. 25:31-46.) All creation raises a chorus of praise to the power-ful and compassionate God.

PRAYER/PRACTICE

The approach of Thanksgiving provides a good time to practice prayers of praise and thanksgiving. Try writing a prayer of your own or use this one as a beginning.

> God of Creation, you fill the earth with trees of plenty and fields of abundance. Your gifts fill baskets of delight and bushels of nourish-ment. Remind us to pause in thanks for all your blessings: For the gift of sun and rain that produces such abundance. For the gift of many peoples whose customs, foods, and wisdom enrich our lives. For the gift of sharing, witnessed long ago between Native Americans and Pilgrims, which makes community possible. For the gift of family, large and small, who serve as a signs of your extended care. For all these things and more, we offer our praise and thanks to you. Amen.

November 19

REMEMBER

Ezekiel (B.C.E.), an Old Testament prophet, priest, and visionary, saw the dry bones of Israel coming back together and prophesied that God would put a new heart and spirit into the people.

READ

Psalm 138:7-8

PONDER

Though abundant praise flows in this psalm, the psalmist does not forget that we will continually have to "walk in the midst of trouble" (v. 7). We will face difficult choices; others' choices will also affect us for good or harm. In the midst of trouble, God remains present. In the midst of dry bones, God brings together new possibilities. In the quandary of directions and decisions, God's steadfast love is present to guide and protect. We affirm with the psalmist, "You will do everything you have promised; LORD, your love is eternal. Complete the work that you have begun" (v. 8, GNT).

PRAYER/PRACTICE

For the next few days I invite you to look at the need and the practice of self-examination. "Self-examination is not morbid introspection or self-condemnation, but the honest, fearless confrontation of the self, and its abandonment to God in trust."[11] Often in Christian practice, however, reflecting on one's day has turned into an exercise of finding fault, looking for sins, feeling bad, and hopelessly trying to do better the next day. The long tradition of "examination of conscience" became an unpleasant task in front of a critical, judgmental, and often disappointed and condemning God. Fortunately, many contemporary spiritual writers have uncovered a new breadth and a renewed understanding of the gift of self-examination.

For today, in preparation for looking at your life, know that God loves you, whether your day has been good or bad or some of both.

November 20

REMEMBER

Leo Tolstoy (1828–1910), a Russian novelist *(War and Peace, Anna Karenina),* returned to his Orthodox roots and sought to live the heart of the gospel as expressed in the Sermon on the Mount. His writings about nonviolence and civil disobedience later influenced Gandhi.

READ

Psalm 139:1-6

PONDER

God makes the first move, takes the first step, searching for us (v. 1). Even our deep hunger and longing for God comes as a response to the One who looks for us and knows us. God knows our thoughts, our paths, our words—even what time we get up in the morning! (vv. 2-4). To be known so well is amazing, awesome, overwhelming, even frightening (v. 6). Thank goodness (thank God) that the One who knows us is the God of love and forgiveness, the God whose judgment of our personal lives remains blessedly tempered with mercy. God searches for us, knows us, and still loves us. The psalmist proclaims, "Such knowledge is too wonderful for me" (v. 6). Amen to that!

PRAYER/PRACTICE

Psalm 139 offers a wonderful beginning for self-examination. God knows us and desires our self-awareness. Many writers distinguish between an "examination of conscience" that serves as a penitential assessment of one's faithfulness and an "examination of consciousness" that seeks a broader awareness of God's presence in all the ups and downs of our life. In either practice, "self-examination is not an invitation to psychoanalysis, problem solving, self-lecturing, or ego-absorption. The whole point of self-examination is to become more *God-centered* by observing the moments when we are or are not so."[12]

To practice the confessional side of self-examination, reflect on your day, your behaviors and attitudes, in light of the Ten Commandments (Exod. 20:1-17).

November 21 •

REMEMBER

Corita Kent (1918–1986), a sister of the Immaculate Heart of Mary, became known for her art, which combined colorful and abstract shapes with messages from the Bible and culture. Her silk-screen prints highlighted women's rights and peace and even graced a postage stamp.

READ

Psalm 139:7-12

PONDER

God not only seeks us but even pursues us. One thinks of the image from Francis Thompson's poem, "The Hound of Heaven," in which God relentlessly pursues humanity until humanity abandons itself to God's love. There is nowhere we can go to avoid God (v. 7). Even ignoring God or denying God's existence will not keep God away. In every country, on every shore, at the farthest limits of the sea or sky, God dwells (v. 9). At times of darkness, both the long hours of night and the internal darkness of illness, depression, or grief, God abides with us, and the darkness is as light to God (v. 12). Great comfort resides in these verses. God continually looks for us, waits for us, watches over us, abides with us. Let those truths sink to the core of your being and speak to any doubts or fears of your worth. You matter to God!

PRAYER/PRACTICE

Eastern Orthodox Christians have historically used the Beatitudes both as a liturgical aid to confession and as a guide to self-examination. Yesterday you tried the Ten Commandments as a pattern to reflect on your day. Today use the Beatitudes (Matt. 5:1-12) as a lens to review your day. Notice the times you served as a peacemaker as well as the times you failed to bring peace or even stirred up anger and distrust. Give thanks for your times of faithfulness; confess the times of weakness.

Remember, an examination of conscience opens a time when "a soul comes under the gaze of God and . . . is pierced to the quick and becomes conscious of the things that must be forgiven and put right before it can continue to love One whose care has been so constant."[13]

November 22

REMEMBER

Eberhard Arnold (1883–1935), helped establish the Bruderhof, a Christian community in Germany based on simplicity, nonviolence, and imitation of the Sermon on the Mount. Harassed by the Nazis, the Bruderhof eventually established communities in the United States.

READ

Psalm 139:13-18

PONDER

"I praise you, for I am fearfully and wonderfully made" (v. 14). A small girl in Vietnam, an old man in Russia, an Aymara Indian in Bolivia, and a young man in South Africa offer that prayer. All around the world people pray this psalm, affirming the God who knit us together in our mother's womb (v. 13). "Wonderful are your works," O God (v. 14). You may have complained about your body, its size or shape, its aches and pains, yet this psalm calls all to thank God for their bodies, intricately woven in the hidden depths (v. 15). God knows us from the beginning, lays out our days, and journeys with us to the end (v. 16).

PRAYER/PRACTICE

The *Spiritual Exercises* of Saint Ignatius shaped the monastic tradition of examen of conscience. The first step of this way of prayer gives thanks to God for the gifts and graces of life and of the day. The second step prays for the grace of insight to know your sins and asks God to enlighten and teach you. The third step enters a time of self-examination in the light of Christ. You examine the day to see how you have responded to God's loving presence, avoiding a too scrupulous or too preoccupied focus on your faults. "Rather, it [the examen] is but a prayerful exploration of *all* of our day, in order to discover not only what is in need of healing, but also what may have been neglected or ignored, or what might be celebrated."[14] The fourth step asks God for pardon or gives God thanks. The fifth step resolves to do better, to trust in God's promise of a new day, of new help and guidance.

Set aside some time to pray this way at the end of your day.

November 23

REMEMBER

Saint Columban (c. 543–615), an Irish monk and missionary to Europe, founded monasteries in France and Italy. Those monasteries kept a Celtic rule, which was stricter than the Rule of Saint Benedict.

READ

Psalm 139:19-22

PONDER

Perhaps the awareness of God's power sets the psalmist off on a tangent. If God is all-knowing and all-powerful, then God should do something about the wicked (v. 19). Liars, schemers, and blasphemers abound. God's enemies become the psalmist's enemies. The psalmist can justify such hatred, "perfect hatred" (v. 22), because the law of love has not yet been preached. Jesus brings a radical correction to an eye for an eye and perfect hatred of the enemy. Jesus says, "Love your enemies, do good to those who hate you, bless those who curse you, pray for those who abuse you" (Luke 6:27-28).

PRAYER/PRACTICE

After spending time in self-examination, one may feel the desire for confession. Roman Catholics and others have a process and tradition of private confession. Many Protestant churches offer a time of common confession and pardon as part of public worship. Yet there exists an age-old tradition, before confession became formalized and professionalized, of confessing one's heart to another trusted person and then receiving prayer and absolution. Christians can still confess and offer absolution to one another, and the power of a face-to-face interaction can bring about tremendous release and renewal.

Does some sin or fault in your past trouble you, hindering your relationship with God? Would talking to another person and asking for prayer provide a step toward healing? Ask God in prayer for guidance in finding a person.

November 24

REMEMBER

Etty Hillesum (1914–1943), a young Jewish woman in Amsterdam, kept a diary of her inner responses to the horror around her and witnessed to the power of love. Her book, *An Interrupted Life,* offers wisdom and expresses hope for a new and kinder day.

READ

Psalm 139:23-24

PONDER

The psalmist, thankfully, reverts to reflection on God's seeking and knowing. God's intimate knowledge of each person ceases to frighten the psalmist. Rather, the psalmist turns toward God and invites, even challenges, God to search, test, and probe the psalmist's own heart and actions (v. 23). We can pray this psalm as a way of asking God to evaluate our thoughts and deeds and to correct us if "there is any wicked way" in us (v. 24). Praying the psalm gives God opportunity to hold a light to our shadows and doubts and lead us back to "the way everlasting" (v. 24).

Psalm 139 has offered comfort, assurance, and strength to many pilgrims on the road to God.

PRAYER/PRACTICE

The examination of consciousness constitutes a time of God-focused awareness of external events and experiences and an awareness of your own thoughts, beliefs, and feelings. You look for awareness of God's grace in your day and for ways you noticed or failed to respond.

One pattern for examination of consciousness bases itself on the way Jesus met with his disciples (Mark 6:30-32). Gather the events and experiences of the day, and offer a prayer of thanks. Next, imagine reporting to Jesus on your successes and failures, your highs and lows. Report any patterns and observations that seem to recur. Finally, rest with Jesus in quiet and prayer. "Allow him to release you from your failures, heal your hurts, and empower you for the challenges ahead."[15]

Try this pattern at the end of your day.

November 25

REMEMBER

Thanksgiving, observed in the United States on the fourth Thursday of November, celebrates an abundant harvest and remains a day to give thanks for native peoples who shared much with the early settlers in America.

READ

Psalm 140:1-5

PONDER

The evil mentioned in this psalm seems not so much directed against an individual as against the nation. The evildoers and the violent stir up wars continually (vv. 1-2). Violence resides in their thoughts, in their speech, and in their plans. The psalm testifies to the all-consuming nature of violence and to our desire to be protected from such violence. We know from the lives of Jesus, Gandhi, and Martin Luther King Jr. that only love can dispel violence. We ask for God's protection (v. 4), but we must also actively oppose violence by working for love and reconciliation and by carrying out acts of kindness and mercy.

PRAYER/PRACTICE

Another practice of self-examination of consciousness is a modern reworking of the examination of conscience. First, list ten or twelve major events of the day, including times of prayer and other activities. Second, reflect on the events "without judging yourself, avoiding feelings, or making excuses."[16] Third, give thanks for the day, for your life, and for God's presence through it all. Fourth, confess your sin, acknowledging your faults in thoughts, words, and deeds. Finally, seek the meaning of the events as you reflect on what God says to you or calls you to do through each experience.

Keeping a journal of your reflections is a helpful practice. You might also do this kind of self-examination at the end of a week instead of each night. Try this pattern.

November 26

REMEMBER

Sojourner Truth (1797–1883), a leading American abolitionist, became a strong proponent of women's rights. Though born a slave, she gained freedom and became a powerful preacher and reformer.

READ

Psalm 140:6-8

PONDER

In times of trouble, in times of persecution, we pray, "Give ear, O LORD, to the voice of my supplications" (v. 6). Our needs do not exhaust God's listening ear and responsive heart. In times of trouble, God remains a sure defense, a strong deliverer (v. 7). In times of persecution and distress, we may even grow stronger, more ready for battle (v. 7). We gain clarity about the foe. We gird ourselves for battle, using the most unusual weapons: the belt of truth, the breastplate of righteousness, the shoes of the gospel of peace, the shield of faith, the helmet of salvation, and the sword of the Spirit, which is the Word of God (Eph. 6:10-17).

PRAYER/PRACTICE

Wendy Wright suggests using the Lord's Prayer as a pattern for self-examination.[17] As you pray the Lord's Prayer, write the answers to the following questions in your journal. "Our Father in heaven, hallowed be your name"—How have you noticed God's holy presence in your life this week? "Your kingdom come, your will be done . . ."—How have you sought for God's will, worked for God's kingdom? "Give us this day our daily bread"—What is the bread that sustained you? With whom did you break bread, and to whom did you give bread today? "Forgive us our sins as we forgive those who sin against us"—How have you experienced God's forgiveness and offered forgiveness to others? With whom do you still need to reconcile? "Save us from the time of trial and deliver us from evil"—Where was your faith tested? In what ways were you delivered from difficulty? "For the kingdom, power, and glory are yours, now and forever"—Give thanks for God's kingdom and power, and thank God for the blessings you have received.

November 27

REMEMBER

Hosea (B.C.E.), an Old Testament prophet, personally lived out Yahweh's intention to take back unfaithful Israel by taking back his prostitute wife. God spoke through Hosea of faithfulness in the midst of unfaithfulness.

READ

Psalm 140:9-13

PONDER

The psalmist's anger spills over into curses and wishes for disaster upon the evildoers. We may have felt like flinging a few burning coals (v. 10) several times in our own lives. Once again, the psalmist does not know the radical notion of praying for enemies. And once again, the writer offers his anger and despair to God because God will act, though often with more grace and forgiveness than the psalmist desires. The Israelites knew that God acts, that God cares for the needy and executes justice for the poor (v. 13). They knew this because they had experienced God's care and compassion. And they knew that God wanted them to act with equal care and compassion, even as they hurled curses and coals at the violent and wicked.

PRAYER/PRACTICE

As you try the various practices of self-examination, beware of slipping into a self-absorbed anxiety about your sins and faults. Beware of false humility. "Whenever we become fascinated by our sins or sucked into despair over our weaknesses, we may be sure that false humility is at work."[18] We can develop a form of spiritual pride as we wallow in guilt, obsess over faults, and believe ourselves to be unforgivable or unredeemable.

Teresa of Avila suggests a remedy: "Stop thinking about your misery, insofar as possible, and turn your thoughts to the mercy of God, to how He loves us and suffered for us."[19]

In your self-examination it remains important to balance your awareness of sin with acceptance of God's grace. As you practice one of the examination patterns today, remember God's abundant grace.

November 28

REMEMBER

Thomas R. Kelly (1893–1941), a Quaker teacher, missionary, and author, wrote *A Testament of Devotion,* a classic devotional guide to the spiritual life.

READ

Psalm 141:1-2

PONDER

This psalm, with its reference to an evening sacrifice, has been used for evening prayer since the earliest days of the church. Some need or fear presses, and the psalmist makes a persuasive and poetic plea: "Let my prayer be counted as incense before you, and the lifting up of my hands as an evening sacrifice" (v. 2). To the Hebrews, incense symbolized an ascent to God. Our prayers rise upward like the smoke from incense, and the fragrance fills the holy space as God's presence hovers over and around the worshiping community. The psalmist hopes the urgent prayer arrives at heaven with a fragrance as sweet as the evening incense at worship.

We may enjoy using incense in our prayer time, but thank God we do not have to plead, coerce, or trick God to hear us.

PRAYER/PRACTICE

You can carry out a time of self-examination in your journal. Answer these questions in your journal:

- When did you sense God's presence in the day's events?

- When did you sense God's presence in your feelings?

- How have you sensed God's call today? How did you respond?

- For what event today do you most need God's healing? [20]

November 29

REMEMBER

Dorothy Day (1897–1980), cofounder of the Catholic Worker movement, challenged the church to great acts of charity and confronted institutions with their injustice. Her devotion to Christ's teachings in the Sermon on the Mount led her to become an active pacifist and frequent participant in civil disobedience.

READ

Psalm 141:3-4

PONDER

Words have power. The psalmist asks God, "Help me to guard my words whenever I say something. Don't let me want to do evil or waste my time doing wrong with wicked people" (vv. 3-4, CEV). Evidently the psalmist feels tempted to associate with the wicked and to partake of some unholy feast. I suspect that Dorothy Day asked God to watch and strengthen her words so that she might awaken a callous and deaf church and city to the plight of the poor. The newspaper she and Peter Maurin (May 9) started contained words of challenge and rebuke. Too many people ate rich delicacies while the poor had little but what they received at the Catholic Worker soup kitchen. New York and the nation would never be quite the same, thanks to the strong words of Dorothy Day and the prophetic witness of the *Catholic Worker*.

PRAYER/PRACTICE

Practicing an examination of consciousness under the guidance and gaze of the gentle Spirit can lead to a healthy self-awareness and a surer foundation for living truthfully and faithfully in God's world. One gift of self-awareness is a growing capacity for compassion as you become less likely to judge others and have less need to rationalize your behavior. "Self-examination is an occasion for spiritual refreshment. . . . Its purpose is always to bring us into greater intimacy with the Lover of our souls, so that we can learn to walk according to God's path for us."[21]

Choose one of the patterns of examination from this month to use for your daily or weekly self-examination.

November 30

REMEMBER

Andrew (first century), a fisherman and one of the twelve apostles, introduced Jesus to Peter, his brother. According to tradition, Andrew carried the gospel to northern Greece and southern Russia.

READ

Psalm 141:5-7

PONDER

"Let the faithful correct me" (v. 5). The temptations of the wicked must seem enticing, for the psalmist not only calls on God for help (v. 1) but now asks for the guidance, counsel, and correction of the community of faith. The flattery of the wicked needs to be countered by the honesty of the faithful. In alliance with the righteous, the psalmist will be able to stand firm and speak the truth. A community of twelve, including Andrew, learned how to pray for enemies and to speak the truth. Perhaps only in community can we have the courage to speak the truth.

PRAYER/PRACTICE

The examination of consciousness wonderfully aids the practice of spiritual direction. Consistent daily reflection will yield insights and troubles, patterns and surprises that become the seedbed for discussion with a director.

One spiritual director, Tilden Edwards of the Shalem Institute, encourages a short form of the examen. Gently remind yourself of God's presence, and then let any event or moment from the day arise in your mind. Notice whether you were present to God or others in the midst of the moment, and if you were not, pray a simple breath prayer, like "Lord, have mercy." If you demonstrated awareness of or responsiveness to God's grace, "smile to God with thanksgiving."[22] Repeat the process for the various situations that arise. Pay attention to any surprises, any patterns, any special graces of the day.

Try this pattern of examination, and then reflect on the eight patterns suggested this month. Choose one or two patterns to add consistently to your life of prayer.

December

Winter God, in the darkest time of year
you brought in starlight, angel song, and baby cries.
Stay with me as I journey to new birth
and celebrate this year of saints, psalms, and prayer.
In the silence and stillness,
fashion my prayer into a carol of praise
and focus my life so that I may act as a herald of Christ, the
child of peace and the prophet of justice. Amen.

December 1

REMEMBER

Charles de Foucauld (1858–1916) lived as a hermit in the Sahara desert, and his writings did much to revive desert spirituality. De Foucauld's famous Prayer of Abandonment remains a testimony of trust and yielding to God.

READ

Psalm 141:8-10

PONDER

Evil usually boomerangs. If you sow wickedness, you reap wickedness. So the psalmist prays to be kept out of the traps of the wicked, which will eventually snare the evildoers (vv. 9-10). It would be appropriate to sing the spiritual "Guide my feet while I run this race." But, even more important then avoiding trouble, the psalmist directs us to keep our focus on God. "My eyes are turned toward you" (v. 8).

Many have found this prayer of Charles de Foucauld helpful in keeping their gaze on the divine:

> My Father, I commend myself to you, I give myself to you, I leave myself in your hands. My Father, do with me as you wish. Whatever you do with me, I thank you, I accept everything. I am ready for anything. I thank you always. So long as your will is done in me and in all creatures, I have no other wish, my God.[1]

PRAYER/PRACTICE

Offer this prayer of thanks for the beginning of Advent.

> God of December darkness and Christmas light, journey with me through this last month of the year. Deepen my longing, heighten my expectation, and make pregnant my hope. I know that within my heart is a Bethlehem: a place where light shines with tender memories. A place where angelic voices sing loud and clear. A place of wonder and awe, delight and calm. A place where the humility of the shepherds and the wisdom of the Magi embrace. God of December darkness and Christmas light, journey with me during these days so that I may know and prize my Bethlehem moments. Amen.

December 2

REMEMBER

Maura Clarke, Ita Ford, Jean Donovan, and Dorothy Kazel, four Christian workers killed in El Salvador in 1980, served the poor and took inspiration from Archbishop Oscar Romero (Mar. 24). They lived their commitment to caring for the human rights of workers.

READ

Psalm 142:1-4

PONDER

I heard someone say, "I only pray when I am in trouble. Since I am in trouble all the time, I am in constant prayer." Though these statements intend to be a little humorous, they speak to the situation of the psalmist and, at times, to us. "I pray to you, LORD. I beg for mercy. . . . Even if you look, you won't see anyone who cares enough to walk beside me" (vv. 1, 4, CEV). This prayer finds a home in those caught in the snares of depression, disillusionment, grief, loneliness, despair, or oppression (like the poor in El Salvador). Feeling cut off from everyone, the psalmist turns to God. Amazingly, what often seems like the last straw really becomes the first step to realizing that God is our help and our salvation. The early church saw Jesus in this psalm, for even though he felt abandoned on the cross, still he cried out to God. Trouble can serve as a doorway to God.

PRAYER/PRACTICE

Longing, a key word in December, shapes the deepest parts of prayers of petition and intercession. In the midst of the hustle and bustle of December, you may find that your longing for Christmas takes on deeper meanings. For the next few days I invite you to explore your longings, your deepest prayers.

"Come, thou long-expected Jesus, born to set thy people free."[2] This Advent hymn by Charles Wesley links longing for Jesus with the longing for freedom—freedom from fears, sins, prejudices, anger, diseases. I invite you to create an alternative Christmas list: a list of your deepest longings.

December 3

REMEMBER

Saint Francis Xavier (1506–1552), one of the first persons to take the vows of a Jesuit, served successfully as missionary to India and Japan. He became the patron saint of foreign missions.

READ

Psalm 142:5-7

PONDER

No verses here express joyous confidence in God's action; no verses give praise and thanks for what God has done or will do. The psalmist experiences desolation with only a hint of hope in the heartfelt cry for help, "You are my refuge, my portion in the land of the living" (v. 5). Abandoned by friends, the psalmist expresses one more glimmer of hope in the last verse. It comes through a small community: "The righteous will surround me" (v. 7). God works through other people at moments when we feel alone and isolated. According to tradition, Saint Francis of Assisi (Oct. 4) memorized this psalm, finding it to be a source of comfort in his lonely begging and a source of strength for the ragged band of simple and just persons who followed him.

PRAYER/PRACTICE

Doctors now diagnose people with SAD, or seasonal affective disorder. Sufferers of SAD, affected by the lack of sunlight during the darker days of winter, experience depression-like symptoms. In a real sense they long for light.

The Advent hymn "O Come, O Come Emanuel" refers to Jesus as Dayspring. The songwriter invites the coming Lord to clear away the gloom, to bring cheer and light

We long for an end to gloomy feelings. We long for light to illumine our path. We long for a new day, for freedom from the threats of terror and the politics of hatred. We long for the dawning of forgiveness and the brightness of peace. We long for light, for our Dayspring.

Today add to your alternative Christmas list and try to soak up a little sunlight if possible.

December 4

REMEMBER

Wolfgang Amadeus Mozart (1756–1791), an Austrian composer, used religious themes in many of his works. His final composition, *Requiem*, reveals his anguish and brilliance.

READ

Psalm 143:1-6

PONDER

The seventh and last of the group of penitential psalms does not specifically mention sins, but it conveys a sense of deep trouble and a willingness to confess. The psalmist uses evocative language to describe a hopeless condition: "in darkness like those long dead" (v. 3); "my spirit faints within me; my heart within me is appalled" (v. 4); "my soul thirsts" (v. 6). These phrases communicate a winter of the soul, a longing for light and refreshment. This psalm feels December-like, summarizing our deep longing for God. It invites us to "meditate on the works of [God's] hands"(v. 5), to trust God to act as in the past (v. 5), and to reach out for the coming Christ child.

PRAYER/PRACTICE

Music stirs and touches the deepest longing of the human spirit. Violins and oboes never fail to tug at my heart. Mozart's *Requiem* can bring tears to my eyes. Likewise, the hymns and songs of the Advent/Christmas season can awaken our longings and touch our souls. Since the fifteenth century, Christians have sung "O Come, O Come, Emmanuel" with its deep longing and its majestic refrain of hope: "Rejoice! Rejoice! Emmanuel shall come to thee, O Israel."[3] Our deepest longing finds fulfillment in the birth of the Christ child.

Our deep longing does not dwell in the fragrance of evergreen or the beauty of brightly wrapped presents; rather, it lies in the hope of renewed relationships, release from resentments, a world at peace, a touch of God. Add to your list of longings, and sing "O Come, O Come, Emmanuel" or another Advent hymn.

December 5

Charles Schulz (1922–2000), a cartoonist, created the comic strip *Peanuts,* which included Linus, a thinker/theologian who often sorts out the bumbling Charlie Brown or tames the arrogant Lucy.

READ

Psalm 143:7-12

PONDER

Petition remains a central part of the life of prayer. We do not pray with a stoical self-sufficiency but rather with an awareness of our need as we ask for God's help. We know we do not have all the resources; we know that we make mistakes. The Psalms teach us how to petition God and how to do so with boldness and urgency. "Answer me quickly, O LORD; my spirit fails" (v. 7). "Teach me the way I should go" (v. 8). "Save me . . . teach me . . . lead me . . . preserve my life . . . bring me out of trouble" (vv. 9-11). The psalmist uses strong verbs, imploring God to act and believing that God hears and responds. "Let me hear of your steadfast love in the morning, for in you I put my trust" (v. 8). We petition God and we listen every morning, trusting in grace sufficient for the day.

PRAYER/PRACTICE

Prayers of longing form a part of our petitions. In the midst of much to do, I long for peace and joy. This prayer helps me, and perhaps it will help you form your own prayer of longing.

> O God, let some joy loose. Let it rise to the surface and shake me out of preoccupation with lists and tasks. Forgive me for my heavy-hearted approach to your season of joy and light. Help me not to let long lists and calendar events overwhelm the wonder of your birth. Smiling God, let some joy loose in me, and let it rub off on others.

Add to your alternative list of longing and read the *Peanuts* comic strip. Consider watching a video of *Charlie Brown's Christmas* or doing something to let some joy loose today.

December 6

REMEMBER

Saint Nicholas (fourth century), the bishop of Myra who, according to legends, secretly helped the poor and became a model for our gift-giving Santa Claus.

READ

Psalm 144:1-4

PONDER

It is time to recover Saint Nicholas. As our consumer culture overdoses on Santa Claus, red-nosed reindeer, the Grinch, and presents, we can offer a wonderful gift by telling the story of this saintly man who had Jesus' compassion for the poor. According to one legend, Bishop Nicholas learned of a poor man who could not afford to provide the usual dowries for his three daughters. Without dowries, they could not marry. Fearing the daughters might be sold as slaves, the bishop threw a bag of gold through an open window in their house one night and then hurried away. Not long afterward the eldest daughter got married. Twice more the bishop dropped a bag of gold into the poor man's house. The father, curious about the identity of his generous benefactor, watched his house and caught the bishop as he left gold the third time. Nicholas begged him to keep this a secret, but much to the embarrassment of Nicholas, the news got out.

PRAYER/PRACTICE

Today look for opportunities to tell children about Saint Nicholas, considered by many persons to be the original Christmas gift-giver (after God, of course). Find a children's storybook about Saint Nicholas and read it to some young folk. Remain open to connecting Saint Nicholas with Santa Claus.

One practice that grows out of the real Saint Nicholas story involves performing acts of kindness, especially anonymous ones. Encourage yourself (and any family members) to perform an anonymous act of kindness each day this week in honor of Saint Nicholas.

December 7

REMEMBER

Leslie Weatherhead (1893–1976), a minister, writer, and broadcaster in London, remains best known for his wise book *The Will of God*.

READ

Psalm 144:5-8

PONDER

Lines of good poetry bear repeating. Much of this psalm borrows lines from other psalms—Psalms 8; 18; and 39, for example. Composing a psalm for the king in Jerusalem, the psalmist gathers together verses that ask for help, freedom, and rescue (v. 7) in time of distress and need. These verses bless God as rock, fortress, and deliverer (vv. 1-2). Perhaps this psalm, with its images of rock, storms, and lightning, came to the mind of Augustus Toplady when a fierce storm blew up as he walked across the English countryside. Taking refuge in the shelter of two massive rocks, Toplady thought of words that became a famous hymn: "Rock of Ages, cleft for me, let me hide myself in thee."[4]

PRAYER/PRACTICE

Waiting appears as another essential element in December and in our prayer life. God desires good for us, but often God's timing differs from ours. We orient our lives to speed. We want faster computers, fast food, instant coffee. We want what we want now, so waiting becomes hard. Waiting in our prayer life and waiting for Christmas become disciplines we return to every December. For what do we wait? Do we wait for a baby to be born? Do we wait for peace to dwell in the whole world and in our fractured, busy lives? Do we wait for a rebirth of joy, a rekindling of hope?

Today notice the times you spend waiting: waiting for a light to change from red to green, waiting in line at a store, waiting for the phone to ring or the printer to print. Each time you find yourself waiting, ask God to wait with you. See if this changes the nature of your waiting.

You may also use your breath prayer during times of waiting.

December 8

REMEMBER

Advent, four weeks long, prepares the church and Christians for the birth of Jesus. Also remember Madeleine L'Engle (b. 1918), a writer whose children's fantasy books and books for adults wrestle with questions of faith and practice.

READ

Isaiah 9:1-7

PONDER

The early church saw in this prophecy of Isaiah a wonderful description of Jesus. The expectant and hopeful language points to Jesus as the Messiah, the long-expected child, the Prince of Peace. Authority rests on his shoulders, and he has indeed brought light to those in darkness, lifted the burdens from the shoulders of the Israelites, and established the kingdom of justice and righteousness. The powerful and beautiful language begs for music to accompany it. Many have composed music for this text; Handel's *Messiah* remains the most notable. Listen to it if you can today.

PRAYER/PRACTICE

Use this Advent prayer or compose your own.

> Holy God, life contains so much whirl and frenzy. Do I ever take the time to look deep into another's eyes? Do I ever linger with a child, befriend darkness, cry on another's shoulder, acknowledge my loneliness? I move so swiftly from one moment to the next, rushing past feelings, looking through people, obsessed with the next event, consumed with the shallow triumph of accomplishing one more task.
>
> God of light, take me into the wilderness of your love where I can be purged of false pride and consuming greed. Help me see your light so that I can live a life of radiant joy and flowing compassion. Open me to the Wonderful Counselor, Mighty God, Prince of Peace. Open me to the One whose Advent makes all people whole. Amen.

December 9

REMEMBER

Eleanor Roosevelt (1884–1962), wife of President Franklin D. Roosevelt, made a name for herself as a writer and activist. She played a major role in drafting the Universal Declaration of Human Rights, which the United Nations adopted in 1948.

READ

Isaiah 11:1-9

PONDER

The struggle for human rights finds support in another Advent text from Isaiah. A new leader will come from the line of David, from the stump of Jesse. This leader will have the spirit of God within, a spirit of wisdom and understanding, of counsel and might (v. 2). The new ruler will show special concern for the poor and the meek and will judge from a righteous heart, not according to who has the best lawyer or the most money (v. 4). The rule this leader establishes will be good for the whole earth; the animals will live at peace, and even children will be safe. The idea of the peaceable kingdom not only provides a beautiful word picture in Isaiah but lifts up a goal to keep striving for. Persons of persistence and courage like Eleanor Roosevelt have worked toward this goal.

PRAYER/PRACTICE

In her book *When the Heart Waits,* Sue Monk Kidd suggests there are postures of waiting.[5] The first posture occurs in the story of Jesus visiting the home of Mary and Martha (Luke 10:38-42). Mary breaks social taboos by joining the circle of men seated at the feet of Jesus. She devotes her whole mind and heart to listening to Jesus.

This posture of waiting lifts up a contemplative focus on the true and good. In the midst of many small times of waiting during the day, this contemplative posture seeks awareness of the constant presence of God, awareness of the deeper hunger for God, awareness of the wonder and blessing all around. Take time today to sit for a while in contemplative openness. Use your breath prayer or centering prayer. Imagine yourself sitting at the feet of Jesus.

December 10

REMEMBER

Thomas Merton (1915–1968), a Trappist monk and mystic, touched the world as an author and spiritual guide. He became an early prophetic voice for peace and nonviolence, and his devotional books still help lead people to a deeper union with Christ.

READ

Psalm 144:9-11

PONDER

"I will sing a new song to you, O God" (v. 9). At surprising times and from unexpected sources, a new song emerges. Thomas Merton sang a new song that captivated a large audience. In his autobiography *The Seven Storey Mountain,* he told how a well-educated, proud, contemporary, and selfish man left everything behind to become a Trappist monk. In post–World War II America, this book touched a yearning for spirituality that had just begun to be articulated. Following the orders of his superiors, Merton continued to write about the spiritual journey, of connections between the contemplative life and the life of the everyday person, of solidarity with each person, which led to his prophetic words about peace and nonviolence. In his later years he became deeply interested in Eastern spirituality and died while on a trip to Thailand.

PRAYER/PRACTICE

A second posture of waiting, according to Sue Monk Kidd, comes from the story of Jesus in the garden of Gethsemane. Jesus says, "Sit here while I pray" (Mark 14:32). At times in our lives waiting becomes too tough to do alone. We find it hard to wait for the doctor's report, to stay in the same job until another one opens up, or to pray when God seems absent. During such times it is good to know that we can wait while Jesus and others carry on in prayer. Waiting does not mean giving up but deepening our trust.

What prayer do you imagine Jesus praying for you? Consider journaling a dialogue between Jesus and you about his prayer for you.

December 11

REMEMBER

Sister Alicia Domon (d. 1977), a French nun, worked with children with mental disabilities and ministered to the poor in Argentina. She joined the Mothers of the Disappeared, an organization of women who protested the repression of the Argentinean military dictatorship. Armed men seized Sister Alicia and twelve other women; they "disappeared."

READ

Psalm 144:12-15

PONDER

The psalm ends by expressing hope for God's blessings upon children (v. 12), upon the land (v. 13), upon the city, (v. 14), and upon the people (v. 15). It provides a rich, imaginative text that with a little adaptation could be given as a blessing to any community of faith.

Sometimes blessings must be fought for to be assured. Alicia Domon and many others have worked to ensure that all of God's children may grow in freedom. To this day, in the face of opposition, the Mothers of the Disappeared keep up a visible protest, a silent witness to the fact that though grown sons and daughters have disappeared, they abide in memory, never forgotten.

PRAYER/PRACTICE

The story of blind Bartimaeus (Mark 10:46-52) portrays an active posture of waiting. When he hears that Jesus is passing by, Bartimaeus shouts and attracts attention, reminding us that not all waiting remains passive or quiet. Often we must take action to prepare for an anticipated vision. For Christmas, we can decorate the house, light Advent candles, display a manger or crèche sets, put up a Christmas tree. Those actions reveal an active posture of waiting. We begin to live with the joy we know is coming.

What activities would help prepare your mind, heart, and home for the birth of Christ? Don't try to do too many or to do them all at once. Allow for some space in your active waiting.

December 12

REMEMBER

In 1531 Juan Diego, an Aztec Indian and Christian convert, encountered a woman on the hill of Tepeyac, outside of Mexico City. Dressed as a young Indian maiden, she identified herself as the Virgin Mary. She asked Diego to go to the bishop and request that a shrine be built where she stood. As Diego tried to persuade the bishop that the mother of Christ had appeared to him, a picture of the Virgin miraculously formed on his cloak. The image gave the Aztecs hope that Christianity was for them as well as their oppressors.

READ

Luke 1:46-55

PONDER

When Juan Diego told the bishop about his vision, the bishop could not understand his dialect and did not believe in the poor Indian's vision. The poor, the foreigner, and visionaries know the experience of waiting. They wait for a better life, for a more gracious multilingual world, for someone to trust their vision. Our economic biases, our racial prejudices, our "English-only" decrees often prohibit us from hearing the radical word of God, a new word for our time.

Some traditions recognize Mary as a friend of the lost and forgotten. Her prayer, recorded in Luke, can help us reshape our attitudes and our waiting. According to Mary, God shows mercy, lifts up the humble, fills the hungry, and sends the rich away empty.

PRAYER/PRACTICE

Reread Mary's song in Luke 1. Pray the song with your name in mind. Begin as Mary does, "My soul magnifies the Lord, and my spirit rejoices in God my Savior, for [God]. . . ." Add your own prayer, telling what God has done for you that causes you to burst forth in song. Create your own song of praise and record it in your journal. If you are musically inclined, try singing your song of praise.

Today, if possible, read more about Our Lady of Guadalupe and the vision of Juan Diego.

December 13

REMEMBER

Saint Lucy (fourth century), one of the virgin martyrs in Sicily, died during the persecution of Emperor Diocletian. Scandinavian countries remember Saint Lucy (Santa Lucia) on this day by having girls wear white dresses with red sashes, put on a crown of candles, and carry breakfast to their family.

READ

Psalm 145:1-7

PONDER

Each verse of this psalm of praise and gratitude begins with a successive letter of the Hebrew alphabet. The psalm contains several phrases from other psalms. Praise extends from generation to generation (v. 4). God's mighty acts bear repeating from age to age. We pick up the chords of praise from previous generations and sing them to future generations, changing the tones, livening the beats, and freshening the words. From the perspective of heaven, all this praise must seem like "the voice of a great multitude, like the sound of many waters and like the sound of mighty thunderpeals crying out, 'Hallelujah!'" (Rev. 19:6).

PRAYER/PRACTICE

Lighting candles at this time of year seems especially meaningful. Many Christians light candles on an Advent wreath to mark the four weeks until Christmas. Often they include a white candle in the center of the wreath to symbolize Christ, the Light of the world. Tonight gather family or friends around a table on which you have placed a large candle, and provide a candle for each person. Sit in darkness for a moment; then as someone lights the central candle, say, "You are the Light of the world, and we take our light from you." After each person lights a candle from the central candle, invite everyone to name places in the world or situations where light is needed. After each place or situation is named, all may raise their candles and say, "Light of the world, chase away the darkness."

December 14

REMEMBER

Saint John of the Cross (1542–1591), a Spanish friar and mystic, sought to reform the Carmelite order along with Teresa of Avila (Oct. 15). Christians remember him for his passionate, poetic writing about prayer, especially the dark night of the soul.

READ

Psalm 145:8-13

PONDER

If one refrain permeates the entire collection of the Psalms, it is probably this: "The LORD is gracious and merciful, slow to anger and abounding in steadfast love. God is good in every way and compassionate to all" (v. 8, NRSV; v. 9, AP). Because of God's mercy and compassion toward the whole of creation, "all your works . . . and all your faithful" (v. 10) give their thanks, praise, and blessing. Praise becomes a collaboration of creation and people rising up in grateful prayer. The sun and moon, trees and birds, poets and musicians, dancers and children lead the way in a drama of adoration and blessing. For God is gracious, merciful, and compassionate, abounding in steadfast love to all.

PRAYER/PRACTICE

For the next few days I invite you to consider what John of the Cross called the dark night of the soul. Many persons share this experience in prayer, which differs from having a few difficulties or encountering obstacles in prayer. (See Sept. 13 Prayer/Practice.) Whereas you used to sense God's presence and direction, in the dark night of the soul you feel God's absence. Your prayers lack feeling, imagination, and lightness. No insights arise to carry you through the day; no sense of the holy emerges. You experience no sense of peace or consolation but mostly just dryness, emptiness, darkness. As one person put it, "Nothing 'worked.' I tried to pray (useless), to meditate (nothing), to find beauty in the world around me (again, nothing)."[6]

If you have experienced or are currently experiencing a dark night of the soul, these next few days may offer hope.

December 15

REMEMBER

Micah (B.C.E.), a prophet in the southern kingdom after the northern kingdom of Israel had fallen to Assyria, condemned the greed and politics of the rich.

READ

Psalm 145:14-21

PONDER

In the closing verses, the psalmist proclaims God's goodness and kindness in meeting human need. God "raises up all who are bowed down" (v. 14). Again and again the prophets testify to God's dominant concern for the poor and oppressed. Nations will be judged on how well they execute justice for the poor, the widows, and the strangers. Micah, in chapter 6, speaks what the psalm sings.

The human need for food remains part of God's generous providing. Perhaps you have said or heard Psalm 145:15-16 prayed as a blessing at a table laden with food: "The eyes of all look to you, and you give them their food in due season. You open your hand, satisfying the desire of every living thing." Consider adding these verses to your repertoire of mealtime blessings.

PRAYER/PRACTICE

The experience of the dark night of prayer happens to people who have a relationship with God. The dark night does not come as punishment for being unfaithful, skipping church, or neglecting prayer. Sometimes the dryness just happens. Other times an external circumstance such as a death, a move to a new home or job, an illness, or a crisis may prompt a dark night. Your prayer life—indeed all of your life—seems dry, and you feel powerless to make things work out right, to make God come close.

It helps to know that many others have experienced a dark night, even saints. John of the Cross and others left markers to help guide you through this experience. What has occasioned your dark night? Who accompanies you through the dark night?

December 16

REMEMBER

Charles Wesley (1707–1788), one of the founders of the Methodist movement in England, penned thousands of hymns, including the Christmas carol "Hark! The Herald Angels Sing."

READ

Psalm 146:1-4

PONDER

Because political campaign promises frequently fail to accomplish their extravagant dreams, many persons become skeptical or cynical and certainly distrustful of campaign advertising. The psalmist, blunt and to the point, states, "Do not put your trust in rulers, mere mortals; they cannot save" (v. 3, AP). That statement does not mean we should abstain from voting or from participating in politics. Rather, we should not allow admiration, respect, and hope for a leader to elevate to uncritical acceptance and hero worship. Only God deserves our ultimate trust and allegiance. Too often those in high places find that power corrupts rather than ennobles. Keeping our eyes on the God of compassion helps clear our vision to act and vote most wisely in the political arena.

PRAYER/PRACTICE

"This paradoxical journey in darkness is a time of God's powerful, albeit hidden, work in our lives. God's work in us occasions an intensive re-patterning of our whole being."[7] In the midst of the dark night, God repatterns your worldview, reorients and refocuses your life and your prayer. You become less defined by what you do; you redirect your identity toward God. Instead of having low or high self-esteem, you discover that your esteem lies in God. Trust God that something occurs in the darkness even though you cannot feel or sense it. You move from knowing about God to an unknowing that does not base itself on ideas, thoughts, or feelings. You move toward a way of loving and being, living less from your head and more from your heart.

Rest in the knowledge that God works in the darkness.

December 17

REMEMBER

Dom Bede Griffiths (1906–1994), an English monk, spent most of his years in India, setting up East-West dialogues, founding Christian ashrams, and living in the style of an Indian holy man.

READ

Psalm 146:5-10

PONDER

Bede Griffiths saw Christ as representing fulfillment of the religious quest. He believed the universal Christ was already present in the Hindu soul, waiting to be discovered. Yet he felt the Hindus had much to teach Christians about the interior life and the sacredness of life. Griffiths sought to serve as a bridge to truth and share with Hindus the Christian understanding of God who "executes justice for the oppressed, who gives food to the hungry . . . sets the prisoners free. . . . lifts up those who are bowed down. . . . watches over the strangers . . . upholds the orphan and the widow" (vv. 7-9). These verses form the core ethical teaching of Christianity and become a model for Christians to live out so that they can offer an authentic and compelling witness to other people and other faiths.

PRAYER/PRACTICE

In the face of the dark night of the soul, our normal tendency is to flee from the emptiness. Sandra Cronk elaborates:

> We search for something to fill the void. We try harder to engage in all the old pursuits and types of prayer. We attempt new techniques of prayer or search for new activities to give life meaning. We assume that we can manipulate ourselves, the world, and even God to bring meaning into our lives again. We believe we can force the answers to our questions if we try hard enough.[8]

We may try to fill the void with alcohol, drugs, or possessions; become depressed; or even contemplate suicide. We need companions to remind us that God still works in the darkness.

December 18

REMEMBER

Corrie ten Boom (1892–1983), a Dutch Christian and watchmaker, helped her father and sister hide Jews in their home until 1944, when they all were arrested and sent to prison. Corrie survived prison and concentration camp, wrote about her experience in *The Hiding Place,* opened a home for people who had been imprisoned during the war, and traveled around the world as an evangelist.

READ

Luke 3:1-18

PONDER

Every December we encounter again the wild man of the desert, John the Baptist. We talk about his clothing, his food, and his sharp words. Was he a circus freak, an attention grabber, a possessed man? John understood himself as a "voice . . . in the wilderness," one called to prepare the way for a dramatic change and a new Messiah. He modeled a simple lifestyle, a repentant heart, and a clear focus. He urged his followers to live justly and confronted the powerful with their abuses. John's words about repentance still confront us. Have we prepared our hearts for the birth of the Messiah? Have we changed our ways, made the crooked places straight and the rough places smooth?

PRAYER/PRACTICE

John the Baptist may inspire a confession or a prayer of reflection. Begin with words like the following, or write your own prayer.

> God of the wilderness, make me more than just curious. Take me to the depths of repentance, for I have settled for comfort and convenience rather than following the poverty of Christ. I have opted for routine piety and tame faith rather than long nights of prayer and fruitful days of wilderness silence. I have traded trust in you for the lesser gods of achievement, recognition, and security.
>
> God of the wilderness, speak to my heart and strengthen my commitment to seek and follow your star, to worship and adore at the cradle, and to live a transformed life. Amen.

December 19

Isaiah (B.C.E.), a contemporary of Micah, experienced a vision in the Temple that led him to call Israel to repent of its injustice and unfaithfulness. His prophecies about hope for the future and a future king (Isa. 9:2, 6) hold a special place in Advent worship preparation.

READ

Isaiah 61:1-4, 8-11

PONDER

Jesus used Isaiah's stunning prophecy to announce his own ministry (Luke 4:16-21). Jesus stands in the long line of prophets who passionately pleaded for the nation and the people to carry out justice, who brought good news to the oppressed, liberty to the captives, and release to the prisoners (v. 1). God, abounding in compassion, wants to bring the poor and the forgotten a garland instead of ashes, the oil of gladness instead of mourning, the mantle of praise instead of a faint spirit (v. 3). God, the lover of justice, hates robbery and wrongdoing (v. 8). From Isaiah to Jesus to us, the call to justice continues. God calls us to a new way of living, a more compassionate way of caring, a more radical way of welcoming and including all people.

PRAYER/PRACTICE

God invites you to befriend the darkness rather than flee from it. Focusing on positive images of shadows and darkness may help. You might meditate on being in the womb of God and imagine a new self being born. Or as you think about a seed growing in the dark earth, you might find it prayerful to work in a garden. The simple act of planting seeds and tending plants can become an act of hope, a way of prayer. The Gospels reveal that Jesus prayed on the night of his arrest, and he also arose from the dead sometime during the night. Can you trust that Jesus exists as your nighttime darkness as well as your light?

Many have found nonthinking, nonrational prayer practices to be helpful in the dark times. Activities such as walking, knitting, chanting, and gardening can serve as companions in the dark.

December 20

REMEMBER

Raoul Wallenberg (1912–c. 1947), a Swedish Christian, volunteered for a diplomatic mission in Budapest during World War II. He saved thousands of Hungarian Jews by issuing them Swedish passports. After his arrest when the Soviets entered Budapest, he disappeared.

READ

Luke 1:5-25

PONDER

Mary gets away with the question, but Zechariah does not. Both ask the angel, "How can this be?" (Luke 1:18, 34, AP). Mary receives an incredible answer. Zechariah gets a lecture and nine months of silence. As a priest Zechariah devoted himself to worshiping and serving God. Perhaps religion had become all routine and duty, but Zechariah should have known that God acts in surprising and astounding ways. He should have remembered the stories about God freeing the Israelites from slavery, feeding them in the desert, and leading them to a new home. The elders among us can help keep hope alive. God has not finished with the world and still holds a few surprises in store. Stay awake!

PRAYER/PRACTICE

In the darkness you need a large portion of trust to believe that God remains at work. Jean Blomquist writes:

> In this time of unknowing, I am *being taken in* by a vibrance I cannot see, a harmony I cannot hear, a succulence I cannot taste, a vastness I cannot feel, an intimacy I cannot touch. . . . Perhaps I never will know in the same ways I have known before, but perhaps I am *being known as* I have never experienced being known before. . . . May I trust the Holy, may I trust the darkness, may I trust that this is a "close and holy darkness."[9]

Give thanks for times of patience and trust when you could not see the way ahead but still believed that God was guiding you through the valleys of darkness into a new dawn.

December 21

REMEMBER

The winter solstice marks the time of year when the hours of night are the longest. Light a candle for this longest night of darkness.

READ

Luke 1:67-79

PONDER

My brother's church conducts a "Longest Night" service, a special worship service for those whose year has been filled with darkness. People who have experienced the deaths of family members and friends; those who have lost jobs; or those coping with serious illness, addictions, loneliness, depression, or broken relationships receive an invitation to the Longest Night service. The candlelight service offers words of hope, support, and encouragement. Those seeking healing have opportunity to be prayed for and anointed.

The Benedictus (the Latin name of Zechariah's prayer) provides an appropriate prayer for such services, especially the part where Zechariah says, "The dawn from on high shall break upon us, to shine on those who dwell in darkness and in the shadow of death and to guide our feet into the way of peace"(vv. 78-79, AP). God will come to us.

PRAYER/PRACTICE

For ancient peoples, the winter solstice evoked fear. Would the sun come back? Would they still have light and warmth?

Today light candles of hope. Consider creating your own Longest Night service. What dark nights have you experienced this year? What scriptures give you hope or encouragement? Invite friends or family members to share with you. As each person recalls a memory of darkness, he or she lights a candle and shares a word of hope, telling what helped him or her through the darkness. Close with this prayer:

> O God of winter darkness, send your starlight as candlelight into our world. O God, you sent Jesus, Light of the world, to guide us into the ways of peace. We are blessed, and we are grateful. Amen.

December 22

REMEMBER

Chico Mendes (1944–1988) organized rubber workers into a union and used nonviolent tactics to save the Amazon rain forests in Brazil. He merged compassion for the poor with an ecological vision and became known as the "Gandhi of the Amazon" before his murder.

READ

Luke 1:26-37

PONDER

Wouldn't it be a blessing to hear and believe that you are wonderful every day? Or to hear the words of the angel, "Greetings, favored one! The Lord is with you" (Luke 1:28)? The angel speaks good news and truthful words. God looks with favor upon you, wonderful you. God abides with you.

You are also less than wonderful sometimes, full of doubts and suspicions, anger and fear. When negative feelings and thoughts threaten to make you forget that you are God's favored one, recall the angel's final word to Mary: "For nothing will be impossible with God" (Luke 1:37).

This assurance helps you carry on in the midst of doubts and fears, especially if you face corporate power and big landowners who want to burn the rain forest so they can graze cattle. Chico Mendes set out to do the impossible. Can we who are favored and blessed do any less?

PRAYER/PRACTICE

Getting ready for Christmas involves both individual and community effort. The church helps keep the focus on Jesus by providing Advent wreaths, devotional books, and special services. The church provides a place to teach young and old about the true meaning of Christmas. Support from the family of God strengthens individual preparations for the good news.

Today give thanks for the holy season of Advent and its call to prepare your heart. Give thanks for your faith community and the support it has given you in this busy season. Take a deep breath. Let God's peace rest upon you before you return to any to-do lists.

December 23

REMEMBER

Rabbi Abraham Heschel (1907–1972), a Hasidic rabbi, escaped from Poland during the Nazi terror and taught in Jewish and Christian seminaries in the United States. He championed interfaith dialogue, served as an observer at Vatican Council II, marched alongside Martin Luther King Jr., and actively protested against racism and war. Heschel's writings invite readers to rest in God's love and live out God's compassion.

READ

Luke 1:38-45

PONDER

After Mary said, "Let it be" (v. 38), she hurried off quickly to see Elizabeth. No mention occurs of her planning the trip or encountering difficulties on the road. Mary bears good news, news that appears too good to keep to herself or bear alone, especially when she may wonder whether she can do what God asked. To be an unmarried, pregnant woman in Nazareth would not have been an enviable situation. The angel's wonderful news becomes hard to accept because of societal prejudices and mores. Mary needed support, so she enlarged her community to celebrate and nurture the good news.

PRAYER/PRACTICE

Offer a prayer of invitation, or use this one to begin.

> Holy Child of Bethlehem, come to me. Unlock the door of my heart. Come, let your love shine in me and in all the world to ease fears and calm worries.
>
> Come, fill me with a joy that knows no bounds.
>
> Come, give me oil of gladness instead of mourning.
>
> Come, fill me with light that brightens every corner of darkness.
>
> Come, lift me from the routine into the splendor of your holy light.
>
> Come, turn me from extravagant preparations to the simple wonder of your humble birth.
>
> Holy Child of Bethlehem, I open my life to your coming.

December 24

REMEMBER

Pray for an expectant mother and her hope and excitement for the coming day. Remember the poor and refugees seeking a place to stay.

READ

Matthew 1:18-25

PONDER

"Do not be afraid." This refrain echoes throughout the birth narratives and even throughout the Gospels. Angels speak these words to Joseph, to Zechariah, to Mary, and to the shepherds. God comes to abide with us. "I am about to do a new thing; now it springs forth, do you not perceive it?" (Isa. 43:19). Often we do not see God's new activity, and we respond with fear when we hear about changes. We can be thankful that Joseph understood the word *Emmanuel* and that when he awoke from his dream, he knew that God indeed was with him and Mary, so he could hang on for the ride, unafraid of whatever God was about to do.

PRAYER/PRACTICE

Attend a Christmas Eve service. Write a prayer or share this meditation with others:

> Can one night make a difference? Can one star outshine all others? Can one child shake up the world? Yes, a thousand times yes!
>
> This child, sung to by choirs and worshiped by all; this child, Christ child, born of Mary, welcomed by the poor and the mighty— this child can change the world, can change lives. This Christ child can redeem us all.
>
> Oh, that our tongues were like bells to ring out the joy and that our hands were like drums to sound out the beat of new life. Oh, that our voices sounded like the heavenly choir and that our hearts could hold the wonder of it all. Oh, that our knees were strong enough to kneel forever in wonder and that our eyes could open wide enough to see glory shining in every star.
>
> Can one night make such a difference? Yes, a thousand times yes! The Christ child was born, Redeemer of us all.

December 25

REMEMBER

The Christ child is born. Glory to God in the highest! Peace to all people, especially the people of Bethlehem and the Holy Land.

READ

Luke 2:1-20

PONDER

Into our world, where we usually stay busy and frequently feel tired, God comes. God comes to us where we are, somewhere between darkness and light. God comes to us as we are, anxious and worried, hopeful and blessed. God comes to us as wonderful and surprising as angels singing to shepherds on a hill. God comes to us now as a small baby in a manger.

Let us marvel at the Holy Child, worship on bended knee, and sing with the angels. Let us be blessed by the gaze of the Christ child. God looks at us with love and great joy that spreads to all people.

PRAYER/PRACTICE

On Christmas morning, our family moves to each manger scene or figure of baby Jesus in the house, where we say, "Welcome, Baby Jesus." We light a white candle in the center of our Advent wreath to symbolize Christ as the Light of the world. We do those simple acts before opening any presents. What rituals do you observe at Christmastime to keep the focus on this most amazing God who comes to us as a child?

Pray this prayer, or create your own prayer to the Christ child:

Holy Child, source of eternal joy and everlasting hope, look upon me with tender eyes. Bring your gentle light to the hidden corners of my life and render my fear small and powerless. Holy Child, touch any who are wounded and lift the hurts and resentments, including my own. Heal and forgive me so that my words may be clear and my actions kind. Holy Child, be near any who grieve, and be near those whose health or poverty dims the angelic chorus. Cause my heart to leap in wonder, my eyes to fill with tears of joy, and my soul to swell with love. O Holy Child of Bethlehem, be born in me today. Amen.

December 26

REMEMBER

Stephen (first century), one of the deacons ordained in the church of Jerusalem, helped administer the distribution of alms to the poor and food to the widows and became the first Christian martyr. Scripture describes him as "full of grace and power" (Acts 6:8).

READ

Acts 6 and 7

PONDER

Like today's churches, the early church experienced struggles. Early Christians had to work out their relationship to Judaism, figure out how to care for the needy in their midst, relate to the growing number of Greek-speaking Christians (the Hellenists), and decide what kind of mission they would have to the Gentiles. Leaders like Stephen, a Greek-speaking Jew who converted to Christianity, provided important service and insight for the decisions and ministry of the young church. Stephen not only helped in the practical matters of caring for the widows and the poor, but he advocated spreading the gospel to all people, preached articulately and persuasively, and received a vision of Jesus at the right hand of God. No wonder he was stoned to death.

PRAYER/PRACTICE

Some cultures set aside the day after Christmas to remember persons who provide service throughout the year. In England, December 26 is called Boxing Day—it is an occasion to give boxed gifts to letter carriers, garbage collectors, newspaper delivery persons, and so forth.

On this day after Christmas, consider carrying on the ministry of Stephen by giving gifts to those who make your life and community better. A letter of thanks to city officials, a gift for the letter carrier, a note to your doctor and nurse, and a visit to someone in a nursing home—all of these actions can extend the joy of Christmas. Since the season of Christmas lasts for twelve days, consider doing one act of kindness for the next twelve days.

December 27

REMEMBER

John (first century), a fisherman and apostle, possibly wrote the fourth Gospel. Scripture refers to him as the disciple Jesus loved.

READ

Psalm 147

PONDER

Tradition tells us that John outlived all the other twelve apostles, was exiled on the island of Patmos, and finally settled in Ephesus, where he presided over the church. According to some stories, John repeatedly preached the same sermon: "Love one another." When church members asked him to preach another message, he supposedly replied, "When you have mastered this lesson, we can move on to another."

In Psalm 147, the psalmist describes God's power as an outpouring of compassion upon the outcasts, the brokenhearted, and the down-trodden (vv. 2, 3, 6). The psalmist sees God's wonder in stars, animals, snow, wind, and water (vv. 4, 9, 16, 18). God delights not in strength or speed (or big bank accounts or large mansions) but in relationship with people, especially children (vv. 11, 13). How good it is to sing praise to this amazing, loving God!

PRAYER/PRACTICE

The end of the year offers a good opportunity to evaluate and review the year. A year-end review can help you get a picture of your journey with Christ. Many Twelve-Step groups encourage a similar review— step four involves "making a searching and fearless moral inventory of ourselves." While a year-end review may be less complete and less rigorous than a "searching and fearless moral inventory," it nevertheless lets you look at your life under the loving gaze of God.

Begin by asking God to accompany you through the evaluation process. Ask God to help you see your areas of weakness and strength. Know that as you place your hope in God's forgiveness and renewal, God releases you from the past and sets you free for a new future.

December 28

REMEMBER

The "Holy Innocents" (first century) were the children put to death as a result of King Herod's efforts to destroy the One born to be king of the Jews. Fearing for his own throne, Herod ordered all male children two years old and under in the Bethlehem district to be killed. Ultimately Herod did not win, but the sound of weeping described in Matthew 2:18 breaks our hearts.

READ

Matthew 2:13-18

PONDER

The Matthew account of the slaughter of Hebrew children parallels the Egyptian pharaoh's slaughter of innocent children when Moses was born (Exod. 1:15–2:10). Matthew portrays Jesus as the new Moses, a liberator of the people, and "a light for revelation to the Gentiles and for glory to your people Israel" (Luke 2:32). Jesus stands in a long line of prophets and liberators, but he is so much more. His compassion extends to all, and his way is love. Jesus invites us to reach out on behalf of children still targeted for death today. Hunger, disease, and war kill. Infant mortality rates remain high, and children continue to be born into poverty and despair. Holy innocents deserve our remembering and our care.

PRAYER/PRACTICE

Reflect on the past year by completing these exercises in your journal. (1) List significant persons in your life for the past year. How have they supported and/or challenged you? (2) List pivotal events or changes in your life and your feeling about them. (3) Remember and celebrate your greatest joys. Offer a prayer of thanks for each one. (4) Name your greatest challenges, pains, and disappointments during the past year. Can you offer a prayer of thanks or see how God has worked through the difficulties? (5) Describe your experience of God this past year. Has God seemed near or distant? (6) Think of a symbol, word, or phrase that pictures or summarizes this year.

December 29

REMEMBER

Saint Thomas Becket (1118–1170), archbishop of Canterbury, England, criticized Henry II for trying to control the church. The king's men murdered this man of honesty and integrity in Canterbury Cathedral.

READ

Psalm 148

PONDER

Did the psalmist leave out anything in this glorious song of praise? Everyone and everything in heaven and on earth join in this cosmic hymn of praise. Though the images seem to cascade down from all sides, an order pervades. The psalmist has in mind the story of creation, beginning with the heavens, the sun, moon, and stars; descending to the sea, mountains, trees, and animals; and ending with humans, kings and ordinary people, young and old alike. May our voices and our lives continually shout praises to the Creator.

PRAYER/PRACTICE

Questions and images from scripture can also help you review the year. Jesus turned to two of John the Baptist's disciples who followed him and asked them, "What are you looking for?" (John 1:38). Reflect on your deepest longings and hopes for the past year. What did you hope would happen in your work life, in your relationships with family and friends, in your relationship with God?

The disciples said to Jesus, "Lord, teach us to pray" (Luke 11:1). Use their request as an opportunity to reflect on your prayer life and your practice of the spiritual disciplines presented in this book. In what new ways have you learned to pray?

Jesus asked the man who had been ill for thirty-eight years, "Do you want to be made well?" (John 5:6). Using this question, reflect on places of struggle in this past year. What were your experiences of healing, growth, and forgiveness? What parts of your life would you like to be better? Thank God for walking with you this past year, and ask God for the grace to move toward wholeness in all parts of your life.

December 30

REMEMBER

John Main (1926–1982), an English Benedictine monk, established a new community in Canada using the Christian mantra as a style of prayer.

READ

Psalm 149

PONDER

Possibly this new song supplied words for a new year's festival celebrating the mighty God and the triumph over evil. Or perhaps the psalmist composed these words to celebrate some military victory or to encourage the Israelites as they battled their enemies. Though we do not know the context, we feel the excitement of praise and the struggle for justice. The psalmist writes about the people of God praising God with music and dancing (v. 3) and gives a call to battle (v. 7). For us, the two-edged sword symbolizes the Word of God, which sees our heart and knows our intentions (Heb. 4:12). God still calls us to be people of prayer and praise, people of justice and compassion. God calls us to face problems that plague the human family: greed, pollution of our fragile planet, poverty, despair, loneliness, and hunger.

PRAYER/PRACTICE

Offer a prayer for the coming year, for the winter season, for a star to guide you, or use this prayer.

> God of the winter sky, place a star on the horizon, for I need your light to guide me. I carry the darkness of resentment and anger, the shadows of fear and self-doubt. I need your light to show my community and me that you tenderly love us.
>
> God of the winter sky, place a star on the horizon, for our world needs the assurance of your shining presence. Shine gently on those who grieve. Shine brightly on all who struggle for bread to eat, land to till, work to do. Shine with a strong light on all those who struggle for justice, who work for peace, who bind up the wounds.
>
> God of the winter sky, place a star above me so that I may go into the new year with your light to guide me. Amen.

December 31

REMEMBER

Sandra Cronk (1942–2000), Quaker teacher and writer, opened her students to the insights of Quakers and other "plain religion" folk, the depths of prayer, and the pathway through the dark night. She taught at Pendle Hill, a Quaker center for study and contemplation, for many years. She was my teacher.

READ

Psalm 150

PONDER

It's time for the "Hallelujah Chorus" with mass choirs and full orchestra. Psalm 150 pulls out all the stops in praising God. The seven instruments mentioned—the wind, string, and percussion instruments known in biblical times—are just the beginning of this crescendo of praise. A climactic statement summarizes the psalm and provides a fitting end to the Psalter: "Let everything that breathes praise the LORD!" (v. 6). The fifth book of the Psalms closes with this glorious doxology of praise, providing a wonderful end to our journey through the Psalms and a wonderful beginning to a new year of praise.

PRAYER/PRACTICE

Create your own prayer for the new year, or use the following:

> Take me into a new year, Gracious God. Help me to continue looking for meaning, seeking peace, praying for light, dancing for joy, working for justice, and singing your praise. I go into the new year filled with expectations, a touch of worry, and a bundle of hope. I do not journey into the new year alone but with you as my guide, with a commitment to my disciplines, with a community of family, friends, and faith. Take me into the new year, Creator of beauty and wonder. Bless me with the companionship of Jesus, and gift me with the guidance and power of the Spirit. Amen.

Make some promises with God about your faith journey for the new year. May you know God's blessings on your way.

Appendixes

Appendix A
Suggested Resources

This list of books, movies, and groups gives further information and assistance in learning more about a saint or prayer practice.

January 3: Sullivan, George E. *The Day the Women Got the Vote: A Photo History of the Women's Rights Movement.* New York: Scholastic, 1994.

January 5: Lanza del Vasto, Joseph Jean. *Warriors of Peace: Writings on the Technique of Nonviolence.* Edited by Michel Random and translated by Jean Sigwick. New York: Alfred A. Knopf, 1974.

January 7: Hurston, Zora Neale. *Their Eyes Were Watching God.* Chicago: University of Illinois Press, 1991.

January 8: Muste, Abraham John. *The Essays of A. J. Muste.* Edited by Nat Hentoff. Indianapolis, Ind.: Bobbs-Merrill Co., 1967.

January 12: Underhill, Evelyn. *The House of the Soul: Concerning the Inner Life.* Minneapolis, Minn.: Seabury Press, 1984.

January 13: Keating, Thomas. *Open Mind, Open Heart: The Contemplative Dimension of the Gospel.* New York: Continuum International Publishing Group, 1994.

Steere, Douglas V., ed. *Quaker Spirituality: Selected Writings.* Classics of Western Spirituality. New York: Paulist Press, 1984.

January 14: Bentley, James. *Martin Niemöller.* New York: Oxford University Press, 1984.

January 15: King, Martin Luther, Jr. *Strength to Love.* Philadelphia: Fortress Press, 1981.

January 19: Spiritual Directors International, P.O. Box 25469, Seattle, WA 98125. Phone: (425) 455-1565. E-mail: office@sdiworld.org.

January 20: Johnson, Jan. *Madame Guyon.* Minneapolis, Minn.: Bethany House Publishers, 1999.

January 24: *Francis de Sales, Jane de Chantal: Letters of Spiritual Direction.* Translated by Péronne M. Thibert. Classics of Western Spirituality. New York: Paulist Press, 1988.

January 27: Bunyan, John. *The Pilgrim's Progress.* Cutchogue, N.Y.: Buccaneer Books, 1976.

January 29: Forest, Jim. *Praying with Icons.* Maryknoll, N.Y.: Orbis Books, 1997.

January 30: Gandhi, Mahatma. *An Autobiography: The Story of My Experiments with Truth.* 2d ed. Boston: Beacon Press, 1993.

Gandhi. Directed by Richard Attenborough. 188 min. Columbia Tri-Star, 1982. Videocassette.

February 2: Sources for "Canticle of Simeon": *The United Methodist Hymnal.* Nashville, Tenn.: United Methodist Publishing House, 1989.

The Upper Room Worshipbook: Music and Liturgies for Spiritual Formation. Nashville, Tenn.: Upper Room Books, 1985.

February 3: Brother Lawrence. *The Practice of the Presence of God.* Grand Rapids, Mich.: Fleming H. Revell, 1989.

February 4: Williams, Juan. *Eyes on the Prize: America's Civil Rights Years, 1954–1965.* New York: Penguin Group, 1988.

February 5: For more information about Taizé, see the Web site at www.taize.fr or write the Taizé Community, 71250 Taizé, France.

> **Distributor of Videos, Books, and CDs/cassettes of Taizé music**
> GIA Publications, Inc.
> 7404 South Mason Avenue
> Chicago, IL 60638
> Phone: (800) 442-1358
> Web site: www.giamusic.com

February 7: Hall, Mary. *The Impossible Dream: The Spirituality of Dom Helder Camara.* Maryknoll, N.Y.: Orbis Books, 1980.

February 9: Walker, Alice. *The Color Purple.* New York: Harcourt Brace Jovanovich, 1982.

February 11: Aelred of Rievaulx. *Spiritual Friendship.* Translated by Mary Eugenia Laker. Kalamazoo, Mich.: Cistercian Publications, 1974.

February 15: Andrews, C. F. *The Sermon on the Mount.* New York: Macmillan Co., 1942.

February 18: Morrison, Toni. *Beloved: A Novel.* New York: Plume, 1988.

February 20: Broyles, Anne. *Journaling: A Spiritual Journey.* Nashville, Tenn.: Upper Room Books, 1999.

February 21: Malcolm X. *The Autobiography of Malcolm X.* As told to Alex Haley. New York: Ballantine Books, 1992.

Cone, James H. *Martin and Malcolm and America: A Dream or a Nightmare.* Maryknoll, N.Y.: Orbis Books, 1991.

February 22: Scholl, Inge. *The White Rose: Munich, 1942–43.* 2d ed. Translated by Arthur R. Schultz. Middletown, Conn.: Wesleyan University Press, 1983.

February 27: Wuellner, Flora Slosson. *Prayer, Stress, and Our Inner Wounds.* Nashville, Tenn.: The Upper Room, 1985.

March 1: Herbert, George. *Herbert: Poems and Prose.* Selected by W. H. Auden. Harmondsworth, England: Penguin, 1973.

March 2: Seuss, Dr. *A Hatful of Seuss: Five Favorite Dr. Seuss Stories.* New York: Random House, 1997.

Good books on *lectio divina*: Hall, Thelma. *Too Deep for Words: Rediscovering Lectio Divina.* Mahwah, N.J.: Paulist Press, 1988.

Vest, Norvene. *Gathered in the Word: Praying the Scripture in Small Groups.* Nashville, Tenn.: Upper Room Books, 1996.

March 3: Baldwin, Lou. *Saint Katharine Drexel: Apostle to the Oppressed.* Philadelphia, Pa.: The Catholic Standard and Times, Inc., 2000.

Holt, Mary van Balen. *Meet Katharine Drexel: Heiress and God's Servant of the Oppressed.* Ann Arbor, Mich.: Servant Publications, 2002.

March 6: Caussade, Jean-Pierre de. *Abandonment to Divine Providence.* New York: Doubleday Publishing, 1993.

March 8: Covey, Alan., ed. *A Century of Women.* Atlanta: TBS Books, 1994.

March 10: Bradford, Sarah H. *Harriet Tubman: The Moses of Her People.* Gloucester, Mass.: Peter Smith Publisher, 1981.

March 11: Dunnam, Maxie. *The Workbook of Intercessory Prayer.* Nashville, Tenn.: Upper Room Books, 1979.

March 14: Mills, Kay. *This Little Light of Mine: The Life of Fannie Lou Hamer.* New York: Dutton/Plume, 1994.

March 22: Williams, Daniel Day. *The Spirit and the Forms of Love.* New York: Harper & Row, 1968. A wonderful introduction to process theology.

March 24: Romero, Oscar. *Voice of the Voiceless: The Four Pastoral Letters and Other Statements.* Translated by Michael J. Walsh. Maryknoll, N.Y.: Orbis Books, 1985.

Romero. Directed by John Duigan. 102 min. Vidmark/Trimark, 1989. Videocassette.

March 26: Check your church library or local bookstore for children's books and Bibles. Here is one of my favorite children's Bible storybooks:

Batchelor, Mary. *The Children's Bible in 365 Stories.* Colorado Springs, Colo.: Lion Publishing, 1995.

March 30: *Thea Bowman, Shooting Star: Selected Writings and Speeches.* Edited by Celestine Cepress. Winona, Minn.: St. Mary's Press, 1993.

March 31: Taylor, Ronald B. *Chavez and the Farm Workers.* Boston: Beacon Press, 1975.

April 2: Carretto, Carlo. *Letters from the Desert.* Maryknoll, N.Y.: Orbis Books, 2002.

April 4: Cone, James H. *Martin and Malcolm and America: A Dream or a Nightmare.* Maryknoll, N.Y.: Orbis Books, 1991.

King, Martin Luther, Jr. *Where Do We Go from Here: Chaos or Community?* New York: Harper & Row, 1967.

April 5: Here are some of my favorite recordings of the Psalms:

Consiglio, Cyprian. *Behind and Before Me.* Available from Oregon Catholic Press, P.O. Box 18030, Portland, OR 97218-0030. Phone: (800) 548-8749. Web site: www.ocp.org.

Farrell, Bernadette. *God Beyond All Names.* Available from Oregon Catholic Press.

Haugen, Marty, and David Haas. *Psalms for the Church Year,* Volume 1. Available from GIA Publications, Inc., 7404 South Mason Ave., Chicago, IL 60638. Phone: (800) 442-1358. Web site: www.giamusic.com

Hurd, Bob, and Ken Canedo. *Alleluia! Give the Glory.* Available from Oregon Catholic Press.

Joncas, Michael. *Come to Me.* Available from GIA Publications, Inc.

April 6: *Hadewijch: The Complete Works.* Translated by Columba Hart. Classics of Western Spirituality. New York: Paulist Press, 1980.

April 7: Hallie, Philip P. *Lest Innocent Blood Be Shed: The Story of the Village of Le Chambon and How Goodness Happened.* New York: HarperCollins Publishers, 1994.

April 8: Bonhoeffer, Dietrich. *Life Together: A Discussion of Christian Fellowship.* San Francisco: HarperSanFrancisco, 2003.

Gass, Robert. *Chanting: Discovering Spirit in Sound.* New York: Broadway Books, 2000.

April 11: Sparough, J. Michael, and Bobby Fisher. *The Body at Prayer: Guided Meditation Using Gesture, Posture, and Breath, with Original Music for Prayer.* Audiocassettes available from St. Anthony Messenger Press, 28 W. Liberty St., Cincinnati, OH 45202. Phone: (513) 241-5615.

Teilhard de Chardin, Pierre. *The Divine Milieu.* New York: HarperCollins Publishers, 2001.

April 14: *The Miracle Worker.* Directed by Arthur Penn. 107 min. MGM/Universal Artists Studios, 1962. Videocassette.

April 15: Daws, Gavan. *Holy Man, Father Damien of Molokai.* Honolulu, Hawaii: University of Hawaii Press, 1984.

April 19: Cummings, Charles. *The Mystery of the Ordinary.* New York: HarperCollins Publishers, 1982. A good book on walking and prayer.

April 20: *Käthe Kollwitz: Graphics, Posters, Drawings.* Edited by Renate Hinz and translated by Rita and Robert Kimber. New York: Pantheon Books, 1981.

April 25: McLain, Gary. *The Indian Way: Learning to Communicate with Mother Earth.* Santa Fe, N.M.: John Muir Publications, 1990. Explains prayer in the four directions.

Zeilinger, Ron. *Sacred Ground.* Chamberlain, S.Dak.: Tipi Press, 1986.

April 26: Stringfellow, William. *A Keeper of the Word: Selected Writings of William Stringfellow.* Edited by Bill Wylie Kellermann. Grand Rapids, Mich.: William B. Eerdmans, 1999.

April 28: Keneally, Thomas. *Schindler's List.* New York: Simon and Schuster, 1982.

Zaillian, Steven (screenplay). *Schindler's List.* Directed by Steven Spielberg. 197 min. Universal Studios, 1993. Videocassette.

April 29: Flinders, Carol L. *Enduring Grace: Living Portraits of Seven Women Mystics.* San Francisco: HarperSanFrancisco, 1993.

May 2: Thomas à Kempis. *The Imitation of Christ: In Four Books.* Translated by Joseph N. Tylenda. New York: Vintage Books, 1998.

May 3: Tamez, Elsa. *The Scandalous Message of James: Faith without Works Is Dead.* New York: Crossroad Publishing Co., 2002.

May 4: Miller, Timothy. *How to Want What You Have: Discovering the Magic and Grandeur of Ordinary Existence.* New York: Avon Books, 1996.

May 5: Hays, Edward. *Prayers for the Domestic Church: A Handbook for Worship in the Home.* Rev. ed. Leavenworth, Kans.: Forest of Peace Publishing, 1989. A good resource for blessing prayers.

May 6: Thoreau, Henry David. *Walden and Civil Disobedience.* New York: New American Library, 1999.

May 9: Maurin, Peter. *Easy Essays.* Chicago: Franciscan Herald Press, 1977.

May 13: Julian of Norwich. *Showings.* Translated by Edmund Colledge and James Walsh. Classics of Western Spirituality. New York: Paulist Press, 1978.

May 14: Brooke, Avery. *Learning and Teaching Christian Meditation.* Rev. ed. Cambridge, Mass.: Cowley Publications, 1990.

May 15: Nouwen, Henri J. M. *Behold the Beauty of the Lord: Praying with Icons.* Notre Dame, Ind.: Ave Maria Press, 1987.

A source for religious and spiritual icons and art: Bridge Building Images, Inc., P.O. Box 1048, Burlington, VT 05402-1048. Phone: (800) 325-6263. E-mail: bbi@bridgebuilding.com.

May 19: Keating, Thomas. *Open Mind, Open Heart: The Contemplative Dimension of the Gospel.* New York: Continuum International Publishing Group, 1994.

May 22: Buber, Martin. *Tales of the Hasidim.* New York: Knopf Publishing Group, 1961.

May 24: Harper, Steve. *Devotional Life in the Wesleyan Tradition: A Workbook.* Nashville, Tenn.: Upper Room Books, 1995.

May 28: Percy, Walker. *Message in the Bottle: How Queer Man Is, How Queer Language Is, and What One Has to Do with the Other.* New York: Picador, 2000.

June 2: De Mello, Anthony. *The Song of the Bird.* Garden City, N.Y.: Image, 1984.

———. *Sadhana, A Way to God: Christian Exercises in Eastern Form.* Garden City, N.Y.: Image, 1984.

June 6: Retreats International, P. O. Box 1067, Notre Dame, IN 46556. Web site: www.retreatsintl.org

June 7: Roberts, Elizabeth, and Elias Amidon, eds. *Earth Prayers from around the World: 365 Prayers, Poems, and Invocations for Honoring the Earth.* San Francisco: HarperSanFrancisco, 1991.

June 9: Cousineau, Phil. *The Art of Pilgrimage: The Seeker's Guide to Making Travel Sacred.* Berkeley, Calif.: Conari Press, 2000.

Douglas, Deborah, and David Douglas. *Pilgrims in the Kingdom: Travels in Christian Britain.* Nashville, Tenn.: Upper Room Books, available February 2004.

Westwood, Jennifer. *Sacred Journeys: An Illustrated Guide to Pilgrimages around the World.* New York: Henry Holt & Co., 1997.

Music of the Iona Community is available from GIA Publications, Inc., 7404 South Mason Ave., Chicago IL 60638. Phone: (800) 442-1358. Web site: www.giamusic.com

June 12: Frank, Anne. *The Diary of Anne Frank.* San Diego, Calif.: Harcourt Trade Publishers, 1995.

June 17: Outler, Albert, ed. *John Wesley.* New York: Oxford University Press, 1980.

June 18: Spiritual Directors International, P.O. Box 25469, Seattle, WA 98125. E-mail: office@sdiworld.org.

June 19: Guenther, Margaret. *Holy Listening: The Art of Spiritual Direction.* Cambridge, Mass.: Cowley Publications, 1992.

June 21: In addition to Margaret Guenther's excellent book *Holy Listening* (see information above, under June 19), see also:

Jones, W. Paul. *The Art of Spiritual Direction.* Nashville, Tenn.: Upper Room Books, 2002.

June 25: Both of these books have limited availability:

Lynch-Watson, Janet. *The Saffron Robe: A Life of Sadhu Sundar Singh.* Grand Rapids, Mich.: Zondervan, 1975.

Singh, Sadhu Sundar. *At the Feet of the Master.* Translated by Arthur and Rebecca Parker. Edited by Halcyon Backhouse. London: Hodder & Stoughton, 1985.

June 26: Norris, Kathleen. *Amazing Grace: A Vocabulary of Faith.* New York: Riverhead Trade, 1999.

———. *Dakota: A Spiritual Geography.* Boston, Mass.: Houghton Mifflin Co., 1994.

———. *The Cloister Walk.* New York: Riverhead Trade, 1997.

June 27: Keller, Helen. *The Story of My Life: The Restored Classic.* New York: W. W. Norton & Co., 2003.

July 3: Peacock, Larry J. "Family Spirituality: A Questionnaire." *Weavings* 3, no. 1 (January/February 1988): 37–39.

July 5: Hays, Edward. *Prayers for the Domestic Church: A Handbook for Worship in the Home.* Rev. ed. Leavenworth, Kans.: Forest of Peace Publishing, 1989.

Huck, Gabe. *A Book of Family Prayer.* New York: Seabury Press, 1979.

July 8: Vanier, Jean. *From Brokenness to Community.* Mahwah, N.J.: Paulist Press, 1992.

July 11: Chittister, Joan D. *The Rule of Benedict: Insights for the Ages.* New York: Crossroad Publishing Co., 1992.

July 18: Johnson, Jan. *Growing Compassionate Kids: Helping Kids See beyond Their Backyard.* Nashville, Tenn.: Upper Room Books, 2001.

July 20: Tsu, Lao. *Tao Te Ching.* Translated by Stephen Mitchell. New York: HarperPerennial, 1994.

July 22: Author and illustrator Tomie dePaola has produced a number of children's books on biblical and religious themes.

Batchelor, Mary. *The Children's Bible in 365 Stories.* Colorado Springs, Colo.: Lion Publishing, 1995.

July 24: International network of hosts and travelers: Servas, Inc., 11 John Street, Room 505, New York, NY 10038. Phone: (212) 267-0252. E-mail: info@usservas.org

July 25: Edwards, Tilden. *Sabbath Time.* Rev. ed. Nashville, Tenn.: Upper Room Books, 2003.

Muller, Wayne. *Sabbath: Finding Rest, Renewal, and Delight in Our Busy Lives.* New York: Bantam Books, 2000.

July 27: Flinders, Carol L. *Enduring Grace: Living Portraits of Seven Women Mystics.* San Francisco: HarperSanFrancisco, 1993.

July 29: De Leeuw, Ronald, ed. *The Letters of Vincent van Gogh.* New York: Penguin USA, 1998.

July 31: *Ignatius of Loyola: Spiritual Exercises and Selected Works.* Edited by George E. Ganss et al. Classics of Western Spirituality. Mahwah, N.J.: Paulist Press, 1991.

August 1: *Patch Adams.* Directed by Tom Shadyac. 115 min. Universal Studios, 1998. Videocassette.

August 2: Baldwin, James. *The Fire Next Time.* Austin, Tex.: Holt, Rinehart & Winston, 2000.

———. *Go Tell It on the Mountain.* New York: Dell Publishing, 1985.

August 5: Cousins, Norman. *Anatomy of an Illness: As Perceived by the Patient.* 20th ed. New York: W. W. Norton & Co., 1995.

August 6: Coerr, Eleanor. *Sadako and the Thousand Paper Cranes.* 25th Anniversary Edition. New York: Penguin Group, 2002.

August 8: Nouwen, Henri. *The Road to Peace: Writings on Peace and Justice.* Edited by John Dear. Maryknoll, N.Y.: Orbis Books, 2002.

August 9: Herbstrith, Waltraud. *Edith Stein: A Biography.* 2d ed. San Francisco: Ignatius Press, 1992.

August 13: Lindbergh, Anne Morrow. *Gift from the Sea.* New York: Knopf Publishing Group, 1991.

August 14: Hanley, Boniface. *Maximilian Kolbe: No Greater Love.* Notre Dame, Ind.: Ave Maria Press, 1982.

August 16: Doherty, Catherine de Hueck. *Poustinia: Encountering God in Silence, Solitude, and Prayer.* 3d ed. Combermere, Ontario: Madonna House Publications, 2000.

————. *Soul of My Soul: Reflections from a Life of Prayer.* Notre Dame, Ind.: Ave Maria Press, 1985.

August 18: Dillard, Annie. *Pilgrim at Tinker Creek.* New York: HarperTrade, 1998.

————. *Holy the Firm.* New York: HarperTrade, 1998.

August 22: Chevalier, Tracy. *Girl with a Pearl Earring.* New York: Plume, 2001. A good novel about Jan Vermeer.

August 23: Weil, Simone. *Waiting for God.* New York: HarperTrade, 2000.

August 25: Servas, Inc., 11 John Street, Room 505, New York, NY 10038. Phone: (212) 267-0252. E-mail: info@usservas.org

August 26: Eck, Diana L. *Encountering God: A Spiritual Journey from Bozeman to Banaras.* Boston: Beacon Press, 1994.

Magida, Arthur J., and Stuart M. Matlins, eds. *How to Be a Perfect Stranger: A Guide to Etiquette in Other People's Religious Ceremonies.* 2 vols. Woodstock, Vt.: Jewish Lights Publishing, 1996.

Smith, Huston. *The Illustrated World's Religions: A Guide to Our Wisdom Traditions.* San Francisco: HarperSanFrancisco, 1995.

August 28: Borg, Marcus J. *Meeting Jesus Again for the First Time: The Historical Jesus and the Heart of Contemporary Faith.* San Francisco: HarperSanFrancisco, 1995.

Buechner, Frederick. *Listening to Your Life: Daily Meditations with Frederick Buechner.* San Francisco: HarperSanFrancisco, 1992.

Foster, Richard J. *Prayer: Finding the Heart's True Home.* San Francisco: HarperSanFrancisco, 2002.

Hays, Edward. *The Old Hermit's Almanac: Daily Meditations for the Journey of Life.* Leavenworth, Kans.: Forest of Peace Publishing, 1997.

Lamott, Anne. *Traveling Mercies: Some Thoughts on Faith.* New York: Random House, 1999.

Nhat Hanh, Thich. *The Miracle of Mindfulness: An Introduction to the Practice of Meditation.* Boston: Beacon Press, 1999.

Nouwen, Henri J. M. *The Life of the Beloved: Spiritual Living in a Secular World.* New York: Crossroad Publishing Co., 1992.

Thompson, Marjorie. *Soul Feast: An Invitation to the Christian Spiritual Life.* Louisville, Ky.: Westminster John Knox Press, 1995.

August 29: Ellsberg, Robert. *All Saints: Daily Reflections on Saints, Prophets, and Witnesses for Our Time.* New York, Crossroad Publishing Co., 1997.

Gangloff, Mary Francis. *Remarkable Women, Remarkable Wisdom: A Daybook of Reflection.* Cincinnati, Ohio: St. Anthony Messenger Press and Franciscan Communications, 2001.

Nouwen, Henri J. M. *Sabbatical Journey: The Diary of His Final Year.* New York: Crossroad Publishing Co., 2000.

August 30: Coelho, Paulo. *The Alchemist: A Fable about Following Your Dream.* 10th ed. San Francisco: HarperSanFrancisco, 2003.

Endo, Shusaku. *Silence.* Translated by William Johnston. Marlboro, N.J.: Taplinger Publishing Company, 1980.

Irving, John. *A Prayer for Owen Meany.* New York: Ballantine Books, 1999.

Kidd, Sue Monk. *The Secret Life of Bees.* New York: Penguin USA, 2003.

Kingsolver, Barbara. *The Poisonwood Bible.* New York: HarperCollins Publishers, 2000.

L'Engle, Madeleine. *A Wrinkle in Time.* New York: Random House Children's Books, 1998.

———. *A Wind in the Door.* New York: Random House Children's Books, 1976.

———. *A Swiftly Tilting Planet.* New York: Random House Children's Books, 1979.

Wood, Douglas. *Old Turtle.* Duluth, Minn.: Pfeifer-Hamilton Publishers, 1992.

August 31: Rilke, Rainer Maria. *Rilke's Book of Hours: Love Poems to God.* Translated by Anita Barrows and Joanna Macy. New York: Putnam Publishing Group, 1996.

September 2: O'Connor, Elizabeth. *Cry Pain, Cry Hope.* Washington, D.C.: Servant Leadership School, 1987.

September 8: Brown, Robert M. *Spirituality and Liberation: Overcoming the Great Fallacy.* Louisville, Ky.: Westminster John Knox Press, 1988.

September 10: Egan, Eileen. *Such a Vision of the Street: Mother Teresa—The Spirit and the Work.* New York: Doubleday, 1985.

September 12: Woods, Donald. *Biko: Cry Freedom.* New York: Henry Holt & Co., 1987.

September 17: *Hildegard of Bingen: Mystical Writings.* Edited by Fiona Bowie and Oliver Davies and translated by Robert Carver. New York: Crossroad Publishing Co., 1990.

September 18: Hammarskjöld, Dag. *Markings.* Translated by Leif Sjoberg and W. H. Auden. New York: Alfred A. Knopf, 1964.

September 19: Smith, Huston. *The Illustrated World's Religions: A Guide to Our Wisdom Traditions.* San Francisco: HarperSanFrancisco, 1995.

Bohler, Carolyn Stahl. *Opening to God: Guided Imagery Meditation on Scripture.* Rev. ed. Nashville, Tenn.: Upper Room Books, 1996. A book on images of God.

September 20: Nouwen, Henri J. M. *The Genesee Diary: Report from a Trappist Monastery.* New York: Doubleday Publishing, 1981.

————. *The Inner Voice of Love: A Journey through Anguish to Freedom.* New York: Doubleday Publishing, 1999.

————. *Life of the Beloved: Spiritual Living in a Secular World.* New York: Crossroad Publishing Co., 1992.

————.*The Way of the Heart.* New York: Ballantine Books, 1985.

September 24: Steere, Douglas. *Dimensions of Prayer: Cultivating a Relationship with God.* Nashville, Tenn.: Upper Room Books, 2002.

September 29: Borysenko, Joan. *Pocketful of Miracles: Prayers, Meditations, and Affirmations to Nurture Your Spirit Every Day of the Year.* New York: Warner Books, 2001. Contains prayers and reflections about the four archangels.

October 1: *The Story of a Soul: The Autobiography of Saint Thérèse of Lisieux.* Translated by Michael Day and edited by Mother Agnes of Jesus. Rockford, Ill.: TAN Books & Publishers, 1997.

October 2: French, R. M., trans. *The Way of a Pilgrim: And the Pilgrim Continues His Way.* San Francisco: HarperSanFrancisco, 1991.

October 4: Bodo, Murray. *The Way of St. Francis: The Challenge of Franciscan Spirituality for Everyone.* New York: Doubleday Publishing, 1985.

October 5: Fischer, Kathleen M. *Women at the Well: Feminist Perspectives on Spiritual Direction.* Mahwah, N.J.: Paulist Press, 1988. Good insights on discernment.

October 6: Steere, Douglas, ed. *Quaker Spirituality: Selected Writings.* Classics of Western Spirituality. Mahwah, N.J.: Paulist Press, 1984.

October 8: Lernoux, Penny. *Cry of the People: United States Involvement in the Rise of Fascism, Torture, and Murder and the Persecution of the Catholic Church in Latin America.* New York: Doubleday Publishing, 1980.

October 11: Nhat Hanh, Thich. *The Miracle of Mindfulness: An Introduction to the Practice of Meditation.* Translated by Mobi Ho. Boston: Beacon Press, 1999.

————. *Going Home: Jesus and Buddha as Brothers.* New York: Berkley Publishing Group, 2000.

October 15: Bielecki, Tessa. *Teresa of Avila: Mystical Writings.* Spiritual Legacy Series. New York, Crossroad Publishing Co., 1994.

Green, Thomas. *When the Well Runs Dry: Prayer Beyond the Beginnings.* 2d ed. Notre Dame, Ind.: Ave Maria Press, 1998.

October 17: Jalal al-Din Rumi, Maulana. *The Essential Rumi.* Translated by Coleman Barks. San Francisco: HarperSanFrancisco, 1997.

October 18: Morris, Danny E., and Charles M. Olsen. *Discerning God's Will Together: A Spiritual Practice for the Church.* Bethesda, Md.: Alban Institute, 1997.

October 19: Lewis, C. S. *The Chronicles of Narnia.* 7 vols. Grand Rapids, Mich.: Zondervan, 1994.

October 21: Buechner, Frederick. *Listening to Your Life: Daily Meditations with Frederick Buechner.* San Francisco: HarperSanFrancisco, 1992.

October 22: Thurman, Howard. *The Growing Edge.* Richmond, Ind.: Friends United Press, 1974.

———. *Disciplines of the Spirit.* Richmond, Ind.: Friends United Press, 1977.

October 29: Lee, Dallas. *The Cotton Patch Evidence.* New York: Harper & Row, 1971.

Girzone, Joseph F. *Joshua: A Parable for Today.* New York: Doubleday Publishing, 2002.

Kazantzakis, Nikos. *The Greek Passion.* Piscataway, N.J.: Transaction Publishers, 1999.

November 2: Muir, John. *The Wild Muir: Twenty-two of John Muir's Greatest Adventures.* El Portal, Calif.: Yosemite Association, 1994.

November 4: Bloom, Anthony. *Beginning to Pray.* Mahwah, N.J.: Paulist Press, 1982.

November 5: Cronin, Deborah K. *Holy Ground: Celtic Christian Spirituality.* Nashville, Tenn.: Upper Room Books, 1999.

November 7: Hays, Edward. *The Old Hermit's Almanac: Daily Meditations for the Journey of Life.* Leavenworth, Kans.: Forest of Peace Publishing, 1997.

———. *The Great Escape Manual: A Spirituality of Liberation.* Leavenworth, Kans.: Forest of Peace Publishing, 2001.

November 10: Bainton, Roland Herbert. *Here I Stand: A Life of Martin Luther.* New York: Penguin USA, 1995.

November 17: For a copy of the SisBros covenant, write Larry Peacock c/o Upper Room Books, 1908 Grand Avenue, Nashville, TN 37212.

Wingeier, Doug. "Social Activism and Mutual Support: Twenty-five Years in a Covenant Community." *Communities* no. 108 (Fall 2000). Published by Fellowship for Intentional Community, RR 1, Box 156-W, Rutledge, MO 63563-9720. Phone: (660) 883-5545. E-mail: fic@ic.org

For further information about the Iona Community: The Iona Community, 4th Floor Savoy House, 140 Sauchiehall St., Glasgow, Scotland UK G2 3DH. E-mail: ionacomm@gla.iona.org.uk

November 24: Hillesum, Etty. *An Interrupted Life: The Diaries of Etty Hillesum, 1941 to 1943.* New York: Atria Books, 1988.

November 28: Kelly, Thomas R. *A Testament of Devotion.* San Francisco: HarperSanFrancisco, 1996.

November 29: Forest, Jim. *Love Is the Measure: A Biography of Dorothy Day.* Maryknoll, N.Y.: Orbis Books, 1994.

December 5: Schulz, Charles M. *A Charlie Brown Christmas.* Directed by Bill Melendez. 25 min. Paramount Studio, 1965. Videocassette.

December 8: L'Engle, Madeleine. *A Wrinkle in Time.* New York: Random House Children's Books, 1998.

———— with Carole F. Chase. *Glimpses of Grace: Daily Thoughts and Reflections.* San Francisco: HarperSanFrancisco, 1997.

December 10: Merton, Thomas. *New Seeds of Contemplation.* Rev. ed. New York: New Directions Publishing, 1974.

December 11: Thornton, Lawrence. *Imagining Argentina.* New York: Bantam Books, 1991. A good novel about the disappeared in Argentina.

December 12: Elizondo, Virgilio P. *Guadalupe: Mother of the New Creation.* Maryknoll, N.Y.: Orbis Books, 1997.

December 14: John of the Cross. *Dark Night of the Soul.* Translated by E. Allison Peers. Mineola, N.Y.: Dover Publications, 2003.

December 18: ten Boom, Corrie. *The Hiding Place.* Directed by James F. Collier. 145 min. Twentieth Century Fox, 1975. Videocassette.

December 20: Marton, Kati. *Wallenberg: Missing Hero.* New York: Arcade Publishing, 1995.

December 23: Heschel, Abraham Joshua. *I Asked for Wonder: A Spiritual Anthology.* Edited by Samuel H. Dresner. New York: Crossroad Publishing Co., 1983.

December 27: Howard-Brook, Wes. *Becoming Children of God: John's Gospel and Radical Discipleship.* Maryknoll, N.Y.: Orbis Books, 1994.

Appendix B
Prayer Practices in This Book

January
Breath prayers
Centering prayer
Praying with the Psalms
Befriending lament psalms

February
Practicing the presence of God
Journaling

March
Lectio divina—praying with
    scripture
Prayers of intercession
Service and kindness

April
Music and prayer
The body at prayer—movements
    and postures
Prayer in the four directions

May
Gratitude
Contemplation and meditation

June
Retreats
Spiritual direction

July
Family and prayer
Graces and bedtime prayers
Seasonal prayers
Sabbaths/vacations

August
Play and creativity
Prayers for peace
Prayers of compassion
Hospitality

September
Learning and growing in prayer
Four movements in prayer
Obstacles in prayer
Angels

October
Discernment and prayer
Clearness committees

November
Saints
Developing a rule of life
Examen—Prayers of reflection

December
Prayers of waiting
Dark night of the soul

Appendix C

Index of Saints and Events

Temple, William–Aug. 30
ten Boom, Corrie–Dec. 18
Teresa of Calcutta, Mother–Sept. 10
Teresa of Avila–Oct. 15
Theophan the Recluse–July 9
Thérèse of Lisieux–Oct. 1
Thomas–July 3
Thomas à Kempis–May 2
Thomas Aquinas–Jan. 28
Thoreau, Henry David–May 6
Thurman, Howard–Oct. 22
Timothy and Titus–Jan. 26
Tolstoy, Leo–Nov. 20
Trocmé, André–Apr. 7
Truth, Sojourner–Nov. 26
Tubman, Harriet–Mar. 10
Tutu, Desmond–Oct. 7
Twain, Mark–July 4

U
Underhill, Evelyn–Jan. 12

V
Valentine–Feb. 14
Vanier, Jean–July 8
Vermeer, Jan–Aug. 22
Veronica–July 12
Vianney, John–Aug. 4
Vincent de Paul–Sept. 27

W
Walker, Alice–Feb. 9
Wallenberg, Raoul–Dec. 20
Weatherhead, Leslie–Dec. 7
Weil, Simone–Aug. 23
Wenceslaus–Sept. 28
Wesley, Charles–May 24, Dec. 16
Wesley, John–May 24, June 17
Wesley, Susanna–Aug. 15
Whitehead, Alfred North–Mar. 22
Wilberforce, William–July 30
Woolman, John–Oct. 6

X
Xavier, Francis–Dec. 3

Other Events and Persons
Advent–Dec. 8
Alcoholics Anonymous–June 10
Aldersgate Day–May 24
All Saints' Day–Nov. 1
Annunciation, Feast of the–Mar. 25
Any saint from this month–Jan. 31
Anyone born on leap year–Feb. 29
April Fools' Day–Apr. 1
Archangels–Sept. 29
Artists and poets–Oct. 23
Author, *Cloud of Unknowing*–July 2
Autumn equinox–Sept. 22
Birth of Christ–Dec. 25
Birth of Mary–Sept. 8
Black History Month–Feb. 1
Campaign for Nuclear
    Disarmament–Feb. 28
Celtic Christians–May 1
Celtic martyrdoms–May 20
Celtic wisdom–Three Candles–
    Sept. 19
Children–Sept. 1
Cinco de Mayo–May 5
Declaration of Independence–July 4
Earth Day–Apr. 22
Expectant Mothers–Dec. 24
Father's Day–June 20
Grandparent–Jan. 23
Hiroshima–Aug. 6
Holy Innocents–Dec. 28
International Fellowship of
    Reconciliation–Oct. 9
International Women's Day–Mar. 8
International Workers Day–May 1
Jesuit Martyrs of San Salvador–
    Nov. 17
Jewish Holocaust Memorial
    Day–May 7

Appendix D
Sourcebooks on Saints, Psalms, and Prayer

SOURCEBOOKS ON SAINTS

Ellsberg, Robert. *All Saints: Daily Reflections on Saints, Prophets, and Witnesses for Our Time*. New York: Crossroad Publishing Co., 1997.

Gangloff, Mary Francis. *Remarkable Women, Remarkable Wisdom: A Daybook of Reflection*. Cincinnati, Ohio: St. Anthony Messenger Press and Franciscan Communications, 2001.

McBrien, Richard P. *Lives of the Saints: From Mary and Francis of Assisi to John XXIII and Mother Teresa*. San Francisco: HarperSanFrancisco, 2001.

Sisters of Notre Dame of Chardon, Ohio. *Saints and Feast Days: Lives of the Saints: With a Calendar and Ways to Celebrate*. Chicago: Loyola Press, 1985.

SOURCEBOOKS ON PSALMS

Brueggemann, Walter. *The Message of the Psalms: A Theological Commentary*. Minneapolis, Minn.: Augsburg Fortress Publishers, 1984.

Chittister, Joan D. *Psalm Journal*. Chicago: Sheed and Ward, 1988.

Heffey, Mary Winefride. *Understanding the Psalms: A Commentary*. Staten Island, N.Y.: Alba House, 1981.

Jaki, Stanley L. *Praying the Psalms: A Commentary*. Grand Rapids, Mich.: William B. Eerdmans Publishing Co., 2001.

Link, Mark. *The Psalms for Today: Praying an Old Book in a New Way*. Valencia, Calif.: Tabor Publishing, 1988.

Peterson, Eugene H. *Praying with the Psalms: A Year of Daily Prayers and Reflections on the Words of David*. San Francisco: HarperSanFrancisco, 1993.

————. *A Long Obedience in the Same Direction: Discipleship in an Instant Society*. Downers Grove, Ill.: InterVarsity Press, 2000.

Rust, Renee. *Making the Psalms Your Prayer*. Cincinnati, Ohio: St. Anthony Messenger Press, 1988.

Sheridan, John. *A Lay Psalter*. Huntington, Ind.: Our Sunday Visitor, Inc., 1985.

Stuhlmueller, Carroll. *The Psalms*. Quincy, Ill.: Franciscan Herald Press, 1979.

SOURCEBOOKS ON PSALM TEXTS

Merrill, Nan C. *Psalms for Praying: An Invitation to Wholeness.* New York, Continuum International Publishing Group, 2000.

International Commission on English in the Liturgy. *The Psalter: A Faithful and Inclusive Rendering from the Hebrew into Contemporary English Poetry, Intended Primarily for Communal Song and Recitation.* Chicago: Liturgy Training Publications, 1995.

SOURCEBOOKS ON PRAYER AND PRACTICE

Borysenko, Joan. *Pocketful of Miracles: Prayers, Meditations, and Affirmations to Nurture Your Spirit Every Day.* New York: Warner Books, 1994.

Broyles, Anne. *Journaling: A Spiritual Journey.* Nashville, Tenn.: Upper Room Books, 1999.

Brussat, Frederic, and Mary Ann Brussat, *Spiritual Rx: Prescriptions for Living a Meaningful Life.* New York: Hyperion Press, 2000.

Cronk, Sandra. *Dark Night Journey: Inward Re-Patterning toward a Life Centered in God.* Wallingford, Pa.: Pendle Hill Publications, 1993.

DelBene, Ron, with Mary and Herb Montgomery. *The Hunger of the Heart: A Workbook.* Nashville, Tenn.: Upper Room Books, 1995.

Dyckman, Katherine M., and Patrick L. Carroll, *Inviting the Mystic, Supporting the Prophet: An Introduction to Spiritual Direction.* Mahwah, N.J.: Paulist Press, 1981.

Fischer, Kathleen M. *Women at the Well: Feminist Perspectives on Spiritual Direction.* Mahwah, N.J.: Paulist Press, 1988.

Hays, Edward. *Prayers for the Domestic Church: A Handbook for Worship in the Home.* Leavenworth, Kans.: Forest of Peace Books, 1989.

Kelly, Thomas R. *A Testament of Devotion.* San Francisco: HarperSanFrancisco, 1996.

Kidd, Sue Monk. *When the Heart Waits: Spiritual Direction for Life's Sacred Questions.* San Francisco: HarperSanFrancisco, 1992.

Leech, Kenneth. *Soul Friend.* Harrisburg, Pa.: Morehouse Publishing, 2001.

———. *True Prayer: An Invitation to Christian Spirituality.* Harrisburg, Pa.: Morehouse Publishing, 1995.

Mogabgab, John S., ed. *Communion, Community, Commonweal: Readings for Spiritual Leadership.* Nashville, Tenn.: Upper Room Books, 1995.

Newell, J. Philip. *Celtic Prayers from Iona.* Mahwah, N.J.: Paulist Press, 1997.

Nouwen, Henri J. M. *Life of the Beloved: Spiritual Living in a Secular World.* New York: Crossroad Publishing Co., 1992.

Peacock, Larry J. *Heart and Soul: A Guide for Spiritual Formation in the Local Church.* Nashville, Tenn.: Upper Room Books, 1992.

Peterson, Eugene H. *Working the Angles: The Shape of Pastoral Integrity.* Grand Rapids, Mich.: William B. Eerdmans Publishing Co., 1987.

Redmont, Jane. *When in Doubt, Sing: Experiencing Prayer in Everyday Life.* New York: HarperCollins Publishers, 1999.

Rupp, Joyce. *Out of the Ordinary: Prayers, Poems, and Reflections for Every Season.* Notre Dame, Ind.: Ave Maria Press, 2000.

Steere, Douglas. *Dimensions of Prayer: Cultivating a Relationship with God.* Nashville, Tenn.: Upper Room Books, 2002.

Thompson, Marjorie J. *Soul Feast: An Invitation to the Christian Spiritual Life.* Louisville, Ky.: Westminster John Knox Press, 1995.

Notes

INVITATION

1. Robert Ellsberg, *All Saints: Daily Reflections on Saints, Prophets, and Witnesses for Our Times* (New York: Crossroad Publishing Co., 1997), 5.

2. Ibid., 6.

3. Jalal al-Din Rumi, "The Sunrise Ruby" in *The Essential Rumi*, trans. Coleman Barks et al. (New York: Quality Paperback Book Club, 1998), 101.

JANUARY

1. Esther de Waal, *A Seven-Day Journey with Thomas Merton* (Ann Arbor, Mich.: Servant Publications, 1992), 14.

2. A. J. Muste quoted in Ellsberg, *All Saints,* 73.

3. Ron DelBene with Mary and Herb Montgomery, *The Hunger of the Heart: A Workbook* (Nashville, Tenn.: Upper Room Books, 1995), 147–49.

4. Jane Wagner, *The Search for Signs of Intelligent Life in the Universe* (New York: Harper & Row Publishers, 1986), 206.

5. Martin Niemöller, *Exile in the Fatherland: Martin Niemöller's Letters from Moabit Prison,* trans. Ernst Kaemke, Kathy Elias, and Jacklyn Wilferd, ed. Hubert G. Locke (Grand Rapids, Mich.: William B. Eerdmans Publishing Co., 1986), viii.

6. Martin Luther King Jr. quoted in Ellsberg, *All Saints,* 153.

7. Martin Luther King Jr., *Strength to Love* (New York: Pocket Books, 1964), 132.

8. Saint Brigit quoted in Kenneth Leech, *Soul Friend: The Practice of Christian Spirituality* (San Francisco: Harper & Row Publishers, 1977), 50.

9. Henri J. M. Nouwen, *Life of the Beloved: Spiritual Living in a Secular World* (New York: Crossroad Publishing Co., 1992), 30–31.

10. Carroll Stuhlmueller, *The Psalms, Read and Pray,* no. 7 (Chicago: Franciscan Herald Press, 1979), 26.

FEBRUARY

1. Nouwen, *Life of the Beloved,* 31.

2. Brother Lawrence, *The Practice of the Presence of God,* rev. ed., trans. Robert J. Edmonson, ed. Hal M. Helms (Orleans, Mass.: Paraclete Press, 1985), 145.

3. Flora Wuellner, "A Suggested Way to Pray through the Day," retreat handout. Used by permission of the author.

4. Ibid.

5. Anne Broyles, *Journaling: A Spiritual Journey* (Nashville, Tenn.: Upper Room Books, 1999), 11.

6. Stuhlmueller, *The Psalms,* 36.

7. Wuellner, "A Suggested Way to Pray through the Day."

MARCH

1. Marjorie J. Thompson, *Soul Feast: An Invitation to the Christian Spiritual Life* (Louisville, Ky.: Westminster John Knox Press, 1995), 39.

2. Ibid.

3. Douglas V. Steere, *Dimensions of Prayer: Cultivating a Relationship with God,* rev. ed. (Nashville, Tenn.: Upper Room Books, 1997), 69.

4. Walter Brueggemann, *The Message of the Psalms* (Minneapolis, Minn.: Augsburg Publishing House, 1984), 19.

5. Oscar Romero quoted in Ellsberg, *All Saints,* 132.

6. Frederic and Mary Ann Brussat, *Spiritual Rx: Prescriptions for Living a Meaningful Life* (New York: Hyperion, 2000), 151.

7. *Sister Thea Bowman, Shooting Star: Selected Writings and Speeches,* ed. Celestine Cepress (Winona, Minn.: St. Mary's Press, 1993).

8. Cesar Chavez quoted in Ellsberg, *All Saints,* 180.

APRIL

1. Joyce Rupp, *Out of the Ordinary: Prayers, Poems, and Reflections for Every Season* (Notre Dame, Ind.: Ave Maria Press, 2000), 103.

2. Ibid., 103–4.

3. Rumi, "Each Note," in *The Essential Rumi,* 103.

MAY

1. Henry David Thoreau, *Walden, and On the Duty of Civil Disobedience* (New York: Harper & Row Publishers, 1965), 67.

2. *The Confessions of St. Augustine,* trans. J. G. Pilkington (New York: Boni & Liveright, 1927), 1.

3. Rupp, *Out of the Ordinary,* 182.

4. Julian of Norwich, *Showings,* trans. Edmund Colledge and James Walsh, Classics of Western Spirituality (New York: Paulist Press, 1978), 225.

5. Desmond Tutu, ed., *An African Prayer Book* (New York: Doubleday, 1995), xvii.

6. Jane Redmont, *When in Doubt, Sing: Prayer in Daily Life* (New York: HarperCollins Publishers, 1999), 59.

7. *The Cloud of Unknowing and the Book of Privy Counseling*, ed. William Johnston (New York: Image Books, 1973), 48–49.

8. Laurence Freeman, *Light Within: The Inner Path of Meditation* (New York: Crossroad, 1987), xii.

9. Thich Nhat Hanh, *The Miracle of Mindfulness: A Manual on Meditation*, rev. ed., trans. Mobi Ho (Boston: Beacon Press, 1987), 12.

10. Charles Wesley, "O for a Thousand Tongues to Sing," in *The United Methodist Hymnal* (Nashville, Tenn.: United Methodist Publishing House, 1989), no. 57.

JUNE

1. Anthony de Mello, *The Song of the Bird* (Garden City, N.Y.: Image Books, 1984), 3–4.

2. Wendell Berry's poem "The Peace of Wild Things" can be found in *Earth Prayers: From around the World, 365 Prayers, Poems, and Invocations for Honoring the Earth*, ed. Elizabeth Roberts and Elias Amidon (San Francisco: HarperSanFrancisco, 1991), 102.

3. *Anne Frank: The Diary of a Young Girl*, trans. B. M. Mooyart (New York: Pocket Books, 1952), 233.

4. Kathleen Fischer, *Women at the Well: Feminist Perspectives on Spiritual Direction* (New York: Paulist Press, 1988), 3.

5. Thompson, *Soul Feast*, 104–5.

6. John Wesley, "Catholic Spirit," sermon 39 in *The Works of John Wesley*, vol. 4 (Grand Rapids, Mich.: Zondervan Publishing House, n.d.), 493.

7. Eugene H. Peterson, *Working the Angles: The Shape of Pastoral Integrity* (Grand Rapids, Mich.: William B. Eerdmans Publishing Co., 1987), 117.

8. Debra K. Farrington, *Romancing the Holy* (New York: Crossroad Publishing Co., 1997), 49, note 2.

9. Letter from Sandra Cronk, beloved Quaker teacher, guide, and friend who died in 2000.

10. Margaret Guenther, presentations made to the Academy for Spiritual Formation, Burlingame, California, November 1–5, 1995.

11. Ibid.

12. Thompson, *Soul Feast*, 115.

13. Stuhlmueller, *The Psalms*, 65.

JULY

1. Richard of Chichester quoted in Eugene H. Peterson, *Praying with the Psalms: A Year of Daily Prayers and Reflections on the Words of David* (San Francisco: HarperSanFrancisco, 1993), July 5 entry.

2. Ibid., July 7 entry.

3. Thomas Ken, "Praise God from Whom All Blessings Flow," altered, *Chalice Hymnal* (St. Louis, Mo.: Chalice Press, 1995), no. 47.

4. Charles Cummings, *The Mystery of the Ordinary* (San Francisco: Harper & Row, Publishers, 1982), 107.

5. Gabe Huck, *A Book of Family Prayer* (New York: Seabury Press, 1983), 42.

6. Edward Hays, *Prayers for the Domestic Church: A Handbook for Worship in the Home* (Leavenwood, Kans.: Forest of Peace Publishing, 1979), 163.

7. J. Philip Newell, *Celtic Prayers from Iona* (New York: Paulist Press, 1997), 57.

8. Anne Broyles, *Growing Together in Love: God Known through Family Life* (Nashville, Tenn.: Upper Room Books, 1993), 64.

9. Based on Thich Nhat Hanh, "Walking with a Child," quoted in Redmont, *When in Doubt, Sing*, 245.

10. Abraham Joshua Heschel, *I Asked for Wonder: A Spiritual Anthology* (New York: Crossroad Publishing Co., 1987), 34–35.

11. Barbara Troxell, "Sabbath: Contemplation, Companionship, and Compassion," in *Wellsprings* (Nashville, Tenn.: Division of Ordained Ministry, 2001), 9.

AUGUST

1. Brussat, *Spiritual Rx*, 201–2.

2. Cecil Frances Alexander, "All Things Bright and Beautiful," *The United Methodist Hymnal* (Nashville, Tenn.: United Methodist Publishing House, 1989), no. 147.

3. Henri Nouwen, *The Road to Peace: Writings on Peace and Justice,* ed. John Dear (Maryknoll, N.Y.: Orbis Books, 1998), 59.

4. Ibid., 60.

5. Ibid., 61–62.

6. Peterson, *Praying with the Psalms*, August 12 entry.

7. Nouwen, *The Road to Peace*, 64.

8. William Blake, "Auguries of Innocence," in *A Concise Treasury of Great Poems: English and American,* ed. Louis Untermeyer (New York: Pocket Books, 1953), 193.

9. "Universal Peace Prayer," in *Peacemaking: Day by Day* (Erie, Pa.: Pax Christi USA, n.d.), 73.

10. See Joan Borysenko, *Pocketful of Miracles: Prayers, Meditations, and Affirmations to Nurture Your Spirit Every Day of the Year* (New York: Warner Books, 1994), 60. Here is the version Dr. Borysenko uses:

> May I be at peace, May my heart remain open,
> May I awaken to the light of my own true nature,
> May I be healed, May I be a source of healing for all beings.

11. Ibid., 61.

12. Peterson, *Praying with the Psalms,* August 30 entry.

13. Rainer Maria Rilke quoted in Beth E. Rhude, *Live the Questions Now: The Interior Life* (New York: Women's Division, Board of Global Ministries, United Methodist Church, 1980), 11.

14. Julia Esquivel, *Threatened with Resurrection: Prayers and Poems from an Exiled Guatemalan* (Elgin, Ill.: Brethren Press, 1982), 61.

15. Emily Dickinson, *The Complete Poems of Emily Dickinson,* ed. Thomas H. Johnson (Boston: Little, Brown and Company, 1960), 116.

SEPTEMBER

1. Brussat, *Spiritual Rx,* 238.

2. Mother Teresa of Calcutta, *Life in the Spirit: Reflections, Meditations, Prayers,* ed. Kathryn Spink (San Francisco: Harper & Row Publishers, 1983), 45.

3. Steere, *Dimensions of Prayer,* 30.

4. Redmont, *When in Doubt, Sing,* 121.

5. Peterson, *Praying with the Psalms,* September 27 entry.

6. Henri J. M. Nouwen, *Sabbatical Journey: The Diary of His Final Year* (New York: Crossroad Publishing Company, 1998), 5–6.

7. Adele Gonzalez, "Deepening Our Prayer: The Heart of Christ," pt. 3 of *Companions in Christ, A Small-Group Experience in Spiritual Formation: Participant's Book* (Nashville, Tenn.: Upper Room Books, 2001), 129.

8. Thomas R. Kelly, *A Testament of Devotion* (New York: Harper & Row Publishers, 1941), 60.

9. Thompson, *Soul Feast,* 31–51.

10. Ibid., 33–35.

11. Ibid., 36.

12. Ibid., 44.

13. Ibid., 45.

14. Ibid., 46–47.

15. Thomas Merton, address to nuns, quoted in M. Basil Pennington, *Centering Prayer: Renewing an Ancient Christian Prayer Form* (Garden City, N.Y.: Doubleday & Co., 1980), 37.

OCTOBER

1. Thomas à Kempis, *The Imitation of Christ* (Nashville, Tenn.: Thomas Nelson Publishers, 1981), 28–29.

2. DelBene with Montgomery, *When You Have a Decision to Make,* 13.

3. Katherine Marie Dyckman and L. Patrick Carroll, *Inviting the Mystic, Supporting the Prophet: An Introduction to Spiritual Direction* (New York: Paulist Press, 1981), 72–73.

4. Larry Peacock, "Prayerful Decision-Making," *Alive Now!* (January/February 1992): 60–61.

5. Dietrich Bonhoeffer, *Life Together,* trans. John W. Doberstein (London: SCM Press, 1954), 27.

6. *Armagosa,* written and directed by Todd Robinson, Triple Play Pictures, 1999, documentary.

7. Anthony de Mello, "Seedlings," in Michael Harter, ed., *Hearts on Fire: Praying with Jesuits* (St. Louis, Mo.: Institute of Jesuit Sources, 1993), 33.

8. Parker J. Palmer, "The Clearness Committee: A Communal Approach to Discernment," in John S. Mogabgab, ed., *Communion, Community, Commonweal: Readings for Spiritual Leadership* (Nashville, Tenn.: Upper Room Books, 1995), 131.

9. Wendy M. Wright, "Desert Listening," in Mogabgab, *Communion, Community, Commonweal,* 125.

10. Palmer, "The Clearness Committee," in Mogabgab, *Communion, Community, Commonweal,* 132.

11. Ibid., 132–33.

12. Ibid., 135.

13. Ibid., 134.

14. A good introduction and guidance to the Clearness Committee is found on pages 159–62 of *Companions in Christ, A Small-Group Experience in Spiritual Formation: Leader's Guide* (Nashville, Tenn.: Upper Room Books, 2001).

15. Peterson, *Praying with the Psalms,* November 9 entry.

NOVEMBER

1. Mark Link, *The Psalms for Today: Praying an Old Book in a New Way* (Valencia, Calif.: Tabor Publishing, 1989), 168.

2. Adapted from "A Personal Ritual for All Saints' Day," in Rupp, *Out of the Ordinary*, 37–38.

3. William O. Paulsell, "Ways of Prayer: Designing a Personal Rule," in Mogabgab, *Communion, Community, Commonweal*, 43.

4. Thompson, *Soul Feast*, 138.

5. Pope John XXIII, *Journal of a Soul*, quoted by Paulsell in Mogabgab, *Communion, Community, Commonweal*, 41.

6. Peterson, *Praying with the Psalms*, November 23 entry.

7. John V. Sheridan, *A Lay Psalter* (Huntington, Ind.: Our Sunday Visitor, Inc., 1985), 196.

8. Marjorie Thompson, "Making Choices," in *Pathways Network Newsletter* 2, no. 1 (February 1998): 7.

9. Thompson, *Soul Feast*, 144.

10. Martin Luther King Jr. quoted in Thompson, *Soul Feast*, 140.

11. Kenneth Leech, *True Prayer: An Invitation to Christian Spirituality* (San Francisco: Harper & Row, Publishers, 1980), 135.

12. Thompson, *Soul Feast*, 85.

13. Douglas V. Steere, *On Beginning from Within*, 3rd ed. (New York: Harper & Brothers Publishers, 1943), 80.

14. Deborah Smith Douglas, "The Examen Re-examined," in Mogabgab, *Communion, Community, Commonweal*, 48.

15. Wendy M. Wright, "Exploring Spiritual Guidance: The Spirit of Christ," pt. 5 of *Companions in Christ: Participant's Book*, 268.

16. Thompson, *Soul Feast*, 94.

17. Wright, "Exploring Spiritual Guidance," *Companions in Christ: Participant's Book*, 258.

18. Thompson, *Soul Feast*, 96.

19. Teresa of Avila, *The Way of Perfection, Meditations on the Song of Songs, The Interior Castle*, vol. 2 of *The Collected Works of St. Teresa of Avila*, trans. Kieran Kavanaugh and Otilio Rodriguez (Washington, D.C.: Institute of Carmelite Studies, 1980), 190.

20. Adapted from an unpublished work by Kathleen Flood, Nashville, Tennessee, April 2000, cited in Wright, "Exploring Spiritual Guidance," *Companions in Christ: Participant's Book*, 277.

21. Thompson, *Soul Feast*, 97.

22. Adapted from Wright, "Exploring Spiritual Guidance," *Companions in Christ: Participant's Book*, 288–89.

DECEMBER

1. Charles de Foucauld, *Meditations of a Hermit*, trans. Charlotte Balfour (New York: Orbis Books, 1981), 24.

2. Charles Wesley, "Come, Thou Long-Expected Jesus," in *The United Methodist Hymnal*, no. 196.

3. "O Come, O Come, Emmanuel," in *The United Methodist Hymnal*, no. 211.

4. Augustus M. Toplady, "Rock of Ages, Cleft for Me," in *The United Methodist Hymnal*, no. 361.

5. Sue Monk Kidd, *When the Heart Waits: Spiritual Direction for Life's Sacred Questions* (San Francisco: HarperSanFrancisco, 1990), 130–43.

6. Jean M. Blomquist, "The Close and Holy Darkness," in *Weavings* 17 (January/February 2002): 16.

7. Sandra Cronk, *Dark Night Journey: Inward Re-Patterning toward a Life Centered in God* (Wallingford, Pa.: Pendle Hill Publications, 1991), 1.

8. Ibid., 41.

9. Blomquist, "The Close and Holy Darkness," *Weavings*, 21.

About the Author

Larry James Peacock is pastor of Malibu United Methodist Church, Malibu, California. For over twenty years he has visited monasteries and retreat centers to chant the Psalms and learn a daily rhythm of prayer. Among the places he has traveled are the Taizé Community in France and the Iona Community in Scotland. A spiritual director since 1988, Larry has served on the faculty for both the Five-Day and Two-Year Academy for Spiritual Formation (sponsored by Upper Room Ministries) and has led numerous retreats.

Beyond college and seminary, Larry's continuing education includes a sabbatical at Pendle Hill, a Quaker center for study and contemplation; the Two-Year Academy for Spiritual Formation; and the Institute for Spiritual Direction and Retreat Leadership. Larry is the author of two other Upper Room books: *Heart and Soul: A Guide to Spiritual Formation in the Local Church* and *Companions in Christ: Getting Started Guide.* Among the books to which he contributed are *The Upper Room Spiritual Formation Bible, The Upper Room Disciplines, The Wisdom of Jesus: Sourcebook of Worship Resources,* and *Inspirations for Daily Living.* He has also authored numerous articles in *Weavings, Alive Now, The Upper Room Daily Devotional Guide,* and *Church Worship.* For ten years he has published *Water Words,* fresh, inclusive liturgy for the church seasons.

Larry is married to author Anne Broyles; they have two children. He is a part-time potter and an occasional juggler.

Other Titles of Interest

Order online at upperroom.org/bookstore
or call Customer Service at (800) 972-0433
Monday–Friday.

These books are also available at Cokesbury
and other Christian bookstores.

Sacred Journeys: A Woman's Book of Daily Prayer

by JAN L. RICHARDSON

Author Jan Richardson describes this book as "not so much a
collection of devotional pieces as it is a story, and stories. . . .
These pages tell the stories of some of the women I have
encountered in my own journey . . . women who have stretched
me with their stories, their questions, their lives, their sacred
journeys."

ISBN 0-8358-0709-6 • Paperback • 448 pages

Journaling: A Spiritual Journey

by ANNE BROYLES

Unlike most books, which are either a journal or a book about
journaling, *Journaling* is both. It contains helpful ways to journal
and sufficient space for practicing each method. Methods include
journaling from the events of daily life, journaling in response to
scripture, journaling with guided meditations, journaling from
dreams, journaling in response to reading, and journaling
conversations or dialogues.

ISBN 0-8358-0866-1 • Paperback • 144 pages

A Guide to Prayer for All Who Seek God

by RUEBEN P. JOB and NORMAN SHAWCHUCK

This book offers a daily pattern for those seeking a rhythm of devotion and personal worship. Each day offers guidance for an opening affirmation, a petition of prayer, and daily scripture selections. Excerpts are included from such writers as Frederick Buechner, Joyce Rupp, Henri Nouwen, Mother Teresa, Howard Thurman, C. S. Lewis, Dietrich Bonhoeffer, John Wesley, and many others.

ISBN 0-8358-0999-4 • Leatherette Cover • 432 pages

The Upper Room Dictionary of Christian Spiritual Formation

KEITH BEASLEY-TOPLIFFE, Editor

With the help of more than fifty scholars from many denominations, The Upper Room has prepared a basic introduction to Christian spiritual formation: your guide to great spiritual teachers of the past and present, to important topics in spirituality, and to ways of praying and leading groups in prayer and spiritual growth.

ISBN 0-8358-0993-5 • Hardcover • 320 pages

Upper Room Spiritual Classics, Series 1

A Longing for Holiness: Selected Writings of John Wesley
(ISBN 0-8358-0827-0)

The Soul's Passion for God: Selected Writings of Teresa of Avila
(ISBN 0-8358-0828-9)

The Sanctuary of the Soul: Selected Writings of Thomas Kelly
(ISBN 0-8358-0829-7)

Hungering for God: Selected Writings of St. Augustine
(ISBN 0-8358-0830-0)

Making Life a Prayer: Selected Writings of John Cassian
(ISBN 0-8358-0831-9)

Also available as 5 titles in a slipcase: ISBN 0-8358-0832-7

Upper Room Spiritual Classics, Series 2

Encounter with God's Love: Selected Writings of Julian of Norwich
(ISBN 0-8358-0833-5)

The Riches of Simplicity: Selected Writings of Francis and Clare
(ISBN 0-8358-0834-3)

A Pattern for Life: Selected Writings of Thomas à Kempis
(ISBN 0-8358-0835-1)

The Soul's Delight: Selected Writings of Evelyn Underhill
(ISBN 0-8358-0837-8)

Living Out Christ's Love: Selected Writings of Toyohiko Kagawa
(ISBN 0-8358-0836-X)

Also available as 5 titles in a slipcase: ISBN 0-8358-0853-X

Upper Room Spiritual Classics, Series 3

Loving God Through the Darkness:
Selected Writings of John of the Cross
(ISBN 0-8358-0904-8)

Seeking a Purer Christian Life: The Desert Mothers and Fathers
(ISBN 0-8358-0902-1)

Total Devotion to God: Selected Writings of William Law
(ISBN 0-8358-0901-3)

Walking Humbly with God: Selected Writings of John Woolman
(ISBN 0-8358-0900-5)

A Life of Total Prayer: Selected Writings of Catherine of Siena
(ISBN 0-8358-0903-X)

Also available as 5 titles in a slipcase: ISBN 0-8358-0905-6